BECOMING VEGAN

THE COMPLETE GUIDE TO ADOPTING
A HEALTHY PLANT-BASED DIET

Brenda Davis, R.D.

Vesanto Melina, M.S., R.D.

Book Publishing Company
Summertown, Tenn.

Cover design: Estelle Carol
Interior design: Warren Jefferson and Cynthia Holzapfel

Published in the United States by
Book Publishing Company
PO Box 99
Summertown, TN 38483
1-888-260-8458
www.bookpubco.com

ISBN 1-57067-103-6

09 08 07 06 05 04 03 02   4 5 6 7 8 9

Davis, Brenda, 1959–
        Becoming vegan / Brenda Davis, Vesanto Melina.
            p. cm.
        Includes index.
        ISBN 1-57067-103-6
         1. Vegetarianism. I. Melina, Vesanto, 1942- II. Title.
        RM236 .D38 2000
        613.2'62--dc21   00-058555

CONTENTS

ACKNOWLEDGEMENTS

To everyone who contributed time, attention, and energy to this project, we offer our heartfelt appreciation.

Sincere gratitude to those who made this book possible:

Cynthia Holzapfel, our editor, Bob Holzapfel, our publisher, Michael Cook, Warren and Barbara Jefferson, Gwynelle Dismukes, Barb Bloomfield, and Anna Casini. It is a continuing pleasure and privilege to work with every one of you, both professionally and personally.

Love and gratefulness to our families:

Paul Davis (Brenda's husband) and David Melina (Vesanto's husband), for support, advice, encouragement, and hours of computer assistance. David, your example and experience as a 20-year vegan offered us incredible practical insight and tremendous inspiration. Leena Davis (Brenda's daughter) for thoughtful review of the teen section and for taking over many household chores. Cory Davis (Brenda's son), for fresh squeezed juices, shoulder rubs, and loving care that made each day a little brighter. Chris Crawford (Vesanto's son and Kamloops artist) and Kavyo Crawford (Vesanto's daughter, scuba diving instructor, and sailor); thanks for the joy of having both of you in our lives.

Deepest appreciation to our cherished advisors and those sharing many hours of invaluable insight:

The late Jay Dinshah and Freya Dinshah, Dr. Paul Appleby, John Borders, Jennie Sawyer, Dr. Michael Klaper, Dr. Mark Messina and Ginny Messina, M.S., R.D., Victoria Harrison, R.D., Dr. Paul Harrison, Parveen Girn, Sooze Waldock, artist Dave Brousseau (Vegan Food Guide Pyramid), and Estelle Carol, cover artist.

Special thanks to those who contributed to specific chapters, providing thoughtful reviews and suggestions:

Dr. Susan Barr, Dr. Winston Craig, Dr. Reed Mangels, Dennis Gordon, M.Ed., R.D., Corinne Eisler, R.D., Bob Bessed, Kevin Fichtner, Ketti Goudey, M.S., R.D., John Westerdahl, M.P.H., R.D., Dr. Neal Barnard, Lisa Dorfman, M.S., R.D., Samara Felensky-Hunt, R.D., Nancy Guppy, R.D., Mark Berman, Catherine Grainger, Julie Rosenfeld, Alex Herschaft, Lucy Goodrum, Liz da Silva, R.D., Dr. Bill Harris, Kristen Yarker, Bonnie Cheuk, Lauren Holm, Dr. Tim Key, Susan McFee, Valerie McIntyre, Amanda Benham, R.D., Barbara Txi Hannah, Shirley and Al Hunting, Wendy Laidlaw, Barb McCoy, Guy Frederickx, Kathleen Quinn, R.D., Jean Freemont, R.D., Monika Woolsley, M.S., R.D., Joseph Pace, Mike Koo, Maureen Butler, Davida Gypsy Brier, John Davis, Bruce Friedrick, Anne Marie Gentry, Dr. Stephen Walsh, Amanda Benham, and Dr. Sarwar Gilani.

Warm acknowledgement to those who gave of their time and energy to support this project:

Dr. Karl Seff, Fran Costigan, Joseph Forest, Sarah Ellis, M.S., R.D., Dr. Dean Ornish, Francis and Carol Sue Janes, Rose Kane, Graham Kerr, Karin Rowles, Ron Pickarski, Jennifer Raymond, M.S., Cherie Soria, Joanne Stepaniak, M.S.Ed., Yves Potvin, Howard Lyman, Suzanne Havala, M.S., R.D., Carol Coughlin, R.D., Sylvia Lambert, Peter and Irene Andor, Michelle Eng, and La Vonne Gallo.

Becoming vegan is an expression of one's profound reverence for life. For some, it is a deliberate step towards the preservation of this planet. For others, it is a declaration of respect for all living things. For many, it reflects a commitment to personal health. Whatever the reason, a vegan lifestyle is a huge leap into a world that is very different from the one in which most of us grew up. Every step you take towards a more compassionate world is one of celebration.

We wish you much peace and joy in your journey.

May *Becoming Vegan* serve as a powerful ally and traveling companion.

Brenda Davis and Vesanto Melina

Brenda Davis, R.D.

Brenda Davis is a registered dietitian in private practice. She is coauthor of the best seller, *Becoming Vegetarian,* and the Chair of the Vegetarian Nutrition Dietetic Practice Group of the American Dietetic Association. Brenda is a recognized leader in her field and an internationally acclaimed speaker. She has worked as an academic nutrition instructor, a public health nutritionist, a clinical dietitian, and a nutrition consultant. Brenda specializes in essential fatty acid nutrition and lifecycle challenges, and has published numerous articles on these and other topics relating to vegetarian nutrition. She has been vegetarian for 11 years, during which time she has been in transition to becoming vegan. Brenda lives with her husband and two teenagers in Kelowna British Columbia.

Vesanto Melina, M.S., R.D.

Vesanto Melina is a registered dietitian and coauthor of *Becoming Vegetarian, Cooking Vegetarian,* and *The Good Cook Book* by Yves. She coordinated the vegetarian section of the *Manual of Clinical Dietetics, 6th edition,* a joint project of the American Dietetic Association and Dietitians of Canada. Vesanto is an internationally known speaker and consultant to individuals, government, and the food industry on vegetarian nutrition and foods. She has taught nutrition on the faculty of the University of British Columbia and Bastyr University near Seattle. Vesanto has been vegetarian for 22 years and vegan for 7 years. She lives in Langley, British Columbia.

Her website (designed by David Melina) is at www.nutrispeak.com.

DEDICATION

To those who inspire us,
with lives guided by conscience and compassion

Donald Watson

Dr. Frey Ellis

Jay and Freya Dinshah

Bob and Cynthia Holzapfel and the vegetarian and
vegan pioneers of The Farm

Pioneering vegetarians and vegans of the American,
British, and Australian Dietetic Associations, and
Dietitians of Canada

CHAPTER
1
Vegan Roots

Pioneers of social reform are courageous individuals who are more concerned about truth, justice, and humanity than about how they will be perceived by others. Without these strong and brilliant minds in our society, women would not vote, only the wealthy would be educated, and slavery would still be legal. For many years, vegetarian and vegan pioneers have been committed to the eradication of another great injustice: one that is committed against the animals so many people call food. It began thousands of years ago with minds like Pythagoras, Buddha, Plato, and Plutarch. But it was not until the mid–1800s that a significant turning point came in Western culture.

It was September 30, 1847, in England when a group of 140 people gathered together to express their respect for their own well-being (and that of animals) by asserting their unwillingness to eat flesh. This was the inaugural meeting of the Vegetarian Society, a

> **Vegetarian:** One who abstains from the use of flesh, fish, and fowl as food, with or without the use of eggs and dairy products.

group formed to publicly support meatless eating. The word "vegetarian," which had been coined in 1842, was adopted by the Society; it is a term derived from the Latin "vegetus," meaning "whole, sound, fresh, lively."

The Vegetarian Society created a publication of its own titled *The Vegetarian Messenger*. Its message was simple—live and let live—and its members strove to lead by example. A primary force in the Society, Joseph Brotherton (1783-1857), was the first Member of Parliament to speak against capital punishment. Like many other vegetarian leaders, he was interested in a range of humanitarian and compassionate reforms and worked to improve the harsh working conditions of children.

Brotherton was born into a family of humble means, much like the segment of society he worked to help. As a young adult at the beginning of the

19th century, he had been influenced by the Reverend William Cowherd, a minister in Salford in the industrial north of England. Reverend Cowherd attracted a large congregation of members who took a vow not to eat meat. It was an era of extreme hardship for the poor, and Cowherd's offer of free vegetable soup gave parish members considerable practical support.

The influence of Reverend Cowherd extended beyond what his early parishioners could have imagined. Another of his disciples, The Reverend William Metcalfe, set sail in 1817 for America with others from the Bible Christian Church. Two early, influential converts in the Philadelphia area were Sylvester Graham (fiery preacher, raw foods enthusiast, and originator of wholemeal Graham crackers) and Bronson Alcott (father of Louisa May). For a time Alcott even attempted to create a vegan community, an endeavor that must have been extremely challenging in that era! These men, along with others they inspired, became the nucleus for the American Vegetarian Society that formed in 1850. The society took shape in an environment of widespread poverty and hardship, badly adulterated food, and alcoholism, but the times also inspired great leaders and idealists who eventually led movements to emancipate slaves and promote women's suffrage and universal education for children.

Interest in vegetarianism fluctuated over the next century and a half. In the 1880s, as many as 34 vegetarian restaurants in London afforded, among other things, a safe and economical place for working women to eat. Arnold Hills (1857-1927), athlete, industrialist, and raw foods enthusiast, wrote in support of "living foods" and against the widely held idea that meat was essential for muscle building. Members of the Vegetarian Cycling Club held world records; vegetarian magazines reported the benefits of meatless diets for endurance sports.

George Bernard Shaw (1856-1950) was converted to vegetarianism while reading the passionate words of Shelley, whose diet had been near-vegan. Shaw's writings offer both common sense and humor.

"Don't attribute every qualm you feel to a breakdown of your constitution through want of meat."

"This is the true joy in life; being used for a purpose recognized by yourself as a mighty one, and being a force of nature instead of a feverish, selfish little clod."

A contemporary and friend, Mohandas (later Mahatma) Gandhi, was raised as a vegetarian. The philosophy of not eating animal flesh is in harmony with the Hindu concept of "Ahimsa" or harmlessness, a cornerstone of Gandhi's Indian culture. His travels to study law in London came at a time of growing interest by Westerners in Eastern philosophy, ethics, and religion. Gandhi expressed the view that humanity's natural food should be strictly nonanimal

and the expectation that with further understanding of nutrition, knowledge of how to
accomplish this would eventually come to
light, enabling people to follow their con-
sciences more consistently.

> **Ahimsa** is a Sanskrit term meaning
> nonharming or noninjuring and can
> be interpreted as "dynamic harmless-
> ness." The practice of Ahimsa includes
> avoiding specific foods and products,
> being considerate of the lives of
> humans and animals, and actively par-
> ticipating in beneficial action.

By the 20th century, the prevention of
malnutrition became a growing priority for
North American and British governments. In
England, for example, the diets of the poor
were near-vegetarian; however, these diets were the result of economic hardship rather than ethical choice and were nutritionally inadequate, consisting
primarily of white bread and tea! Some infants were fed a "milk" of flour and
water; overall dietary, medical, and living conditions resulted in the death of
one baby out of every four. By the beginning of World War I, a new meal-plan-
ning guide based on food groups was developed and promoted by the U.S.
Department of Agriculture. Awareness of the benefits of newly identified vitamins and minerals had effects on both sides of the Atlantic. Scientific research
illustrating the severe effects of protein deficiency made headlines. Analysis of
different foods revealed that meat and dairy products were rich protein sources,
and feeding trials showed that children could grow faster when fed these foods.
In response, authorities supported increased production and distribution of animal foods as a solution for many nutritional problems.

At the same time, some members of the vegetarian movement showed a
reluctance to use animal products beyond flesh foods. Between 1909 and 1912,
The Vegetarian Messenger showed support for a diet free of not only meat, but
also eggs, milk, butter, and cheese, listing a number of ethical and health objec-
tions to the use of these animal products. In Britain, ethical considerations
played a major role in the motivation of vegetarians, while in North America
more emphasis was placed on health benefits, for example by The American
Natural Hygiene Society.

Though the interest in plant-based diets continued for a committed few,
the majority of the population was won over to a dietary pattern in which animal products were easily accessible and highly prized. By the 1940s and 1950s,
food policies which were ostensibly developed to ensure an adequate food supply included substantial subsidies for animal products. From about 1955, factory
farming focused more on productivity and mechanization, and less on providing livelihoods for rural families. People became increasingly distanced from
the origins of their food. Scientific research was focused on obtaining *enough*
of various nutrients for adequate growth and health. Relatively little attention

was given to diseases of nutritional excess, environmental destruction, and the lives of farm animals.

VEGAN AWAKENINGS

Within the vegetarian movement, some recognized the error in logic that would have us believe cows and chickens "give" us their milk and eggs. They noted that the females of these species are killed for food when productivity declines, the males earlier than that, and took the view that animals do not exist to be used by people. In November, 1944, a small group established the Vegan Society in London, and the word "vegan" was first coined by founding member Donald Watson. Members of the Society wished to eliminate exploitation of any kind in order to bring about a more reasonable and humane society and the emancipation of humans and animals. The Society emphasized the moral, spiritual, social, health, and economic advantages of living by humane principles.

The Society was grateful to add to its membership Dr. Frey Ellis, who took a special interest in vegan health. He educated vegans about the health benefits of vegan diets, about the care necessary in bringing up children as vegans, and about vitamin B_{12}, which had been discovered in 1949. Dr. Ellis was a medical doctor at Kingston hospital and a consultant hematologist for the region. He conducted much of the early research on vegan health as time went by, including graduate students who worked under his direction. Dr. Ellis became a council member and vice president of the Vegan Society in 1961 and was its president from 1964 until he died in 1978. This gentle man worked to show the scientific world that a vegan diet could be nutritionally adequate. At the same time, he provided some needed guidance to vegans.

> **The aims of The Vegan Society are:**
>
> • To advocate that man's food should be derived from fruits, nuts, vegetables, grains, and other wholesome nonanimal products and that it should exclude flesh, fish, fowl, eggs, honey, and animals' milk, butter, and cheese.
>
> • To encourage the manufacture and use of alternatives to animal commodities.

> **Veganism** may be defined as a way of living which seeks to exclude, as far as possible and practical, all forms of exploitation of, and cruelty to, animals for food, clothing, or any other purpose.
>
> In dietary terms, it refers to the practice of dispensing with all animal produce, including meat, fish, poultry, eggs, animal milks, honey, and their derivatives.
>
> *International Vegetarian Union*

In 1960 the American Vegan Society was founded in the United States by Jay Dinshah, a vegan since 1957. He was soon joined by his new English bride, Freya, whose vegetarian family had been neighbors of Dr. Ellis and his family in England. Both Dinshahs had been lifelong vegetarians before becoming vegan. Then, as now, the Society encouraged active participation in Ahimsa as a part of vegan living and views this way of life as an urgent, worldwide necessity. It established the following "six pillars of the compassion-ate way" using "Ahimsa" as an acronym:

Abstinence from animal products

Harmlessness with reverence for life

Integrity of thought, word, and deed

Mastery over oneself

Service to humanity, nature, and compassion

Advancement of understanding and truth

> **A vegan diet** is derived from fruit, vegetables, grains, legumes, nuts, seeds, and other wholesome nonanimal products.

In 1975, a World Vegetarian Congress was held at the University of Maine in Orono by a new umbrella organization called the North American Vegetarian Society (NAVS). Jay Dinshah was founding president. This event attracted members totaling 1,500 participants and 90 speakers from 30 countries. Serena Coles' lecture to the Congress, entitled "Blueprint for A Humane World," propelled many toward veganism. Environmental, ethical, and health reasons for not using animal foods were strongly presented. Although eggs and dairy were optionally available at the 13-day event, dishes prepared and catered by Freya Dinshah were all vegan and led to a set of recipe cards, "Vegetarian Cooking for 100." These recipes later came to be used by thousands of universities, hospitals, nursing homes, and prisons.

To quote participant Ann Cottrell Free:

"Lives were changed for a variety of philosophical and health reasons. But perhaps the main reason for the success of Orono was the realization that we were not alone and that we were in the vanguard of a healthier future no longer based on the enslavement of other beings."

ANIMAL FOODS...UNCOVERING THE COSTS

In waves throughout the '70s and '80s, new segments of the population became aware of the devastating consequences of our animal-centered diets. Frances Moore Lappé's book, *Diet for a Small Planet* (1971), introduced many to the effects on the environment and human hunger, and interest in vegetarianism began to grow in middle class America. *Laurel's Kitchen* (1976) examined the human health issues and nutritional considerations involved in planning a balanced vegetarian diet. This was followed by numerous successful cookbooks, such as *Moosewood Cookbook* (1977), which provided immensely appealing recipes using milk products and eggs along with plant foods. Soon people

> **How is "vegan" pronounced?**
> In North America and the U.K, the correct pronunciation is "vee-gun." You may hear other pronunciations as well, such as "vee-gn," "vay-gn," and "vee-jan."

discovered that quiche, grilled cheese sandwiches, and three-cheese lasagne could contribute to weight gain and a rise in cholesterol as easily as a meat-centered diet. Because dairy products lack iron and interfere with absorption of this mineral, iron-deficiency anemia became a problem for some vegetarians who relied on dairy, rather than legumes, as primary protein sources. Nutrition textbooks of the day often included information about vegetarian diets in the "fad diet" section of the book. Readers were cautioned that vegetarianism was risky and even downright dangerous for children.

The Farm: Vegan Community

The Farm, a community of 1,500 people located in southern Tennessee, played a vital role in the early '70s in proving the viability of a vegan diet by becoming the largest group of intentional vegans known up to that point. Importantly, it was certainly the first group to include large numbers of children, including babies, and pregnant and lactating women. The Farm collaborated with the Centers for Disease Control in publishing the results of a study on the growth rates of its children in a 1989 issue of *Pediatrics* magazine (vol. 84, no. 3), with the conclusion that vegan children eating a varied diet could grow at rates comparable to nonvegan children. (See O'Connell et al, Table 2.1, page 18).

Seventh-day Adventist Contributions

Members of the Seventh-day Adventist church have made outstanding contributions in the area of vegetarian nutrition. A central part of this religious tradition, founded in the mid-1900s, is taking care of the body as a temple of the Holy Spirit. Based on the understanding that the original diet of humans was plant-based, approximately 30% of Seventh-day Adventists are vegetarian, 50% use meat less than once a month, and 1-2% are vegan. Adequate rest, sunshine, water, and an avoidance of smoking, caffeine, and alcohol are part of the lifestyle, with the result that these are considered to be among the healthiest people in North America.

The classic work on adequacy of plant protein was done in a joint venture between the Seventh-day Adventist Loma Linda University in California and Harvard University. Dr. Mervyn Hardinge and his associates contributed much to our understanding of vegetarian nutrition. He demonstrated that vegetarian diets were adequate for adults, pregnant women, and adolescents, and that vegetarian diets provided all the necessary amino acids. For many years, it was not easy to win acceptance for the excellent research that was done on the overall sufficiency of plant-based diets. However, with perseverance and time, the immense value of the extensive investigation done in the field of vegetarian

Fast Facts…"Food" Animals

General

Food animals slaughtered, North America 1999: more than 10 billion
Animals killed for food worldwide, 1998: 43.2 billion
Proportion of all antibiotics that are used in animal agriculture: 40%
Proportion of these antibiotics that are used to promote rapid growth: 80%

Veal Calves, Dairy Cows, and Cattle

Calves taken from their mothers within 24 hours of birth: 90%
Calves that never suckle from their mothers' udders: 50%
Natural life span of cow: 20 years
Fate of a dairy cow at 5 to 6 years of age: ground beef
Fate of most male calves at 4 months of age: veal
Livestock farms that are confined feedlot operations (U.S.): over 70%
Cattle feed operations that account for over 40% of cattle sold (U.S.): 2%.

Laying Hens

Eggs per year per laying hen before factory farming: 70
Eggs per year per laying hen today: 250
Percent of laying hens that suffer broken bones in their cage: 30%.
Male chicks (from laying hens) killed per year by suffocation, gas, or grinding in the U.S.: 200 million
Male chicks used per day for fertilizer, chicken food, and pet food in Canada: 40,000

Chickens (U.S.)

Mass of breast tissue of 8-week-old chicken today compared with 25 years ago: 7 times
Broiler chickens that have trouble walking: 90%
Chickens still alive at the scald tank: 20%
Number of chicken farms, 1969 to 1992: 35% decrease
Number of chickens slaughtered, 1969 to 1992: 200% increase

Pigs (U.S.)

Producers with over 50,000 hogs in 1988: 7%
Producers with over 50,000 hogs in 1997: 37%
Number of hog farms now compared to 50 years ago: 4%
Pigs with pneumonia at time of slaughter: about 70%
Pigs who are lame at time of slaughter: 50%
Pounds of corn and soy to produce one pound of pork: 7 pounds

Manure

Rating of agriculture, crops, and livestock as a source of water pollution in the U.S.: No. 1
Approximate tons of manure from North American food animals per year: 1.5 billion
Approximate tons of solid sewage waste from North American humans per year: 0.73 billion
Feces and urine from livestock for each 0.3 kg serving of meat: 16 kg

Related Human Issues

Cumulative trauma disorders among poultry workers, compared to national average: 16 times
Children dying of starvation or malnutrition per day, worldwide: more than 33,000
Portion of U.S. grain crop fed to animals destined for slaughter: 70%
Estimated U.S. health care costs per year related to excessive meat consumption: $60-$120 billion

nutrition has been recognized. Among the most impressive research to date on vegetarian and vegan populations is that from the Adventist Health Studies. These studies have demonstrated important health advantages of vegetarian and vegan diets. (See pages 21, 30, and 33.). While Adventists have traditionally been lacto-ovo vegetarians, dietary philosophy has stated, "…the time will come when we may have to discard some of the articles of diet we now use, such as milk and cream and eggs."

The Seventh-day Adventists operate prestigious universities around the world, including Loma Linda University, and numerous hospitals and holistic retreats. The Seventh-day Adventist Dietetic Association, a nonprofit organization of vegetarian dietitians, has been an invaluable source of nutrition information for health professionals for 40 years. They offer numerous inexpensive health education forums, conferences, and cooking classes, run natural food stores, create vegetarian diet manuals, cookbooks, audiovisual materials, and books for health professionals and the public. The Adventist community also introduced soymilk (having learned of it in China) and made available delicious, easy-to-use vegetarian meat substitutes.

The Well-Being of Animals

In 1987, *Diet for A New America* by vegan activist John Robbins drew attention not only to human health, hunger, and environmental issues relative to animal-centered diets, but also to the plight of farm animals in current food production systems, including laying hens and dairy cows. It was a shock for most people to learn of the routine debeaking of chickens (followed by weeks of pain for the birds) and to discover that millions of fluffy male chicks are killed on their first day of life by suffocation, gas, or grinding. It was equally shocking to learn that the veal industry is merely a by-product of the dairy industry and that laying hens and milk cows live just one quarter of the natural life span of their species. Robbins related the ethical arguments of vegetarianism to the current day realities of animal agriculture, building on some of the powerful earlier work by Peter Singer (*Animal Liberation*) and others. For individuals who professed to love animals, these realities made it difficult to continue consuming milk, eggs, and other foods produced from such a system. The vegan way of life had finally reached mainstream America.

The Health of the Planet

In 1997 several environmentalists, concerned with the damaging effects of animal waste, were honored with Pulitzer prizes for their writings about pig manure. With a billion cows, pigs, and sheep and over nine billion birds slaughtered each year in North America, the problem has became too vast to ignore. Contaminated drainage from feed lots, stockyards, and slaughterhouses has ended up at our doorsteps, in our well water, ground water, bays, lakes, rivers, and streams. Animal agriculture has immense and damaging impacts on groundwater supplies and dwindling aquifers, fuel resources, and wildlife. These problems are reflected in government documents.

The Health of People

With each succeeding year, scientific research examining the link between diet and disease strengthened the arguments in favor of plant-centered diets. Governments and health organizations around the world began to clearly promote plant-based diets as supportive to human health. Evidence confirming the nutritional adequacy of well-planned vegetarian and vegan diets has become too overwhelming to refute. (See Chapter 2.)

COMMON SENSE AND COMPASSION COME TO MARKET

Across North America and Europe, more and more people are voting with their grocery dollars for highly nutritious, appealing vegan foods. In discussing top trends for the new millennium, Elizabeth Sloan of *Food Technology* says,

"'Fresh' will be forced to get 'fresher' while vegetarian, organic and locally grown foods will abound."

"More than half of restaurants with an average check of $15+, and 45% of those below, report more frequent ordering of vegetarian dishes. Grilled veggie sandwiches were the 'rising star' among all sandwiches, while grain- and legume-based dishes graced 14% of the menus nationwide in Ré-I's Menu Census. Vegetarian category sales grew by 31% to $166.3 million, and by nearly 20% in natural food stores, during the year ending June 1998."

Food Technology, 53:(8) (1999): 40, 48

Modern vegetarianism reflects these intertwined influences:

- scientific evidence of the importance of diet in maintaining health;
- interest in a blend of Eastern and Western philosophy and religion;
- concern over the destruction of the environment through human "progress";
- shock over factory farming conditions;
- concern with oppressed groups, from starving children to farm workers, damaged by pesticides.

A look at the website of the International Vegetarian Union (www.ivu.org) cannot fail to impress you with the power and diversity of the vegetarian movement world-wide and the immense breadth of its base.

VEGETARIANISM AND VEGANISM…GROWING TOGETHER

It is interesting to note that while 90 to 95% of vegetarians are lacto-ovo vegetarian who include eggs and dairy in their diets, as a group there is a tendency to shift away from animal foods altogether. It is no mere coincidence that the availability and sales of nondairy beverages, nondairy frozen desserts, vegan patties, veggie sandwich slices, and other all-plant options have escalated over the past decade. Meals at a growing number of vegetarian festivals held throughout the U.S., Canada, the U.K., Europe, Australia, and Asia are becoming exclusively vegan. The same is true for meetings of vegetarian associations, such as the monthly potlucks of EarthSave groups throughout the U.S. and Canada. Catering services, airline food operations, and institutions include tasty plant-only menu items because these will be most widely accepted by vegans, vegetarians, and those with allergies to eggs and dairy. At a potluck gathering or dinner party, a delicious vegan item is likely to have universal appeal.

The demand for animal-free products is increasing rapidly among the entire vegetarian population. For most of us, it is a gradual but very natural progression, particularly if the reasons for our dietary choices extend beyond human health issues. Anyone concerned about animal well-being cannot deny the unnatural, and in many ways cruel, conditions of today's dairy cows, veal calves, and laying hens: massive doses of hormones and antibiotics, battery cages, assembly line slaughter, genetically engineered cows with distended udders, and calves living out their brief lives in tiny stalls. Nor can we ignore the devastating environmental affects of raising these animals in the numbers we do today.

In 1847, the rejection of flesh foods was linked with the conviction that the killing of living, feeling creatures was neither necessary nor morally acceptable for human survival and well-being. The Vegetarian Society advocated "the adoption of a principle that will tend essentially to true civilization, to universal brotherhood, and to the increase of human happiness generally." It comes as no surprise that a century and a half later, people with similar ethics about the well-being of all sentient life support the adoption of all-plant diets. Furthermore, now we know how to do this, in excellent health! We have helpful tools, such as blenders and food processors in our kitchens, that make things a *lot* easier. Many types of vegan eating patterns are being successfully adopted; some

are centered almost entirely around whole foods or raw foods, and others
include many fortified and convenience products.

Vegan Nutrition

Significant books written to provide nutritional expertise to vegans were *Vegan
Nutrition* (1988, The Vegan Society) by Cambridge trained Gill Langley; *Simply
Vegan* (1991, The Vegetarian Resource Group) by Debra Wasserman and Dr.
Reed Mangels; and *Nutrition and Wellness…A vegetarian way to better health*
(1999, Golden Harvest Books) by Dr. Winston Craig, to mention but a few. In
1996, Dr. M. Messina and V. Messina coauthored the extremely well-docu-
mented book, *A Dietitians' Guide to Vegetarian Diets*. (For more on this, see page
272.) Dietitian Suzanne Havala has not only written many books, but has
coauthored position papers on vegetarian nutrition for the American Dietetic
Association, clarifying for dietitians and other health professionals the safety of
vegan diets. For many dietitians the "risky diet" is no longer seen to be that
without animal products; the "risky diet" is the diet packed with animal products. The Vegetarian Nutrition Dietetic Practice Group (VNDPG), an
important voice within the American Dietetic Association, serves as a vital
resource for reliable nutrition information on vegetarian and vegan diets. The
VNDPG was established in 1991 and has nearly 1,800 members, including
many vegan dietitians.

Feeding the Planet

With the global population estimated to rise to more than eight billion by
2025, we are currently setting a poor example for the billions in less affluent
nations who are trying to emulate Western lifestyles. These people see some
advantages of meat-centered diets, but not the immense disadvantages that
accompany such eating patterns. We are now aware that we can raise strong,
healthy children on vegan diets and that the widespread adoption of well-
designed, plant-based diets could be a far more efficient use of the world's food
resources and part of a solution for the tragedies of human hunger.

Vegans are the new pioneers of the vegetarian movement, forging ahead
with courage, ingenuity, and inventiveness, making it easier for all others to
dine, dress, and conduct their lives without animal products.

THE VEGAN JOURNEY…CELEBRATING EVERY STEP

The journey towards a vegan lifestyle is a unique and personal experience for
each and every one of us. Some see it as an integration of one's gentle and
kindly nature with courage, the courage to make choices that reflect one's

deepest beliefs. It is a journey that is filled with emotionally charged challenges. When animal products are present in everything from gelatin-based camera film to glues, you may wonder if being vegan is possible at all! Be assured that it is possible to be a dietary vegan, and it gets easier each day to find alternatives for a host of animal products. There are many whose diets are free of animal foods, an estimated 2½ million people in North America and ¼ million in Britain. Many people's closets don't contain a shred of leather, silk, or wool. Growing numbers avoid soaps and household products that contain animal ingredients. Improved food labeling regulations, requiring the listing of all ingredients, allow people to know what goes into the products they buy. Vegetarian and vegan websites offer travelers information on everything from airplane meals and restaurants to bed-and-breakfasts at your destination. (For more on this, see page 273.)

Fast Facts...Food Choices

Meatless Meals

Vegetarian meals served, 1999, United Airlines: 491,300
Vegan meals served, 1999, United Airlines: 192,250
Households (U.S.) eating four or more meatless dinners per week, 1994: Over 20%
Males (U.S.) who always order a dish without meat, fish, or fowl, 1999: 5%
Females (U.S.) who always order a dish without meat, fish, or fowl, 1999: 6%
U.K. population (of about 57 million) that is vegetarian: 5%
U.S. adults who don't eat meat, poultry, fish, dairy, eggs, honey (vegans): 0.9%

Changing Food Consumption Patterns

Decrease in per capita consumption of veal calves 1970-1998 (U.S., retail weight): ▼ 67%
Decrease in per capita consumption of sheep, 1970-1998 (U.S., retail weight): ▼ 58%
Decrease in per capita consumption of cattle, 1970-1998 (U.S., retail weight): ▼ 58%

Grocery Trends

Increase in veggie burger sales in 1999 (U.S.): 10%
Increase in veggie burger sales in 1999 (Canada): 12%
Increase in sales of veggie breakfast items (vegetarian bacons and sausages) in 1999 (U.S.): 20%
Increase in sales of vegetarian alternatives for ground beef in 1999 (U.S.): 35%
Increase in sales of chicken substitutes that are vegetarian in 1999 (U.S.): 71%
Increase in sales of veggie sandwich slices in 1999 (U.S.): 79%
Safeway stores (Canada and U.S.) that sell tofu, soymilk, vegan burgers, and hot dogs: 100%
Tesco and Sainsbury's stores (U.K.) that sell soymilk, tofu, vegan burgers, and hot dogs: 100%.
Kroger stores (Atlanta & Nashville regions) that sell vegan burgers and hot dogs: 100%

Embark on your vegan journey with a spirit of adventure and a sense of humor. Allow the transformation to occur with the joy of knowing that every step you take makes a difference. When you make choices out of love of human life, animal life, or the life of this planet (or all three), you make this world a better place, and there is no greater cause for celebration.

SELECTED REFERENCES

For a complete list see www.nutrispeak.com/veganrefs.htm. See also general references for the whole book on page 276.

Ahimsa. (July-December 1978:1, 3). Published by The American Vegan Society, PO Box 369, Malaga, N.J. 08328-0908.

Cummings, D. *Environmental Impacts of Large Animal Production*. USDA–Center for Emerging Issues, 1998.

Eng, K. "Nutrition, manure, environment do not equal a simple equation." *Feedstuffs*, October 21, 1996.

Environmental risks of livestock and poultry production; see www.senate.gov/~agriculture/animalw.htm

International Vegetarian Union website at www.ivu.org/

Marcus, E. *Vegan, The New Ethics of Eating*. McBooks Press, 1998.

Newberry, R.C., and A.B. Webster, N.J. Lewis, C.V. Arnam. "Management of Spent Hens." *Journal of Applied Animal Welfare Science* 2 (1) 1999:13-29.

Spencer, Colin. *A Heretic's Feast*. University Press of New England, 1995.

Stepaniak, Joanne. *The Vegan Sourcebook*. Lowell House, 1998.

Lee, E., and C. Phillips. "Dietary Choice: It Affects the Planet's Health Too." *Vegetarian Nutrition Health Letter* (Loma Linda University) 4(1999):1-3.

CHAPTER
2

Perspectives on Vegan Health

"Attitudes toward vegetarian diets have progressed from ridicule and skepticism to condescending tolerance, to gradual and sometimes grudging acceptance, and finally to acclaim."

Dr. Mervyn Hardinge, esteemed pioneer of
vegetarian nutrition, Third International
Congress on Vegetarian Nutrition, 1997

Perspectives on vegetarian and vegan diets have shifted 180° over the course of a few short decades. Only a generation ago, vegan diets were classified as "fad diets," and strong warnings against such regimes could be found in almost every major nutrition textbook. Governments and health organizations went to some length to discourage the use of such diets, especially among children and pregnant and lactating women. Not a word was uttered about the possible benefits that might result from vegan or vegetarian eating patterns. One source of concern was deeply entrenched beliefs that humans require animal protein, especially during times of rapid growth. In addition, there were scattered reports of malnourished vegan infants, which some considered proof that such dietary patterns do not work.

It was not until scientists discovered that they had overestimated both the protein needs of infants and children and the quality of animal protein relative to plant protein that these biases were reappraised. Over time, research provided evidence that well-constructed vegan diets could not only foster good health for people of all ages, but may afford significant benefits for disease risk reduction. Reports of malnutrition were not reflective of well-planned vegan diets, rather of restrictive, poorly planned patterns. Today, dietetic and medical organizations support the use of appropriately planned vegan diets, and recognize their potential to be highly protective and even therapeutic for those with chronic diseases.

When assessing the health implications of any diet, there are two key considerations:

Is it safe and adequate? To be acceptable, a diet must provide sufficient calories and nutrients. At the same time, it must avoid excess harmful dietary components.

Does it support optimal health? The ultimate goal is to grow to maximum potential, reach peak performance (mentally and physically), experience little or no illness, and recover rapidly from injury. It is extraordinarily difficult to determine whether a given eating pattern supports optimal health. The best we can do is to compare the health consequences of various diets. While most diets can be made safe and adequate, fewer will truly promote optimal health.

ARE VEGAN DIETS SAFE AND ADEQUATE?

The main criticism of vegan diets is that they are not safe or adequate, and that relative to nonvegan diets, they increase the risk of malnutrition. The argument goes something like this:

Meat, eggs, and milk are the only sources of complete protein—the kind of protein infants and children need to grow properly. Meat is our most concentrated source of iron and zinc. Milk is our best source of calcium. These nutrients are often lacking in the diets of poor people who cannot afford animal foods. When we add a little meat, eggs, and/or dairy products to the diets of people who exist on a few starchy staples, children grow better and there is less malnutrition. In addition, plant foods are completely lacking in vitamin B_{12}. Obviously if we need a nutrient and we can't get it from plants, that should tell us that humans are meant to be nonvegetarians.

While these arguments seem logical, they tell only a small part of the story. It is true that many diets based on a single starchy staple (such as a root vegetable, rice, or white bread) lack protein, iron, zinc, and calcium, so adding meat and milk (concentrated sources of these nutrients) will improve their nutritional adequacy. However, adding nutrient-rich plant foods such as tofu, nut butters, legumes, leafy greens, and fortified soymilk would accomplish the same thing without necessitating policies that harm the environment. If we are to provide effective solutions to global hunger problems, these solutions must be sustainable. The fact that the plants we eat lack vitamin B_{12} is not a sign that we need to eat animal foods. Neither plants nor animals synthesize the vitamin —it is made by bacteria. It just happens that animals and their food are contaminated with B_{12}-producing bacteria. Our plant foods may also be contaminated with these bacteria, but we generally wash away the vitamin B_{12} during food preparation. The simplest way to deal with lack of vitamin B_{12} is to use the tried and true solution that has been adopted successfully for lack of vitamin D, folate, or iodine with the general population—add it to the food supply. Nondairy beverages, breakfast cereals, and meat substitutes all are now being fortified with vitamin B_{12}.

Many people fail to recognize that there is as much potential for malnutrition with Western-style diets as with vegan diets. According to the State of the World 2000 (Worldwatch Institute), there are three kinds of malnutrition:

Hunger—a deficiency of calories and protein. Hunger affects some 1.2 billion people worldwide. In countries with the greatest hunger problems, more than 50% of the population is underweight.

Overconsumption—an excess of calories, often accompanied by deficiency of vitamins and minerals. Overconsumption also affects 1.2 billion people worldwide. In countries with the greatest amount of overeating, more than 50% of the population is overweight.

Micronutrient deficiency—a deficiency of vitamins and minerals. This form of malnutrition affects 2 billion people worldwide and overlaps with both hunger and overconsumption. It is the result of insufficient variety in the diet and/or an excess of fat and sugar, crowding out foods that would otherwise contribute essential nutrients.

Two types of malnutrition among vegans deserve attention: *hunger and micronutrient deficiencies.* Technically, hunger (protein-calorie malnutrition) need occur only with insufficient access to food. In the vegan population, hunger is uncommon. It can occur, for example, when infants and children are given very-low-fat, high-fiber diets or when calories are restricted to achieve a model-thin body. Micronutrient deficiencies may be observed among vegans when insufficient sources of vitamins B_{12} or D are provided or when the diet is centered around junk foods and/or refined carbohydrates and lacking in fruits, vegetables, nuts, seeds, and legumes.

Two types of malnutrition are relatively common among nonvegetarians: *overconsumption and micronutrient deficiencies.* Overconsumption dramatically increases risk for numerous chronic diseases and is the fastest growing form of malnutrition in the world. It is most commonly seen in diets that are centered around animal foods, processed foods, and fast foods, and diets that are low in fiber and high in fat, cholesterol, sugar, and salt. In such diets, micronutrient deficiencies are associated with lack of variety (i.e., burgers and fries) or with too much refined food (high-fat, high-sugar foods that squeeze out valuable whole grains, vegetables, fruits, and legumes).

Both vegan and nonvegetarian diets can lead to malnutrition—vegan diets tending towards undernutrition and nonvegetarian diets tending towards overnutrition. Both have the potential to adequately nourish a population, if appropriately planned—and to be risky, if poorly planned.

Vegan Nutrition Intake and Status...a summary of the research

Table 2.1 summarizes and gives perspective on classic studies on vegan diets. Whereas research on single nutrients is covered in later chapters, these studies focus on overall dietary adequacy. When interpreting results, it is important to note significant limitations to the research.

LIMITATIONS OF RESEARCH

What we know about the health consequences of vegan diets comes from a very limited number of scientific studies and observations. The information provided must be interpreted with caution for several reasons:

- The number of participants is generally small (under 50 people) and may or may not be reflective of the entire vegan population.

- Studies do not always distinguish life-long vegans from short-term vegans who may have become vegan as a therapeutic measure or to reduce risk of disease. In these individuals, rates of chronic disease may be similar to the general population or even higher.

- Studies do not always provide crucial details about food intake. For example, vegans could be living on pasta and bread rather than whole plant foods, whereas the nonvegetarians studied may be eating plenty of whole plant foods, plus a little fish.

Lessons We Have Learned from Studies on Vegans

The vast majority of studies assessing the dietary intakes and nutritional status of vegans reassure us that well-planned vegan diets can supply adequate nutrition, even during vulnerable times such as pregnancy, lactation, infancy, and childhood. It is important to recognize, however, that as with nonvegetarian or lacto-ovo vegetarian diets, vegan diets can be both adequate and inadequate. Care must be taken to ensure sufficient energy, vitamin B_{12}, and vitamin D, especially in children of weaning age (1-3 years). Other nutrients that may require attention include protein, essential fatty acids, riboflavin, and certain minerals, particularly calcium, zinc, and iodine (in Europe and other places where salt is not iodized). Fortunately, the primary nutrition challenges for vegans are relatively easy to overcome. In fact, many of the nutrients of concern are now being added to foods commonly consumed by vegans (i.e., calcium, riboflavin, and vitamins B_{12} and D to soymilk, and iron, zinc, and vitamin B_{12} to meat substitutes).

Table 2.1 *Summary of Research on Vegan Diets Compared to Nonvegan Diets*

Author/ Location	No. of Participants	Positive (+) & Negative (-) Results for Vegans
Studies Showing Overall Adequacy of Vegan Diets		
Hardinge and Stare, USA, 1954	25 vegans, 30 lacto-ovo vegetarians, 30 nonvegetarians	+ iron, vitamins A and C, thiamin - protein, calcium, and riboflavin (in a few vegans)
Guggenheim et al, Jerusalem, 1962	119 vegans	+ all nutrients except riboflavin. (Note: calcium = 825 mg per day) - riboflavin
Ellis et al, Great Britain, 1970	26 vegans 24 nonvegetarians	+ all nutrients; weight 8-10 lb (3.6-4.5 kg) less than nonvegetarians (who also had low folate levels) - B_{12} (in 3 vegans)
Sanders and Ellis, Great Britain, 1978	34 vegans (3-84 years) 23 nonvegetarians	+ all nutrients studied: B_{12}, iron, folate - serum B_{12} low though not deficient, supplementation advised
Abdulla et al, Sweden, 1981	6 vegans	+ Potassium, magnesium, copper, and folate (protein and calories deliberately low) - zinc, iodine, and vitamin B_{12}
Carlson et al, United Kingdom, 1985	10 vegans, 9 lacto-ovo vegetarians, 18 nonvegetarians	+thiamin, folate, vitamin C, iron, fiber - vitamins B_2, B_{12}, and D
T.A.B. Sanders, Britain, 1988	39 vegan infants and children	+ normal growth and development, not deficient - calories, calcium, vitamin D, and energy were below the recommended levels
O'Connell et al., USA, 1989	404 vegetarian children aged 4 months- 10 years (288 vegans, 116 lacto-ovo vegetarians)	+ adequate growth, no significant difference in height and weight by age 10. Compared with U.S. child, greatest differences in height were seen at 1-3 years, showing importance of weaning foods.
Draper et al., Britain, 1993	38 vegans, 52 lacto-ovo vegetarians, 34 semivegetarians	+ magnesium, iron, copper, vitamin B_6, E - riboflavin, iodine, calcium, vitamin B_{12}, D
Haddad et al., USA, 1999	25 vegans 20 nonvegetarians	+ fiber, vitamin C, A, folate, magnesium, copper, iron, and manganese - zinc and calcium (females only), B_{12} in 40% of vegans Note: nonvegetarian women also low in calcium
Studies Showing Inadequacy of Restrictive Vegan Diets		
Shinwell and Gorodischer, Israel	72 vegan infants, aged 3-16 months of age	- Infants suffered protein-energy malnutrition, growth retardation, iron-deficiency anemia, zinc, B_{12}, and vitamin D deficiency. Infants weaned at 3 months to homemade soymilk (13.7 kcal/100 ml compared 65-70 kcal/100 ml for breast milk).
P.C. Dagnalie et al., Netherlands	macrobiotic, near-vegan infants and children in 15 studies	- Infants and children were severely malnourished (most severe in infants 6-18 months old). Home-prepared soy or nut "milks" were used and nutritional supplements generally avoided.

IMPLICATIONS OF VEGAN DIETS ON CHRONIC DISEASE

There is a strong and consistent message, demonstrated by many years of solid scientific research for almost every major chronic disease that plagues affluent populations. Animal-centered diets, rich in saturated fat and cholesterol and low in fiber, increase the risk of chronic diseases; plant-centered diets, low in saturated fat and cholesterol, and rich in dietary fiber and phytochemicals, decrease the risk of these diseases.

The vast majority of major health organizations in the Western world now recognize this link and promote a plant-based diet as optimal for health. In June of 1999, five of the top health organizations in the U.S. jointly endorsed a nutritious eating plan meant to help stave off the diseases that kill most people—heart disease, stroke, cancer, and diabetes. The Unified Dietary Guidelines were released by the American Cancer Society, the American Dietetic Association, the American Academy of Pediatrics, the National Institutes of Health, and the American Heart Association.

The guidelines suggest limiting total fat to not more than 30% of calories and saturated fat to not more than 10% of calories. They also advise 55% or more of daily calories come from complex carbohydrates such as grains, fruits, and vegetables, salt be limited to a teaspoon a day (6 grams), and only enough calories be consumed to maintain a desirable body weight. To accomplish these goals, the following recommendations are made:

- Eat a variety of foods.
- Choose most of what you eat from plant sources.
- Eat five or more servings of fruits and vegetables each day.
- Eat six or more servings of bread, pasta, and cereal grains each day.
- Eat high-fat foods sparingly, especially those from animal sources.
- Keep your intake of simple sugars to a minimum.

More recently, the U.S. government released the updated, official U.S. Dietary Guidelines, which are available at:

www.health.gov/dietaryguidelines.

These national guidelines are consistent with the Unified Dietary Guidelines in their strong emphasis on consumption of a variety of vegetables, fruits, and whole grains daily and reduction in the use of animal products, especially those rich in saturated fat and cholesterol. Many health experts believe that these guidelines would be even stronger if government ties to animal agricultural industries were less powerful. Nonetheless, the Guidelines have come a long way, and there is little question that things are moving in the right direction.

Vegan diets come closer to national nutrition recommendations for fat, cholesterol, trans fatty acids, protein, and fiber than any other diet. They consist almost exclusively of the foods that authorities urge us to make the foundation of the diet—vegetables, fruits, legumes, and whole grains. These foods are naturally high in fiber, phytochemicals, vitamins, and minerals, low in saturated fat, and cholesterol free.

The information on vegan diets and chronic disease, while still in very early stages, is quite impressive. There is convincing evidence that vegan diets are useful in the prevention and/or treatment of numerous chronic diseases, including heart disease, hypertension, stroke, cancer, obesity, diabetes, gallbladder disease, arthritis, kidney disease, gastro-intestinal disorders, and asthma. The only negative findings related to chronic disease appear to be for osteoporosis. However, these findings seem to be associated with poorly planned vegan diets, and the potential drawbacks for bone health appear to be easily averted. We will consider the evidence relating to four diseases: heart disease, cancer, diabetes, and osteoporosis. (Excellent resources that address the other diseases are listed at the end of the chapter.)

HEART DISEASE

Heart disease is the number one killer in most affluent nations. In North America, it accounts for about 40% of all deaths. An extensive body of research confirms the strong favorable effect plant-based diets have on heart disease risk reduction. Much of the information we have comparing the incidence of heart disease in people consuming various diets comes from two important Seventh-day Adventist studies:

• Adventist Mortality Study, comparing health of Adventists with general population (Snowden, 1984)

• Adventist Health Study, comparing health of vegetarian, vegan, and nonvegetarian Adventists (Fraser, 1992).

Only a few studies have looked specifically at the incidence of heart disease in vegans. Data from four of these studies is shown Table 2.2. (Key, 1999). These are the two Seventh-day Adventist studies (*California, 53,490 participants*); the Oxford Vegetarian Study (Thorogood, 1994; *U.K., 11,047 participants*), and The Heidelberg Study (Chang-Claude, 1992; *Germany, 1,757 participants*). Note that the majority of participants, vegetarian and nonvegetarian, shared an interest in health or came from similar social/religious backgrounds. Results were adjusted for age, sex, smoking, alcohol use, activity level, and education.

Table 2.2 *Percent Difference in Heart Disease and Stroke Compared with Regular Meat-Eaters (n=31,766)*

Diet Category	Heart Disease	Stroke
Vegans (n=753)	-26%	-30%
Lacto-ovo vegetarians (n=23,265)	-34%	-13%
Fish-eaters (no meat) (n= 2,375)	-34%	+4%
Occasional meat eaters(meat less than 1/wk) (n=8,135)	-20%	-3%

★Note: this analysis did not include the "health food shoppers" because of the uncertainty of their dietary classification.

While these findings suggest that vegan diets offer much stronger protection against stroke than other dietary patterns, both lacto-ovo vegetarian diets and vegetarian diets with fish appear to offer greater protection against heart disease. Earlier research by Thorogood et al, 1987, estimated the incidence of heart disease to be 57% lower in lifelong vegans and 24% lower in lifelong lacto-ovo vegetarians compared with nonvegetarians, based on total cholesterol levels. The discrepancy between what was expected and what research to date has found may be attributed to the length of time the participants have been vegan and the relatively small number of vegan participants relative to the non-vegans. Further research verifies this higher than expected risk for heart disease among some vegans. Blood cholesterol level is not the only dietary factor affecting the risk of CVD, as heart attacks and strokes often occur in people with normal blood cholesterol levels. There are a broader set of risk factors affected by diet, each of which is influenced by a vegan eating pattern.

Fast Facts from the Adventist Mortality and Health Studies

Compared with the general population
Fatal heart attacks suffered by vegan Adventist men: less than 20%
Fatal heart attacks suffered by lacto-ovo vegetarians: about 40%

Compared with nonbeef eaters
Fatal heart attacks in men who ate beef at least 3 times a week: 60-70% more.
Fatal heart attacks in women who ate beef at least 3 times a week: 30% more.

Compared with those who became vegetarian after age 50
Risk of fatal heart disease among men who became vegetarian before age 20: about 50%
Risk of fatal heart disease among men who became vegetarian before age 30: about 30%

Compared with people who rarely ate nuts
Reduction in fatal and nonfatal heart disease among people who ate nuts
at least 4 times a week: 50%

RISK FACTORS REDUCED BY A VEGAN DIET
Blood Cholesterol Level

It is estimated that for every 1% increase in blood cholesterol, heart disease risk increases by 2-3%. The most important dietary factors that raise blood cholesterol are saturated fat, cholesterol, and trans fatty acids. Of all dietary groups, vegans have the lowest intakes of saturated fat, trans fatty acids, and cholesterol. The most powerful cholesterol-lowering agents are soluble fiber, plant protein (especially soy protein), polyunsaturated fats, and phytochemicals, all of which are found exclusively or primarily in plant foods. It comes as no surprise that vegans have the lowest total and LDL cholesterol levels of all dietary groups, including lacto-ovo vegetarians and fish-eaters. In 5 studies from 1987-1999, average blood cholesterol of vegans ranged from 3.5 mmol/l (135 mg/dl) to 4.3 mmol/l (165 mg/dl), compared with 4.6 mmol/l (177 mg/dl) to 5.3 mmol/l (205 mg/dl) for nonvegetarians.

Oxidation of LDL Cholesterol

When LDL cholesterol becomes oxidized by free radicals, the product is highly damaging to blood vessels, inducing plaque formation. The susceptibility of LDL cholesterol to oxidation depends on both the levels of LDL cholesterol present and the presence of antioxidants such as vitamin E, carotenoids, vitamin C, flavonoids, and polyphenolic compounds. In addition, high intakes of heme iron may increase LDL oxidation. (Heme iron is found only in meat, fish, and poultry.) Antioxidants come primarily from plant foods, so concentrations of these protective substances are typically higher in vegan diets than in nonvegetarian diets. Recent studies showed vegans to have higher blood levels of antioxidants and lower levels of lipid peroxidation than nonvegetarians.

Hypertension (high blood pressure)

Both coronary artery disease and stroke are increased by high blood pressure. While vegan and vegetarian populations have slightly lower blood pressures than nonvegetarians (5-10 mm Hg less), rates of hypertension are lower still, (only one-third to one-half those of nonvegetarians). The healthier body weight of vegans and vegetarians appears to be an important contributing factor. Other aspects of diet that may control blood pressure are higher fiber; higher potassium, magnesium, and phytochemical intakes; lower total and saturated fat consumption; and possibly reduced sodium intakes. (Vegans may not consume less sodium with high intakes of convenience foods.)

Obesity and High Waist-to-Hip Ratio

The risk of heart disease and hypertension are both associated with excessive body weight. Compared with lacto-ovo vegetarians and nonvegetarians, vegans are leaner and have lower waist-to-hip ratios. It is thought that low obesity rates are related to these characteristics of vegan diets: high fiber content (improves satiety), lower fat content (reduces caloric density), and higher glucagon secretion. (Glucagon increases blood glucose concentration, promotes appetite control, and increases fat oxidation.)

RISK FACTORS THAT REQUIRE FURTHER RESEARCH
Blood Clotting Tendency

Most serious cardiovascular events (heart attacks, strokes, etc.) begin with the formation of a blood clot. Blood clots form and dissolve in blood all the time and generally do no harm. However, when injuries to blood vessels occur, this balance is disrupted, increasing the tendency for blood platelets to stick together (platelet aggregation). This is the initial step in clot formation. Once a clot is formed, it may attach to an artery wall or travel through the blood vessels, with the potential of becoming lodged and blocking blood flow. When blood flow to the heart is blocked, a heart attack occurs; when it occurs in the brain, the result is a stroke.

It has long been hypothesized that blood clotting tendencies would be decreased in vegetarians, and more so in vegans, due to a favorable ratio of saturated fat (which causes platelets to aggregate) compared to polyunsaturated fats. However, the few studies done have failed to support this theory. A possible explanation is that low vegan intakes of omega-3 fatty acids, which are about half the intakes of nonvegetarians, result in decreased production of potent hormone-like substances that reduce platelet aggregation. Li and coworkers, 1999, concluded that vegetarians, especially vegans, might be advised to increase their dietary intake of omega-3 fatty acids in order to reduce platelet aggregation. (See more on this on page 61.)

Homocysteine Levels

Homocysteine is an amino acid produced by the body during the breakdown of methionine, a sulfur-containing essential amino acid that is concentrated in animal foods. There is strong evidence that elevated homocysteine is an independent risk factor for heart disease and may increase the risk of heart attack or stroke by two to three times. Research has failed to show a relationship between methionine intake and homocysteine levels but is centered more on intakes of three B vitamins that help us get rid of this damaging by-product.

Blood levels of homocysteine are determined largely by folate, vitamins B_{12}, and B_6. Initially, researchers expected vegetarians and vegans to have low levels of homocysteine because they consume less methionine and almost twice as much folate as nonvegetarians. Instead, studies show average homocysteine levels of vegans to be either similar to or higher than nonvegetarians. Two studies (by Mezzano and by Mann, both 1999) found significantly higher homocysteine levels in vegetarians compared to meat eaters, with vegans having the highest levels. Though vegan intakes of folate and B_6 amounts are generally good, vegans may have reduced vitamin B_{12} status, increasing risk for elevated homocysteine. Vitamin B_{12} is involved in the conversion of homocysteine back to methionine. With insufficient B_{12}, conversion appears to be slowed, and homocysteine levels rise. On the other hand, one would expect vegan diets to reduce homocysteine levels if all three B vitamins are abundantly supplied.

Overall Risk for Heart Disease and Stroke

Vegans have reduced risk for heart disease and stroke due to their high-fiber, low-saturated fat, cholesterol-free, phytochemical-rich diets. They have lower total and LDL cholesterol levels, lower blood pressure, less obesity, better waist/hip ratios, and lower levels of certain blood clotting factors. However, vegans appear to have higher platelet aggregation factors and may have higher homocysteine levels, which could, at least partly, counteract the benefits. The message is crystal clear:

The vegan diet has tremendous potential for reducing heart disease risk. For full benefit:

- *Ensure adequate intake of vitamin B_{12}.* (Use a supplement and/or B_{12}-fortified foods.)

- *Ensure sufficient intake of omega-3 fatty acids and improve the balance of essential fatty acids.* (For more on this, see Chapter 4.)

Vegan Diets in the Treatment of Cardiovascular Disease

Vegan and near-vegan diets have proven highly effective in treating cardiovascular diseases as shown by studies listed in Table 2.3.

Though Dr. Dean Ornish has subsequently added full-fat soyfoods and small amounts of flaxseed oil to the original diet, no studies to date have examined the effectiveness of higher-fat vegan diets (containing nuts, seeds, etc.) for the treatment of heart disease. Mediterranean-style diets have been shown to be among the most protective diets against heart disease. Though not exclusively vegetarian, these are centered around relatively unprocessed plant foods, including nuts, seeds, olive oil, and avocados. In the Lyon Heart Study, by the

Table 2.3 Vegan and Near-Vegan Diets in the Treatment of Cardiovascular Disease

Year and Researcher	E =Experimental Group	C = Control Group (where used)	Results
1990/1995 Dean Ornish	Near-vegan diet (less than 10% fat, limited skim milk and egg white), stress management, ½ hour daily exercise, and group therapy.	30% calories from fat diet, less than 200 mg cholesterol/day.	After 1 year, 82% of E showed regression of heart disease, whereas C showed progression. LDL cholesterol dropped 37% in E, only 6% in C. Angina *decreased* by 91% in the E, increased 165% in C. In a 4-year follow-up, C had twice as many cardiac events as E.
1995 John McDougall	12-day live-in program, vegan diet, 5% fat and 60 g. fiber per day.		Patients experienced average decreases in total cholesterol of 11% and a 6% drop in blood pressure.
1999 Caldwell Esselstyn	12-year ongoing study using very-low-fat vegan diet coupled with cholesterol-lowering medication.		Approximately 70% showed reversal of disease. In the 8 years preceding study, 11 participants experienced 48 cardiac events (total). During 10 years of study, only 1 noncompliant patient experienced cardiac event.

end of two years on the Mediterranean diet patients had an unprecedented 76% lower risk of dying of a heart attack or stroke when compared with patients on a "prudent Western-type diet." Mediterranean diets are higher in monounsaturated fat and omega-3 fatty acids, and lower in omega-6 fatty acids than vegan diets. It is reasonable to assume that a vegan "Mediterranean-style" diet, constructed to avoid B_{12} shortages and to ensure sufficient omega-3 fatty acids, could produce even more impressive results. Such a diet would actually be lower in saturated fat and cholesterol and higher in fiber than traditional Mediterranean diets.

CANCER

There is rarely a soul in the Western world who is not touched by cancer. It is the second leading cause of death in the developed world. In North America, one in four people will die of cancer. Worldwide, cancer strikes 10 million people every year. Unlike heart disease, it shows few signs of abating in the more affluent countries. In the developing world, both diseases are on the rise. Cancer risk varies dramatically across populations and changes quickly when people move to areas with very different lifestyles. In the past, cancer was seen as an indiscriminate killer, but current scientific evidence suggests:

• *most cancer is preventable, with about three cases in four directly related to lifestyle choices;*

• *controllable factors of greatest impact appear to be smoking, diets rich in animal foods and low in vegetables and fruits, inactivity, obesity, and exposure to hazardous materials;*

• *experts estimate that improving diet and exercise alone could prevent 30-40% of all cancers;*

• *just eating more vegetables and fruits could eliminate 20% of cancers. Avoiding tobacco could bring this figure up to 60-70%.*

Diet and Cancer...state of the art

The most comprehensive document on diet and cancer published to date, *Food, Nutrition and the Prevention of Cancer: a global perspective,* was released by the World Cancer Research Fund (WCRF) and the American Institute of Cancer Research (AICR) in 1997. This report by a panel of experts chaired by Dr. John Potter based its findings on over 4,500 credible scientific studies. It details patterns of diet and cancer throughout the world and examines the effects of various aspects of diet on 18 cancer sites. It provides recommendations, both for those who create health policies and for consumers. Table 2.4 provides a summary for the top 12 cancer sites, listed in order of their relative occurrence worldwide. The "Estimated Percent Preventable by Diet" provides a range of estimates as determined by a number of scientific studies.

Epidemiological studies (looking at population groups or subgroups) provide first-line evidence of the impacts of food and nutrition on cancer risk. With a few important exceptions, less affluent countries of Africa, Latin America, and Asia tend to have high rates of cancers of the mouth, pharynx, larynx, esophagus, stomach, liver, and cervix. The wealthier countries of Europe, North America, Australia and surrounding areas have relatively high rates of cancers of the colon and rectum, prostate, breast, and endometrium. Lung cancer, due mainly to tobacco, is the most common cancer in the world. As countries become more industrialized and urbanized, cancer rates tend to increase. Where diet is concerned, three things have become irrefutable:

• *Vegetable and fruit consumption is associated with lower risk of cancer at almost every site.*

• *Alcohol is highly detrimental for cancers of many sites (not just liver).*

• *Meat and animal fats are detrimental.*

Based on their findings, the panel made 14 recommendations for risk reduction, listed on the facing page.

Table 2.4 Findings on Diet and Cancer from the WCRF and AICR's Report
The strength of the link between diet and cancer is shown by *possible link*, probable link, and **convincing evidence of a link**. (Evidence that is suggestive but insufficient has been excluded.)

Top 12 Cancer Sites	Estimated % Preventable by Diet (low to high)	Dietary Factors Linked to Decreased Risk	Dietary Factors Linked to Increased Risk
Lung	20–33%	**Vegetables and fruits** Carotenoids in food *Vitamin C and selenium in food*	*Alcohol, Total and saturated fat, Animal fat, Cholesterol*
Stomach	66–75%	**Vegetables and fruits, Refrigeration** Vitamin C in food *Carotenoids in food* *Whole grains, Tea*	Salt and salting *Grilling and barbecuing meat and fish* *Starches*
Breast	33–50%	Vegetables and fruits *Carotenoids in foods, Fiber*	Alcohol, Obesity, *Meat* *Total, saturated and animal fat*
Colon, rectum	66–75%	**Vegetables,** *Carotenoids in food* *Starches, Fiber*	Alcohol, Meat, *Grilling (BBQ or broil), Total, saturated, and animal fat, Sugar, Obesity, Eggs*
Mouth and pharynx	33–50%	**Vegetables and fruits** *Vitamin C in food*	**Alcohol** *Hot maté (extremely hot tea)*
Liver	33–66%	*Vegetables*	**Alcohol,** Aflotoxin
Cervix	10–20%	Vegetables and fruits *Carotenoids and vitamin C in food*	
Esophagus	50–75%	**Vegetables and fruits** *Carotenoids and vitamin C in food*	**Alcohol** *Hot maté (extremely hot tea)* *Cereals*
Prostate	10–20%	*Vegetables*	*Meat, Total, saturated, and animal fat* *Milk and dairy products*
Bladder	10–20%	Vegetables and fruits	*Coffee*
Pancreas	33–50%	Vegetables and fruits *Vitamin C in food, Fiber*	*Meat* *Cholesterol*
Larynx/ Nasopharynx	33–50%	Vegetables and fruits	**Alcohol**

The most consistently protective dietary components appear to be:		**The most consistently harmful dietary components appear to be:**	
Vegetables	16 sites	Alcohol	7 sites
Fruits	12 sites	Meat, animal fat, and saturated fat	5 sites
Carotenoids in food	6 sites		
Vitamin C in food	5 sites	Total fat, grilling and barbecuing, and dairy products	4 sites
Fiber or whole grains	4 sites		
Whole grains	1 site	Salt and salting	2 sites

WCRF and AICR Dietary Recommendations for Cancer Risk Reduction in Individuals

Food Choices

• Choose predominantly plant-based diets rich in a variety of vegetables and fruits, pulses (legumes), and minimally processed starchy staple foods.

• Eat 400-800 grams (15-30 ounces) or five or more portions (servings) a day of a variety of vegetables and fruits, all year round.

• Eat 600-800 grams (20-30 ounces) or five or more portions (servings) a day of a variety of cereals (grains), pulses (legumes), roots, tubers, and plantains. Prefer minimally processed foods. Limit consumption of refined sugar.

• If eaten at all, limit intake of red meat to less than 80 grams (3 ounces) daily. It is preferable to choose fish, poultry, or meat from nondomesticated animals in place of red meat.

• Limit consumption of fatty foods, particularly those of animal origin. Choose modest amounts of appropriate vegetable oils.

Alcohol

• Alcohol consumption is not recommended. If consumed at all, limit alcoholic drinks to less than two drinks a day for men and one for women.

Food Processing and Preparation

• Limit consumption of salted foods and use of cooking and table salt. Use herbs and spices to season foods.

• When levels of additives, contaminants, and other residues are properly regulated, their presence in food and drink is not known to be harmful. However, unregulated or improper use can be a health hazard, and this applies particularly to developing countries.

• Do not eat charred food. For meat and fish eaters, avoid burning of juices. Consume the following only occasionally: meat and fish grilled (broiled) in direct flame; cured and smoked meats.

Food Storage

• Do not eat food, which, as a result of prolonged storage ambient temperatures, is liable to contamination with mycotoxins.

• Use refrigeration and other appropriate methods to preserve perishable food as purchased and at home.

Weight and Exercise

• Avoid being underweight or overweight, and limit weight gain during adulthood to less than 5 kg (11 pounds).

• If occupational activity is low or moderate, take an hour's brisk walk or similar exercise daily, and also exercise vigorously for a total of at least one hour in a week.

Dietary Supplements

• For those who follow the recommendations presented here, dietary supplements are probably unnecessary and possibly unhelpful for reducing cancer risk.

Note: The panel also discourages production, promotion, and use of tobacco in any form.

Vegans and Cancer...what we know

In light of the findings to date on specific food components and cancer, one would expect that the vegan diet would afford the greatest protection of all. While it appears very promising, the research that looks specifically at vegan diets is too limited to draw conclusions at this point.

In 1999 Key analyzed data from five prospective studies of mortality in vegetarians and nonvegetarians. While cancer mortality in vegans is assessed separately, the small population of vegans (753) relative to lacto-ovo vegetarians (23,265) and nonvegetarians (42,276) makes the findings merely suggestive.

The two largest prospective studies to date looking at the mortality of vegetarians were the Seventh-day Adventist (SDA) Mortality Study (comparing vegetarian Adventists with nonvegetarians in the general population) and the Adventist Health Study (comparing vegetarian and nonvegetarian Adventists). Pertinent findings from these studies are given on the next page.

Straight Answers to Common Cancer Questions

Do vitamin and mineral supplements help prevent cancer?

While we are not yet 100% certain, most do not appear to be helpful. The exception may be folate, as shown by the Nurses' Health Study of over 88,000 women (Giovannucci, 1995). Researchers compared nurses with folate intakes less than 200 mcg/day and greater than 400 mcg/day (including supplements); higher intakes were linked with a 30% reduced risk of colon cancer. Numerous other large trials, using other vitamin and mineral supplements such as beta-carotene and vitamin E have provided disappointing results; indeed, beta-carotene was found harmful in some studies. These nutrients have been shown to be protective *when provided in foods.* It appears that in foods, vitamins, minerals, and phytochemicals work together in very complex ways to reduce cancer risk. For example, flaxseed contains two substances that are known anticarcinogens—alpha-linolenic acid (an omega-3 fatty acid) and lignans. While these two substances have independent protective effects, they are even more effective when consumed together in flaxseed. If you take supplements, choose a multivitamin/mineral combination providing close to recommended intakes and avoid high-dose single nutrient supplements.

There has been a lot of press about a couple of studies showing no relation between fiber and colon cancer. Is it true that fiber offers no protection?

No, it is not true. Headlines declaring that fiber doesn't matter reached millions of people after results from the Nurses' Health Study showed no protective effect against colon cancer with higher fiber intakes. Unfortunately, the media failed to tell the whole story and the scientific community is still trying

Fast Facts from Adventist Mortality and Health Studies

Lung Cancer

- Risk for nonsmoking nonvegetarians compared to nonsmoking vegetarians: 50%
- Risk with low fruit consumption—less than 3 servings per week: 100%

(Note: Fruit consumption had a strong protective effect in this nonsmoking population.)

Prostate cancer

- Risk in nonvegetarians compared to vegetarians: 54%
- Risk with frequent consumption of soymilk—greater than 1 serving per day: 70%
- Risk with frequent consumption of legumes—greater than 3 times per week: 50%

(Note: Higher intakes of dried fruits and tomatoes and lower intakes of fish were also protective.)

Colon cancer

- Risk in nonvegetarians compared to vegetarians: 88%
- Risk in nonvegetarians who ate red meat less than once a week compared to vegetarians: 37%
- Risk in nonvegetarians who ate red meat more than once a week compared to vegetarians: 86%
- Risk in nonvegetarians who ate white meat less than once a week compared to vegetarians: 50%
- Risk in nonvegetarians who ate white meat more than once a week compared to vegetarians: 200%

(Note: Legume consumption was associated with a reduced risk of colon cancer in meat eaters, but this effect was not observed when large amounts of white meat were consumed.)

Bladder Cancer

- Risk in nonvegetarians eating meat 3 or more times per week compared with vegetarians: Double
- Risk in coffee drinkers (2 or more cups per day) compared to those who do not drink coffee: Double

Pancreatic Cancer

- Risk in those eating legumes, dried fruit, and vegetable protein products at least 4 times a week compared with people seldom eating these foods: 20%

Ovarian Cancer

- Nonvegetarians consuming meat 4 or more times a week compared with vegetarians: 66%

(Note: Death rates increased with egg consumption.)

Breast Cancer

- Lifetime risk in overweight 30-year-old (BMI over 50th percentile) compared with normal weight 30-year-old: 57%

to pick up the pieces. The results of this study must be viewed with caution for several reasons:

- Years of solid research suggest a link between high dietary fiber and lower rates of colon cancer. The result of one study does not negate this weight of evidence.

- The Nurses' Study relied on a food frequency questionnaire done on three occasions in the 1980s, with standards now considered by many scientists to be unreliable.

- In the high-fiber group, total intake was only 25 grams a day; cereal fiber less than 5 grams a day! Many experts believe this is simply not enough fiber to offer significant protection.

- During the first 14 years of the study, participants were not questioned about their use of fiber supplements.

- All dark breads were coded as being high in fiber. In fact, some dark breads are simply white flour with molasses added. The variation in fiber content of dark breads can range from about 1 to 7 grams per slice.

- Eighty percent of participants changed their fiber intake over the course of the study.

A more recent study (Jansen, 1999) in over 12,000 men in 7 countries had far different results. Jansen looked at mortality from colorectal cancer over a 25-year period and found that an increase of 10 grams of fiber a day was associated with a 33% lower death rate. When data from men with the highest fiber intakes (over 50 grams per day) was excluded, no such protective effect was observed. Researchers concluded that to defend against colorectal cancer, intakes of more than 30-40 grams of fiber a day may be necessary. (See pages 157 to 160 for vegan menus, along with fiber provided by each.)

Can vegan diets both prevent and reverse cancer?

Although there is some evidence that vegan diets are effective in preventing certain cancers, there is no evidence from larger studies showing that vegan diets can reverse cancer. A few anecdotal reports of individuals on vegan macrobiotic diets have been published. It may be unrealistic to expect any diet to reverse cancers that are induced by a combination of factors, including those that are distinct from diet, such as environmental contaminants or tobacco.

Are raw foods more protective against cancer than cooked foods?

We don't know. The evidence to date is for vegetables, raw or cooked. Some components appear to work better from raw foods and some work better from cooked foods. For example, carotenoids appear to be more available from cooked carrots and cooked tomatoes than from raw products. In garlic, certain phytochemicals are destroyed in cooking; others are formed. Without question, there is a trade off. Studies have not been sufficiently large or consistent enough to provide evidence for recommendations. For now, the bottom line is: eat more vegetables—raw, cooked, or both!

Should we avoid peanuts and tree nuts because of their aflatoxin content?

Aflatoxins have been implicated only for liver cancer, and even then, only in people with chronic hepatitis B. It appears to be a problem primarily where peanuts are dietary staples and they are stored in moist, warm areas, becoming moldy. In North America (with the possible exception of the southeastern U.S.), intake of aflatoxins is low. Nuts are an extremely valuable part of a vegan diet and should be included, rather than avoided. Be sure to purchase fresh nuts and store them in a cool, dry place, preferably in the freezer or refrigerator.

DIABETES

Diabetes is the seventh leading cause of death in the U.S. and an important risk factor for heart disease, stroke, kidney disease, blindness, and leg and foot amputations. There are two types of diabetes:

- *Type 1* (insulin-dependent diabetes mellitus or IDDM)—a lack of insulin production by the pancreas
- *Type 2* (noninsulin-dependent diabetes mellitus—NIDDM)—insulin resistance (pancreas produces insulin but the body is unable to use it efficiently)

Type 1 diabetes accounts for only about 10% of all cases. There are considerable global differences in Type 1 diabetes, and several observations have linked these differences to milk consumption. While some research indicates a pattern of increased diabetes with greater milk consumption, the pattern is not entirely consistent. A recent study by Elliot (1999) found that while total milk protein consumption did not consistently correlate with diabetes incidence, the consumption of specific milk proteins (beta-casein A + B) did. Different breeds of cows produce varying amounts of beta-casein A + B. These proteins produce a peptide called beta-casomorphin-7, which has immune-suppressing activity. While further research is warranted to determine the proportion of Type 1 diabetes caused by these milk proteins, we can expect that Type 1 diabetes would be less common among those who are raised as vegans without milk protein intake.

Type 2 diabetes is a disease that is seen with a frequency that varies tremendously across population groups, from virtually zero to as much as 50%. Approximately 80% of those suffering from Type 2 diabetes are overweight. Excess body weight is the single most important risk factor for Type 2 diabetes, especially for those who carry their weight in their upper body (apple shape), rather than hips and thighs (pear shape). Risk of diabetes is approximately doubled for those who are moderately overweight, tripled for those with frank obesity. For Type 2 diabetes, the most effective treatment is weight loss.

> ## Fast Facts from the Seventh-day Adventist Prospective Diabetes Study
>
> Risk of diabetes in male vegetarians vs. nonvegetarians: 53% lower.
> Risk of diabetes in female vegetarians vs. nonvegetarians: 55% lower
> Risk of diabetes in vegetarians aged 50-69 vs. similar aged nonvegetarians: 76% lower.
> Relative risk of diabetes in vegetarians vs. nonvegetarians:
> 45% for males and 71% for females★
> *★Listed as cause of death on the death certificate and adjusted for age*

Incidence of Diabetes in Vegans and Vegetarians

Worldwide, the lowest frequency of Type 2 diabetes is with populations eating near-vegan diets. Whether this is due strictly to lower body weight is not yet clear. Some convincing evidence exists that very-high-fiber diets may, in themselves, be protective. When populations such as these adopt a high-fat, low-fiber North American-style diet, diabetes risk quickly escalates. If they revert to their original diet, incidence of diabetes is once again reduced.

For Western vegetarians, evidence comes from a large study of Seventh-day Adventists (Snowdon, 1985). As yet there are no similar studies looking at the incidence of diabetes in Western vegan populations; however, there are several reasons that vegans may be at reduced risk:

- less obesity
- lower intakes of saturated fat (may increase insulin secretion, potentially leading to insulin insensitivity★)
- much higher intakes of fiber, especially soluble fiber (improves blood glucose response★)
- higher intakes of magnesium in well-designed vegan diets (insufficient magnesium may lead to insulin resistance★)
- higher intakes of unrefined foods (whole grains, legumes, vegetables, nuts, seeds) with low glycemic index★

★For more on these topics, see chapters 4, 5, 6, and 13.

TREATMENT OF DIABETES WITH VEGAN DIETS

Studies using low-fat vegan, vegetarian, or near-vegetarian diets for treatment of cardiovascular disease have resulted in marked improvements in blood glucose control and reduced requirements for hypoglycemic medications. Most

> ## *Vegan Dietary Guidelines for Type 2 Diabetes*
>
> - Achieve and maintain a healthy body weight. Reduce caloric intake as needed.
>
> - Meet nutrient needs by following the Vegan Food Guide on pages 154-55. Eating a wide variety of foods will help ensure a sufficient intake of trace minerals.
>
> - Aim for approximately 50-60% complex carbohydrates, 25-30% fat (mostly monounsaturated fats, with not more than 7% saturated fat and minimal trans fatty acids), and 10-20% protein.
>
> - Choose whole grains such as quinoa, barley, wheat berries, oat groats, rye berries, etc. when possible. Avoid refined carbohydrates such as bread, pasta, pretzels, bagels, crackers, etc., made from refined white flour.
>
> - Include moderate amounts of foods rich in monounsaturated fat (nuts, avocados, etc.) Watch portion sizes, especially for those who are overweight.
>
> - Include sufficient omega-3 fatty acids in the diet. People with diabetes may have difficulty with conversion of omega-3 fatty acids and should aim for at least 2.2 grams of alpha-linolenic acid per 1,000 calories or use long chain omega-3s from microalgae. (See pages 65-66.)

included lifestyle changes, such as increased exercise. In 1999 Nicholson carried out a pilot study with seven experimental subjects on a low-fat vegan diet without additional lifestyle changes and four control subjects on a conventional low-fat diet. The experimental group had an average of 28% reduction in fasting blood glucose (from 10.7 to 7.75 mmol/L/ 195 to 141 mg/dl). Of six on oral hypoglycemic agents, one discontinued and three reduced medication; of two on insulin, both reduced the amount. The control group had a 12% decrease in fasting blood glucose with no reductions in medication. While this study was small, it provides a good basis for further research studies.

OSTEOPOROSIS

Osteoporosis is a crippling disease that produces severe bone loss, robbing the body of as much as 30-40% of bone tissue. It is estimated that one in four North American women will develop osteoporosis in her lifetime, and by the age of 90, one in three will have suffered a hip fracture.

Propaganda from the dairy industry has led people to believe that osteo-porosis is a dairy deficiency disease. When one examines the worldwide incidence of osteoporosis, it becomes clear that this is simply not true. In many regions (e.g., Africa) where diets are predominantly plant-based and low in cal-cium and dairy, osteoporosis rates are low, while in many affluent Western countries where diets are high in both calcium and dairy foods, osteoporosis is much more prevalent. This fact has given rise to a theory among some vege-tarians that milk actually *causes* osteoporosis and that eliminating milk offers protection against this devastating condition. Proponents claim that milk pro-tein causes so much urinary calcium loss that any potential benefit is negated. This theory is equally untrue. Milk is neither cause nor cure for osteoporosis. The calcium losses induced by milk protein are miniscule in comparison to the total calcium content of milk. The protein in a cup of milk induces a urinary calcium loss of about 8-10 mg; it contains 300 mg calcium, about a third of which is absorbed. On the other hand, when one considers ethical concerns, environmental issues, and the health benefits of plant foods, there are many preferable calcium sources: fortified soymilk, green leafy vegetables, calcium-set tofu, legumes, almonds, and figs. These come packaged with protective phyto-chemicals rather than saturated fat, trans fatty acids, and cholesterol!

While calcium is important to bone health, that's not the whole story. Bones are composed of a protein matrix (35%) embedded with mineral salts (65%). Calcium is the most abundant mineral, but phosphorus and lesser amounts of magnesium, sodium, potassium, sulfate, fluoride, and chloride are also present. Vitamin D is critical to the deposition of calcium into the bone. Boron also appears to play a lesser role. Other dietary factors—excessive pro-tein or sodium—can negatively influence bone health. (For bone building, we need enough protein, but not too much!). Bones act as calcium banks, with deposits and withdrawals being made continually. Beyond diet, physical exer-cise (especially weight-bearing activity), reproductive hormones, and avoidance of smoking also play significant roles in bone health.

Research on the Bone Health of Vegans

Although there is little data available on the bone health of vegans, especially lifelong vegans, the research is not as encouraging as one might hope. To date, seven studies have been carried out assessing the bone health of vegans. Of these, three studies found no significant differences in bone mineral densities of the vegans and lacto-ovo vegetarians examined. Four studies found significant-ly lower bone mineral densities (10-20% lower on average) in vegans compared to lacto-ovo vegetarians, nonvegetarians, or both. In one study of over 800 women in China, the average bone mineral densities of women on dairy-free diets were approximately 20% lower than in those consuming dairy. In a Taiwanese study of more than 250 women, long-term vegans had 2½ times the risk of lumbar spine fracture and almost 4 times the risk of low bone mass of the femoral neck. Interestingly, very low protein intakes were shown to be detrimental to bone health.

The weight of the evidence suggests that vegans do need to be concerned about long-term bone health. It is important to note that almost half of the studies showing relatively poor bone health in vegans were done on less privileged people in the Orient with very restrictive diets and calcium intakes of 400 mg or less per day. Average calcium intakes of the Western vegans studied, although somewhat higher, were consistently less than half the current Acceptable Intakes (AIs). We would expect to see very different outcomes in vegans with lifelong use of fortified nondairy milks and orange juice, and other carefully selected calcium-rich plant foods. However, until the evidence becomes available, we cannot assume vegan diets will necessarily promote optimal bone health. It is important to adopt healthy lifestyle practices, both in avoiding common pitfalls and building on the natural advantages of plant-based diets.

Avoiding Potential Pitfalls

Vegan diets can contribute to poor bone health when inappropriately planned. The following factors appear to have the greatest negative impact.

- *Very low calcium intakes (350-500 mg/day).* These low calcium intakes may suffice for active people with genetically large bone frames, plant-based diets low in sodium, low but adequate protein intakes, and regular exposure to sun light. These low intakes will not likely be adequate for Western vegans, especially those with small bones, low body weight, low intakes of calories and other nutrients, little sun exposure, and/or sedentary lifestyles.

- *Insufficient vitamin D from sun exposure or fortified foods.* Vitamin D supports the absorption of bone-building minerals and positive calcium balance.

- *Inadequate energy intakes.* A lack of calories can lead to underweight (more common among vegans), which is a risk factor for osteoporosis.

- *Too little protein.* While too much protein can increase urinary calcium losses, protein is needed for formation of collagen (the protein component of bones).

- *Lower blood estrogen levels.* Vegans and other vegetarians may have lower estrogen levels and total reproductive hormones over their life span. Estrogen stimulates bone-building cells, so there is a connection between decreased estrogen and decreased bone density. Typically in vegetarians, menstruation begins a little later and menopause begins a little earlier, resulting in decreased lifetime exposure to estrogen. This can raise the risk for osteoporosis, though it reduces risk for breast cancer. Estrogen replacement therapy for post-menopausal women remains controversial for the same reasons.

Building on the Advantages

Vegan diets have excellent potential for supporting bone health. The following factors offer the greatest protection.

- *Moderate protein levels.* Vegan diets provide close to recommended intakes for protein, but are rarely excessive.

- *Lower sodium content.* Much dietary sodium comes from processed foods. Vegans tend to eat more whole plant foods and fewer processed foods, thus sodium intake is generally lower than that of nonvegetarians.

- *Less acid production.* Meat-centered diets produce a higher acid load than plant-based diets due to higher content of sulfur-containing amino acid. This acid results in increased urinary calcium losses.

- *Higher levels of certain protective vitamins.* Folate and vitamins C and K are associated with improved bone health; all three are higher in vegan diets than nonvegetarian diets.

- *Higher levels of certain protective minerals.* Minerals such as boron, magnesium, and potassium are protective and are higher in vegan diets than nonvegetarian diets. Boron (found in flax, fruits, leafy vegetables, nuts, and legumes) has been shown to reduce urinary calcium losses and may increase estrogen levels.

- *Richer in protective phytochemicals, particularly isoflavones (the mild plant estrogens in soy).* These isoflavones appear to inhibit the breakdown of bone tissue.

- *Lower alcohol and caffeine intakes.* Vegans tend to have lower intakes of alcohol and caffeine, both of which can contribute to bone loss.

The Bottom Line

Vegan diets offer both advantages and disadvantages where bone health is concerned. However, vegans can expect to enjoy excellent bone health throughout life by following the Vegan Food Guide (pages 154-55) and getting plenty of weight-bearing exercise, some of it in the sun. Whether one relies on whole, calcium-rich plant foods and sunlight, or vegan products that are fortified with calcium and vitamin D, achieving excellent bone health can be accomplished with relative ease.

RECOMMENDED RESOURCES

Vegan nutrition in health and disease is a lively and dynamic field of research.
To keep up to date and for information on many other topics, such as kidney disease, gastro-intestinal conditions, and immune/inflammatory diseases, we suggest subscriptions to three outstanding resources. All are written by leading experts and are reliable and readable.

- *Issues in Vegetarian Dietetics*: newsletter (Vegetarian Dietetic Practice Group of the American Dietetic Association); www.vegetariannutritiondpg.org

- *Loma Linda University Nutrition and Health Letter*: newsletter; subscribe at 888-558-8703 or vegletter@sph.llu.edu

- *The Vegetarian Journal*: magazine; subscribe at 410-366-VEGE or vrg@vrg.org

SELECTED REFERENCES

See also general references for the whole book on page 276.

Chiu, J. F. "Long-term vegetarian diet and bone mineral density in post-menopausal Taiwanese Women." *Calcif. Tissue Int.* 60 (1997): 245-9.

de Lorgeril, M. et al. "Mediterranean diet, traditional risk factors, and the rate of cardiovascular complications after myocardial infarction: final report of the Lyon Diet Heart Study." *Circulation* 99 (6) (1999) 779-785.

Esselstyn, C. B. Jr. "Updating a 12-year experience with arrest and reversal therapy of coronary heart disease." *Am. J. Cardiol.* 84 (3) (1999): 339-41.

Hu, J. F. et al. "Dietary calcium and bone density among middle-aged and elderly women in China." *Am. J. Clin. Nutr.* 58 (1993): 219-227.

Lau, E. M. "Bone mineral density in Chinese elderly female vegetarians, vegans, lacto-vegetarians and omnivores." *Eur. J. Clin. Nutr.* 52 (1998): 60-4.

Li, D. et al. "The association of diet and thrombotic risk factors in healthy male vegetarians and meat-eaters." *Eur. J. Clin. Nutr.* 53 (1999): 612-619.

Mann, J. I. "Dietary determinants of ischaemic heart disease in health conscious individuals." *Heart* 78 (5) (1997): 450-5.

McDougall, J. "Rapid reduction of serum cholesterol and blood pressure by a twelve-day, very low fat, strictly vegetarian diet." *J. Am. Coll. Nutr.* 14 (5) (1995): 491-6.280(23)130

Mezzano et al. "Vegetarians and cardiovascular risk factors: hemostasis, inflammatory markers and plasma homocystein." *Thromb. Haemost.* 81 (6) (1999): 913-7.

O'Connell, J. M. "Growth of vegetarian children: The Farm Study." *Pediatrics* 84 (3) (1989): 475-481.

Sanders, T. A. B. "Growth and development of British vegan children." *Am. J. Clin. Nutr.* 48 (3 Suppl) (1988): 822-5.

CHAPTER
3

Plant Protein: the Source of
All Essential Amino Acids

The word "protein" is derived from the Greek word protos, meaning "primary" or "first." Perhaps this refers to the first question asked of most vegans: "Where do you get your protein?" In fact, this question can be answered very simply: "From *all* of the whole plant foods I eat." International guidelines tell us to get 10–15% of our calories from protein. As you can see in Table 3.6 (pages 46–47), 10–40% of calories in most plant foods are derived from protein. By consuming enough calories from the vegan foods listed in this table, it's easy to get more than enough protein.

Some folks will be satisfied with your response and gladly move on to some other topic of conversation, like "Where do you get your calcium?" Others will just keep firing away protein questions like those below, and you'll feel a whole lot better being completely equipped with the answers:

How much protein do we need?

Which amino acids have to be in dietary protein, in what amounts, and do we get all of these from plant foods?

What about the digestibility of plant protein?

Do vegan diets provide enough protein?

Can a vegan diet be too low in protein?

How do vegans successfully meet their protein needs in the real world?

Do some people, such as those with certain blood types, need more protein or require animal protein?

Are there advantages—and disadvantages—to very-high-protein diets?

In answering these questions, we'll begin by looking at two aspects of our need for protein. First is the *quantity* or weight of protein that we require in our diets. Second is whether specific amino acids, the building blocks of protein, are present in adequate amounts to meet our protein-manufacturing requirements. Along with protein digestibility, this is referred to as protein *quality*.

QUANTITY: HOW MUCH PROTEIN DO WE NEED?

Adults require protein for a multitude of purposes, primarily the maintenance of tissues: muscle, bone (which is composed of protein and minerals), blood cells, and all other cells throughout the body. Protein needs are stated in terms of grams (g) of protein per kilogram (kg) body weight. Based on extensive research, the U.S. Recommended Dietary Allowance (RDA) for adult protein intake has been set at 0.8 grams per kilogram body weight per day. (See Table 3.1 for pound-kilogram conversion.) This figure includes a safety margin for variations in the digestibility of foods, a 25% increase to cover what different individuals might require, plus a little extra on top of that. (For ease in calculation, you may use 1g protein/kg body weight to get an approximate amount.)

The protein in foods such as tofu, textured soy protein, meat substitutes, and refined grains is as digestible as that in animal products. Vegans who eat plenty of these highly digestible plant foods can use the figure of 0.8g/kg to determine their recommended protein intakes. Whole grains, beans, and vegetables have a tremendous range of health benefits, including an abundance of fiber, phytochemicals, trace minerals, and vitamins. At the same time, these foods are slightly less digestible than some of the more refined and processed plant foods. Thus, with diets composed of whole plant foods, some experts suggest that a factor of 10-15% be added to cover differences in protein digestibility. (See more about this on pages 44-45.) **For vegans on predominantly whole foods diets, a figure of 0.9 g protein per kg body weight is suggested (Table 3.1).** This allows us to calculate the recommended protein intake for an adult of any weight.

Table 3.1 Equivalent Weights in Pounds and Kilograms With Vegan Protein Recommendation

Pounds	Kilograms	Protein g (0.9 g/kg)
1	0.45	0.9
2.2	1.0	2.2
105	47.6	43
120	54.4	49
135	61.2	55
150	68.0	61
165	75.0	67.5
180	81.6	73
195	88.4	80
210	95.3	86

Recommended Protein Intake at 0.9 g/kg body weight

For a person weighing 135 lbs (61 kg): multiply 61 x 0.9 = 55 g protein.

For a person weighing 165 lbs (75 kg): multiply 75 x 0.9 = 68 g protein

For yourself:

a) weight in pounds ____ lb divided by 2.2 lb/kg to give weight in kg = ____kg

b) multiply ____kg x 0.9 = ____g is your recommended protein intake

(For ease in calculation, you may use 1g protein/kg body weight.)

Additional protein is required to build new tissue at times of growth. Specific requirements for pregnancy, lactation, infancy, childhood, and adolescence are covered in Chapters 10 and 11. Athletes who are in the process of building muscle (pages 248-49) and people who are underweight and want to gain (page 238) also require additional protein above the 0.8-0.9 g/kg. Those who are recovering from burns or surgery may need as much as 20% of their caloric intake to be derived from protein in order to rebuild tissue.

QUALITY

To meet our needs, which amino acids have to be in dietary protein?

The building blocks for protein consist of 22 different amino acids. Of these, nine must be supplied in the diet and are known as essential amino acids (EAAs). The remainder can be formed in our bodies from these EAAs and other dietary components. Each protein, which may be hundreds of amino acids in length, is comprised of a specific sequence and arrangement of these 22 building blocks. Whether it is an enzyme or a cell component, every protein's complex structure supports the roles it must play, such as creating a tiny field of electrical attraction.

Earlier in the century, the quality of a particular protein was assessed by looking at its ability to support weight gain in young rats. The method was called the PER (Protein Efficiency Ratio). The rats gained weight quickly (for example, doubling their weights in a week) and grew fur, which required substantial amounts of two amino acids, methionine and cysteine. As we eventually discovered, EAA requirements of furry, rapidly growing rats are quite different from those of humans at any age; for example, amounts of methionine needed are 50% higher than human requirements.

In the last decade, the PER has been replaced by the PDCAAS (Protein Digestibility Corrected Amino Acid Score), which is now accepted as the official method for evaluating protein quality for humans by the World Health Organization and the FDA. This updated method is based on

Table 3.2 Essential Amino Acids(EAAs): Suggested Pattern of Requirements for Humans Past Infancy FAO/WHO/UNU Recommended Pattern

EAA	Amount in 1 g protein mg
Tryptophan	11
Histidine	19
Methionine + Cysteine*	25
Isoleucine	28
Threonine	34
Valine	35
Lysine	58
Phenylalanine + Tyrosine*	63
Leucine	66

*Some of our requirement for methionine can be filled by the amino acid cysteine, and some of our requirement for phenlyalanine can be filled by the amino acid tyrosine. Thus these two amino acids are listed, in addition to the nine essential amino acids, however, they are not considered essential themselves.

human needs, not rat requirements.* The score is arrived at by measuring the amounts of different essential amino acids in one gram of a particular protein (corrected for digestibility) and comparing that with the amounts of these amino acids per gram of protein required for growth and good health by a person two years of age or older. It is understood that any protein that meets the needs of growing two-year-olds will meet and exceed adult requirements and therefore be more than adequate. A model of this scoring pattern is given for tofu in Table 3.2. Names of the nine EAAs are shown on the left side of the table. If one gram of protein provides enough of all the essential amino acids to meet the standard, then the protein is given a score of 1 (or 100%).

What amounts of these amino acids must be present?

In practical terms, this means that if we consume exactly enough tofu, for example, to exactly meet our RDA for protein (at 0.8g/kg body weight) and no other dietary protein at all, tofu alone will provide all the EAAs we need. Milk and eggs also have scores of 1 (100%).

To figure out how to meet our daily protein needs with tofu alone, it helps to know that 1 cup (248 grams) of firm tofu provides 40 g protein. Someone who needs 50 grams of protein could meet needs with 1¼ cups firm tofu. This may seem like a fair amount of tofu to eat; however, consider this. Egg has long been considered the "gold standard" for protein quality. One medium egg provides 5.5 g protein, so someone who needs 50 g of protein would have to eat 9 eggs that day to meet their entire need for protein, including every EAA. Cow's milk protein also receives a protein quality rating of 1 (100%). One cup (244 g) of 2% milk provides 8.1 g protein, so someone who needs 50 grams of protein would have to drink 6 cups of 2% milk to meet their daily requirement.

Table 3.3   Comparison of EAAs in Tofu's Soy Protein with Suggested Pattern from Table 3.2

EAA	EAA in Tofu mg/g protein	EAA x 92% (Digestibility Score) mg/g protein	Suggested Pattern mg/g protein
Tryptophan	16	15	11
Histidine	29	27	19
Methionine + Cysteine	27	25	25
Isoleucine	50	46	28
Threonine	41	38	34
Valine	50	46	35
Lysine	66	61	58
Phenylalanine + Tyrosine	82	75	63
Leucine	76	70	66

Report of Joint FAO/WHO Expert Consultation, Protein Quality Evaluation, Food and Nutrition Paper 51, FAO of the United Nations, 1991

Our model is simplified. Digestibility can vary from one amino acid to another; however, there is considerable debate among experts about exact digestibility factors to be used, derived from different methods. This example illustrates the PDCAAS scoring system. In reality, most foods have scores of less than 1. Generally, soy products are rated between 90% and 100%, with soy protein concentrates and soy protein isolates having particularly high scores (depending on the manufacturing process used). Say a protein has a PDCAAS of 0.9 (90%) or more, as most soyfoods do. If you consume enough of that single protein to meet the RDA plus 10%, you'll get the recommended quantity of protein, including every essential amino acid.

It's possible to meet all of one's protein needs from primarily one plant food—and not just on paper. In human feeding experiments, such as the five-week Michigan State University Bread Study, adults met their amino acid needs with 90-95% of the dietary protein from wheat, the remainder coming from fruits and vegetables. However, using just one food (animal *or* plant) to meet protein needs would get pretty dull! The majority of studies assessing single protein sources have been done with animals. (A caged rat can't really complain about being served the same item for weeks on end.) In reality, meeting needs for all essential amino acids is easily done with the normal assortment of plant foods that humans select, even on a rather simple diet that meets caloric requirements.

Essential Amino Acids from Plant Foods

When our diets contain a variety of foods, the amino acids derived from digesting all the different proteins are pooled in fluids between body cells and in the intestine. This pool can be drawn on to build muscle, replace cells and enzymes, and generally meet our needs. Every plant food does not exactly match the suggested pattern; however, when the diet provides an assortment of plant proteins over the course of a day (based on the Vegan Food Guide, pages 154-55), all amino acids are present in abundance. Beyond this, it is not necessary to carefully combine grains and beans (protein complementation) at one meal to get the perfect mix of amino acids, as was thought in the last century. This idea became popular with the book *Diet for a Small Planet*, which emphasized the need for variety in a way that became unnecessarily complicated. Author Frances Moore Lappé was being overly cautious in order to avoid criticism from the "nutrition establishment." She later explained, "In combating the myth that meat is the only way to get high-quality protein, I reinforced another myth" (of the need for protein complementation at the same meal).

For those who want to explore the amounts of protein and EAAs in specific foods, a helpful resource is the USDA. Nutrient Database for Standard Reference at www.nal.usda.gov/fnic/cgi-bin/nut_search.pl.

In our tissues, the EAAs from animal foods and plant foods are indistinguishable. In fact, the amino acids in all animal protein are derived from plants, whether they originated from a cow that ate beans and grains, or from a fish that ate a smaller fish that ate seaweed. People often assume that plants are lacking in some amino acids because that is what they have been told for years. It comes as a surprise to some that plants are the source of all EAAs. In fact, the reason these are termed "essential" is that they are essential in the diet for humans and for animals, whose physiology is similar. Clearly, we don't need meat or any animal foods to get EAAs—plant foods provide every one.

> *"Although it is frequently pointed out that plant protein can provide all human nutrition needs; it is nevertheless the case that the misconception persists that they are nutritionally inferior to animal proteins. This is the result of both complex social and cultural attitudes towards meat and the scientific tradition of protein-quality evaluation in animals."*

Professor D.J. Millward,
University of Surrey, U.K., *Meat or wheat for the next millenium?*
Proceedings of the Nutrition Society 1999; 58:249-260.

What about the digestibility of plant protein?

The people who developed tofu in the Orient thousands of years ago were certainly on to a good thing. Processing makes the protein in tofu far more digestible than in the original soybeans. The same is true for soy protein isolates and concentrates that are used in making veggie meats. Though we may think of "natural" as better, when it comes to soy digestibility, a little processing does wonders!

To complete this section on protein quality, see typical examples of protein digestibility in Table 3.4. To be on the safe side, many experts recommend that vegans add a factor of 10-15% to the protein RDA, particularly when the protein intake is

Table 3.4 *Protein Digestibility in Foods*

Foods	Digestibility
Soyfoods	90-98%
White bread	97%
Whole wheat bread	92%
Oatmeal	86%
Canned lentils	84%
Soybeans	78%
Black, garbanzo, kidney, and pinto beans, canned	72-89%
Meat, fish (for comparison)	94%

predominantly from whole foods, rather than from the more processed soy-foods, veggie meats, and refined grains.

It is tempting to assume that because white bread and processed soyfoods provide more digestible protein, they are better choices than the whole foods. This is not the case. While processing foods increases the digestibility of their protein, it strips them of numerous valuable vitamins, minerals, and phyto-chemicals. However, for some people, including some of these more processed products can help balance a diet that would other-wise be too bulky, which can be a concern with small children or people whose caloric needs are high.

Table 3.5 Calorie and Protein Intakes of Vegans

Group (numbers)	Calories	% calories from protein	Grams protein
Summary from 12 Studies			
Males & Females (217)	2298	11.9%	68
Males (85)	2646	11.5%	76
Females (84)	1980	11.6%	57
Oxford Study			
Males (45)	2580	11.3%	73
Females (69)	1911	12.2%	58

Do vegan diets provide enough protein?

Table 3.5 provides a summary of average vegan protein and calorie intakes in 12 studies of vegan diets conducted over the past half century in the U.S., U.K., Canada, New Zealand, and Australia. Averaged, the figures show protein and calorie intakes that are right on target in meeting dietary recommendations. Results from The Oxford Vegetarian Study of 6,000 vegetarians and 5,000 nonvegetarians in the United Kingdom between 1980 and 1984, showed sim-ilar intake patterns for 114 vegans in the group. A look at the vegan menus in Chapter 9 will convince you that recommended protein intakes can be met and exceeded at a range of caloric intakes.

Plant Protein…Perfect for People!

There are different ways of stating the amount of protein in foods. You may see it listed as grams of protein per serving, grams of protein per 100 calories, or percentage of calories derived from protein (see Table 3.6). Whichever system is used, there are some plant foods that "measure up" well against animal foods. It is also clear that to meet an individual's RDA for protein (usually about 50 to 70 grams per day), it certainly helps to include the plant protein powerhouses—tofu, veggie "meats," lentils, and other legumes—though this is not essential. On average, we need about 3 to 4 grams of protein for every 100 calories we con-sume. On weight loss diets, use the high end of this range or a little more.

Table 3.6 Protein and Percentage of Protein, Fats, and Carbohydrates in Foods

Food & Category	Measure (Serving)	Protein grams	Protein grams per 100 Calories	% Calories From Protein	% Calories From Fat	% Calories From Carbohydrate
Vegetables						
Bean sprouts, raw	1 c	3.2	10.1	32%	4%	64%
Broccoli, raw	1 c	2.6	10.6	33%	9%	58%
Carrot, raw, 7.5"	1	0.7	2.4	9%	4%	87%
Cauliflower, ckd	½ c	1.1	8.0	26%	15%	59%
Corn, ckd	½ c	2.7	3.1	11%	9%	80%
Green/yellow beans, ckd	½ c	1.2	5.4	18%	6%	76%
Eggplant, ckd	½ c	0.4	3.0	10%	6%	84%
Kale, raw	1 c	2.2	6.6	22%	11%	67%
Mushrooms, ckd	½ c	1.7	8.0	26%	13%	61%
Potato, baked, med.	1	2.8	2.1	8%	1%	91%
Potato, sweet baked, med	1	2.0	1.7	7%	1%	92%
Romaine lettuce, raw	1 c	0.9	11.6	36%	10%	54%
Spinach, raw	1 c	1.6	13	36%	10%	54%
Turnip, ckd, mashed	½ c	0.8	3.4	12%	3%	85%
Legumes, Tofu, Tempeh, Veggie "Meats"						
Cranberry beans, ckd.	1 c	16.5	6.9	27%	3%	70%
Garbanzo/chickpeas, ckd	1 c	14.5	5.4	21%	14%	65%
Lentils, ckd	1 c	17.9	7.8	30%	3%	67%
Navy beans, ckd	1 c	15.8	6.1	24%	4%	72%
Kidney beans, ckd	1 c	15.4	6.8	27%	3%	70%
Pinto beans, ckd	1 c	14.0	6.0	23%	3%	74%
Soybeans, ckd	1 c	28.6	9.6	36%	43%	21%
Tofu, firm	½ c	19.9	10.9	40%	49%	11%
Tofu, silken firm	½ c	17.4	11.1	45%	40%	15%
Tempeh	½ c	15.8	9.6	36%	32%	32%
Yves deli slices	4 (2 oz)	14.6	20.6	84%	2%	14%
Vegan wieners, veggie dogs (selected)	1 (1½ oz)	9.1-10.9	16.4-20.6	73-90%	0-18%	8-17%
Vegan burgers (selected)	1 burger	11.0-13.0	7.9-11.4	32-40%	0-24%	36-68%
Veggie ground round	2 oz.	12.0	19.0	76%	2%	22%
Seitan (dry mix)	¼ c	15.9	14	56%	6%	38%
Recommended Distribution in Overall Diet				*Protein* 10-15%	*Fat* 15-30%	*Carbohydrate* 55-75%

Food & Category	Measure (Serving)	Protein grams	Protein grams per 100 Calories	% Calories From Protein	% Calories From Fat	% Calories From Carbohydrate
Nuts, Seeds, and Butters						
Almonds	¼ c	7.4	3.5	13%	74%	13%
Brazil nuts	¼ c	5.1	2.1	8%	86%	6%
Cashew nuts	¼ c	5.2	2.7	10%	69%	21%
Flaxseed	2 Tbsp.	3.8	4.0	15%	59%	26%
Hazelnuts	¼ c	4.4	2.1	8%	83%	9%
Pecans	¼ c	2.6	1.4	5%	88%	7%
Pine Nuts	¼ c	8.2	4.2	16%	75%	9%
Pistachios	¼ c	3.6	6.6	13%	71%	16%
Pumpkin seeds	¼ c	8.5	4.5	17%	71%	12%
Sesame tahini	3 Tbsp	8.1	3.0	11%	78%	11%
Sunflower seeds	¼ c	8.0	4.4	17%	71%	12 %
Nondairy Milks						
Soymilks (selected)	½ c	2.5-4	1.3-4	19-21%	21-24%	55-60%
Grain milks (selected)	½ c	0.5-2	0.4-1	6-14%	0-12%	74-94%
Grains & Products						
Barley, pearled, ckd	½ c	3.6	1.8	7%	3%	90%
Millet, ckd	½ c	4.2	3.0	12%	8%	80%
Oats, ckd	½ c	3.0	4.2	17%	14%	69%
Quinoa, ckd	½ c	3.0	3.5	14%	14%	72%
Rice, brown, ckd	½ c	4.5	2.1	8%	7%	85%
Rice, white, ckd	½ c	2.2	1.8	8%	2%	90%
Whole wheat flour	¼ c	4.1	4.0	15%	5%	80%
Bread, whole wheat	1 slice	2.7	3.9	15%	14%	71%
Bread, white	1 slice	2.5	3.1	12%	12%	76%
Fruits						
Apples	1 med	0.3	0.3	1%	4%	95%
Oranges	1 med	1.2	2.0	7%	2%	91%
Bananas	1 med	1.2	1.1	4%	4%	92%
Berries	½ c	0.4	2.0	7%	10%	83%
Animal Foods (for comparison)						
Milk, 2%	½ c	4.0	6.2	25%	35%	40%
Cheese, cheddar	¾ oz	5.3	6.4	25%	73%	2%
Egg, medium	1	5.5	8.4	35%	62%	3%
Ground beef	2 oz.	10.6	8.0	33%	67%	0%
Chicken, roasted	2 oz.	15.3	12.5	52%	48%	0%
Cod baked/broiled	2 oz.	12.9	21.7	92%	8%	0%
Salmon baked/broiled	2 oz.	15.5	12.6	52%	48%	0%
Recommended Distribution in Overall Diet				Protein 10-15%	Fat 15-30%	Carbohydrate 55-75%

Can a vegan diet be too low in protein?

The American Dietetics Association's position paper on vegetarian nutrition states, *"Plant sources of protein alone can provide adequate amounts of essential amino acids if a variety of plant foods are consumed and energy needs are met."* Diets based on the Vegan Food Guide (pages 154-55) easily provide enough protein. It is possible for vegans to fall short on poorly designed diets. The most common reasons for insufficient protein are:

1. If total caloric intake is insufficient for any reason, such as anorexia nervosa (see page 220), depression, isolation, poverty, or lack of appetite due to illness.

2. If higher-protein plant foods aren't included or are included in insufficient amounts. For example, when:

• most calories come from junk foods—soda pop, chips, French fries, donuts, pastries, and candy.

• protein is believed to be a nonissue and the diet is built around salads and fruit;

• beans are avoided because they are poorly digested, cause too much gas, or seem difficult or too time-consuming to prepare;

• people travel or eat in restaurants most of the time and have difficulty finding vegan options, so they end up living on salads and stir-fried vegetables.

How do vegans successfully meet protein needs in the real world?

We can get our RDA of protein by eating veggies, but it may take a shopping cart full of greens! Here are ways to get 10 grams of protein:

• 2 cups of cooked broccoli or spinach (cooking makes veggies more compact)

• 3 to 4 cups of mung bean sprouts, raw broccoli, or cooked kale

• 4½ cups of cooked mushrooms

• 11 cups of Romaine lettuce

• 8 oranges or bananas

• 2 cantaloupes

• 11 cups of berries (best eaten while sitting in the midst of the berry patch)

PLAN YOUR PROTEIN POWERHOUSES

While some raw foods enthusiasts fill the table with great, glorious salads, for most vegans it's important to find concentrated protein foods that work for them as well. If beans give you gas, try veggie "meats" and the smaller legumes such as lentils, as many people find these more digestible. If preparation is a challenge, explore the many vegan burgers, dogs, and slices now in supermarket coolers and freezers. For travelers and restaurant eaters, there are simple things you can do to increase your protein intake. (Also see page 273.)

- Take along soynuts, pumpkin seeds, peanuts, and other nuts and seeds as your primary snack foods.
- Try tofu jerky and vegan protein bars.
- Remember to order vegan food when you fly. The airline may call it vegan, vegetarian, or strict vegetarian.
- If you can't find a place that's entirely vegetarian, frequent ethnic or California-style restaurants more often. Most offer great veggie options.
- If you are stuck at a steak house, ask if the chef could toss some nuts or beans into your stir-fry or salad; often they have chick-peas on hand.
- Invest in a few food containers with tight-fitting lids so that you can easily take along protein-rich foods such as hummus, marinated tofu, or a legume-based dish from home or a local deli. When you're out, you'll find that the rest of a meal is easily available—salads, veggies, baked potatoes.

Look through Table 3.6 and discover protein solutions for the challenges you face. Often these are the same foods that are good sources of iron and zinc. For those people who "fail" at being vegan, think they get too hungry, or don't have enough stamina on a vegan diet, often the problem is not getting enough of the plant foods that are concentrated protein sources. This takes us to some very timely questions.

Do some people, such as those with certain blood types, need more protein or require animal protein?

The answer is yes and no. Yes, some people do need more protein than others. For every nutrient—vitamins, minerals, protein—there is quite a range in individual requirements. For this reason the RDAs are based on average needs, with a substantial safety margin to cover those who require more. Because of normal human variability, some people do well with plenty of the higher-protein plant foods (whether legumes or the more processed alternatives), others function best with a diet centered around grains, and still others thrive with mostly veggies and raw foods. A great variety of eating patterns can be developed using the Vegan Food Guide on pages 154-55 as a basic model to ensure that needs for all nutrients are met. It can be helpful to experiment with different styles of vegan eating and see what makes you feel best.

No, there is *no* scientific evidence that people with certain blood types need animal protein. As noted on page 44, the basic building blocks for our protein-building needs are the same essential amino acids that are present in both animal and plant foods, and those present in animal flesh originated from plants. People of all blood types have done well, and continue to do well, on vegan diets—a show of hands at any vegetarian gathering proves that quickly enough. Though the blood type theory was catchy enough to sell books, it is not backed up by reliable science.

It's also true that some people are at a loss when it comes to shopping for and preparing nourishing vegan meals or don't know how to obtain balanced vegan meals when eating out. So they think vegan (or vegetarian) diets don't work for them or aren't sufficiently nourishing. It's not that it can't be done, it's just that they haven't learned how to do it. This is not entirely surprising because most of what we learned about food and cooking while growing up was geared to meat-centered diets, not vegan diets. Thus, most people need to spend some time acquainting themselves with this new way of eating. Attending cooking classes, reading, and learning about practical issues and nutrition through vegetarian events can make a big difference in gaining new skills.

Books that tell us to avoid carbohydrates and focus on meat protein tend to be written by those with little expertise (or interest) in the tremendous contribution that plant protein foods can make towards weight management, leveling of blood glucose, or reduction of chronic disease risk. These writers characterize meats as "protein foods," whereas a glance at Table 3.6 shows that what's *really* distinctive about meat is the high fat levels. Where these books ring a note of truth is that they steer people away from sugar and other refined carbohydrates. They are also striking a chord with some vegetarians whose diets have been too low in protein-rich plant foods.

Are there advantages and disadvantages to very-high-protein diets?

WHERE THEY WORK

High-protein diets have their usefulness. People require extra protein at times of growth (see Chapters 10 and 11), while healing after injury, or when building muscle (see Chapters 15 and 16). Even at times of increased need, the amount required tends to be less than 2 grams protein per kg body weight.

Often, where total protein needs are elevated, total energy needs are also increased (as is the case for many endurance athletes). The extra food consumed to meet caloric requirements is generally more than sufficient to ensure that protein needs are met. Where necessary, high-protein diets can be constructed using tofu, tempeh, and veggie meats; you can see high-protein vegan menus at various caloric levels on pages 157-60. With soy protein powders, intakes can be higher still. Certainly vegan diets can easily be constructed to rival nonvegetarian diets in both quality and quantity of protein.

WHERE THEY DON'T WORK

Because meat-eaters often eat twice as much protein as recommended by the RDA, and a rash of popular (but poorly researched) diet books have recently hit the market, health experts are discovering big problems with high-protein, low-carbohydrate diets:

• When carbohydrate intake drops as low as 10-15% of calories, a condition called ketosis may result. This condition can also occur during starvation or in diabetes mellitus, where there simply isn't enough carbohydrate to fuel the brain. Lacking carbohydrate, the body breaks down fat, and by-products (called ketone bodies) build up in the bloodstream. The brain, which depends on glucose as its fuel, doesn't do well under these conditions. Ketosis can lead to dizziness, headaches, nausea, fatigue, sleep problems, and bad breath. If it continues, it can result in dehydration, gout, hypotension (low blood pressure), electrolyte imbalances, and possible kidney and liver damage.

• High-protein, low-carbohydrate diets are often deficient in components that protect us against disease. The carbohydrate-containing foods in Table 3.6 have been hitting the headlines because of their protective vitamins, phytochemicals, and fiber. For these reasons, they continue to be our most valuable energy sources.

• Diets that are very high in protein may actually provide excessive amounts of the sulfur-containing amino acids methionine and cysteine. These amino acids are most concentrated in animal foods, and their breakdown into sulfur-containing compounds causes the urine to become acidic, increasing urinary excretion of calcium. In addition, methionine is metabolized into homocysteine, the presence of which is a well-accepted risk factor for heart disease. The more limited presence of methionine and cysteine in many plant foods was once thought to be a disadvantage. However, that perspective has shifted and we are now aware that while we need sufficient amounts of these sulfur-containing amino acids, excess intakes of them may turn out to be detrimental to health.

• Animal protein raises blood cholesterol level, while plant protein lowers it. Animal protein also comes packaged with saturated fat and cholesterol—two dietary components well linked with many chronic diseases, especially heart disease.

There is no question that consuming sufficient protein is essential to optimal health. However, this does not imply "the more, the better." Indeed, protein intakes closer to the RDA, or approximately 10-15% above the RDA, may turn out to be not only adequate, but preferable for most vegans, unless they have elevated requirements.

CHAPTER
4

Big Fat Lies... cutting through the confusion

For many individuals, becoming vegan is about taking another step along the road to better health. Dairy and eggs are key sources of saturated fat and cholesterol, so their removal is viewed as the final conquest over these potentially damaging food components. While a person might assume that a vegan diet would end their concerns about fat, as it turns out, it simply shifts the focus. Debates about the amounts and types of fats that best support health are very active within vegan and vegetarian communities. Where the amount of fat is concerned, there are two well-recognized, opposing camps—the very-low-fat camp and the high-fat "Mediterranean-diet" camp. Discussions surrounding the optimal sources of fat for vegans are no less intense, particularly where essential fatty acids, tropical fats, and specific plant oils are concerned.

This chapter presents the latest findings on the current issues and controversies concerning fats in the vegan diet, namely:

• How much fat is optimal?
• Can vegan diets supply sufficient essential fatty acids?
• What are the best fat sources?

Before exploring each of these in detail, here is basic information on fats.

A FATTY ACID PRIMER

Fats and Oils: a family of compounds that do not dissolve in water, including notable members listed below.

Fatty Acids: a basic component of fats and oils. Foods contain three types of fatty acids in varying amounts: saturated, monounsaturated, and polyunsaturated. Fatty acids are built of a chain of carbon atoms with hydrogen and oxygen molecules attached. The degree of "saturation" of a fatty acid depends on the amount of hydrogen attached to the carbon atoms.

Saturated Fat (SFA): molecules completely packed or "saturated" with hydrogen. Fats containing mainly SFA are generally hard at room temperature. These fats are often considered "bad fats" because they have consistently been linked to an increased risk of heart disease and some forms of cancer. Animal products are the main sources of saturated fats in Western diets. Vegans rarely need to concern themselves with avoiding saturated fats, as plant-based diets generally contain very little. Most higher-fat plant foods contain about 5-20% of fat as saturated fat (compared with 20-30% in fish, 33% in chicken, 50% in meat, and 66% in dairy). The one important exception is tropical oils. Coconut fat is over 85% saturated, palm kernel oil over 80%, and palm oil about 50%. These foods are rarely a major part of any North American diet, in most cases accounting for less than 2% of the fat.

Monounsaturated Fatty Acids (MFA): fatty acids having one spot in the carbon chain where hydrogen is missing (one point of "unsaturation"). Fats high in these MFA are generally liquid at room temperature and semi-solid when refrigerated. These are generally considered "good fats"; they are beneficial to health and can protect against chronic diseases, especially heart disease. These are neutral or slightly beneficial in their effects on total cholesterol levels and do not decrease HDL ("good") cholesterol; in fact, they may even slightly increase it. There is some evidence that monounsaturated fats reduce blood pressure and enhance blood flow. Monounsaturated fats have been shown to improve blood sugar control in people with diabetes without the increase in triglyceride levels that often occurs with high-carbohydrate diets. While diets high in some fats are associated with various forms of cancer, monounsaturated fats do not increase and may decrease cancer risk. The main dietary sources are olives, olive oil, canola oil, avocados, most nuts (except for walnuts and butternuts), high-oleic sunflower oil, and high-oleic safflower oil.

Polyunsaturated Fat (PUFA): fat molecules having more than one spot in the carbon chain where hydrogen is missing (more than one point of "unsaturation"). Fats high in these PUFA are liquid at room temperature and when refrigerated. Reviews concerning their health effects are inconsistent. When they replace saturated fats and trans fatty acids in the diet, a drop in blood cholesterol levels occurs. However, their impact on other risk factors for cardiovascular disease is varied. Some studies show that they increase cancer risk, others show them to be protective. Their effect on other diseases seems no less contradictory. Much of the confusion can be explained by learning more about the two families of polyunsaturated fatty acids and specific family members. The main dietary sources are vegetable oils, seeds, nuts, grains, legumes, and other plant foods.

Essential Fatty Acids (EFA): the two polyunsaturated fatty acids required in the diet. One is linoleic acid, a parent in the omega-6 fatty acids family. The other, alpha-linolenic acid, is a parent in the omega-3 fatty acids family. The family names describe the first point of unsaturation on the carbon chain. Both families may be considered "good fats" necessary to health. Before the days of refined vegetable oils, people consumed small, but roughly equal, amounts from these two families. This provided a healthy balance of these essential fats. Two forces have upset this delicate balance. First, the highly unsaturated omega-3 fatty acids are diminished in the food supply because they are highly vulnerable to oxidation and rancidity, therefore are usually removed during food processing. Second, the availability of omega-6 fatty acids has increased, especially after the huge push in the 1970s to replace saturated fats with omega-6-rich vegetable oils. The result: our current food supply provides 10-20 times as much omega-6 fatty acids as omega-3 fatty acids. This crowding out of nutritious omega-3s has serious implications for health and chronic disease, as these generally have more favorable health effects than do the omega-6 fatty acids. For vegans this is an important consideration, as without special care, the imbalance in an all-plant diet may be even more pronounced.

Long-Chain Polyunsaturated Fatty Acids: larger polyunsaturated fatty acid molecules. These fatty acids originate from either of two places. We can convert parent fatty acids to longer-chain fatty acids in the body, or we can consume these long-chain fatty acids directly from food. In the omega-6 family, we may either convert linoleic acid to arachidonic acid (AA) or AA can be consumed directly from animal products such as meat and dairy products. In the omega-3 family, we may convert alpha-linolenic acid to eicosapentaenoic acid (EPA) and docosahexaenoic acid (DHA). These can be consumed directly from fish or microalgae, the single-celled organisms that provide EPA and DHA to fish. These long-chain fatty acids are not considered "essential" because we can make them from the parent fatty acids, with the possible exception of DHA for premature infants. However, they are very important to health.

Trans Fatty Acids: an undesirable type of monounsaturated fatty acids that have had the hydrogen atoms rearranged during food processing. Trans fatty acids are produced when liquid oils are hydrogenated to form hard, stable fats. Fats containing these were developed to improve shelf life of foods, increase melting point of fat (good for deep-frying), and permit high temperature cooking. From the food industry's viewpoint, these fats are attractive. From a health perspective, they are a disaster. Gram for gram, trans fatty acids appear to be 2 to 4 times as damaging as saturated fatty acids. With trans fatty acids accounting for 4% of calories in North American diets, it is estimated that they are responsible for up to 10% of deaths from heart disease. In the U.S diet, about 90% of trans fatty acids come from the hydrogenated fats in processed and fried foods and the remaining 10% come from meat and dairy products. Our most concentrated sources are margarine, shortening, crackers, cookies, granola bars, chips, snack foods and deep-fried foods. As many of these foods contain eggs or dairy products, they are excluded from vegan diets.

Cholesterol: a sterol that is necessary to the structure of every cell. As the human body makes about 800 mg of cholesterol a day, there is no need for any cholesterol in the diet. Cholesterol comes only from animal foods and is concentrated in eggs and organ meats. High intakes increase risk for chronic diseases, especially of the heart and blood vessels.

Cardiovascular Disease (CVD): diseases of the heart (coronary heart disease—CHD) and blood vessels (coronary artery disease—CAD), including hypertension (high blood pressure) and stroke. The most common form of CVD is atherosclerosis or hardening of the arteries.

LDL cholesterol: a cholesterol carrier that is largely responsible for depositing cholesterol in artery walls. It is often referred to as "bad cholesterol" because elevated LDL is associated with increased risk of CVD.

HDL cholesterol: a carrier of cholesterol that helps remove cholesterol from the arteries, returning it to the liver for removal from the body. It is referred to as "good cholesterol" because high levels decrease risk of heart disease, while low levels can increase risk.

Triglycerides: the main form of fat in foods and in the body, each molecule consisting of three fatty acids plus a carbohydrate backbone. Elevated triglycerides in the blood can increase risk of CVD.

THE FAT DEBATE: HOW MUCH FAT IS OPTIMAL IN THE VEGAN DIET?

The question of optimal fat intake is among the most hotly debated issues in vegetarian nutrition. On one side are the proponents of very-low-fat diets (10-15% fat or less), generally advising against the use of concentrated fats, oils, and higher-fat plant foods such as nuts, seeds, avocados, and olives; full-fat soyfoods are often limited too. On the other side are those advocating much higher-fat "Mediterranean" style diets (30-40% fat) with low saturated fats, negligible trans fatty acids, but liberal use of olive oil, nuts, seeds, avocados, and olives (plus cheese and dairy products in nonvegan diets).

Very-Low-Fat Vegetarian Diets

Research showing the phenomenal success of very-low-fat vegetarian diets (often in combination with other lifestyle changes) in treating patients with severe heart disease made these diets extremely popular among Western vegans and vegetarians. In 1990, Dr. Dean Ornish proved that diet and lifestyle changes (a vegetarian diet with less than 10% fat, stress management, aerobic exercise, and group therapy) could not only slow the progression of athero-sclerosis but significantly reverse it. After one year, 82% of Ornish's patients who made these changes experienced "regression" of their disease (an actual reduction in artery plaque and improvement in blood flow), while a control group who ate a "heart healthy diet containing no more than 30% fat and less than 200 mg of cholesterol daily" continued to get worse. Over the next four years, improvements continued for people in the very-low-fat group, while those in the control group got progressively worse and experienced twice as many heart attacks or other serious events, such as a stroke or heart failure. In 1995, Dr. John McDougall reported an average decrease in total cholesterol of 11% and a 6% drop in blood pressure in 500 subjects following a 5% fat vegan diet for only 12 days. In 1999, Dr. Caldwell Esselstyn reported on a 12-year ongoing study of 11 patients on a very-low-fat vegan diet, coupled with cho-lesterol-lowering medication. Approximately 70% experienced reversal of their disease. In the eight years prior to the study, these patients had a total of 48 car-diac events, while in over a decade of the trial, only one patient (someone not complying with the diet) experienced a heart attack or other serious event.

Though these very-low-fat diets were designed for therapeutic use, many vegetarians and vegans have embraced them as the "gold standard" for healthy eating and promote them as ideal for people of all ages.

Mediterranean-Style Diets

In apparent conflict with the low-fat diet findings, studies of certain populations suggest that some high-fat diets are also protective. Key's classic Seven Countries Study provided powerful evidence for a relationship between diets high in sat-urated fat, blood cholesterol levels, and the incidence of coronary artery disease. Yet, surprisingly, the lowest mortality rate was not in the country with the low-est total fat intake, but on the island of Crete where people consumed a Mediterranean-style diet, high in fat but low in damaging saturated fats, trans fatty acids, and cholesterol. These findings challenged the notion that amount of fat is the most important dietary predictor of blood cholesterol levels and raised the possibility that the type of fat could be even more important.

One of the most important tests of this theory was the Lyon Heart Study (1996). In this study, 302 post-heart attack patients ate a modified version of a Mediterranean-style diet based on grains, vegetables, fruits, legumes, and fish, with olive oil, canola oil, and canola-based margarine as added fats. As controls, another 303 patients were assigned to an American Heart Association Step 1-type Diet. Nutritional characteristics of the two diets, based on intakes of 144 (Mediterranean) and 83 (control) patients, in the final visit (after 46 months) are shown in Table 4.1.

Table 4.1 The Lyon Heart Study—Dietary Intakes★

	Mediterranean-Style Diet	Prudent Step-1-Type Diet
Total Fat	30%	34%
Cholesterol	203 mg	312 mg
Saturated Fat	8%	12%
Monounsaturated Fat	11%	13%
Polyunsaturated Fat	6%	5%
Omega-6:omega-3	4:1	18:1
Fiber	19 g	16 g

★Based on the nutrient intakes of 83 control and 144 experimental patients in the final visit (46 m follow up)

By the end of two years, those on the Mediterranean diet had an unprecedented 76% lower risk of dying of a heart attack or stroke. Follow-up not only confirmed cardiac protection up to four years after the first heart attack, but also showed a 61% reduction in cancer risk.

Mediterranean diets provide a compelling argument in favor of higher-fat diets. However, the real message is that it is a big mistake to ignore the type of fat and the balance of essential fatty acids. Clearly, it is not nuts, seeds, avocados, olives, or soybeans that are responsible for the epidemic of chronic disease that plagues us.

Making Sense of the Dichotomy

While it may appear that this debate is about diametrically opposed eating patterns, very-low-fat vegetarian diets have more in common with Mediterranean-style diets than is generally recognized. Both are based on vegetables, legumes, fruits, and whole grains, and both provide abundant plant protein, fiber, phytochemicals, vitamins, and minerals—all protective to health. Neither is high in saturated fat, trans fatty acids, cholesterol, or animal protein, dietary components that may contribute to chronic disease. Both keep linoleic acid (the essential fatty acid that is too high in most plant-based diets) down to a healthy level. The Mediterranean diet includes monounsaturated fat-rich food and oils and is richer in omega-3 fatty acids (the fatty acids that tend to be too low in plant-based diets). From research to date, we know that monounsaturated fat is not harmful and may be beneficial, and that omega-3 fatty acids are highly protective. The health advantages provided by foods rich in monounsaturated fats (i.e. nuts, avocados, and olives) and omega-3 fatty acids (flaxseeds, walnuts, soy products) may be as much related to the abundance of valuable vitamins, minerals, phytochemicals, protein, and fiber, as to their fat content.

For many scientists, the debate centers on the optimal amount of fat to prevent, treat, or reverse chronic diseases. It is often assumed that the diet that will reduce disease risk is also best for the entire population. While this may make sense for an overindulgent adult population with high risk of chronic disease, a healthy vegan population with people of all ages has very different nutritional needs. In establishing appropriate guidelines for fat, we must not only consider disease reduction, but also ensure proper growth and development of infants and children, achieve adequate nutrient intakes, and maximize absorption of nutrients and phytochemicals.

Optimal Fat Intakes for Vegans

When we consider all factors important to achieving and maintaining excellent health throughout the life cycle, neither very-low-fat vegetarian/vegan diets nor high-fat Mediterranean-style diets are optimal for the general vegan population. Both have potential disadvantages.

POTENTIAL PROBLEMS WITH VERY-LOW-FAT DIETS

Very-low-fat diets may:

- Provide excessive bulk and insufficient calories, particularly for infants, children, and those with very high energy requirements.
- Contain inadequate essential fatty acids (especially omega-3 fatty acids), particularly during infancy, childhood, pregnancy, and lactation.
- Compromise absorption of fat-soluble vitamins, minerals (including iron, zinc, manganese, and calcium), and phytochemicals.
- Reduce the nutritional value of the diet when "fat phobic" consumers select nonfat cookies, cakes, chips, etc., while obsessively avoiding nutritious, higher-fat plant foods such as avocados, olives, nuts, seeds, and tofu.
- Cause a drop in HDL cholesterol ("good cholesterol") and a rise in triglycerides, increasing risk for cardiovascular disease.* This is not generally a

---

The primary function of HDL is the removal of excess cholesterol from the bloodstream. When there is less cholesterol to remove, there is less need for HDL cholesterol. Thus, a drop in HDL is not always detrimental to health.

concern when the primary sources of carbohydrates are whole plant foods. Problems arise when the diet is based on refined grains such as bread, bagels, pasta, and pretzels.

POTENTIAL PROBLEMS WITH HIGH-FAT DIETS

High-fat diets may:

• make it very difficult to meet nutrient needs, particularly if much of the fat comes from oil, margarine, mayonnaise-type spreads, etc. These foods are very concentrated calorie sources but contain few nutrients;

• lead to excessive caloric intakes, contributing to obesity in some individuals;

• increase risk for other chronic diseases (e.g., cancers of the lung, prostate, breast, colon, and rectum);

• result in a rise in free radical reactions★ and oxidative damage to body tissues, potentially increasing risk of heart disease, cancer, diabetes, arthritis, age-related health problems, and neurological disorders;

The Best of Both Worlds…meeting halfway in between

While there are advantages to both very-low-fat vegan diets and higher-fat Mediterranean-style diets, most experts agree that the level of fat intake that is most protective to health lies somewhere in between.

The World Health Organization (WHO), in their 1990 report "Diet, Nutrition and the Prevention of Chronic Diseases," recommended a total fat intake between 15-30% of calories. In 1995 the Food and Agriculture Organization (FAO) in collaboration with the WHO recommended an upper limit of 30% fat for sedentary individuals and 35% for active individuals (if they are not eating more calories than needed, have adequate essential fatty acid and nutrient intakes, and get less than 10% of their calories as saturated fat). Most Western governments and national and international health organizations advise limiting fat to not more than 30% of total calories. They also caution not to restrict fat during the first two years of life. (Human breast milk provides 45-50% of its energy from fat.) After the age of two and until full height is reached, fat should gradually be reduced to 30% of total calories or less.

Remember that disease risk is as strongly associated with sources of fat as with the amount of fat in the diet. If the primary source of fat is whole plant foods (nuts, seeds, soy, avocados, and olives), one can expect to maintain excellent health eating a relatively high proportion of total calories as fat (i.e., 30%

★*Free radicals are molecules containing one or more unpaired electrons that react quickly with molecules. (Most molecules are stable, containing only paired electrons.) This creates more free radicals, setting off a destructive chain of oxidative damage to tissues. Free radicals react easily with polyunsaturated fats (which are unstable molecules).*

of calories). In contrast, when fat is derived from animal sources and processed fats (i.e. hydrogenated oils), adverse health consequences could be realized with relatively moderate total fat intakes.

Optimal fat intakes for vegans fall nicely into the 15–30% of calories from fat range. For those with chronic disease or obesity it may be prudent to aim for the lower end of this range, while those struggling to maintain or gain weight may need to aim for the upper end of the range. It is important to note that healthy vegans may do better with slightly higher fat intakes than are desirable for nonvegetarians. Vegan diets are bulky and the fat from nutrient-rich whole plant foods such as nuts, seeds, and soyfoods gives a necessary balance. The best way to ensure that fat does not dilute the nutrient density of the diet is to make nuts, seeds, soyfoods, and other higher-fat plant foods your main source of dietary fat.

Current Fat Intakes

While the differences in the total fat content of vegan, lacto-ovo vegetarian, and nonvegetarian diets are not as remarkable as might be expected, the differences in the types of fat are noteworthy. Table 4.2 on page 64 shows significant variations in cholesterol, saturated fat, and trans fatty acids intakes between these dietary groups, vegan intakes being more consistent with nutrition recommendations. One study examining trans fatty acids in body fat found lacto-ovo vegetarians to have one-third less trans fatty acids in their tissue than nonvegetarians, and vegans eating no refined foods to have no detectable levels. Note that vegan intakes of trans fatty acids can vary considerably with intake of processed foods. While there are few specific recommendations for trans fatty acid intakes, most authorities agree that current intakes should not be increased, and many agree that the optimal intake is zero.

THE NEGLECTED NUTRIENTS: CAN VEGANS GET ENOUGH ESSENTIAL FATTY ACIDS?

While there is no question that vegan diets are closer to recommendations for the dietary fat components listed previously, the same cannot be said regarding essential fatty acids (EFA). Indeed, many experts believe that vegetarians, and especially vegans, could be at a considerable disadvantage. There are two specific issues here: getting enough essential fatty acids and getting a healthy balance of these fatty acids. Essential fatty acid nutrition is tricky business and a lively field of research. To help you understand the concerns, here's a basic update.

Recall (from the primer on page 54) the parents of the two essential fatty acid families, linoleic acid (LA) and alpha-linolenic acid (LNA). Both are necessary for the formation of healthy cell membranes and are vital to the maintenance of cell integrity, permeability, shape, and flexibility. They are also critical to the development and functioning of the brain and nervous system, and are

Fatty Acid Abbreviations
Omega-6 Fatty Acids
Linoleic acid – LA
Arachidonic acid – AA
Omega-3 Fatty Acids
Alpha-linolenic acid – LNA
Eicosapentaenoic acid – EPA
Docosahexaenoic acid – DHA

involved in the production of hormone-like substances called eicosanoids that regulate many vital organ systems. A deficiency of LA results in impaired growth, fatty liver, skin lesions, and reproductive failure. LNA deficiency, although less well understood, appears to cause impaired visual and brain development, and neurological disorders.

The long-chain fatty acids in each of these families are very important to health and have more of an effect on body functions than their parent fatty acids. The long-chain omega-6 fatty acid AA and the omega-3 fatty acid EPA can be converted to eicosanoids. Those formed from AA are very potent, increasing blood pressure, inflammation, platelet aggregation, blood clotting, and cell proliferation, while those formed from EPA are less potent, protecting against these responses. Getting a good balance of parent omega-6 and omega-3 fatty acids is important because each family competes for the enzymes necessary to convert parent forms to longer chain fatty acids. If one parent fatty acid is plentiful while the other is scarce, much more of the plentiful fatty acid will be converted. For example, in North American diets (including vegan and vegetarian diets), there is a far greater proportion of linoleic acid relative to alpha-linolenic acid, thus more AA will be formed relative to EPA. This may increase risk for chronic diseases, including heart disease, cancer, diabetes, osteoporosis, and numerous immune and inflammatory disorders.

Docosahexaenoic acid (DHA) is not converted to eicosanoids but is an important structural component of the gray matter of the brain, the retina of the eye, and specific cell membranes, and is found in high levels in the testes and sperm. Low levels of DHA have been associated with several neurological and behavioral disorders such as depression, schizophrenia, Alzheimer's disease, and Attention Deficit Hyperactivity Disorder (ADHD). It is also linked to reduced visual and brain development in infants. Thus, while these long-chain fatty acids are not technically "essential" nutrients, we must ensure sufficient levels by relying on conversion from parent fatty acids or by consuming them directly from foods.

Plants provide little, if any, long-chain fatty acids (with the exception of single-celled ocean plants and some seaweeds), so ensuring sufficient conversion to these forms is especially important for people eating vegan or near vegan diets. The most significant factors that can interfere with conversion are:

Dietary Factors

- excessive intake of omega-6 fatty acids (this alone can reduce conversion by 40-50%)
- excessive saturated fat, cholesterol, and trans fatty acids
- insufficient intakes of calories and protein
- deficiencies of vitamins (pyridoxine or biotin) and minerals (zinc, magnesium, copper, calcium)
- alcohol (inhibits activity of conversion enzymes delta-5- and delta-6-desaturase)

Other Factors

- stage of life (infants have limited ability to convert; conversion ability also declines in old age)
- metabolic disorders (people with diabetes have reduced delta-6-desaturase function)
- chronic disease (certain disease states may affect ability to convert)
- genetics (some genetic disorders can seriously impair the conversion process)
- smoking (reduces conversion ability)

Getting enough of the right stuff?

Historical evidence suggests that both essential fatty acids were plentiful in early human diets. It was not until the turn of the 20th century that things started to change. With the advent of food processing and the emphasis on longer shelf life, unstable omega-3 fatty acids were seen as a disadvantage. Thus their presence in the food supply gradually diminished. At the same time, omega-6-rich vegetable oils gained a strong hold on the market, and the balance between the two essential fatty acids began to tilt precariously. Now, almost all North American diets provide a poor balance of these essential fatty acids. Vegan and vegetarian diets generally contain even more omega-6 fatty acids, thus balance can be even worse (although it need not be).

Diagram 4.1 Metabolism of Essential Fatty Acids

Omega-6 Fatty Acid Family	Omega-3 Fatty Acid Family
Linoleic Acid (LA) (sunflower, safflower, corn, and grape-seed oils, seeds, walnuts, grains) ↓	Alpha-Linolenic Acid (LNA) (flaxseed, hempseed, and canola oil, walnuts, butternuts, greens, soy) ↓
Gamma-linolenic acid (GLA) (primrose and borage oils) ↓	Eicosapentaenoic acid (EPA) → less potent eicosanoids (fish, seaweed, microalgae) ↓
Arachidonic acid (AA) → more potent eicosanoids (animal fats)	Docosahexaenoic acid (DHA) (fish, eggs, microalgae)

Recommended Intakes of Essential Fatty Acids

The World Health Organization recommends that a minimum of 4% of calories come from total polyunsaturated fatty acids. Health Canada suggests a minimum 3% of calories from omega-6 fatty acids and 0.5% from omega-3 fatty acids or 1% for infants who do not receive a direct source of EPA and DHA. While the U.S. government has not yet established recommended intakes for essential fatty acids, the National Institute of Health (NIH) proposed "Acceptable Intakes" in 1999. These are 2-3% of total calories for LA, 1% of total calories for LNA, and 0.3% of total calories for EPA plus DHA. They recommended a dietary intake of total EPA and DHA of at least 650 mg/day, and a minimum of 300 mg of DHA/day during pregnancy and lactation. This recommendation assumes intake of fish, as microalgae sources that might be used by vegans and other vegetarians are not commonly used. Most experts agree that where there is no EPA or DHA in the diet, the intake of alpha-linolenic acid should be at least 1-2% of calories, and possibly more in pregnancy. To be consistent with the NIH recommendations, allowing for typical conversion rates, total intakes of LNA would need to be adjusted upwards to about 3-4% of calories.

Scientists use the ratio of omega-6:omega-3 fatty acids to assess the balance between essential fatty acids in the diet. The World Health Organization suggests a ratio between 5:1 and 10:1, the Canadian government advises between 4:1 and 10:1, and the NIH (based on their "Acceptable Intakes") suggests between 2:1 and 3:1. Giving careful consideration to current research, recommendations, and the essential fatty acid intakes and status of vegans, we advise a ratio between 2:1 and 4:1, and no higher than 6:1.

> *Optimal omega-6 to omega-3 ratio: 2:1 - 4:1*

Actual Intakes of Essential Fatty Acids

As shown in Table 4.2, vegan ratios are far from optimal, unbalanced by high intakes of the omega-6 fatty acids that are so widely distributed in plant foods. Total intakes from the omega-3 fatty acid family provide a similar proportion of calories for all three dietary groups. Intakes of long-chain omega-3 fatty acids come from eggs (one large supermarket egg providing about 50 mg DHA) and from fish. (See Table 4.3 for food sources.)

Vegan and Vegetarian EPA and DHA Status

Compared to serum levels of nonvegetarians, vegan levels of long-chain omega-3s are low, indicating limited conversion. A total of five studies have examined the long-chain omega-3 fatty acid status of vegans compared with

Table 4.2 *Fat Intakes of Vegans, Lacto-Ovo Vegetarians and Omnivores*

	Recommended Intakes	Vegan	Lacto-Ovo Vegetarian	Omnivore
Total Fat	15-30%	28-32%	30-34%	34-36%
Cholesterol	less than 300 mg	0	100-200	200-400 mg
Saturated Fat	less than 7-8%	4-8%	8-12%	10-14%
Trans Fatty Acids	0%	0-2%	2-4%	4-8%
Omega-6	3-5%	10-12%	8-10%	5-7%
Omega-3	1-2%	0.5-1%	0.5-1%	0.5-1%
LNA	2.2 g+	1-3	1-3	1-3
EPA	-	0	3	46
DHA	-	0	33	78
Omega-6/ Omega-3	2:1-6:1	14:1-20:1	10:1-16:1	7:1-14:1

nonvegetarians. In 4 of the 5 studies, the levels of DHA and EPA were between 22% and 55% that of nonvegetarians (well under half in most cases). The one study that found slightly higher levels of DHA and EPA in vegans (62-65% that of nonvegetarians) was done on children (aged 11-15 years). The higher DHA and EPA levels in children may be attributable to better conversion in this population and/or to reserves accumulated during the breast-feeding period. Interestingly, levels of AA are very similar in vegans and nonvegetarians, indicating that vegans have no difficulty with the omega-6 conversion.

Sanders (1992) compared the essential fatty acid composition of human breast milk and found that milk from vegan mothers had over double the linoleic acid and alpha-linolenic acid content of the nonvegetarian mothers, but less than half the DHA. The essential fatty acid status of the infants reflected the levels in the milk they received. Vegan infants had less than 30% of the EPA and DHA of nonvegetarian infants.

Does Supplementation with LNA or DHA Improve Essential Fatty Acid Status of Vegans and Vegetarians?

A few studies have looked at the effect of improving the omega-6:omega-3 ratio or adding a direct source of DHA to the diet. The earliest trial by Sanders and Younger (1981) using LNA supplementation in vegans documented a significant increase in EPA but no significant change in DHA. An important study by Ghafoorunissa (1992) showed that by providing an omega-6:omega-3 ratio of 4:1, conversion of LNA to both EPA and DHA could be accomplished. A few studies have looked at the effect of improving the omega-6:omega-3 ratio or adding a direct source of DHA to the diet. Conquer and Holub (1996,

1997) provided vegetarian subjects with microalgae supplements with 1.62 g of DHA/day. DHA in the serum and platelets increased by well over 200%, while EPA levels increased by more than 100%. No similar studies have been done on vegans.

The Question of Conversion: Do Vegans Need a Direct Source of EPA/DHA?

With vegan intakes of EPA and DHA typically being zero and serum levels low, an important question arises: Can vegans sufficiently convert parent fatty acids, LA and LNA, to longer chain fatty acids or do they need a direct dietary source?

While conversion of LA to AA is rarely a problem for vegans (probably due to high ratios of LA in the diet), conversion of LNA to EPA and DHA is far less efficient, with rates shown in the chart to the right. DHA consumed directly from microalgae can be converted back to EPA from DHA.

Most experts agree that adequate conversion can take place, providing sufficient LNA is consumed and factors that can depress conversion enzymes are minimized. Reducing intake of omega-6 fatty acids is especially important. While we know healthy individuals convert some LNA to EPA and DHA, we are not sure if the

Conversion Efficiency of Omega-3 Fatty Acids
LNA → EPA: 5-10%
LNA → DHA: 2-5%
DHA → EPA: 9-12%

amount of conversion that normally takes place promotes optimal health.

What about vegans with high DHA requirements or who are at risk for poor conversion?

Many people have elevated DHA/EPA requirements (e.g., pregnant and lactating women, infants, or those with diseases linked to poor EFA status), while others are at risk for poor conversion (those with diabetes or neurological disorders, infants, and elderly people). We do not know how much LNA is needed to ensure sufficient conversion in such individuals. Possibly conversion is so limited that for optimal health some people require a direct source of DHA. For example, premature infants do not convert alpha-linolenic acid to DHA sufficiently, thus they require a direct source. Fortunately, the best source of all is breast milk—the ideal food for all infants.

If DHA needs are elevated or conversion is lacking, the affected individual has two options:

- *Maximize conversion.* Increase intake of LNA to at least 4-5 g/day (about 2.2 g per 1,000 calories) and reduce intake of LA to not more than 8-10 g/day.
- *Provide a direct source of DHA.* Aim for 100-300 mg/day from microalgae supplements.

In some cases it may be prudent to do both. Though uncommon, it is possible to overdo omega-3 fatty acid intake. If a person minimizes omega-6 fatty acids and is using large amounts of omega-3 fatty acids (i.e., over 2 Tbsp. flax oil/day), resulting in a ratio of omega-6:omega-3 of less than 1:1, insufficient LA conversion can occur. Enzymes preferentially convert omega-3 fatty acids when compared to omega-6 fatty acids. Remember that a balance of 2:1-4:1 (omega-6:omega-3) appears optimal.

Sources of Essential Fatty Acids

The primary sources of the two essential fatty acids, LA and LNA, are plants, on land and in the sea.

The most common sources of long-chain fatty acids, AA, EPA, and DHA are animal foods (although DHA and EPA are also available from sea plants).

Omega-6 Fatty Acids

- LA: seeds (sunflower, safflower, hemp, grape, pumpkin, sesame); nuts (walnuts, butternuts); corn; soybeans; oils extracted from these foods
- AA: meat; poultry; dairy products

Omega-3 Fatty Acids

- LNA: green leaves of plants (dark green leafy vegetables, broccoli); seaweeds; selected seeds (flax, chia, hemp, canola); nuts (walnuts, butternuts); soybeans; oils extracted from these foods
- EPA & DHA: fish; eggs; poultry (if chickens were fed fish meal); seaweed, microalgae (original source for fish)

Note: Specific amounts of fatty acids in foods are listed in Table 4.3 on pages 67-68.

Vegan DHA—Let's get growing!

The original sources of EPA and DHA are not fish but microalgae, microscopic sea plants that are consumed by small fish (which are then consumed by larger fish). While the advantages of fish and fish oil are well known and strongly embraced by the medical community, the original sources of the long-chain fatty acids responsible for these benefits are plants. That is good news for vegans! By cultivating these plants, we would have a renewable, clean source of EPA and DHA. We wouldn't have to worry about the PCBs, DDT, mercury, lead, or other toxic pollutants, or cholesterol that may come packaged with fish. At present, two companies market cultured microalgae—Martek and OmegaTech. (See page 76.) This microalgae is rich in DHA but contains little EPA. Amounts of EPA and DHA in microalgae vary tremendously, but those that are currently being cultured contain 10-40% of the dry weight in DHA. This microalgae is sold as a nutritional supplement in gel caps. (No vegan caps

Table 4.3 *Fatty Acid Composition of Selected Foods*

Food/serving size	% calories from Fat	Saturated Fat (% of total fat)	Mono. Fat (% of total fat)	Omega-6 (% of total fat)	Omega-3 (% of total fat)	LNA gm	EPA mg	DHA mg
Oils								
Canola oil, 1 Tbsp.	100%	7%	61%	21%	11%	1.6	0	0
Corn oil, 1 Tbsp.	100%	13%	29%	57%	0%	0	0	0
Cottonseed oil, 1 Tbsp.	100%	26%	22%	52%	0%	0	0	0
Flaxseed oil, 1 Tbsp.	100%	9%	18%	16%	57%	8.0	0	0
Grapeseed oil, 1 Tbsp.	100%	5%	16%	70%	0%	0	0	0
Hempseed oil, 1 Tbsp.	100%	8%	16%	57%	19%	2.7	0	0
Olive oil, 1 Tbsp.	100%	15%	75%	9%	1%	0.8	0	0
Palm oil, 1 Tbsp.	100%	51%	39%	10%	0%	0	0	0
Palm kernel oil, 1 Tbsp.	100%	85%	11%	2%	0%	0	0	0
Peanut oil, 1 Tbsp.	100%	19%	48%	33%	0%	0	0	0
Safflower oil, 1 Tbsp.	100%	6%	14%	75%	0%	0	0	0
Safflower oil, high oleic, 1 Tbsp.	100%	6%	75%	14%	0%	0	0	0
Sesame oil, 1 Tbsp.	100%	14%	40%	42%	0%	0	0	0
Soybean oil, 1 Tbsp.	100%	14%	23%	51%	7%	0.9	0	0
Sunflower oil, 1 Tbsp.	100%	10%	19%	65%	0%	0	0	0
Sunflower oil, high oleic, 1 Tbsp.	100%	10%	84%	4%	0	0	0	0
Walnut oil, 1 Tbsp.	100%	9%	23%	53%	13%	1.7	0	0
Nuts, Seeds, and Soy								
Almonds, 1 oz. (¼ c)	80%	10%	65%	23%	1%	0.14	0	0
Butternuts, 1 oz. (¼ c)	84%	2%	18%	59%	15%	2.5	0	0
Cashews, 1 oz. (¼ c)	72%	20%	59%	17%	0%	0	0	0
Flaxseed, whole, 2 Tbsp.	41%	9%	18%	16%	57%	5.2	0	0
Flaxseed, ground, 2 Tbsp.	41%	9%	18%	16%	57%	3.8	0	0
Hazelnuts, 1 oz. (¼ c)	87%	7%	75%	14%	0%	0	0	0
Macadamia nuts, 1 oz. (¼ c)	95%	16%	78%	2%	0%	0	0	0
Peanuts, 1 oz. (¼ c)	76%	14%	50%	32%	0%	0	0	0
Pecans, 1 oz. (¼ c)	94%	8%	59%	26%	1%	0.3	0	0
Pistachios, 1 oz. (¼ c)	72%	12%	53%	30%	0%	0	0	0
Pumpkin seeds, 1 oz. (¼ c)	76%	19%	31%	45%	0-5%	0-0.7	0	0
Soybeans, 1 c cooked	47%	14%	22%	50%	7%	1.0	0	0
Tofu, firm ½ c (4.5 oz)	54%	14%	22%	50%	7%	0.7	0	0
Walnuts, 1 oz (¼ c)	90%	6%	14%	58%	14%	2.6	0	0
Seaweeds								
Irish moss, 100 g, raw	< 1%	32%	14%	7%	45%	.001	46	0
Kelp, 100 g, raw	12%	63%	25%	18%	2%	.004	4	0
Spirulina, 100 g, raw	13.5%	49%	12%	23%	15%	0.2	0	0
Wakame, 100 g, raw	13%	32%	14%	8%	46%	.001	186	0

Food/serving size	% Calories from Fat	Saturated Fat (% of total fat)	Mono. Fat (% of total fat)	Omega-6 (% of total fat)	Omega-3 (% of total fat)	LNA g	EPA mg	DHA mg
Fruits and Vegetables								
Avocados, 1 med	86%	16%	63%	12%	1%	0.25	0	0
Greens, 1 c	12-14%	28%	5%	11%	56%	0.1	0	0
Olives, 10 large	84%	13%	74%	8%	0.5%	0.02	0	0
Animal Foods, for comparison								
Eggs, 1 lg	61%	31%	38%	12%	0.7%	.02	5	51
High-fat fish, 3 oz.	40-50%	20%	50%	2%	23%	0.1	500	800
Low-fat fish, 3 oz.	5-10%	20%	20%	6%	50%	0	100	150

are available at the present time.) If desired, it can be squeezed out of the caps and taken as a liquid supplement. OmegaTech is currently working on producing a dried form of microalgae, which we can expect to see on the market in the near future. Seaweeds are even lower in fat than most land vegetables (less than 1-14% of calories from fat) but do contain small amounts of long-chain fatty acids. A 100 g serving provides, on average, about 100 mg of EPA, but little DHA. Seaweeds do not contribute significantly to EPA intakes in the Western world but are important sources where people use large quantities of seaweed on a daily basis (i.e., northern Japan and other parts of Asia).

What can vegans do improve their intake, balance, and conversion of essential fatty acids?

- Avoid using concentrated omega-6-rich oils as your primary fat sources, and limit processed foods.
- Select oils high in monounsaturated fats and omega-3 fatty acids.
- Eat good sources of omega-3 fatty acids each day.
- Consider taking a direct source of long-chain omega-3 fatty acids. Explore your options with seaweeds (for significant amounts of EPA, large amounts are needed) and microalgae (lobby companies to develop vegan-friendly products).

PICK OF THE CROP...WHAT ARE THE BEST FAT SOURCES FOR VEGANS?

Vegan eating patterns can be designed to provide an excellent intake and balance of all fats, including essential fatty acids. The next section provides practical help for fine-tuning dietary fat intakes.

The Fat Sleuth…uncovering the truth about fat in plant foods

For many years, the assumption that all fat is bad has permeated our culture. There is a serious flaw in this thinking. Not all fat is bad; some fat is protective, some necessary to life. This doesn't imply that fat is off the hook. Animal foods laden with saturated fat and cholesterol are still very much in the doghouse, as are processed foods containing trans fatty acids (products of hydrogenation). However, there is an overwhelming body of evidence supporting the health benefits of higher-fat plant foods. While the usefulness of low-fat diets in treating certain chronic diseases must be acknowledged, there is absolutely no evidence to suggest the addition of moderate amounts of higher-fat whole plant foods would be detrimental to healthy vegans or vegetarians. It appears to be quite the contrary.

In Defense of Higher-Fat Whole Plant Foods

The highest quality of fat is that naturally present in fresh nuts, seeds, soybeans, avocados, and olives. These plant foods come packaged by nature to protect them from damaging light, heat, and oxygen. Such foods carry with them valuable vitamins, minerals, phytochemicals, plant protein, essential fatty acids, and fiber. Both epidemiological and clinical studies have confirmed that frequent consumption of these foods provides considerable health benefits. Let's look at the evidence in a little more detail.

NUTS

During the last decade, several large epidemiological studies on tree nuts (studies looking at health practices and rates of disease in populations) have confirmed their powerful contribution to health (see Table 4.4).

Clinical research on specific tree nuts has since been pouring in. Sabate and coworkers examined the effects of walnuts on blood cholesterol levels and found that, when compared to a similar control diet without nuts, those on the walnut diet experienced a total cholesterol reduction of 12% and LDL reduction of 16%. Several other studies using almonds, walnuts, hazelnuts, pecans, macadamia nuts, and peanuts (not a tree nut) have produced similar favorable results.

Although these health benefits may come as a surprise, it's less of a mystery when you look more closely at the composition of these unique foods. Nuts are rich in antioxidants, including selenium and vitamin E (possibly reducing LDL oxidation), plant protein, and fiber. They contain significant levels of the amino acid arginine, which is converted to nitric oxide, a potent dilator of blood vessels that increases blood flow. In addition, their folic acid levels may

Table 4.4 *Epidemiological Studies on Nuts*

Study	No. of participants	Results
The Adventist Health Study 1992	27,000	Participants eating nuts 5 times or more/wk had a 50% reduction in risk of dying from coronary heart disease (CHD) compared to those eating nuts once a/wk or less. When contrasted with 65 other foods, nuts had one of the strongest inverse relationships to CHD.
Iowa Women's Health Study	34,000	Women with the highest nut intakes had a 60% lower risk of CHD compared to women who didn't eat nuts. Adjustments for lifestyle factors and intakes of other foods did not alter the results significantly.
Nurses' Health Study	86,000	Women eating nuts 5 times or more/wk had a 39% reduced risk of fatal CHD and a 32% reduced risk of nonfatal heart attacks compared with those eating nuts less than once a month. Adjustments for lifestyle factors and intakes of other foods did not alter the results significantly.

help reduce levels of homocysteine, a substance in the body that can increase risk for heart disease. Nuts are important sources of copper and magnesium, both shown to protect against heart disease. In addition to the beneficial nutrients mentioned above, nuts and seeds are rich in ellagic acid, lignans, and other phytochemicals known to be anticarcinogens.

SEEDS

Of all seeds, flaxseeds appear to offer the most potential for human health. They have the highest alpha-linolenic acid (LNA) content of any food (57%) and the lowest omega-6:omega-3 ratio (0.28), thus can go a long way towards helping correct the imbalance in essential fatty acids. Flaxseeds are the richest known source of the potent anticarcinogen *lignans*, with 75-800 times the levels of most other plant foods. Lignans have an antiestrogenic effect, possibly reducing the risk of hormone-related cancers. Flax is also loaded with potassium and magnesium and is one of the richest known sources of boron. Flaxseeds lower cholesterol and the LNA in flax has been shown to reduce triglyceride levels, blood pressure, and the tendency to form blood clots. The Lyon Heart study provides evidence that LNA may be protective against sudden death from a heart attack. Research also suggests that LNA may positively affect immune/inflammatory disorders. In addition, flaxseeds appear to improve blood sugar control in people with diabetes.

A genetically modified flax is now being marketed as "a new and improved version of flaxseed oil" under the trade name "Linola oil." This claim is quite deceiving because the "improvement" is solely in how long the oil will last on store shelves. It has been robbed of its precious omega-3 fatty acids (down to only 2% from 57%) and contains about 70% omega-6 fatty acids (resulting in a very unbalanced omega-6:omega-3 ratio of 35:1).

Other less common seeds, including chia seeds (grown in the deserts of Mexico) and hemp seeds, are also rich sources of alpha-linolenic acid. Chia seeds are about 30% omega-3 and hemp seeds are about 20%. All seeds are good sources of vitamins, trace minerals, essential fatty acids, plant protein, phytochemicals, and fiber. They are among our richest vitamin E sources and are loaded with several B vitamins and minerals.

Soy

The soybean is one of the most valuable and versatile foods on the planet. It stands apart from other beans in a number of ways. It is abundant in all essential amino acids, it contains far greater amounts of phytoestrogens called isoflavones (including genistein and daidzein) than any other food, and it is much higher in fat than most other legumes (about 50% of calories). In addition, soy is a rich source of phytosterols (plant sterols), saponins, lecithin, fiber, and numerous vitamins, minerals, and phytochemicals.

Volumes of research accumulated over the past two decades indicate that soyfoods may provide protection against heart disease, hypertension, certain cancers, osteoporosis, kidney disease, and the discomforts of menopause. An intake of about 25-30 g (1 oz) of soy protein/day lowers blood cholesterol in those with high blood cholesterol levels by approximately 10%. More recent studies suggest that soy isoflavones inhibit the oxidation of LDL cholesterol and improve elasticity of the arteries. Soy also shows promise in the prevention and treatment of hormone-related cancers (especially prostate cancer) and colon cancer. Although the mechanism by which soy may reduce cancer risk is unknown, isoflavones such as genestein and daidzein are weak estrogens and can suppress the action of the more potent human form of estrogen. They are also very effective inhibitors of tyrosine kinase, an enzyme consistently linked with tumor growth. Recent research demonstrated beneficial effects of soy on kidney disease: patients with kidney disease experienced a dramatic decrease in protein loss, which increased again when the soy was removed. Soy has also been shown to inhibit bone deterioration and favorably affects calcium metabolism, thus reducing the risk of osteoporosis. The verdict regarding reduction of menopausal discomforts remains a question mark. Although many conflicting results have been reported, it appears as though the effects are favorable, but relatively small.

Avocados

Like other fat-rich plant foods, avocados offer some unexpected surprises. While most people know they are rich in protective monounsaturated fats, they are less aware of their high levels of nutrients and phytochemicals. Avocados contain more folate and potassium per ounce than any other fruit

(60% more than bananas) and are good sources of vitamins C and E. The most exciting news is their phytochemical content. Avocados contain 76 milligrams of beta-sitosterol per 100 grams of fruit—more than four times that of other commonly eaten fruits and double the amount in other whole foods. Phytosterols such as beta-sitosterol can inhibit cholesterol absorption from the intestine, reducing blood cholesterol levels, and some evidence indicates they may inhibit tumor growth. Avocados are also rich in glutathione—triple that of most other fruits. Glutathione functions as an antioxidant, and numerous studies have linked glutathione to the prevention of various types of cancer, including cancer of the mouth and pharynx, and also heart disease.

Olives

Olives contain many protective dietary components including phytosterols,* and polyphenolic compounds. Polyphenolic compounds are potent antioxidants, inhibiting LDL oxidation and reducing the tendency for blood cells to clump together. They have also been shown to lower blood sugar levels. Olives are also rich in plant sterols.

What about coconut and other tropical fats?

The primer on fats showed that coconut fat, palm kernel oil, and palm oil are high in saturated fats. Many people assume that with such high levels of saturated fats, these foods should be strictly avoided. In fact, in less affluent parts of the world where the indigenous diet is plant-based and coconut and other high saturated fat plant foods are staples, the rates of chronic disease are relatively low. By contrast, tropical oils are rarely a major part of any North American diet, accounting for less than 2% of the fat in most cases, and chronic disease rates are high. Clearly, many factors contribute to chronic disease; excessive intakes of saturated fat is only one. When consumed as part of a high-fiber, cholesterol-free, plant-based diet, moderate use of coconut or other saturated fat-rich plant foods does not appear to increase cholesterol levels or heart attack risk. Thus, it is not necessary for vegans to completely eliminate these foods from the diet. The small amount of saturated fat coming from whole plant foods such as coconut, nuts and other fat-rich plant foods may in fact turn out to be of benefit for vegans. They are very stable fats with a low risk of oxidation. (Vegan diets are generally very high in unstable polyunsaturated fats.) On the other hand, for people eating high-fat, high-cholesterol, animal-centered diets, tropical oils simply add fuel to the fire.

*Phytosterols are plant sterols (beta-sitosterol is one of the more common plant sterols), while cholesterol is an animal sterol. Plant sterols can significantly reduce the absorption of cholesterol, thereby potentially reducing its harmful effects.

Concentrated Fats and Oils...any place in a vegan diet?

While the best fat comes from whole foods, some use of concentrated fats and oils can fit into a nutritious vegetarian-eating plan. Oils add extra calories to the diet without much extra food volume, thus can be useful for people who have difficulty eating enough calories on a vegan diet. Oils can also help to improve the absorption of important nutrients and protective phytochemicals. You get far greater health benefits from using salad dressings made of extra-virgin olive oil, fresh lemon juice, garlic and herbs, than from fat-free, water-based chemical concoctions from the supermarket.

Oils are extracted from plant foods, and depending on the method of extraction, lose variable amounts of vitamins, minerals, and phytochemicals in the process. Although refined oils offer important advantages over hydrogenated oils, they provide little nutritional value other than pure fat. Many refined oils available on supermarket shelves are high in omega-6 fatty acids, with minimal omega-3 fatty acid content. For example, sunflower, safflower, grapeseed, and corn oil are 60-75% omega-6, while soy, sesame, and cottonseed oil are 50-60% omega-6. Soy oil is also high in omega-3 fatty acids and is a better choice than other omega-6-rich oils; however, due to its high omega-6 content, it is not the best choice for everyday oil.

If you are using oils, select unrefined, mechanically pressed organic oils when you can. Extra-virgin olive oil is generally the only unrefined oil available on supermarket shelves. The high monounsaturated fat content makes it an excellent choice. Olive oil has been shown to reduce total and LDL cholesterol levels without impacting on HDL cholesterol. It also reduces blood pressure and the risk of a second heart attack. Epidemiological evidence suggests that diets rich in olive oil may reduce cancer risk. Other high-quality fresh-pressed oils are available in natural food stores. (Those with high omega-3 content will be kept refrigerated.) Your best choices are flaxseed, canola, walnut, and hazelnut oil. Your primary cooking oil should be mainly monounsaturated—olive or canola oil. About half of the nonorganic canola oil is produced from genetically engineered crops, so if you want to be sure to avoid these products, buy organic.

When oils are subjected to high-temperature cooking (i.e., when they start to smoke), fats—especially unsaturated fatty acids—are damaged and a number of toxic products are formed. These substances can damage the liver, circulatory system, and the kidneys. Although frying is not recommended, there are some fats that resist destruction more than others. The oils that survive heat best are those richest in saturated and monounsaturated fats, such as tropical oils, olive oil, high-oleic sunflower or safflower oil (those grown to have a high mono content), canola oil (not fresh-pressed), and peanut oil. Most fresh-pressed oils contain too much unsaturated fatty acids to use in high-temperature cooking. The most unsaturated of oils, flax oil, should not be used in cooking at all. It is best reserved for salad dressings or on foods at the table. Boiling and baking are less destructive to oils, since the temperature in baked goods generally goes up only to about 240°F., a temperature that most oils can handle.

PRACTICAL GUIDELINES FOR VEGANS... FAT IN PERFECT BALANCE

1. *Aim for 15-30% of calories from fat for healthy vegan adults (More for infants and children—see Chapter 11).*

What does 15-30% of calories mean in terms of real food? It amounts to about 1 to 2 tablespoons of fat from high-fat plant foods or concentrated oils for every 1,000 calories eaten. This "fat allowance" takes into account the fat naturally present in lower-fat vegetables, fruits, grains, and legumes. If you consume 2,000 kcal, a 15-30% fat diet would allow you the equivalent of 2 to 4 tablespoons of fat per day. The following amounts of higher-fat plant foods provide the equivalent of 1 tablespoon of fat:

   1 oz. (¼ cup) nuts or seeds
   1 cup medium tofu or ½ cup of firm tofu or tempeh
   2 cups regular soymilk
   ½ avocado
   20 olives
   ½ oz. fresh coconut or ¼ oz. dried coconut

2. *Limit intake of saturated fat to no more than 8% of calories; avoid trans fatty acids.*

Saturated Fat: Vegan diets are naturally low in saturated fat (unless large amounts of tropical oils are used). Other plant foods are so low in saturated fat that if total fat is under 30% of calories, saturated fat will easily be kept to less than 8% of calories, and often closer to 5%.

Trans Fatty Acids: Dr. Bruce Holub, trans fatty acid expert from the University of Guelph, Canada, suggests keeping trans fatty acids under 1% of calories. Vegans are definitely the closest to the mark! The main sources of trans fatty acids in the vegan diet are shortening and any foods containing hydrogenated or partially hydrogenated oils (i.e., crackers and chips). Fast food establishments generally use hydrogenated oils for French fries and other deep-fried foods.

To minimize your consumption of trans fatty acids:
• use whole foods as the foundation of the diet;

- become a label reader. Avoid products containing shortening and hydrogenated or partially hydrogenated oils;
- avoid hydrogenated margarine. Use nut or seed butters, flax oil, or olive oil instead. If you do use margarine, select a nonhydrogenated variety;
- avoid deep-fried foods.

3. *Limit intake of omega-6 fatty acids to no more than 3-5% of calories.*

Meeting the recommended 3-5% intake for omega-6 fatty acids is a snap on any vegan diet, even one that is low in fat. Most vegans eat 2-3 times more omega-6 fatty acids than are recommended. How can you be sure that you don't overdo omega-6 fats? Remember two simple rules:

- *Don't use omega-6-rich oils as your everyday cooking or salad oils.*
- *Avoid processed foods and deep-fried foods made with these oils.*

Keeping your omega-6 fatty acid intake to 3-5% of calories allows for a maximum of about 11 g (just over 2 teaspoons) of LA per day in a 2,000 kcal diet. It is easy to get 11 grams of LA without using any omega-6-rich oils at all; for example from ½ cup firm tofu plus 1 oz. peanuts. Using small amounts of omega-6-rich whole foods (i.e., a sprinkling of sunflower seeds and sesame seeds) is fine, however, if you are using large quantities they can quickly disrupt your essential fatty acid balance. To preserve the balance, increase foods rich in omega-3 fatty acids.

4. *Aim for at least 1-2% omega-3 fatty acids (at least 2% omega-3 fatty acids during pregnancy and lactation).*

Average intakes of omega-3 fatty acids are about half the recommended levels. How can you double your intake of this important nutrient? First and foremost, include a reliable source of omega-3 fatty acids in the daily diet. On a 2,000-calorie diet, you need at least 2.2 to 4.4 grams of alpha-linolenic acid.

The following foods provide roughly 2.2 g of alpha-linolenic acid:

• 1 tsp. flaxseed oil	• 1 Tbsp. hemp oil
• 1 Tbsp. flaxseeds (ground)	• 1 cup soybeans
• 20 cups dark greens	• 4 tsp. canola oil
• 12 ounces firm tofu	• ¼ cup walnuts or butternuts

5. *Consider getting a direct source of EPA/DHA during pregnancy and lactation or if you suffer from a disorder or disease linked to a deficiency of these fatty acids.*

Vegan EPA: At present, no direct source EPA supplement is available for vegans. However, about 10% of DHA can be converted back to EPA. The only food source of vegan EPA is seaweed, however it is so low in fat that large amounts need to be consumed to make any significant contribution to EPA intake. Most seaweeds contain approximately 100 mg EPA per 100 g product (but little or no DHA).

Vegan DHA: The only vegan DHA comes from microalgae. When supplementing with a direct DHA source, 100-300 mg/day is generally recommended. Currently there are two companies producing DHA-rich microalgae: Martek (http://www.martekbio.com) and OmegaTech (www.omegadha.com).

6. *Make monounsaturated fat-rich foods your primary sources of dietary fat.*

Monounsaturated fats (from oils and foods) should provide about 50% of your fat intake (about 20-35 grams) in a 2,000 kcal diet. Your best food sources include nuts and nut oils, olive and olive oil, avocados, canola oil, and high-oleic sunflower and safflower oil.

7. *Rely on whole foods for the bulk of your fat.*

Shift to a diet with the highest quality fats available:

• Use nut butters instead of margarine on bread or crackers.

• Make spreads, dips, and dressings using avocados, tofu, or nut butters.

• Use flaxseeds, nuts, and/or wheat germ in baked goods and cereals.

• Use nuts, flaxseeds, avocados, olives, and/or marinated tofu in salads.

SELECTED REFERENCES

Ågren J., M. Törmalä, M. Nenonen, and O. Hänninen. "Fatty acid composition of erythrocyte, platelet, and serum lipids in strict vegans." *Lipids* 30 (1995): 365-369.

Conquer, J., and B. Holub. "Docosahexanenoic acid (omega-3) and vegetarian nutrition." *Vegetarian Nutrition: An International Journal* 1/2 (1997): 42-49.

Gerster, H. "Can Adults Adequately Convert a-Linolenic Acid (18:3n-3) to Eicosapentaenoic Acid (20:5n-3) and Docosahexaenoic Acid (24:6n-3)?" *Intl. J. Vit. Nutr. Res.* 68 (1998): 159-173.

Krajcovicova-Kudlackova, M., R. Simoncic, A. Bederova, and J. Klvanova. "Plasma fatty acid profile and alternative nutrition." *Ann. Nutr. Metab.* 41 (6) (1997): 365-70.

Li, D., M. Ball, M. Bartlett, and A. Sinclair. "Lipoprotein (a), essential fatty acid status and lipoprotein lipids in female Australian vegetarians." *Clin. Sci.* Aug(2) (1999): 175-181.

Ornish, D., L.W. Scherwitz, J. H. Billings, K. L. Gould, T. A. Merritt, S. Sparler, W. T. Armstrong, T. A. Ports, R. L. Kirkeeide, C. Hogeboom, and R.J. Brand. "Intensive lifestyle changes for reversal of coronary heart disease." *JAMA* 280 (23) (1998): 2001-7.

Sanders, T. B. A., and S. Reddy. "The influence of a vegetarian diet on the fatty acid composition of human milk and the essential fatty acid status of the infant." *Dept. Nutr. Dietetics.* 120 (1992): S71-77.

CHAPTER
5

The Two Faces of Carbohydrates

Carbohydrates are the most important source of food energy in the world. The FAO/WHO (Food and Agricultural Organization of the United Nations/World Health Organization) suggests that the diet consist of at least 55% carbohydrates. Government and health organizations from around the world concur. The reason is simple. Populations consuming animal-centered diets, rich in fat and protein and low in carbohydrates, have high rates of heart disease, cancer, diabetes, obesity, and other chronic diseases. By contrast, those consuming plant-based diets, rich in carbohydrates, have significantly lower rates of disease.

One would imagine that such knowledge would take affluent populations by storm and those attempting to lose weight and prevent disease would flock towards plant-centered diets in droves. Ironically, the best-selling diet books of today urge consumers to do the exact opposite. They push meat-centered, high-protein, high-fat diets and claim carbohydrates are at the root of all that ails us.

This chapter cuts to the heart of carbohydrates, considers the myths and realities surrounding them, and sorts through the issues that are foremost on the minds of those who build their diets from plants.

CARBOHYDRATES CLOSE UP

What are carbohydrates?

Carbohydrates are packages of the sun's energy used to support all life on earth. They are created through photosynthesis, a process in which water, carbon dioxide, and the green pigment chlorophyll join forces to trap the sun's energy. The molecule that results is a 6-carbon configuration known as glucose, a simple carbohydrate or sugar. ("Carbo" means carbon and "hydrate" means water.) Plants make other sugars such as fructose and galactose by rearranging the glucose molecule. These single sugar units are called *monosaccharides* ("mono" means one). Two units of sugar are linked together by bonds to make *disaccharides* ("di" means two) such as sucrose, maltose, and lactose. Three to nine molecules of sugar are bound together to form *oligosaccharides* ("oligo" means few) such as raffinose and starchyose. Tens, hundreds, or thousands of sugar molecules are linked together to make *polysaccharides* ("poly" means many). Polysaccharides are further divided into two groups called *starch* and *nonstarch polysaccharides* (NSP). Starch includes all of the polysaccharides that can be completely digested and absorbed, while nonstarch polysaccharides include all of the polysaccharides that cannot be *completely digested and absorbed*. (The bonds in these carbohydrates cannot be completely broken down by body enzymes.) Nonstarch polysaccharides such as cellulose, hemicellulose, and pectin are also known as *fiber*.

Carbohydrates are often classified as *simple carbohydrates*, which include the mono- and disaccharides, and *complex carbohydrates* (oligo- and polysaccharides). Traditionally, this division was used to distinguish nonnutritious simple sugars such as sucrose or table sugar from more nutritious starches and fiber found in whole grains, legumes, vegetables, and fruits. However, these terms are quite meaningless when you take a good look at the carbohydrates in these foods. Vegetables and fruits are generally very low in starches and contain mostly simple sugars. In addition, the absorption rate of starch varies tremendously depending on how a food is processed and prepared, and some starches can be absorbed more quickly than simple sugars in fruits or vegetables. So rather than focusing on simple and complex carbohydrates as "bad guys" and "good guys," we need to look at the overall nutritional value of the food in question, its fiber content, and its affects on blood sugar.

Why are carbohydrates important to human health?

Carbohydrates are the preferred energy supply for most body functions. The only other sources of energy are protein, fat, and alcohol. Protein can be used as a fuel but it is far from ideal, as it is first stripped of its amine group, which is handled by the liver and kidneys, and over time can damage these organs. Fat is used as a fuel, but not for the brain and nervous system, and excessive fat can contribute to many diseases. Alcohol is not a desirable fuel source as it is highly toxic to the body. That leaves us with carbohydrates, which are efficiently and safely used by the entire body for energy. In addition to serving as our major energy source, carbohydrate-rich foods help to improve satiety and control blood sugar, cholesterol and triglyceride levels, and insulin metabolism. They are essential to the healthy workings of the gastrointestinal tract, protecting against constipation and intestinal disorders. Carbohydrates support flora in the large bowel and enable fermentation and the optimal functioning of intestinal cells.

Carbohydrates supply about 4 kcal/g (although a more accurate figure may be 3.75 kcal/g). Those that are only partly digested or not digested at all (nondigestible oligosaccharides, resistant starch, and nonstarch polysaccharides or fiber) are counted in the caloric values of carbohydrate-containing foods. Thus, the usable calories in many high-carbohydrate foods may actually be overestimated. The FAO/WHO in their *Expert Consultation on Carbohydrates in Human Nutrition* (1999) recommends that we reassess the energy value of carbohydrate-rich foods to more accurately reflect this knowledge. They suggest that a figure of 2 kcal/g be used for any carbohydrate that reaches the colon undigested rather than the 4 kcal/g used for completely digestible carbohydrates.

THE CARBOHYDRATE CONTROVERSY: HOW MUCH CARBOHYDRATE SHOULD PEOPLE EAT?

Carbohydrates contribute between 40–80% of the food energy in various parts of the world. In general, this range is reflected by the amount of plant and animal foods people eat. Recall that carbohydrates are made by plants and are not present in animal foods, with the single exception of mammal's milk which contains lactose. Where the foundation of the diet is starchy staples, such as rice or root vegetables, the total carbohydrate content of the diet is at the high end of this range. Where animal foods predominate, carbohydrate intakes tend towards the lower end of this range. Table 5.1 provides a list of the approximate carbohydrate content of selected foods.

Table 5.1 Carbohydrate (CHO) Content of Various Foods

Plant Food	% kcal from CHO	Animal Food	% kcal from CHO
Grains	65–85%	Meat	0%
Vegetables	50–90%★	Poultry	0%
Fruits	90–95%	Fish	0%
Legumes	65–75%	Eggs	3%
Nuts and seeds	10–15%	Cow's milk	29–55%★★
Tofu	11–15%	Cheese	1%
Meat analogs	10–30%		

★*The range of CHO in vegetables is due to differences in protein content (calories from protein vary from about 10-40%).*

★★*The range of CHO in cow's milk is due to differences in fat content (lower fat means a higher proportion of calories from CHO).*

The FAO/WHO recommends that a minimum of 55% of calories and a maximum of 75% of calories come from a variety of carbohydrate sources. The emphasis is on variety, with cereals, vegetables (particularly root vegetables), legumes, fruits, nuts, and seeds making up the bulk of the carbohydrate intake. After reviewing Table 5.1, it becomes very clear why people who eat plant-centered diets easily meet the recommended 55% of calories from carbohydrates, while people consuming animal-centered diets have greater difficulty doing so.

There are two primary reasons for recommending a minimum of 55% of calories from carbohydrates.

• When carbohydrate intakes fall below 55% of energy, protein and fat intakes become excessive and the risk of chronic diseases escalates.

• Carbohydrate-rich plant foods improve intakes of many protective micronutrients, antioxidants, and phytochemicals, in addition to being our most valuable energy sources.

The FAO/WHO recommends 75% of energy from carbohydrates as an upper limit. Their rationale is that greater amounts of carbohydrates could compromise intakes of protein, fat, and other essential nutrients with potentially significant adverse effects on health. For example, at 80% of calories from carbohydrates, only 20% of calories remain for protein and fat (about 10% each). At these levels, fat intake may be too low to provide sufficient essential fatty acids and ensure optimal absorption of vitamins, minerals, and phytochemicals. For people eating completely plant-based diets, 10% protein may be insufficient if the mix of plant foods is limited (e.g,. low lysine with poor legume intake), the overall digestibility of the protein is poor (very bulky diets), or requirements are especially high (in children, athletes, etc.).

Where do vegans stand?

Vegans, on average, consume approximately 60% of their energy as carbohydrates. Carbohydrate intake increases with decreasing intake of dietary fat, so for those eating very-low-fat diets, carbohydrate intakes will be closer to 75% of calories. This compares to about 50-55% for lacto-ovo vegetarians and less than 50% for most nonvegetarians. Vegan diets naturally fall within the 55-75% range, providing a balance of carbohydrates, fat, and protein that is closer to the recommended levels than other dietary patterns.

While for most people high-carbohydrate diets are most desirable, it is important to recognize individual variations in nutrient and energy needs. Some people do better on diets that are somewhat higher in protein and/or fat. For example, people with syndrome X or other disorders of carbohydrate metabolism may do better with a more moderate carbohydrate intake (in the range of 45-55% carbohydrate). For these people, some of the carbohydrates can be replaced with monounsaturated fat from nuts, avocados, and high-monounsaturated oils. For individuals wishing to increase calories from protein, concentrated plant protein foods such as veggie meats made from soy protein isolates or concentrates, soy protein drinks, and tofu can be selected more often.

Is there any basis for the claims that high-carbohydrate diets cause obesity?

In one word, no. It is, however, very interesting that with virtually every respected health organization in the world promoting plant-based, high-carbohydrate diets, the low-carbohydrate regimes such as The Zone, Dr. Atkin's New Diet Revolution, Protein Power, The Carbohydrate-Addicts Diet, and Sugar-Busters are all the rage. What is the appeal of such programs? Perhaps it is simply that the authors are selling something that people want—a license to eat more meat. Low-carbohydrate diets are essentially high-protein, high-fat diets, and the central focus of these plans is meat (which is, of course, 100% protein and fat and completely carbohydrate-free).

The main argument of most of these diet programs is that carbohydrates cause insulin resistance, which in turn causes obesity and other chronic diseases. The research that is generally sited as justification for this claim is that of Dr. Gerald Reaven, professor of medicine at Stanford University. When questioned by the Center for Science in the Public Interest about this possible connection between insulin resistance and obesity, Dr. Reaven clearly stated,

> "...there's not one shred of evidence that insulin resistance causes obesity...Carbs don't make you fat, and insulin doesn't make you fat....Calories make you fat."

If these claims had any basis in fact, the people in the world who eat the most carbohydrate would have the greatest rates of insulin resistance, obesity, and chronic disease. In fact, epidemiological evidence clearly demonstrates that the exact opposite is true. Those populations eating the most carbohydrate have the lowest rates of obesity and chronic disease, and those eating the highest amounts of protein and fat have the highest rates of obesity and chronic disease. Recent studies have shown that after migrating to the U.S., Japanese and Mexican Americans consume significantly more fat and less carbohydrate than what was provided by their traditional diets and that their risk of diabetes, obesity, and heart disease escalates as a result.

While low-carbohydrate diets can produce weight loss, their success is a function of a reduced caloric intake, not a reduced carbohydrate intake, and this success comes at a cost.

Low-carbohydrate diets tend to maximize the dietary components most strongly linked to chronic disease—saturated fat, cholesterol, and animal protein and minimize the dietary components that have been found to be the most highly protective—fiber, phytochemicals, antioxidant nutrients, plant protein, and unsaturated fats.

In a recent debate between Dr. Ornish and Dr. Atkins on CNN's *Crossfire*, Dr. Ornish was challenged with the fact that these diets can aid in weight loss. His response:

> *"There are lots of ways of losing weight. You could go on chemotherapy and lose weight, but I won't recommend it as the optimal way."*

In all fairness, all low-carbohydrate diets shouldn't be lumped together, as some are far lower in carbohydrates and higher in fat than others. The highest fat diets are Protein Power, which racks up 60% of calories from fat and Dr. Atkin's Diet Revolution at 55% of calories from fat. Both of these plans provide 18% of calories as saturated fat. By contrast, The Zone is only 30% of calories from fat and 8% saturated fat (a much safer regime).

For more information, check out the excellent discussion, "Exiting the Zone," by Robyn Landis at www.bodyfueling.com/carbophobia.html.

CARBOHYDRATE COMMONSENSE: WHAT TYPES OF CARBOHYDRATES SHOULD PEOPLE EAT?

While health authorities agree that high-carbohydrate diets are desirable for entire populations, they recognize that their impact on health is largely dependent on the sources of carbohydrates provided. Simple sugars can be obtained from fresh fruit or soda pop and starches from deep-fried donuts or barley. The evidence is overwhelming that when carbohydrates are consumed as a part of whole plant foods, such as legumes, whole grains, vegetables, fruits, nuts, and seeds, they benefit health. On the other hand, when plant foods are refined and the resulting starches and sugars (white flour and concentrated sugar) are used to make a variety of processed foods, they can adversely affect health in a number of ways. For this reason, recommendations to increase carbohydrate intakes are generally accompanied by suggestions to consume whole plant foods and to limit consumption of refined products, sucrose, and other concentrated sugars.

What is the problem with refined carbohydrates and sugars? When you really think about it, all sugars and starches eventually end up as glucose, fructose, or galactose anyway. However, when we extract starches and/or sugars from plants, a few things get left behind: vitamins, minerals, protein, essential fatty acids, phytochemicals, and fiber. In other words, we leave behind the vast majority of protective substances found in plants. What remains is pure carbohydrate and little more. In fact, in the refining of wheat to make white flour, about 75% of all the vitamins and minerals are lost, 90% of the fiber, and 95% of the phytochemicals. Granted, sometimes we add back a few of the vitamins and minerals. For example, when we refine grains such as wheat or rice, we often add back a few B vitamins such as thiamin, riboflavin, niacin, folate, and the mineral iron. This is called *enrichment*. However, we do not add back any of the fiber, phytochemicals, or other vitamins and minerals that were removed (vitamin B_6, pantothenic acid, vitamin E, selenium, magnesium, zinc, potassium, manganese, boron, etc.).

While whole plant foods protect and promote health, excessive consumption of concentrated sugars and starches can damage health. Table 5.2 briefly addresses the health consequences of whole plant foods in comparison to refined sugars and starches.

Digestion and Absorption of Different Sources of Carbohydrates

Absorption of the monosaccharides glucose and galactose is rapid, while fructose is much more slowly absorbed. Disaccharides, oligosaccharides, and polysaccharides must be broken down by digestive enzymes into monosaccharides before they can be absorbed. Absorption occurs along the entire length of the small intestine. However, refined carbohydrates are digested more rapidly in the upper portion of the small intestine. By contrast, whole foods are digested more slowly further along the small intestine.

The relative effect of various carbohydrates on blood sugar is often assessed using a tool called the *glycemic index*. The glycemic index measures the average amount of sugar going into the bloodstream over a two-hour period after eating a food. This amount is compared to some standard food, usually glucose or white bread. The standard food is given a value of 100. The glycemic index is not necessarily a measure of how fast sugar enters the bloodstream, as is commonly assumed. This means that a food causing a wide but gentle blood sugar curve (gradual, but long lasting) can have the same glycemic index as a food causing a sharper spike (quick rise and fall) in blood sugar if the area under the curve is the same.

The glycemic index is often used to determine what foods are best for people with diabetes, hypoglycemia, or other challenges of carbohydrate metabolism. The glycemic index of a variety of foods is provided in Table 5.3

There are a few surprises here, all of which are completely explainable. Many factors affect the absorption of starches and sugars, and thus the glycemic index of any given food.

Table 5.2 Health Consequences of Whole Plant Foods vs. Refined Starches and Sugars

Health Concern	Effects of Eating High-Carbohydrate Whole Plant Foods	Effects of Eating Excessive Refined Starches and Sugar
Obesity	Increases satiety. Delays hunger. Reduces caloric intake. Improves nutrient, phytochemical, and fiber intake (especially important for those on weight loss diets).	Encourages overeating (less filling). Causes greater fluctuations in blood sugar, possibly increasing hunger. Interferes with intake of foods with higher nutrient, fiber, and phytochemical content.
Noninsulin dependent Diabetes Mellitus (NIDDM and Hypoglycemia	Improves blood sugar control, reducing the peaks in blood sugar after eating. May reduce triglycerides. Improves satiety. Promotes healthy body weight.	Impairs blood sugar control, increasing peaks in blood sugar after eating (especially when consumed without protein and fat). Increases triglycerides and decreases HDL cholesterol. May interfere with weight loss efforts.
Heart Disease	Reduces total and LDL cholesterol (especially high-fiber items). Helps reduce intake of saturated fat and cholesterol. Provides antioxidant nutrients and beneficial phytochemicals. May reduce triglycerides. Reduces blood pressure. Promotes healthy body weight.	Increases triglycerides and decreases HDL cholesterol. Refined carbohydrate foods often come packaged with damaging saturated fat and trans fatty acids. May impair weight loss efforts. May promote LDL cholesterol oxidation, due to lack of protective antioxidants and phytochemicals.
Cancer	Phytochemicals and antioxidant nutrients reduce oxidative damage to body tissues and DNA. Phytochemicals reduce cell proliferation, induce detoxifying enzymes, suppress and block harmful substances, and reduce estrogen activity—all highly protective against cancer. Fiber appears protective against colorectal cancer,★ cancer of the pancreas and breast cancer. High-carbohydrate diets may also protect against colorectal cancer.	Sugars and starches contain few of the constituents in plants that protect against cancer. Sugars from refined foods may increase risk of colorectal cancers and possibly cancer of the pancreas. Refined starches may increase risk of stomach cancer.
Other gastro-intestinal (GI) disorders	Intakes of fiber and resistant starch are the most important contributors to stool weight. Decreases constipation, hemorrhoids, and anal fissures. Protects against diverticular disease. Protects against gallstones. May protect against irritable bowel disease and other inflammatory bowel diseases. Fiber may reduce the risk of duodenal ulcers.	When intake is high, total fiber content of diet tends to be low, reducing stool weight and contributing to GI disorders. Increases risk of developing constipation, hemorrhoids, anal fissures, diverticular disease, gallstones, irritable bowel disease, and other inflammatory bowel diseases.
Dental and gum diseases	Reduces dental carries and gum diseases.	Increases dental carries and gum diseases.

★ *See pages 29-31 in Chapter 2 for more information on the controversy surrounding colon cancer and dietary fiber intake.*

- Food processing, cooking, or otherwise reducing food particle size (mashing, pureeing) increases the glycemic index. (Mashed potatoes have a higher glycemic index than boiled potatoes.)

- Ripening of fruit increases their glycemic index. (Ripe bananas have double the glycemic index of underripe bananas.)

- Fat and protein reduce glycemic index. (Chocolate has a lower glycemic index than brown rice.)

- Fiber (especially water-soluble fiber) reduces glycemic index. (Barley has a lower glycemic index than wheat berries.)

- Presence of less digestible starches in foods reduces the glycemic index.

- Higher density of the food (containing less air) reduces glycemic index. (Dense white pasta has a lower glycemic index than fluffy whole wheat bread.)

- Fructose rather than glucose as the principle sugar reduces glycemic index. (Fructose has a glycemic index of about 23, so high-fructose foods such as fruits have a much lower glycemic index than might be expected.)

- Higher amylose content (starch polysaccharide) reduces glycemic index. (Low-amylose white rice has a glycemic index close to 90, while high-amylose rice has a glycemic index close to 60.)

While a glycemic index can be of value, its is greatly limited by these many confounding variables. In addition, the glycemic index is not always reliable from day to day, even when the food and test conditions are held constant.

FOCUS ON FIBER

Dietary fiber has been defined as the part of food that cannot be broken down by human digestive enzymes. Traditionally only nonstarch polysaccharides (cellulose, hemicellulose, pectins, gums, and mucilages) and lignin (which is not a carbohydrate) were included in this definition. Today, most experts recognize resistant oligosaccharides and resistant starches (portions of carbohydrate foods that are not digested and absorbed in the small intestine) as part of total dietary fiber.

Cellulose, a major component of fiber, has a high water-absorbing capacity and a very low solubility in water. Hemicelluloses include both soluble and insoluble components. Soluble hemicelluloses are thought to play an important role in reducing blood cholesterol levels. Pectins, gums, and mucilages are soluble in water and are prized for their ability to form stable gels.

All of these undigestible carbohydrates enter the large intestine, where they are fermented to varying degrees by microflora (bacteria) in the colon. Those with the lowest fermentation rates are the ones that contribute the most to stool bulk. The fibers that are the least fermentable are cellulose and other

Table 5.3   Glycemic Index of Selected Foods* (glucose=100)

Food Product	Glycemic Index	Food Product	Glycemic Index
Grains		*Vegetables*	
Barley	25	Peas or corn, frozen	47–48
Rye berries	34	Sweet potatoes	54
Wheat berries	41	Potatoes, boiled	56
White spaghetti	41	Beets	64
Heavy grain breads	45	Potatoes, mashed	70
Rice, brown	55	Carrots	71
Rice, white	56	*Fruits*	
Oatmeal, all type	61	Grapefruit, plum, each	24–28
Whole wheat bread	69	Apples, oranges, grapes	36–43
White bread	70	Kiwi, banana	52–53
Legumes		Orange juice	57
Peanuts	14	Watermelon	72
Soybeans	18	*Other*	
Most other legumes	26–38	Chocolate	49
Canned baked beans	48	Potato chips	54

*Glycemic indexes provided in this table are adapted from average values provided in the International Tables of Glycemic Index (1995).

insoluble fibers, such as wheat bran. Those that are most rapidly fermented are oligosaccharides, concentrated in beans and vegetables of the cabbage family.

Why is fiber so important to health?

Review Table 5.2, paying attention to the column labeled "Effects of High-Carbohydrate Whole Plant Foods." The vast majority of the protective effects listed here are owed, in large part, to dietary fiber. When the fiber is removed, many of these health benefits are lost. Fiber helps to protect us against almost every major chronic disease that plagues the Western world, including heart disease, cancer, gastrointestinal diseases, diabetes, hypoglycemia, and obesity.

How much fiber should I eat?

The World Health Organization recommends an intake of 27–40 grams of fiber per day for most adults or 15–22 grams of fiber per day per 1,000 kcal consumed. For those consuming between 2,000 and 2,800 kcal, that works out to about 30–62 grams of dietary fiber per day.

If you are eating a vegan or near-vegan diet, chances are that your fiber intake is just what it should be. Vegans consume, on average, about 40–50 grams of fiber per day. By contrast, most lacto-ovo vegetarians consume about 30–40 grams of fiber per day, and most nonvegetarians about 10-20 grams. The high-fiber intakes of vegans are believed to be at least partly responsible for the numerous health benefits of all-plant diets.

Can I get too much fiber?

Yes—it is possible to get too much of almost anything. Excessive fiber can make the diet too bulky, thereby jeopardizing energy intake, especially in small children. It can also reduce the absorption of certain minerals such as calcium, iron, and zinc. However, when compared to refined foods, high-fiber whole foods provide enough extra minerals to more than compensate for any losses incurred. When fiber does bind with minerals, they can be at least partly liberated during fermentation in the large bowel. Short-chain fatty acids (also products of fermentation) help to facilitate their absorption from the large bowel. As a general rule, eating a wide variety of whole plant foods will not result in excessive intakes of fiber. It is important to note, however, that problems with mineral absorption can occur if concentrated fiber, such as wheat bran, is added to whole foods. Wheat bran is particularly high in phytates that inhibit mineral absorption. These concentrated fiber foods are unnecessary and potentially harmful additions to high-fiber plant-based diets.

How do I deal with the gas?

Gas production is a normal, healthy function of the intestines which appears to protect the colon against genetic damage leading to cancer. It dilutes carcinogens, stimulates beneficial bacterial growth, favorably alters the gut pH, and improves the function of the epithelial cells of the colon.

Unfortunately, as wonderful as it may be for health, there is a point at which the negative consequences begin to outweigh any sort of benefits (especially where work and social life are concerned).

There are two main causes of gas: fermentation of carbohydrates that reach the large intestine and swallowing of air. You can reduce the amount of air you swallow by eating more slowly, avoiding carbonated beverages and beer, not chewing gum or sucking on candy, and if you wear dentures, making sure that they fit properly. As for reducing the fermentation of carbohydrates, there are a number of options.

• *Reduce the amount of undigested carbohydrates that reach the colon.* Moderate your intake of foods that are especially problematic. Among the worst offenders are the oligosaccharides (raffinose and starchyose) in beans and vegetables of the cabbage family.

• *Use smaller portions of beans* (i.e., put them in soups, stews, and salads).

- *Use more tofu and textured soy protein,* which contain less of the problem sugars.

- *Use lentils, split peas, or other small legumes rather than larger beans* which seem to cause more problems.

- *Reduce the oligosaccharide content of legumes before they are eaten.* Always soak beans overnight, and pour off the rinse water before cooking them. Not soaking beans can increase the gas they cause as much as 10 times.

- *Don't overeat.* Overeating increases the amount of food that seems to end up undigested in the colon.

- *Take an enzyme such as Beano,* which breaks down the undigestible carbohydrates before they reach the colon.

- *Play detective with yourself.* The main culprit for you could be something you don't really suspect, such as mushrooms, onions, or celery.

- *Improve your bacterial flora.* Eating beans and other fibrous foods *regularly* encourages the growth of bacteria that are more efficient at completely digesting bean sugars (thereby reducing gas production). Start out slowly with small portions, and gradually increase your intake as your system adapts. Begin by adding easier-to-digest legumes to soups, stews, or other dishes once or twice a week. Slowly increase portion sizes and use of larger legumes in the diet.

SELECTED REFERENCES

For a complete list see www.nutrispeak.com/veganrefs.htm. See also general references for the whole book on page 276.

Anderson, J. W., B.M. Smith, and J. Gustasson. "The practicality of high fibre diets." *Am. J. Clin. Nutr.* 59(supp)(1994):1242S-47S.

Foster-Powell, K., and J. Brand Miller. "International tables of glycemic index." *Am. J. Clin. Nutr.* 62 (supp)(1995): 871S-93S.

Harland, B.F., and E.R. Morris. "Phytate: good or bad food component?" *Nutrition Research.* 15 No.5 (1995): 733-754.

Mackay, S., and M.J. Ball. "Do beans and oatbran add to the effectiveness of a low fat diet?" *Europ. J. Clin. Nutr.* 46 (1992): 641-648.

Spencer, H., and C. Norris, J. Durlar, et al. "Effect of oatbran on calcium absorption and calcium, phosphorus, magnesium balance in men." *J. Nutr.* 121 (1991): 1976-1983.

The Joint FAO/WHO Expert Consultation on Carbohydrates in Human Nutrition, April 1997. http://www.fao.org/WAICENT/FAOINFO/ECO-NOMIC/ESN/Carbweb/carbo.pfd

CHAPTER
6

Prospecting for Minerals

By the middle of the 19th century, scientists recognized that protein, fat, carbohydrate, and water alone were not capable of supporting life. By 1900 they learned that the ash that remains after a food is burned is composed of many mineral elements that play vital roles in human nutrition. Of these, 21 minerals are considered essential—vital to life, growth, and reproduction.

There is little question that plants can provide all the essential minerals in adequate amounts. At the same time, there is concern that some vegan diets may fall short, especially where minerals such as zinc and calcium are concerned. In this chapter, we take on the role of the vegan prospector, in search of minerals from plants. The treasure we seek—optimal health—is far greater than gold and something gold cannot buy.

Here are three simple ground rules that will make our quest a whole lot more rewarding:

1. **Eat whole plant foods, following the Vegan Food Guide** (pages 154-55). When foods such as whole grains are refined, minerals are removed. When refined foods are enriched, the only mineral that is added back is iron. Whole foods have their original wealth of minerals.

2. **Make sure your caloric intake is adequate.** When caloric intake is too low, it can be difficult to achieve the recommended intakes for minerals. This is especially a concern when mineral-rich nuts, seeds, legumes, and tofu are excluded or greatly limited in the diet.

3. **Use some foods that are fortified with calcium, zinc, iron, and iodine.** While it is possible to get enough of these minerals without using fortified foods, many people don't. Fortified foods make it simple to achieve recommended intakes. Getting enough calcium, zinc, and in some cases iron and iodine can be a challenge for a lot of people, vegan or not. For these nutrients, fortified foods can save the day.

Now let's get going—consider us your guides.

UNCOVERING CALCIUM DEPOSITS   *Attention Required*

Calcium in Perspective

Calcium is the most abundant mineral in the body and the fifth most common mineral in the earth's crust. Plants take up this calcium as they grow. Humans benefit from this calcium by either:

- consuming calcium-containing plant foods;
- drinking the milk of an animal that has consumed plant sources of calcium;
- in infancy, consuming human milk with calcium originating from various food sources.

Over history and in modern times, calcium salts, such as the calcium carbonate from limestone, have also become part of the diet. For example, when Native Americans ground corn in clay bowls, the resulting corn flour became "fortified" with calcium carbonate, creating a product that resembles the calcium-fortified tortillas that you can buy in supermarkets today. It is believed that prior to the advent of agriculture, humans in many parts of the world had dairy-free diets that were very high in calcium (in the range of 1,500-3,000 mg/day), although the plants that they consumed are not commonly eaten today. In nature's calcium cycle, animal bones and antlers disintegrated, returning calcium to the earth. Throughout our evolution, consuming calcium in suspension, via cow's milk, has not been a cornerstone of the diet of most humans.

Calcium's Role in Bone Building and Maintenance over the Years

Calcium has a structural role in bones by giving hardness (along with other minerals) to a flexible protein matrix or framework. In teeth it has a similar function. Achieving maximum bone strength, or density, takes 20 to 30 years, with about 45% of the gain in bone mass occurring up until 8 years of age, another 45% occurring from age 8 until 16, and a further 10% occurring over the next decade and a half. After age 30, bone mass gradually declines; eating patterns, exercise, and hormonal balance all influence the rate of loss. By accumulating a sufficient mass of healthy, well-mineralized bone during infancy, childhood, and adolescence, we allow for the inevitable, gradual loss that occurs over succeeding years. By getting a strong start, we delay the decline into the fracture region, where breaks occur with a slight fall or even a hug. In our later years, attention shifts to lifestyle choices that help us reduce losses and hold on to the calcium we have.

Calcium's Other Roles

A small proportion (1%) of the calcium in our bodies has functions quite distinct from these structural roles. Calcium is essential to blood clotting (preventing blood loss after an injury), muscle relaxation (without calcium, muscles remain tight after contracting), nerve cell message transmission, and regulation of cell metabolism (such as storage of energy as glycogen). Calcium also appears to play a role in preventing hypertension.

Lactose Intolerance and Lactase Nonpersistence

The food guides of most affluent Western countries would lead us to believe that humans require cow's milk to meet calcium needs. Nutrition education campaigns

Lactose: the predominant sugar in human milk and cow's milk. (Makes up about one-third of the calories in 2% milk.)

Lactase: an enzyme produced in the intestine that digests lactose into simpler sugars, allowing it to be absorbed.

Lactose Intolerance: the inability to digest significant amounts of lactose. Typical symptoms are nausea, bloating, gas, abdominal cramping, and diarrhea within two hours after milk is consumed.

Lactase Persistence: continued production of lactase, past the age of weaning (about four years).

Lactase Nonpersistence: stop in production of the enzyme lactase. If milk is consumed, there may or may not be symptoms of lactose intolerance.

and convincing dairy advertisements further support this notion. However, the practice of dairying appears to be a relatively recent phenomenon, occurring only in specific areas of the world. Where this practice contributed significantly to people's diets, it seems that a genetic adaptation occurred that allowed people to continue drinking milk after the age of weaning. Normally, after our first few years of life, we stop producing the enzyme lactase and lose our ability to digest lactose.

Lactase persistence has shown itself most strongly in two population groups. First, among African nomads, whose survival depended on milk from their herds, it seems that genetic selection favored lactase persistence. In semi-desert areas near the Sahara, little other food was available; animals grazed on cactus and desert plants, providing their herders with protein, minerals, and water. Second, Viking settlers, from anthropological data, show evidence of rickets and osteomalacia (softening of the bones). Minimal winter sunlight limit-

Table 6.1 Prevalence of Lactase Nonpersistence in Various Population Groups

Population Group (Ethnic or Geographic)	Approximate Prevalence of Lactase Nonpersistence
North American Caucasians	20%
North American Hispanics	50%
North American Asian	80%
African Americans	80%
Native Americans	80%
Worldwide	75%

ed their productions of vitamin D, thus decreasing the active absorption of calcium. (See page 143.) It is believed that adaptations in these people included:

• the lighter skin of Scandinavians, permitting increased vitamin D production with less light exposure, and

• an ability to drink animal milk without bloating, gas, abdominal cramping, and diarrhea. This adaptation allowed greater calcium intake.

While there has been migration of people with lactase persistence to countries all over the world, lactase nonpersistence can reasonably be considered the original condition of humans and to be true for most adult humans today.

Points to Ponder

It is believed that the amounts of calcium consumed by humans in the late Paleolithic era were more than double the intakes of today—with no cow's milk at all. Humans evolved in a calcium-rich, salt-poor dietary environment, and our basic metabolism has changed little from that of our late Stone Age ancestors, although diets have changed drastically. At a thought-provoking presentation in Vancouver in 1999, calcium specialist Dr. Robert Heaney gave rough estimates of eating patterns of our hunter-gatherer ancestors in Stone Age times and of people involved with early agriculture in the fertile crescent of the Middle East. Approximations based on different dietary patterns are summarized in Table 6.2. The genetic strains of uncultivated plant foods were different from what you'll find now in produce aisles of supermarkets. In more recent times, an example of foods eaten by North American natives is fiddlehead ferns at 94 mg calcium/100 calories. Calcium-rich foods that are widely available today include kale (270 mg calcium/100 calories), broccoli (171 mg calcium/100 calories), and others shown in Table 6.7.

Intakes of 140 vegans in 9 studies conducted in 5 countries (the U.S., Britain, Canada, Finland, and New Zealand) from 1954 to 1995 show vegan intakes to be about 30 mg calcium per 100 calories, about 80% of typical American intakes.

Though many plant foods used by our ancestors are not widely available today, we do have calcium-rich greens, plus we have advantages not available to our ancestors: fortified products (soy and grain milks, juices, cereals) and calcium-set tofu. It's important to make our calories count by eating nutrient-dense foods, as our ancestors did, rather than wasting calories on sugars and fats. If we wish to get the nutrients we need *without* fortified plant foods, we will need to eat fairly large quantities of calcium-rich plant foods; this is a common practice with some raw foods enthusiasts and vegans.

Table 6.2 Estimated Calcium In Diets

Population Group	Plant Sources of Calcium	Calcium Density (mg calcium per 100 calories)	Approximate Calcium Intake (mg) in 2,000 Calorie Diet	Calcium Intake (mg) in 3000 Calorie Diet
Late Stone Age/Paleolithic Humans	Nuts, seeds, roots, shoots, berries, tubers, uncultivated plants	70-80 mg/100 cal	1,500	2,250
Early agriculturalists 10,000 years ago	Grains, legumes, seeds, fruits, limestone from milling	70 mg/100 cal	1,400	2,100
For comparison				
Current American Intakes	Approximately 25-40% from plant foods, 60-75% from dairy products	37 mg/100 cal	740	1,100
Average intakes of 140 vegans in 9 studies	Plant foods	30 mg/100 cal	600	900

Calcium Intake, Absorption, and Loss...a matter of balance

Calcium status is not simply a matter of calcium intake, but rather of calcium balance. This is a complex interplay of intake, absorption, and excretion, with all three factors having important impacts on bone density.

On average, North Americans absorb about 30% of the calcium that is present in our diets, but when you take into account the amounts lost in urine and feces, the actual amount we *retain* may be as low as 10% of what was in our food. From the calcium that makes its way into our bodies, there can be substantial losses, depending on certain characteristics of our diet, particularly the protein and sodium contents. A single fast food hamburger could result in calcium losses of about 23 mg. However, if we retain only 10% of what was in our diet, that one burger would, in effect, increase dietary calcium needs by 230 mg.

Factors Affecting Calcium Losses

PROTEIN AND ITS ACIDIFYING EFFECT

Protein's negative impact on calcium balance is created by sulfur-containing amino acids. They are present in amounts that vary from one protein to another and have an acidifying effect on the blood. Part of the body's response to more acidic blood is to restore pH balance by drawing calcium from the bones. Calcium acts as a base, so it can effectively neutralize this acid. For every gram of protein in the diet, approximately 1 mg of calcium is lost in the urine. Meat is considered to have an exceptionally strong negative impact on calcium balance because it is a concentrated source of protein and of the sulfur-containing amino acids. However, all protein, including plant protein, which tends to be less concentrated in sulfur amino acids, contributes to urinary calcium losses. Thus, high intakes of protein powders, particularly soy protein, could contribute to losses. While protein is essential for building body tissues, including bone, excessive amounts can have significant drawbacks.

Vegetarian diets tend to be more alkaline, while animal-centered diets tend to be more acidic. In general, vegetables and fruits produce an alkaline ash favorable to calcium balance. Meats are highly acidic, while dairy foods and grains are moderately acidic.

SODIUM AND ITS EFFECT ON CALCIUM LOSSES

When the kidneys excrete excess sodium, 23 to 26 mg of calcium is lost along with every gram of sodium excreted. Examples of salty, high-sodium foods commonly used by vegans are listed in Table 6.3. Many meat substitutes and canned or bottled foods are high in sodium. In order to protect your bones as you age, you would be wise to pay some attention to the salt content of your food. Begin by noticing amounts of sodium on the nutrition panel of food labels, and find seasonings other than salt to add zest to your foods.

Table 6.3   Sodium in a Few Vegan Foods

Food	Amount	Sodium, mg
Table salt	⅙ tsp/1 g	388
Sea salt	⅙ tsp/1 g	388
Tamari or soy sauce	1 tsp	335
Miso	1 tsp	209
Tomato sauce (see label)	1 cup	40-1,680
Canned tomatoes (see label)	1 cup	24-504
Veggie burgers (see label)	1 burger	114-1148
Veggie "meat" slices (see label)	3 oz.	680-980
Potato chips (see label)	3 oz	360-660
Corn chips (see label)	3 oz	182-869
Salsa (see label)	½ c	468-1,280
Recommended maximum average sodium intake/day		about 2,400

SOFT DRINKS, COFFEE, AND CALCIUM LOSSES

For most people, the effect of these beverages on calcium levels is minimal; however, intakes are worth considering in two instances:

1) *If intake of either beverage is particularly high.* While consumption of up to 3 cups of coffee per day appears to have negligible effects on calcium balance, it is possible that higher intakes lead to calcium losses. Reliance on soft drinks such as colas that are high in phosphoric acids can also have a negative effect on calcium balance.

2) *For people with particular concerns about bone health,* these are not the best fluids to consume. Choose calcium-fortified drinks or water instead. Some mineral waters can add to your calcium intake without adding calories.

Calcium Intakes

THE CHALLENGE OF DETERMINING RECOMMENDED CALCIUM INTAKES

Because calcium needs are influenced by a host of factors, it is extremely difficult for nutrition experts to determine exactly how much calcium an individual needs to function at optimal levels and to continue into old age with healthy, strong

Adequate Intakes of Calcium for Adults	
Age	*AI calcium, mg*
19–50 years	1,000
Over 50 years	1,200

bones. In fact, it has been such a challenge that the recommendations are now called "Adequate Intakes" (AI) and are a sort of "best guess," used when there is insufficient data to make a firm recommendation. These Adequate Intakes may seem high. Remember that they are based on the needs of the general North American population, with high amounts of sodium and meat-centered diets providing much more protein than needed. To make things worse, the population is largely sedentary, a factor that works against the retention of minerals in bones.

It is possible that the calcium requirements of vegans and of other vegetarians are lower than those of the general population, particularly if:

• protein intakes are adequate and yet closer to recommendations (see page 40);

• sodium intake is not over 2,400 mg/day, on average;

• there is regular participation in weight-bearing exercise.

However, note that salt, tamari, and miso are vegan food ingredients. Though plant proteins are somewhat lower in the sulfur-containing amino acids, **vegans should not assume they are protected from osteoporosis because of lower protein intakes**. Until there is more evidence upon which to base specific vegetarian requirements, vegans should aim for the Adequate Intakes established in 1998 by the Institute of Medicine for calcium (see the box above) and vitamin D (page 137).

Another factor that complicates the determination of calcium recommendations is that calcium status cannot be easily assessed by routine blood tests, as is possible with iron. Bone density in the later years gives some feedback on the adequacy of early calcium intakes; however, it also reflects our overall diet and lifestyle choices during and since childhood.

Table 6.4 Calcium in vegan menus (pages 157-60)

Calories	Calcium, mg
1,600	1,302
2,200	1,567
2,800	1,374
4,000	1,955

The one-day meal plans for different caloric intakes listed in Chapter 9 provide the amounts of calcium shown in Table 6.4.

SURVEYS ON DIETARY CALCIUM AND RELATED FACTORS

National Institute of Health Surveys during the 1990s showed that on average, in the general American population, females above the age of 12 do not meet recommended intakes for calcium. Men do better, though their intakes drop later in life.

Another way of looking at the adequacy of dietary calcium is to determine the ratio of calcium to protein in our diets. Table 6.5 shows intakes of vegans, lacto-ovo-vegetarians, and nonvegetarians in studies conducted in a range of the wealthier countries between 1954 and 1995, summarized by M. and V. Messina. Nonvegetarians have poorer ratios than lacto-vegetarians because their protein intakes are high. Vegan ratios are poorer because calcium intakes tend to be low. Though this isn't true for all vegans, vegan diets tend to be slightly lower in sodium, a fact that works in favor of calcium retention, rather than loss.

Table 6.5 *Calcium Intakes, Calcium:Protein Ratio, and Sodium Intakes in Vegan, Lacto-Ovo-Vegetarian and Nonvegetarian Diets*

Dietary Pattern and Gender	Calcium Intake (mg/day)	Ratio Calcium (mg): Protein (g)	Sodium Intake (mg/day)
Vegans: female	400-600	9-11:1	1,800-2,400
Vegans: male	600-700	9-12:1	2,800
Lacto-ovo-vegetarians: female	900-1,000	15-17:1	2,000-2,500
Lacto-ovo-vegetarians: male	1,100-1,300	15-17:1	3,000-3,800
Non-vegetarians: female	800-900*	11-12:1	2,000-2,500
Non-vegetarians: male	1,100-1,200	10-12:1	3,000-3,600
Recommended	1,000-1,200	In the range of 16:1 to 20:1	Less than 2,400

Nonvegetarian intakes in these studies were higher than those of typical American women above age 19 whose calcium intakes are in the range of 780 mg/day.

A generation or two ago, calcium–rich and calcium-fortified plant foods were less widely available, making things much more of a challenge for vegans. Now, there is no reason that vegan diets have to be low in calcium, particularly in North America, Europe, and Australia where many calcium–rich vegan options are on the market.

RESEARCH ON CALCIUM INTAKES AND LIFELONG BONE HEALTH OF VEGANS

In Chapter 1, we made the point that vegans are modern pioneers. This is certainly true when it comes to exploring the effects on bone health after many years, or a lifetime, of vegan eating! Very little evidence has accumulated yet, particularly with diets and lifestyles typical of vegans in industrialized countries. There are several studies of Asian vegans with low caloric intakes, low calcium intakes (300-400 mg/day), and bone densities that are significantly lower than those of nonvegetarians. However, too many discrepancies exist to draw conclusions for Western vegans, other than those with inadequate caloric intakes (for example, Westerners with eating disorders).

Absorption of Calcium

OXALATES, PHYTATES, AND TIMING: THEIR IMPACTS ON ABSORPTION

In this complex interplay of factors affecting calcium balance, the third factor we're looking at, after calcium losses and intake, is absorption. The availability of this precious mineral from plant foods is affected by the presence of oxalates and to some extent phytates, which can limit the fraction or percentage of calcium absorbed. Table 6.6 shows the estimated amounts of calcium absorbed from foods based on the research of Dr. Connie Weaver. Dr. Weaver's research compared amounts of foods that provided equivalent quantities of calcium. This is an important point, because we absorb calcium more efficiently when a small amount is taken at a time. This means that you absorb more calcium when calcium-rich foods or supplements are eaten over the course of a day, rather than all at once. For example, you absorb more calcium from four ½-cup servings of fortified soymilk throughout the day than if you had the whole two cups of soymilk (or an equivalent amount of calcium in supplement form) all at once.

Table 6.6 Amounts, Percentage Absorption, and Estimated Absorbable Calcium in Plant Foods and Milk

Food and serving size	Serving g	Calcium content, mg	Fractional absorption, %	Estimated absorbable calcium, mg
Bok choy, ½ c	85	79	53%	42
Broccoli, ½ c	71	35	61%	21
Chinese cabbage flower leaves, ½ c	85	239	40%	95
Chinese mustard greens, ½ c	85	212	40%	85
Kale, ½ c	85	61	49%	30
Fruit punch with calcium citrate malate, ¾ c (6 oz)	180	225	52%	117
White beans, 1 c	220	226	22%	49
Pinto beans, 1c	172	89.4	27%	24
Tofu with calcium, ½ c	126	258	31%	80
Sweet potatoes, ½ c	164	44	22%	10
Spinach,★ ½ c	85	115	5%★	6
Rhubarb,★ ½ c	120	174	8%★	10
Cow's milk, ½ c	120	150	32%	48

★High contents of oxalates present decrease absorption.

BIOAVAILABILITY

Bioavailability is the proportion of a nutrient in a food that we can actually utilize. The calcium in many greens has a relatively high bioavailability, as does the calcium citrate malate used to fortify certain beverages (40-60% or more). The percentage of calcium absorbed from calcium-set tofu and from milk is similar, at 31-32%. Mineral water that contains calcium provides the mineral in a form that is well absorbed. The absorbability of calcium from soy beverages (often fortified with tricalcium phosphate) is a little lower, about 24%. Many common beans, almonds, sesame seeds, and sweet potatoes have lower bioavailability (around 20%). Spinach, beet greens, Swiss chard, and rhubarb are high in oxalates, allowing little of the calcium present to be absorbed; these cannot be counted on as calcium sources.

VITAMIN D: ESSENTIAL FOR CALCIUM ABSORPTION

Vitamin D, discussed on pages 132-39, is required for the active absorption of calcium. As vitamin D is not a natural component of most foods, lack of vitamin D can be an issue for anyone, vegan or not, who neither uses vitamin D-fortified foods or supplements nor gets an adequate amount of sunlight on the forearms and face each day. An example of someone who would likely be low in vitamin D is an elderly person or invalid who is seldom outdoors and who does not use vitamin D-fortified beverages such as soymilk. If sunlight is insufficient and fortified foods are not used, it's a good idea to take a supplement that contains vitamin D along with calcium.

Calcium Intake and Bone Health

Diet is just one of the lifestyle factors impacting lifelong bone health. To complicate things further, there are many nutrients in addition to calcium that help to build bones or affect calcium retention and bone loss. For example, sufficient vitamin D, magnesium, and protein favorably affect bone health. Boron, plentiful in fruits, leafy vegetables, nuts, and legumes, may have a beneficial impact too. Excessive protein and sodium have negative impacts. (For more on osteoporosis, see pages 34-37.) Research does not consistently show that people who consume more calcium have fewer bone or hip fractures, though some studies support this theory. Nonetheless, calcium is a major raw material for bone construction and maintenance, and it simply makes sense to ensure that your diet provides enough calcium to build and maintain bones. Our Stone Age ancestors developed healthy bones with relatively high calcium intakes. Vegans are well advised to aim for the Adequate Intakes of calcium (page 95) and to follow the tips on the next page.

Solid Solutions for Better Bones
Calcium Intake

- Include at least 6 to 8 servings of calcium-rich foods, as described in the Vegan Food Guide (pages 154-55), spread over the course of a day.
- Eat calcium-rich greens every day: kale, collards, broccoli, okra, Oriental greens such as bok choy, and turnip and mustard greens.
- Use calcium-set tofu more often—it is so versatile it can be a part of breakfast, lunch, supper, snacks, or desserts. Soyfoods come with an additional bonus—isoflavones—that further support bone strength.
- Make sure the soy or grain beverage you select is fortified with calcium and the vitamin D that promotes its absorption.
- If you drink commercial fruit juices, select those that are calcium-fortified.
- Explore Table 6.7 to discover other calcium sources. You might keep a bag of figs or almonds in your purse, backpack, or glove compartment; spread your toast with almond butter or with sesame tahini and a thin layer of blackstrap molasses; or use white beans in soups, casseroles, and spreads.
- If you're not getting at least 1,000 mg calcium per day (1,200 after age 50), take a calcium supplement. Calcium citrate malate is an excellent choice, as it is the form most readily absorbed.
- Focus on calcium and other bone-building nutrients in the early years and during pregnancy.

Decreasing Calcium Losses

- Limit high-sodium foods and be moderate in use of salty seasonings (salt, tamari, miso).
- Avoid excessive intakes of protein, but be sure to meet recommended intakes.
- After the age of 30, choose a diet and active lifestyle that help you hold onto the calcium you have.

Additional Lifestyle Choices for Lifelong Bone-Health

- Run, walk, or lift weights.
- Enjoy an average of 10-15 minutes a day of sun on the face and hands for light-skinned people and about 30 minutes a day for dark-skinned people, or take a vitamin D supplement.
- Consume a good overall balance of nutrients by following the Vegan Food Guide (pages 154-55).

Table 6.7 Calcium, Milligrams (mg) per Serving and mg per 100 Calories (419 Kilojoules)

Food and Category	Measure (Serving)	Calcium mg per serving	Approx. Food to Provide 100 Calories	Calcium mg per 100 Calories
Vegetables				
Bean sprouts, raw	1 c/240 mL	14	3.2 c/770 mL	43
Broccoli, raw	1 c/240 mL	42	4 c/960 mL	171
Carrots, raw, 7.5"/19 cm long	1	19	3	63
Cauliflower, ckd	½ c/120 mL	10	3½ c/840 mL	70
Collard greens, ckd	½ c/120 mL	113	2 c/480 mL	457
Corn, ckd	½ c/120 mL	2	½ c/120 mL	2
Green/yellow beans, ckd	½ c/120 mL	28	2⅓ c/560 mL	131
Eggplant, ckd	½ c/120 mL	3	3½ c/840 mL	21
Kale, raw	½ c/120 mL	90	3 c/720 mL	270
Mushroom pcs, ckd	½ c/120 mL	5	2½ c/600 mL	22
Okra, boiled	½ c/120 mL	50	2 c/480 mL	198
Potato, baked, med.	1	12	¾	9
Potato, sweet baked, med	1	32	½ c/120 mL	27
Romaine lettuce, raw	1 c/240 mL	20	12½ c/3 L	257
Spinach, raw★	1 c/240 mL	30★	15 c/3.6 L	446★
Turnip, ckd, mashed	½ c/120 mL	25	2 c/480 mL	105
Seaweed (e.g. wakame), raw	½ c/120 mL	67	3 c/720 mL	360
Nondairy "Milks" (brands vary)				
Fortified soy and grain milks (see label)	½ c/120 mL	100–150	about 1 c/240 mL	130–375
Unfortified soy and grain milks (see label)	½ c/120 mL	5–10	about 1 c/240 mL	12–60
Legumes, Tofu, Tempeh, Veggie "Meats"				
Black beans and black turtle beans, ckd	1 c/240 mL	46–102	⅖ c/100 mL	18–67
Cranberry beans, ckd	1 c/240 mL	89	⅖ c/100 mL	38
Garbanzo/chickpeas,ckd	1 c/240 mL	80	⅖ c/100 mL	30
Lentils, ckd	1 c/240 mL	38	⅖ c/100 mL	16
Navy beans, ckd	1 c/240 mL	127	⅖ c/100 mL	49
Kidney beans, ckd	1 c/240 mL	50	scant ½ c/110 mL	22
Pinto beans, ckd	1 c/240 mL	82	⅖ c/100 mL	35
Soybeans, ckd	1 c/240 mL	175	⅓ c/80 mL	59
Tofu, firm, calcium-set (see label)★★	½ c/120 mL	861	¼ c/60 mL	471★
Tofu, silken firm	½ c/120 mL	40	⅔ c/160 mL	52
Tempeh	½ c/120 mL	77	⅓ c/80 mL	47
Vegan wieners, veggie dogs (selected)	1.4 oz/42 g	17–20	2	34–44
Vegan burgers (selected)	1 (70 g)	20–40	about 1	14–57
Veggie ground round	2 oz/60 g	50	3 oz/90 g	76

★Note that spinach, Swiss chard, beet greens, and rhubarb are not good calcium sources as they are high in oxalates that bind the minerals, making calcium unavailable.

★★Database figures listed here may be higher than many local brands.

Food and Category	Measure (Serving)	Calcium mg per serving	Approx. Food to Provide 100 Calories	Calcium mg per 100 Calories (419 Kilojoules)
Nuts, Seeds & Butters				
Almonds	¼ c/35 g	79–115	2 Tbsp/17 g	38–54
Cashew nuts	¼ c/35 g	8	2 Tbsp/17 g	15
Flaxseed	2 Tbsp/18 g	47	2.4 Tbsp/22 g	56
Hazelnuts	¼ c/34 g	38	2 Tbsp/16 g	18
Pecans	¼ c/27 g	19	2 Tbsp/15 g	10
Pine Nuts	¼ c/34 g	9	2 Tbsp/18 g	5
Pistachios	¼ c/32 g	34	2¼ Tbsp/18 g	19
Pumpkin seeds	¼ c/34 g	15	2 Tbsp/19 g	8
Sunflower seeds	¼ c/36 g	42	2 Tbsp/18 g	21
Sesame tahini★	3 Tbsp/45 mL	50–191	1 Tbsp/15 mL	18–74★
Grains and Products				
Barley, ckd	½ c/120 mL	13	⅓ c/80 mL	9
Millet, ckd	½ c/120 mL	4	⅓ c/80 mL	2
Oatmeal, ckd	½ c/120 mL	9	⅔ c/160 mL	13
Quinoa, ckd	½ c/120 mL	15	½ c/120 mL	15
Rice, brown, ckd	½ c/120 mL	10	½ c/120 mL	10
Rice, white, ckd	½ c/120 mL	8	½ c/120 mL	8
Whole wheat flour	¼ c/30 g	10	¼ c/30 g	10
Life Cereal	¾ c/32 g	100	⅝ c/26 g	83
Soy-N-Ergy	¾ c/32 g	500	⅞ c/37 g	423
Special K Plus	1 c/60 g	600	½ c/30 g	286
Fruits and Juices				
Apples	1 med	10	1 large	12
Bananas	1 med	7	1	6
Cantaloupe	¼ melon	15	½ melon	31
Figs	5	88–137	2–2½	47–56
Oranges	1 med	52	1½	85
Strawberries	½ c/120 mL	10.1	2⅓ c/560 mL	47
Fortified orange juice (see label)	¾ c/180 mL	225–262	⁹/₁₀ c/216 mL	272–318
Other				
Blackstrap molasses	1 Tbsp/15 mL	176	2 Tbsp/30 mL	366
Animal Foods (for comparison)				
Milk, 2%	½ c/120 mL	135	⅘ c/190 mL	208
Cheese, cheddar	¾ oz/21 g	152	1 oz/30 g	152–182
Cottage cheese, 2%	½ c/120 mL	80	½ c/120 mL	80
Yogurt	½ c/120 mL	220	⅔ c/160 mL	291
Beef, chicken or fish	2 oz/60 g	4–8	1–3 oz/30–90 g	3–13

★*Highest figures are from tahini made with unhulled sesame seeds, which may have high oxalates.*

Boning Up On Calcium

In Table 6.7 on the previous pages, the two columns of figures on the left show serving sizes of a variety of foods along with the amounts of calcium in milligrams. Though these figures give a general idea of calcium distribution among foods, note that actual mineral contents can be expected to vary considerably, depending on the genetic variety of the foods, maturity when harvested, and soil and growing conditions.

The column on the right shows the amount of calcium in these same foods per 100 calories. This way of presenting nutrition information is an expression of "nutrient density," a classic way of showing the nutrient content of a food per hundred calories (or per calorie). Because it's the number of calories each day that we eat that's important, not the weight of food, it makes sense to examine the nutrients we get relative to the calories we eat. The greater the nutrient density, the more nutritional value you get for each calorie consumed. In several charts throughout the book, we provide information on nutrient density for various nutrients in a range of foods. You can also see the approximate amount of those foods to provide 100 calories. Though many plant foods contain plenty of calcium per 100 calories, you won't get the calcium you need with tiny little side salads!

IRON NUGGETS   *Planning May be Needed*

Iron's Importance

Of all the essential minerals in foods, iron is probably the most well recognized. Often, iron is the focus of our earliest encounters with the subject of nutrition. First there was Popeye and his never-ending supply of canned spinach. (As you'll see on page 109, spinach isn't such a great iron source, after all.) Then there was grade school nutrition class, where we were taught that we needed to eat meat for its rich supply of iron. Later we heard warnings about vegetarians being at high risk for iron deficiency. If you are still haunted by rusty facts such as these, here's a solid update.

Iron is a "precious metal" when it comes to human health. As part of certain blood cells, it plays a central role in transporting oxygen to the body, releasing this life-giving substance where needed and carrying away the metabolic waste product carbon dioxide. As part of many enzyme systems, iron also plays key roles in the production of cellular energy, in immune system functioning, and in the mental processes surrounding learning and behavior.

Every day we lose miniscule amounts of iron in cells that are sloughed from skin, the intestinal walls, and other places in the body. We are efficient at recycling iron, however, losses must be replaced from food or from food plus supplements. Women of childbearing age have additional iron losses during menstruation, in the range of an extra 30-45 mg of iron each month, making their requirements higher than those of men. Growth and the building of new cells put high demands on both our stored and dietary iron and can deplete the small reserves of infants and children. With teens, there can be the double challenges of growth and notoriously poor eating habits. Naturally, those with blood loss for any reason (for example blood donors and those with ulcers) have increased needs. Athletes also have higher requirements due to increased oxygen demands. (For more on meeting the needs of athletes and specific age groups, see Chapters 10 to 12, and 16.)

Iron Issues

IRON DEFICIENCY ANEMIA

Worldwide, iron is the most prevalent nutritional deficiency. This is not only a problem for populations in low-income countries, but also for those in North America, the U.K., and other industrialized parts of the world. Deficiencies are due to low intakes, low bioavailability, and losses. Worldwide, the groups most susceptible are women who menstruate, pregnant and lactating women, teens, and children aged 6 months to 4 years. This is true for vegetarians and non-vegetarians alike.

IRON OVERLOAD

Getting a lot of iron is not an advantage for everyone. A genetic condition called hemochromatosis causes affected individuals to absorb more iron from food than the body requires. About 10% of the North American population carries one gene for this disorder, while about 1 person in 250 carries 2 such genes. Someone with a single iron-loading gene is at very low risk of iron deficiency. A person with both genes absorbs large quantities of iron, and if left untreated, the condition can be fatal. For these people, the form of iron in meat (called heme iron) is associated with the greatest risk, especially in a diet that is low in the antioxidant vitamin E. This condition has alerted scientists to the fact that factors in plant foods that limit iron absorption, such as phytates, can actually be seen as protective, though it is possible for hemochromatosis to develop in someone on a vegetarian diet.

Iron Status Assessment

Iron deficiency anemia occurs in three progressive stages, with lab results and symptoms described on the next page:

Stage 1: Iron Depletion

Iron stores diminish, indicated by a decrease in the body's serum ferritin. This decrease does not affect how a person feels.

Stage 2: Iron Deficiency

In addition to low serum ferritin, there is a decrease in serum iron and the percentage saturation of transferrin, the iron transport protein. This may be accompanied by a slight decrease in hemoglobin production, a tired feeling, and sensitivity to cold.

Stage 3: Iron Deficiency Anemia

Total blood hemoglobin is below the normal range. Since the body's oxygen-delivery system is diminished, people are likely to feel symptoms such as exhaustion, irritability, lethargy, and headaches. With some dilution of the red hemoglobin in tiny blood vessels, the skin may appear pale.

Surveying the Situation

IRON DEFICIENCY IN POORER COUNTRIES VERSUS AFFLUENT COUNTRIES

Iron deficiency is a serious health problem for 700 million people or about 12% of the entire human population. In some parts of the world, iron deficiency anemia (stage 3, above) occurs in as many as 50% of children and premenopausal women. As well as having a major impact on quality of life, consequences in infants and children can include irreversible learning impairment. Despite some iron intakes that meet recommended levels, diets in these areas are often very limited and the proportion of dietary iron that is actually absorbed may be small. Diets may contain few of the vitamin C-rich fruits and vegetables that greatly increase iron absorption. Health problems, such as parasitic infections, contribute to losses as well.

In North America, Europe, and Japan, the situation is less extreme, though still considerable, with few cases of iron deficiency anemia but an estimated 10% of women and teens being iron deficient (Stage 2, above).

IRON STATUS AND INTAKES OF VEGETARIANS

Studies show little difference in the incidence of iron deficiency between vegetarians and nonvegetarians in developed countries. The primary difference appears to be that vegans and other vegetarians often have iron stores at the low end of the normal range. Low iron stores can be a definite disadvantage in the face of iron stresses, for example heavy menstrual losses, illness, or in some parts of the world, hookworm infection. For those in generally good health and with abundant food available, iron stores at the low end of the normal range do not seem to be a problem and may even protect from free radical damage related to higher iron stores. (This does not mean hemoglobin and serum transferrin should be low.) Since iron deficiency is such a prevalent condition and easily diagnosed, if you have any doubts about your iron status, it's an excellent idea to get feedback on how you're doing by having a lab test done. It is often possible to get photocopies of lab results from physicians and then track your progress.

The amount of iron in vegetarian, and particularly vegan, diets tends to be higher than, or at least equal to, that in nonvegetarian diets. As an example, in a New Zealand study, the mean iron intake in the vegetarians and vegans was 16.8 mg/day and that of the nonvegetarians

Table 6.8 Mean Iron Intakes and Stores (Serum Ferritin) of Australian Male Vegans, Lacto-ovo-vegetarians and Omnivores (Ball et al, 1999)

Diet (and number in study)	Iron Intakes Daily, mg	Serum Ferritin Concentrations, ng/m
Vegans (10)	22.9	65
Lacto-ovo-vegetarians (39)	20.4	64
Omnivores (25)	15.8	121

was 14.6 mg/day. Results from an Australian study by Ball and coworkers are shown in Table 6.8. Findings were similar in comparable research with females, though too few vegans were included to analyze their data separately.

Vegans and other vegetarians may need higher intakes of dietary iron to compensate for the lower bioavailability of iron from plant foods. In a classic study by Sanders, adult vegans had hemoglobin levels comparable to nonvegetarians, and all vegan subjects were above the normal lower limit. Note that dairy products are poor sources of iron and can inhibit iron's absorption, so when they form a large part of the diet, they can contribute to poor iron status.

Recommended Intakes

Recommended Dietary Allowances for Iron
Women 14.4-32.4 mg   Men 14.4 mg

The recommended iron intakes for vegetarian adults are 1.8 times those for the general population due to differences in bioavailability, and are highest for women in childbearing years. Plant-based diets are abundant in iron; our menus provide amounts shown in Table 6.9. Fortified foods can add even more.

Table 6.9 Iron in vegan menus (pages 157-60)

Calories	Iron, mg
1,600	25
2,200	33
2,800	32
4,000	43

Effect of Iron Status on Absorption

Many factors affect the efficiency of iron absorption; the most powerful is our need for iron. Those with greatest need absorb iron most efficiently, as illustrated in a small study by Cook (Table 6.10).

Table 6.10 Percentage of Nonheme Iron Absorbed from a Single Meal

Men, not iron deficient	2.5%
Women, not iron deficient	7.5%
Iron deficient person	21%

Bioavailability: Boom and Bust

As with many other minerals, it's not just the amount of iron in one's diet that is significant, but how well it is absorbed. Iron is found in two forms in foods, heme and nonheme iron. Heme iron has a higher bioavailability (15-35%) than nonheme iron (2-20%). Heme iron is found only in hemoglobin (oxygen-carrying protein of the blood) and myoglobin (oxygen-carrying molecules of the muscle), and thus comes strictly from animal flesh. In addition, meat, fish, and poultry contain a factor (MFP factor) that can increase the absorption of nonheme iron from foods eaten with it. The iron in meat is 50-60% heme iron, and 40-50% nonheme iron. Dietary factors have relatively little impact on the absorption of heme iron.

Nonheme iron is found in both plant and animal foods but is the only type of iron in plant foods, dairy products (which contain very little), and eggs. Many aspects of the diet influence one's absorption of nonheme iron. These include factors present in the iron-containing food itself and in foods eaten at the same time. When these factors are maximized in the diet, they can come together to provide an iron absorption level approaching that of heme iron. After being absorbed and reaching our cells to be used for building hemoglobin and other purposes, it makes no difference whether the iron was originally heme or nonheme.

Making the Most of Iron in Vegan Diets

A glance at Table 6.11 shows that there's no shortage of iron in plant foods! Because of this, vegetarians, and particularly vegans, often have higher total iron intakes compared to nonvegetarians. Vegans have an added advantage because their diets don't include dairy. Milk products are poor sources of iron. They displace iron-rich foods from the diet, and the presence of cow's milk or cheese in the diet has been shown to decrease the absorption of iron from a meal by as much as 50%.

Vegetarians eat plenty of fruits and vegetables and get about 50% more vitamin C than nonvegetarians; vegan intakes are higher still. This is a definite advantage when it comes to iron absorption. For example, 5 ounces of orange juice, containing 75 mg of vitamin C, has been shown to increase the absorption of iron from foods eaten at the same time by a factor of 4. You can also get 75 mg of vitamin C from 1/3 cup of sweet red pepper, a large kiwifruit, a cup of papaya, or a 2-cup serving of salad. (Less will be proportionally less effective.) A half-cup of any of the following provides more than 30 mg vitamin C: broccoli, Brussels sprouts, cauliflower, collards, bell peppers, snow peas, cantaloupe, citrus fruits and juices, guava, strawberries, and vitamin C-fortified juices. Vitamin C is easily destroyed by storage, processing, and cooking. For example, vegetables lose about 50% of their vitamin C when boiled, 30% when steamed, and 15% when microwaved. Losses vary tremendously depending on temperature and duration of exposure to heat and oxygen.

Other factors that enhance iron absorption are citric acids (present in citrus fruits, of course), fructose (fruit sugar), and certain amino acids. These are good reasons to ignore "food combining" (better called "food separating") rules suggesting that you eat fruit separately from other foods!

To a certain extent, phytates and the associated fiber reduce mineral availability from whole grains, legumes, and other plant foods. Phytate is a phosphorus-containing compound present in plant cells. Though phytates and fiber can cause iron to be less well absorbed, this can be offset by substantial amounts of vitamin C in foods eaten at the same time. Furthermore, the effect of phytates is considerably reduced by techniques used frequently in the preparation of vegetarian foods:

- leavening of whole grain breads
- roasting of nuts
- soaking of beans prior to cooking
- fermenting of foods, as with tempeh, miso, and natto
- sprouting of grains, seeds, and legumes

Sprouting has effects beyond breaking down phytate to make iron more available. The germination of lentils has been shown to increase vitamin C content 17.5 times and germination of mung beans by 8.5 times, offering another boost to iron absorption. Sprouting lentils or mung beans is an excellent way to increase absorption of both iron and zinc.

Soyfoods are rich in iron; at the same time they contain components that decrease its absorption. Overall they can be counted on as iron contributors. When soyfoods are fermented, both enzymatic action and yeasting processes increase iron and zinc availability; this occurs in the production of tempeh, miso, natto, and soy sauce. When tofu, soyfoods, and other legumes or grains are eaten along with vitamin C-rich foods, mineral availability is further increased.

The cookware we use, specifically cast-iron, and to a lesser extent stainless steel, can contribute to the iron in our diets. Small amounts of iron from a saucepan or wok enter food being prepared, particularly when we cook acidic foods such as tomato-based spaghetti sauce or sweet and sour sauce. The iron drawn from cookware in this way is bioavailable and can be used by our cells in the same way as other iron in foods.

Dietary Factors That Decrease Absorption

The bioavailability of iron can be reduced by up to 60% by the tannins in black or green teas that are consumed at the same time as iron sources. Small amounts of tannins are present in Indian curry, turmeric, coriander, tamarind, and curry spices. Cocoa and coffee can have the same effect as tea, though to a lesser extent. For those individuals with low iron status, select water—or better still, citrus or vitamin C-fortified fruit juices—as beverages with meals.

Foods high in oxalates—spinach, Swiss chard, beet greens, and rhubarb—contain iron in a bound form that prevents absorption. These are not iron providers, despite their iron contents, so don't count them.

Other factors that can reduce the absorption of nonheme iron are antacids and zinc supplements. For people with low iron levels, it's a good idea to take these interactions into consideration and to avoid the foods and beverages that reduce absorption when consuming iron sources.

Striking It Rich With Iron From Plant Foods

- Eat iron-rich plant foods (see Table 6.11).
- Use iron-fortified foods (enriched grain products and fortified meat substitutes).
- Help your body absorb iron by eating vitamin C-rich foods at the same time.
- Use foods that are leavened, sprouted, soaked, fermented, and roasted.
- If your iron status is low, avoid consuming foods, beverages, and supplements (zinc) that decrease absorption at the same time as iron sources.
- Use cast-iron and stainless steel cookware.
- If in doubt, have your iron status checked.

Prospecting for Iron and Zinc

In Table 6.11 on the next 2 pages, the 3 columns of figures at the left show serving sizes for foods and the amount of iron and zinc, in milligrams, per serving. Though these figures give a general idea of iron and zinc distribution among foods, note that *actual* mineral contents can be expected to vary with the variety of the plants, type of soil, growing conditions, and maturity when harvested.

The 2 columns on the right, "Iron mg (milligrams) per 100 Calories" and "Zinc mg per 100 Calories," are an expression of nutrient density, a classic way of looking at the nutrient content of food per hundred calories (or per calorie). You can also see approximately how much of that food it takes to provide 100 calories. In some cases, a food can be nutrient dense, but if you want to rely on it as a major mineral source, you'll need to eat quite a lot of it! Following the table, we go on to iron's companion nutrient, zinc, which is found in many of the same foods but has quite different roles in the body.

Table 6.11 Iron and Zinc: Food Sources, Milligrams (mg) Per Serving and mg Per 100 Calories★ (Also shows the quantity of food that will provide 100 calories★)   (★419 Kilojoules)

Food and Category	Measure (Serving)	Iron mg per Serving	Zinc mg per serving	Approx. Food to Provide 100 Calories	Iron mg per 100 Calories	Zinc mg per 100 Calories
Vegetables						
Mung bean sprouts, raw	1 c/240 mL	1.0	0.4	3.2 c/720 mL	3.0	1.4
Broccoli, raw	1 c/240 mL	0.8	0.4	4 c/960 mL	3.1	1.4
Carrot, raw, 7.5"/19 cm	1	0.4	0.1	3	1.2	0.5
Cauliflower, ckd	½ c/120 mL	0.2	0.1	3½ c/840 mL	1.4	0.8
Green/yellow beans, ckd	½ c/120 mL	0.8	0.2	2⅓ c/560 mL	3.7	1.0
Kale, raw	1 c/240 mL	1.1	0.3	3 c/720 mL	3.4	0.9
Mushroom pcs, ckd	½ c/120 mL	1.4	0.7	2½ c/600mL	6.5	3.3
Potato, baked, med.	1	1.7	0.4	¾	1.2	0.3
Potato, sweet, baked, med	1	0.5	0.3	½ c/120 mL	0.4	0.3
Romaine lettuce, raw	1 c/240 mL	0.6	0.1	12½ c/3 L	7.7	1.8
Spinach, raw★	1 c/240 mL	0.8★	0.2	15 c/3.6 L	12.3★	2.4
Winter squash, ckd, mashed	½ c/120 mL	0.2	0.2	1¼ c/300 mL	1.0	0.9
Legumes/Tofu/Tempeh						
Aduki beans, ckd	1 c/240 mL	4.6	4.1	⅓ c/80 mL	1.5	1.4
Black/blck turtle beans, ckd	1 c/240 mL	3.6-5.2	1.4-1.9	⅖ c/100 mL	1.6-2.1	0.6-0.9
Cranberry beans, ckd	1 c/240 mL	3.7	2.0	⅖ c/100 mL	1.5	0.8
Garbanzo/chickpeas, ckd	1 c/240 mL	4.7	2.5	⅖ c/100 mL	1.8	0.9
Lentils, ckd	1 c/240 mL	6.6	2.5	⅖ c/100 mL	2.9	1.1
Navy, pinto, kidney, ckd	1 c/240 mL	4.5-5.2	1.8-1.9	⅖ c/100 mL	1.8-2.3	0.7-0.8
Soybeans, ckd	1 c/240 mL	8.8	2.0	⅓ c/80 mL	3.0	0.7
Miso	1 Tbsp/30 mL	0.4	0.5	3⅓ Tbsp/50 mL	1.4	1.7
Tofu, firm (see label)	½ c/120 mL	1.8-13.2	1.3-2.0	¼-½ c/60-120 mL	1.8-7.2	1.3-2.0
Tofu, silken firm	½ c/120 mL	1.3	0.8	⅔ c/160 mL	1.7	1.0
Tempeh	½ c/120 mL	2.2	1.0	⅓ c/80 mL	1.1	0.9
Grains and Products						
Barley, pearled, ckd	½ c/120 mL	1.0	0.6	½ c/120 mL	1.0	0.6
Millet, ckd	½ c/120 mL	0.8	1.1	⅓ c/80 mL	0.5	0.8
Oatmeal, ckd	½ c/120 mL	0.8	0.6	⅔ c/160 mL	1.1	0.8
Quinoa, ckd	½ c/120 mL	2.1	0.8	½ c +/140 mL	2.5	0.9
Rice, brown, ckd	½ c/120 mL	0.5	0.6	½ c/120 mL	0.5	0.6
Rice, white, ckd, enr	½ c/120 mL	1.0	0.4	½ c/120 mL	1.0	0.4
Rye flour, dark	¼ c/60 mL	2.0	1.6	¼ c/60 mL	2.0	1.6
Whole wheat flour	¼ c/60 mL	1.2	0.9	¼ c/60 mL	1.2	0.9
Wheat germ	2 Tbsp/30 mL	0.9	1.8	¼ c/60 mL	1.8	3.5
Nondairy Milks						
Soymilks (see label)	½ c/120 mL	0.5-0.9	0.3-0.9	½-¾ c/120-180 mL	1.1-1.4	0.4-0.7

★Don't count on spinach as an iron source; it's high in oxalates that inhibit absorption, as are Swiss chard, beet greens, and rhubarb.

Food and Category	Measure (Serving)	Iron mg per Serving	Zinc mg per serving	Approx. Food to Provide 100 Calories	Iron mg per 100 Calories	Zinc mg per 100 Calories
Veggie "meats"						
Yves deli slices, each ½ oz /15 g (fortified)	4	3.6	3	5½ slices	4.5	4.1
Yves Good Dog, 1.8 oz /52 g (fortified)	1	3.6	2.2	1¼	4.5	2.8
Garden vegan burger, 2 oz/60 g	1	1.1	0.4	1	1.1	0.4
Yves Burger Burger (fort.) 3 oz/90 g	1	3.6	5.2	1	3.0	4.4
Yves Veggie Ground Round	2 oz/55 g	2.7	3	3 oz/90 g	4.9	4.9
Nuts, Seeds, and Butters						
Almonds	¼ c/35 g	1.4	1.2	2 Tbsp/17 g	0.7	0.6
Cashew nuts	¼ c/35 g	2.1	1.9	2 Tbsp/17 g	1.0	1.0
Flaxseed	2 Tbsp/18 g	1.9	0.4	2.4 Tbsp/22 g	2.2	0.4
Hazelnuts	¼ c/34 g	1.6	0.8	2 Tbsp/16 g	0.8	0.4
Pecans	¼ c/27 g	0.7	1.2	2 Tbsp/15 g	0.4	0.7
Pine Nuts	¼ c/34 g	3.1	1.4	2 Tbsp/18 g	1.6	0.8
Pistachios	¼ c/32 g	1.4	0.7	2¼ Tbsp/18 g	0.8	0.4
Pumpkin seeds	¼ c/34 g	5.2	2.6	2 Tbsp/19 g	2.8	1.4
Sunflower seeds	¼ c/36 g	2.4–2.7	1.8	2 Tbsp/18 g	1.2–1.5	0.9
Sesame tahini	3 Tbsp/45 mL	2.1–2.9	2.0–4.7	1 Tbsp/15 mL	0.8–1.0	0.8–1.7
Fruits						
Apples	1 med	0.2	0.1	1 large	0.4	0.1
Apricot, halves dried	10	1.6	0.3	12	2.0	0.3
Bananas, medium	1	0.4	0.2	1	0.4	0.2
Strawberries	½ c/120 mL	0.3	0.1	2⅓ c/560 mL	1.3	0.4
Figs, dried	5	2.1	0.5	2½	1.1	0.2
Melons, cantaloupe	¼	0.3	0.2	½	0.6	0.5
Orange, medium	1	0.1	0.1	1½	0.2	0.2
Prunes	10	2.1	0.4	5	1.0	0.2
Raisins	¼ c/60 mL	0.9–1.1	0.1	3 Tbsp/15 mL	0.7–0.9	0.1
Other						
Blackstrap molasses	1 Tbsp/15 mL	3.6	0.2	2 Tbsp/30 mL	7.4	0.4
Animal Foods (for comparison)						
Milk, 2%	½ c/120 mL	0.1	0.5	⅘ c/190 mL	0.1	0.8
Cheese, cheddar	¾ oz/21 g	0.1	0.7	1 oz/30 g	0	0.8
Egg, medium	1	0.5	0.5	1½	0.8	0.7
Ground beef	2 oz/60 g	1.1	2.4	1½ oz/45 g	0.8	1.8
Chicken, roasted	2 oz/60 g	0.6	0.7	2 oz/60 g	0.6	0.7
Cod baked/broiled	2 oz/60 g	0.3	0.3	3⅓ oz/100 g	0.5	0.6
Salmon baked/broiled	2 oz/60 g	0.3	0.3	1⅔ oz/50 g	0.2	0.2

ZOOM IN ON ZINC   *Planning May be Needed*

Zinc

Though our bodies contain just 2 to 3 grams of this mineral, it affects many fundamental processes. Zinc is a component of at least 60, and perhaps several hundred, enzyme systems. It is essential to cell division and the generation of new life. Zinc is necessary for the elimination of carbon dioxide, other aspects of respiration, the maintenance of acid-base balance, wound healing, and the functioning of our immune systems. It plays a part in our ability to taste. It helps build protein, blood, and our genetic material, DNA; it is crucial at times of growth and reproduction. Certain tissues and fluids in the body contain relatively high concentrations of zinc; these include the iris and retina of the eye, and also the prostate, sperm, and seminal fluid. In fact, men lose an estimated 0.6 mg of zinc with each seminal emission—about 6% of their recommended intake for the day and 27% of what they might absorb from that intake.

In the plant world, too, zinc is involved with the generation of new life, reflected in its presence in the seeds, nuts, and legumes that germinate and sprout to form new plants. Men can recover that zinc with a little bowl of pumpkin seeds, almonds, cashews, pine nuts, pistachios, or sunflower seeds. (See Table 6.11.)

Because of its involvement when the body is growing, children are particularly vulnerable if they're not getting enough zinc. Zinc deficiency in humans was first recognized in 1961 in Egyptian children, where a combination of factors contributed: low zinc intakes, regular consumption of unleavened bread (which has low mineral availability), an unusual practice of eating clay (which binds zinc), losses of zinc through respiration (in a hot climate), and hookworm infection. The stunted growth that occurs with some children in various regions of the world has been, in part, attributed to low zinc intakes. For example, researchers have estimated that zinc deficiency may play a role in the short statures of 30% of children in China. Insufficient calories and other health problems can also contribute to this outcome.

In North America, serious zinc deficiency of this type is rare. However, marginal zinc deficiency, characterized by slow physical growth, poor appetite, and reduced ability to taste, has been identified on a number of occasions in infants and children. Typically, both vegetarians and nonvegetarians at many stages of life fail to meet U.S. recommended intakes, with vegetarian intakes slightly below those of nonvegetarians. It is not certain whether this is a problem, and if it is a problem, in what way.

Recommended Intakes

The new recommended intakes for zinc are significantly lower than the previous RDAs in the U.S. and slightly lower than previous RNIs in Canada. Some of the difficulty in determining zinc requirements is due to uncertainty about how well zinc is absorbed from different diets. Another part of the mystery is that it's not all that easy to assess a person's zinc status, unlike iron status, which is relatively well understood and easily assessed.

What we are clear about is that the body actually needs about 2.5 mg of zinc per day, and that somewhere between 10% and 40% of the zinc in the diet is actually absorbed. Bioavailability is a big issue when it comes to zinc. The recommendations shown above are based on an estimated absorption rate of 20%. The one-day meal plans throughout this book provide the amounts of zinc shown in Table 6.12.

Table 6.12 Zinc in vegan menus (pages 157-60)

Calories	Zinc, mg
1,600	16
2,200	15
2,800	16
4,000	24

Surveying the Situation

ZINC INTAKES OF VARIOUS POPULATIONS

There is some concern about zinc intakes of the general North American population, which tend to be well below U.S. recommended intakes. Typically, adult men consume between 12-13.5 mg zinc per day and adult women 9-10 mg zinc per day, both exceeding recommended intakes. Four studies conducted in Canada, the U.K., and Australia showed average zinc intakes of 294 nonvegetarian women to be an average of 8.8 mg per day.

ZINC INTAKES OF VEGANS

Some studies suggest that vegans have zinc intakes that compare favorably with patterns of vegetarians and nonvegetarians; others have shown vegan intakes to be 5-20% below the intakes of nonvegetarians. Vegans with particularly low *caloric* intakes also have particularly low *zinc* intakes. In a British study, 18 male vegans averaged 10.1 mg of zinc per day. The average caloric intake of these men, 2,190 calories, was somewhat low for men. Studies of 33 vegan women in Canada, the U.K., and New Zealand showed an average 8.3 mg zinc in diets providing an average of 1,860 calories per day. Since the numbers in these studies are small, they may or may not be representative of larger populations. Haddad and her coworkers found 25 vegans to have similar zinc intakes and plasma zinc, compared to a control group of nonvegetarians.

In the U.S., University of Texas researcher Dr. Jeanne Freeland-Graves found intakes of four male vegans to be a respectable 14.1 mg per day. In contrast, zinc intakes of the four vegan women studied were extremely low (averaging 1.4 mg), and their average caloric intake was below 1,700 calories.

In cases where zinc intakes of North American or British vegans are low, it's clearly not due to a lack of vegan foods on the market but to dietary selection. To quote Freeland-Graves:

"In a study of 79 vegetarians, our laboratory observed that only female vegans had low dietary levels of zinc. These low levels were attributed to heavy reliance on fruits, salad, and vegetables, foods that are poor sources of zinc. In contrast, males ate abundant quantities of legumes and whole grains, foods that are good sources of zinc."

In some studies, high-protein diets have been shown to increase zinc requirements, though there is some evidence to the contrary. Thus, vegans may have an advantage because their protein intakes tend to be closer to recommended levels and are rarely excessive. It also appears that when zinc intakes are low, the body compensates by conserving zinc, for example, by reducing fecal losses.

In summary, zinc intakes of vegans, other vegetarians, and nonvegetarians are lower than recommendations. Intakes of some vegans are extremely low. What does this mean?

Assessment of Zinc Status

There is no single, specific and accurate indicator of zinc status. Thus, determining whether a person has enough zinc to function at optimal levels is a real challenge. Zinc levels in hair, saliva, and blood can be measured; however, all of these methods have limitations. Tests involving zinc-dependent enzymes show some promise as more accurate indicators of zinc status but such tests are not widely available. Of the limited data assessing zinc status of vegetarians and nonvegetarians, some comparisons show no statistical difference between the groups; others show lower zinc status in the vegetarians.

While there is little evidence of outright deficiency among vegetarians, there are many unanswered questions and tremendous potential for research. Clearly, zinc intakes of some vegans are far too low for optimal functioning and the addition of zinc-rich foods to the diet is warranted (Table 6.11). In addition, there are many things vegans can do to make the most of the zinc they do consume.

Bioavailability: Boom and Bust

The balance between factors that *enhance* and those that *inhibit* zinc absorption determines its overall availability from a meal or diet. It's a complex matter and not yet completely understood.

In meals that are high in phytate, zinc, and calcium, a complex of these three substances can be formed that tightly binds zinc, considerably reducing its absorption. This can be true when there are plenty of dairy foods in the diet. For vegans, the best course is to aim for recommended calcium intakes but not to consume excessive amounts of calcium-fortified beverages and tofu manufactured with calcium salts (as is much of the commercial firm tofu available). If calcium supplements are taken, it's best to avoid taking them along with foods that are high in both zinc and phytates (whole grains, wheat bran, and legumes).

Among the most powerful factors increasing bioavailability of zinc from whole plant foods are food preparation and processing methods that break down the zinc-phytate complex. These methods include:

• sprouting (to germinate lentils, mung beans, seeds, nuts, or grains);

• soaking (to prepare beans, grains, nuts, or seeds for use);

• yeasting (to make bread with zinc-rich whole grain flours);

• fermenting (to make sourdough bread, where the lactic acid formed may aid mineral absorption, or in soy products such as tempeh);

• roasting (to toast nuts).

Prospecting for Zinc

One factor that has made it much easier to meet recommended intakes for zinc (along with iron and protein) is the increased availability of zinc-fortified meat substitutes and soy beverages. The meat substitutes come many forms: deli slices, veggie hot dogs, ground round, and burgers. These products offer convenient ways to make children's lunches appealing or to assemble a meal in minutes. Not all veggie meats and soy beverages are zinc-fortified, so read labels. In Canada, fortification of soy and grain beverages includes zinc, whereas this is not the case with many in the U.S.

For many vegans, it's far more appealing to get zinc from whole or raw foods rather than from more processed products. For these people, sprouting and using fermented foods can make a big difference in zinc availability.

Among the most common reasons people fail to get enough zinc and other minerals is their restriction of higher-fat plant foods such as nuts, nut butters, seeds, and even soyfoods and legumes. In a diet that is packed with beef, chicken, and cheese, it may make sense to cut out the big bowls of peanuts as TV snacks. Certainly, this kind of thinking has shaped our attitudes towards nuts. Actually, recent research indicates that of the higher-fat foods just listed, nuts are an extremely wise choice. (See pages 69-70.) In vegan and other vegetarian diets where there aren't a lot of fat calories coming from animal foods, nuts have a great deal to offer in terms of trace minerals, phytochemicals, for their sensory appeal as snacks,

> **Fat conscious people take note:**
> For the percentage of calories in your diet that comes from fat, don't waste your calories on fats and oils that contribute little nutrition. Get value from the all fats in your diet by concentrating on mineral-rich nuts, seeds, and soyfoods, along with flaxseed oil, ground flaxseed, or walnuts for omega-3 fatty acids.

and the creamy quality they give when blended in recipes. It makes sense to include nuts, not leave them out.

Zinc-rich foods are dispersed throughout the plant kingdom: grains, legumes, nuts, and seeds. The Vegan Food Guide (pages 154-55) is designed to provide a balance of the minerals and other nutrients you require and to help you design a diet that easily meets recommended intakes. When you consider all it does for you, it makes sense to:

Think about Zinc

- Expand your food horizons with tasty zinc-rich items you don't normally include, for example, tahini, pumpkin seeds, and a mix of legumes. (See Table 6.11.)
- Make sure your overall caloric intake is adequate.
- Get a few jars and sprout lids, and start sprouting lentils, seeds, and grains.
- Use fermented soyfoods, such as tempeh, miso, and natto.
- Keep trail mix (nuts, seeds, and dried fruit) in your glove compartment, backpack, or desk drawer.
- If your zinc intake falls short of the mark, choose fortified foods.

OTHER MINERAL MARVELS

Earlier in this chapter, we considered three minerals that have been studied extensively and are of particular interest to vegetarians: calcium, iron, and zinc. The mineral boron was mentioned on page 98, and cobalt is a central part of vitamin B_{12} (page 121). On the next few pages, we cover eight more of the 21 minerals that are essential to various life processes. Note that at the time of writing this book, recommendations for intakes of some minerals were under review; over time revisions are expected. Concerning minerals that are not included in this chapter, in some cases little is known about their functions or how much we need. In other cases, the minerals are widely available and deficiencies are not considered to be an issue.

Of the minerals listed on the next pages, iodine deserves particular attention, especially for those who do not use iodized sea salt. Sodium is of interest too, not because we're looking for adequate intakes and good sources, but because we're trying not to get too much!

Chromium   *Planning may be needed*

Function: Supports action of insulin and is a part of glucose tolerance factor.

Adequate Intake: 20 to 35 mcg/day. More may be beneficial for people with heart disease or diabetes.

Sources: Whole grains and whole grain products, nuts (especially pecans), mushrooms, asparagus, prunes, spices, brewer's yeast, beer.

Special Issues: As with other minerals, our need for chromium makes a good case for the use of nuts and whole, rather than refined, grains.

Copper   *Usually plentiful*

Function: Is a part of enzymes needed for action of iron, for protein metabolism, and building of hormones.

RDA: 900 mcg/day

Sources: 1 serving (½ c) of grains provides about 0.1 to 0.3 mcg; 1 serving nuts, seeds, beans, tofu, or tempeh provides 0.5-0.7 mcg (with Brazil nuts and pecans particularly high). Also: sweet potatoes, bananas, raisins, and prunes.

Special Issues: High zinc intakes (e.g., from supplements in excess of the RDA) can prevent copper absorption, resulting in copper deficiency.

Fluoride   *Usually plentiful*

Function: Increases hardness of tooth enamel and mineralization of bone.

Adequate Intake: 3-4 mg/day

Sources: Fluoridated water, fluoride drops and treatments, seaweed, tea (with amounts varying considerably), use of Teflon (which contains fluoride). Studies have shown fluoridated toothpaste to be ineffective in preventing tooth decay.

Special Issues: Some intake of fluoride can help develop hard, decay-resistant teeth.

Iodine   *Planning may be needed*

Function: Is an essential part of thyroid hormones, influencing most organ systems. Extremely important during pregancy.

Adequate Intake: 150 mcg/day. The Tolerable Upper Intake Level (UL) is set at 1,100 mcg.

Recommended Intakes for Nutrients

Recommended Dietary Allowances (RDAs) have been set periodically since 1941 by the National Academy of Sciences.

In Canada, comparable values were the Recommended Nutrient Intakes (RNIs). In recent years, the Institute of Medicine of the National Academy of Sciences, including scientists from the United States and Canada, has expanded on the RDAs, because it has been recognized that for some nutrients, such as calcium, we simply don't know enough yet to set a suitable RDA and for some nutrients it's helpful for supplement users to know safe upper limits for intake. Thus we now have several categories to guide our nutrient intake.

Recommended Dietary Allowance (RDA): the average daily dietary intake level that is sufficient to meet the needs of nearly all (97-98%) of the population. It is determined for healthy people, and amounts vary for men, women, stages of life such as pregnancy, and for different age groups.

Adequate Intake (AI): used when an RDA cannot be determined due to insufficient data. It is a "best guess" and is based on observation of intakes in healthy populations and whatever experimental data is available.

Tolerable Upper Intake Level (UL): the maximum intake of a nutrient that is likely to pose no risk of adverse health effects in almost all individuals in the general population. It should not be considered the recommended amount, but a ceiling to help people avoid taking too much of a nutrient.

Label readers take note: The **Daily Values (DVs)** that are on nutrition panels of food products are another category again. This set of standards is based on an earlier set of RDAs. Though the RDAs and other recommendations are regularly updated as new scientific information comes in, the DVs (also known as "U.S. RDAs) that are used as a standard for labels do not keep pace with these changes. Designing new product labels is a very expensive process, and it would be a nightmare for manufacturers if they had to continually make new labels with every major or minor change in recommendations.

Sources: ¼ tsp. of iodized salt provides 67 mcg or about half the RDA for iodine. In Canada, all table salt is iodized, in the U.S. iodization is optional, and there is not a national program for iodized salt in Britain. Sea salt is not always iodized; look for some that is. Raw and dried sea vegetables (seaweeds, including kelp tablets and powders) are good sources, though digestible amounts of iodine can vary considerably. Without sources such as these, iodine intake from a vegan diet may be only about 10% of the RDA.

Special Issues: Components in raw flaxseed, soyfoods, and foods in the cabbage family can interfere with iodine's action or with thyroid function. This presents a potential problem to iodine-deficient or hypothyroid individuals.

Magnesium   *Planning may be needed*

Function: Is a component of strong teeth and bones, helps convert food to useable energy, passes along nerve impulses, and has other diverse roles.

RDA: Women 310-320 mg/day; Men 400-420 mg/day

Sources: Present in all whole grains, but lost in refining. (A slice of whole wheat bread contains 30 mg, but a slice of white bread 5 mg.) Magnesium is the central atom in the chlorophyll molecule, so greens are good sources; so are other vegetables, nuts, seeds, legumes, fruit, and chocolate.

Special Issues: Magnesium is abundant in plant foods, however where there is reliance on refined foods and sugar, intakes can be low. Status of some vegans is borderline or low.

Selenium   *Usually plentiful*

Function: Protects cells (heart, blood) from oxidative damage and is needed for iodine metabolism.

RDA: 55 mcg/day; *Tolerable Upper Intake Levels:* 400 mcg/day

Sources: Grains, nuts (especially Brazil nuts), and seeds grown in selenium-rich soil. You can get between ⅓ and ½ of the RDA from 1 slice of whole grain bread or 1 cup of oatmeal. However, any table showing selenium contents of foods would have to be regionally specific, as much variation exists.

Special Issues: Amounts of selenium in U.S.- and Canadian-grown crops are considered adequate, despite regional variation; U.K. and European intakes may be lower. Eating foods from different locations helps.

Sodium   *Planning may be needed, especially for salt sensitive people*

Function: Maintains fluid balance outside cells, facilitates the transmission of nerve impulses, and is part of digestive secretions from the pancreas.

RDA: Minimum 500 mg; Maximum 2,400 mg (suggested by National Academy of Sciences) or 3,000 mg (suggested by American Heart Association)

Sources: Table salt (sodium chloride) is 40% sodium by weight and 60% chloride, thus the minimum (500 mg sodium) is met by 1,250 mg of sodium chloride which is ¼ tsp. table salt. For a list of high-sodium foods, see Table 6.3.

Special Issues: Results from 5 studies have shown vegan intakes of sodium to be 1,990 mg sodium on average and within the recommended range of between 500 and 2,400 (or 3,000) mg/day. Vegans relying on veggie meats and processed foods may have high sodium intakes.

Potassium   *Usually plentiful*

Function: Acts with sodium to maintain fluid balance inside cells and to transmit nerve impulses; also plays an important role in muscle contraction, including heart muscle.

RDA: Minimum 2,000 mg (3,500 mg may be preferable)

Sources: Though bananas have somehow become famous as potassium-rich foods, in fact mushrooms, tomatoes, potatoes, green beans, and strawberries all have more potassium per calorie than bananas.

Special Issues: Plenty of fruits and vegetables are packed with potassium, so getting enough of this mineral is no problem for vegetarians!

SELECTED REFERENCES

For a complete list see www.nutrispeak.com/veganrefs.htm. See also general references for the whole book on page 276.

Alexander, D. et al. "Nutrient intake and haematological status of vegetarians and age-sex matched omnivores." *Eur. J. Clin. Nutr.* 48 (1994): 538-46.

Ball, M.J., and M.A. Bartlett. "Dietary intake and iron status of Australian vegetarian women." *Am. J. Clin. Nutr.* 70 (1999): 353-8.

Cook, J.D. "Adaptation in iron metabolism." *Am. J. Clin. Nutr.* 51 (1990): 301-8.

Freeland-Graves, J. "Mineral adequacy of vegetarian diets." *Am. J. Clin. Nutr.* 48 (1988): 859-62.

Gibson, R., U. Donovan, and A. Heath. "Dietary strategies to improve the iron and zinc nutriture of young women following a vegetarian diet." *Plant Foods for Human Nutrition* 51 (1997): 1-16.

Gueguen, L., and A. Pointillart. "The bioavailability of dietary calcium." *J. Amer. Coll. Nutr.* 19 (2000): 119S-136S.

Reddy, M. et al. "Estimation of nonheme-iron bioavailability from meal composition." *Am. J. Clin. Nutr.* 71 (2000): 937-943.

Tucker, K. et al. "Potassium, magnesium, and fruit and vegetable intakes are associated with greater bone mineral density in elderly men and women." *Am. J. Clin. Nutr.* 69 (1999): 727-736.

Weaver, C.M., and K. Plawecki. "Dietary calcium: adequacy of a vegetarian diet." *Am. J. Clin. Nutr.* 59 (1994): 1238S-41S.

CHAPTER
7

Vitamins for Vegan Vigor

The first half of the 20th century has been described as "The First Golden Age of Nutrition." In about four decades of tremendously exciting nutrition research, it was found that tiny amounts of substances in food could reverse serious, even fatal, diseases in a matter of months or even days. The presence of any one of the vitamins in the diet is the difference between life and death, yet our daily requirement for all the vitamins, plus all the minerals covered in Chapter 6, easily fits into a teaspoon.

Recognition of the vitamins began in the early 1900s. First, a fat-soluble component was discovered (eventually called vitamin A), followed by a water-soluble component (B) that eventually turned out to be a mixture of seven vitamins. Next, of course, was vitamin C, which is also soluble in water. Within a few decades, it was recognized that

> **Vitamin:** a carbon-containing substance that is essential to life, is not burned for energy, and must be supplied in the diet.

the essential fat-soluble substances included vitamins eventually named A, D, E, and K. A few more compounds were considered and then excluded. Since they were not absolutely necessary for survival, they didn't fit the admission requirements to be classified as a vitamin.

Vitamins are present in all food groups: B vitamins (other than B_{12}) are abundant in grains and legumes, A and C in vegetables and fruits. Vitamins E and K are present in plant oils, E is found in nuts and seeds, and vitamin K in the oils that are found in small but significant amounts in leafy greens. Thus, vegan diets tend to be overflowing with these life-supporting substances. Just two vitamins require particular attention in plant-based diets: B_{12} and (at northern latitudes) D. At times nutritionists have wondered if riboflavin (vitamin B_2) might be a concern for vegans, because milk is a major source of this nutrient for many North Americans. However, many vegan foods are rich in riboflavin (pages 129-30), and now with riboflavin-fortified soy and grain milks, it's easy to meet recommended intakes without dairy.

Now we'll turn our attention to vitamin B_{12}, which was the last vitamin to be identified (in 1949).

VITAL VITAMIN B_{12} *Attention required*

Vitamin B_{12} is a beautifully complex molecule. Its common name, "cobalamin," reflects the presence of the mineral cobalt in a central position, surrounded by amines (nitrogen-containing compounds). In commercial preparations, a molecule of cyanide (carbon and nitrogen) is attached, resulting in "cyanocobalamin." You will see these names on supplements and fortified foods that contain effective forms of vitamin B_{12}.

Vitamin B_{12} helps build our genetic material, DNA, and is particularly important for cells that reproduce rapidly, such as red blood cells that are produced in our bone marrow. Another significant role for B_{12} is maintenance of the protective sheaths that surround nerve fibers. Working together with other B vitamins, B_{12} helps convert carbohydrate, fat, and protein to energy that our bodies can use. Vitamin B_{12} is involved in other aspects of the metabolism of certain fatty acids and amino acids. For example, B_{12} helps get rid of homocysteine, a potentially damaging breakdown product of the amino acid methionine. As mentioned in chapter 2, excess homocysteine can injure the delicate inner lining of artery walls and be a trigger for heart disease.

Deficiency/Effects of Too Little

With insufficient dietary vitamin B_{12} or inadequate absorption, a consequence is abnormally shaped, large blood cells (because they haven't divided properly). This condition is called macrocytic (large cell) anemia. The abnormal blood cells have decreased ability to carry oxygen, resulting in fatigue. Effects on nerve cells, spinal cord, and brain can be serious, resulting in symptoms of confusion, depression, irritability, inability to concentrate, tingling and numbness in fingers, arms, and legs, lack of sensation, and eventual paralysis. In vitamin B_{12} deficiency, homocysteine starts to build up, atherosclerotic plaque can accumulate, and arteries begin to clog with eventual consequences of heart disease and strokes. In infants there is a potential for serious damage to the nervous system. All of this can be easily avoided while still maintaining a vegan diet.

B_{12} Bulletin

The occasional (inaccurate) book or leaflet still suggests that vegans may get enough vitamin B_{12} without supplements or that very occasional use of fortified foods or supplements is sufficient. *Not true!*

A review of the scientific literature shows that a small, but significant, percentage of vegans, young and old, develop vitamin B_{12} deficiencies. If intake is inadequate, damage can be dramatic, sudden, and in a few unfortunate cases, irreversible. It is somewhat surprising that this continues to happen when *the evidence is perfectly clear that vegans require vitamin B_{12} (cobalamin) in the form of a supplement or fortified food.*

Designing a vegan diet without insuring a reliable source of B_{12} is as unrealistic as trying to live on love and ignore all else! That doesn't work when it's time to pay the rent or the mortgage. Landlords and banks require the currency of dollars. Human beings require the vitamins that are essential to the processes of life.

By definition, a vitamin is essential in the diet! Vitamin B_{12} originates not from animal foods but from bacteria. The way that vegans ensure their supply of this essential nutrient is to make sure that two to three times each week they take a reliable source of B_{12} that has originated from bacteria—and that's what supplements and fortified foods provide. It's that simple. Nonvegetarians also need reliable B_{12} sources; the animal foods they eat contain B_{12} of bacterial origin.

Vegans can be certain to get B_{12} by regular use of vitamin B_{12} (cobalamin, cyanocobalamin) fortified foods or supplements. This needs to be more than "occasionally." For example, 2 cups of B_{12}-fortified soymilk per day provide the approximately 3 mcg we require daily. If tablets are taken, it is recommended that they be taken two to three times a week. Just a small amount can be absorbed at a time, so most of a large dose will not be retained. Getting enough B_{12} is essential at any age and is especially important during pregnancy, infancy, and early childhood where young ones have not yet built up their reserves of vitamin B_{12}.

Recommended Intakes

A microgram (mcg or µg) is one-millionth of a gram or one thirty-millionth of an ounce. In pregnancy, a little extra is

The amount of B_{12} to prevent deficiency is tiny:
2.4 micrograms (mcg) per day;
2.6 mcg in pregnancy
2.8 mcg in during lactation.

required—and because of all the cell division that is occurring at this stage of life, it's needed very much! For those older than 50 years of age, it is recommended that most of their B_{12} come from supplements or fortified foods—or, if absorption has diminished, from injection or other method (page 199). Excess B_{12}, higher than recommended levels, are excreted. High intakes have not been linked with health problems.

Vegan Sources, Past and Present

An odd thing about B_{12} is that if we weren't such clean-living critters, we'd have more B_{12} sources because many more bacteria would contribute to our supply. Cobalamin is created by one-celled organisms: bacteria and fungi. These microscopic organisms are all over the place—in earth, wind, rainwater, and oceans. In centuries past, when foods such as sauerkraut or tempeh were fermented, airborne bacteria would drift in and enter the fermentation process, making these foods potential sources of vitamin B_{12}.

When we eat carrots that are well-cleaned (no bits of dirt), bottled or chlorinated water (few bacteria), and foods that have been fermented in the most hygienic conditions (scrupulously clean stainless steel vats, limited types of one-celled organisms, and quick production), we can't count on these foods and beverages to supply us with B_{12}. And even when our carrots do have bits of dirt on them, soils that have been treated with pesticides and herbicides have less B_{12}-producing bacteria than organic soils.

While our B_{12} sources from soil, air, water, and fermented foods have declined, we now have the advantage of B_{12}-fortified foods and supplements of known reliability, making it far easier to be vegan and to be assured of B_{12} intake in this era.

B_{12} SOURCES FOR NONVEGANS

Diets that include meat or dairy also contain vitamin B_{12} that was produced by microorganisms, for example those in soil or in the intestines of animals. When an animal consumes particles of soil or manure along with grass or feed, B_{12}-producing bacteria are consumed and the vitamin ends up in the flesh or milk from animals.

Deficiency Due to Inadequate Absorption

Over 95% of the cases of B_{12} deficiency do not occur in vegans and are not due to inadequate B_{12} intakes. These are associated with impaired absorption of this vitamin for two reasons.

First, 10-30% of people over the age of 50 lose their ability to absorb the protein-bound form of B_{12} that is present in animal foods, due to reduced stomach secretions (gastric acid and an enzyme called pepsin). These people do fine with the forms of B_{12} used by vegans: fortified foods and supplements.

Second, a condition known as pernicious anemia occurs in 2% of the aging population. (The name "pernicious" arose because potential injury to the body from lack of B_{12} is so serious. In fact, long-term absence of any vitamin is serious!) As these people get older, their stomach linings fail to synthesize a B_{12} carrier protein called "Intrinsic Factor." This can happen with vegans as well as with nonvegans. In normal absorption, Intrinsic Factor is secreted into the stomach contents, attaches itself to B_{12} (along with calcium), and carries the vitamin into the lower part of the small intestine where it helps B_{12} be absorbed across the intestinal lining and into the bloodstream. B_{12} is then carried by TCII (transcobalamin II) carrier protein to cells where it is needed. Where there is lack of Intrinsic Factor, fortified foods or regular supplements are not the remedy. Instead, B_{12} is given by injection (for example, once a month) for fast, certain results.

In some cases, elderly people have been described as "confused," yet where lab results supported a diagnosis of B_{12} deficiency, an injection or megadose of vitamin B_{12} has been a quick cure for the confusion. Symptoms such as depression, irritability, mood swings, restlessness, disorientation, memory loss, difficulty in concentrating, dementia, chronic fatigue, apathy, and insomnia might actually be symptoms of B_{12} deficiency. Where lack of the vitamin was not a cause for the problem, giving the vitamin won't be a solution, though.

It has been estimated that by the age of 127, we would all have lost our ability to absorb this vitamin. Though the ability to absorb B_{12} declines with age, for most vegans the main point to address is to make sure they consume reliable sources of B_{12} from supplements or food (see Table 7.2).

Reuse, Recycle

Our bodies recycle and reuse vitamin B_{12} very efficiently, some people more efficiently than others. A little of the B_{12} in our bodies is secreted through bile into the intestine and then 65-75% of it is reabsorbed. The most efficient recyclers, those who absorb B_{12} very well, can go for three, or even as long as twenty years, without obvious dietary sources. On the other hand, some individuals run out of B_{12} fast when their intakes drop.

Lab Data

It's worthwhile for vegans to become B_{12} experts, take an interest in lab results, and thereby avoid deficiency problems that can so easily be avoided. If one were to stop consuming vitamin B_{12} (cobalamin), one would pass through four progressive stages of depletion:

1. Within days after intake stops, serum depletion occurs and the amount of vitamin B_{12} on the carrier protein TCII drops. (This lab test is known as holoTCII or HTCII and is becoming available in more labs.)

2. Next, cells become depleted; red cell B_{12} concentration and holohaptocorrin (an indicator of B_{12} stores) become low. Total serum B_{12} levels above 190 pg/ml (picograms per milliliter) seem to be consistent with good health for vegans; levels below 100 pg/ml require that immediate action be taken and shots or supplements used.

3. At this stage (biochemical deficiency), DNA synthesis is slowed and there is a serum increase in two substances: homocysteine and methylmalonic acid (MMA). These are both unwanted substances that B_{12} helps get rid of.

4. Next is clinical deficiency with macrocytic (large cell) anemia. This is indicated by a complete blood count (CBC) with red blood cell indices and morphology (lab tests that look at the size and shape of blood cells). With a lack of B_{12}, the serious symptoms set in that were described under "Deficiency/Effects of Too Little."

A situation that complicates diagnosis of B_{12} deficiency is that stage 4 can also reflect the lack of another B vitamin, folate. Both of these B vitamins help in the manufacture of new blood cells. If you lack B_{12} but have plenty of folate intake (which tends to be abundant in vegan diets), your lab results won't show stage 4 (macrocytic anemia). For this reason, it's a great idea to have lab tests that show more than one indicator of B_{12} status, likely HTCII and MMA. In a situation of B_{12} deficiency, although folate can help with cell division, folate can't help with the nerve damage that results from a long-term lack of B_{12}.

According to Dr. Ella Haddad of Loma Linda University:

"It is important to emphasize that several indicators must be evaluated to assess status because individuals respond differently to low intakes. Serum vitamin B_{12} concentrations are helpful in diagnosis of vitamin B_{12} deficiency, but serum methylmalonic acid concentration is a sensitive and specific early indicator of deficit."

There's no question that any adult who has been vegan for several years without supplementation should get lab tests done and start using fortified foods or supplements. With children who haven't built up protective stores of B_{12}, and during pregnancy and lactation, there's no point taking chances with this at all.

B_{12} Status of Vegans

Table 7.1 shows the lab results from 90 people in the U.S. who had been vegan for at least 1 year and as much as 28 years. The 78 people in Groups 1a and 1b had used no B_{12}-fortified food and supplements. Those in Group 1a ended up with total serum B_{12} values below the normal range. The lower limit for normal serum B_{12} is considered by some experts to be 200 pg/ml and by others 190 pg/ml; levels nearer 100 are always cause for concern. Those in Group 1b, who may have been a little more efficient at recycling B_{12}, had values within the lower end of the normal range, with 288 pg/ml as the group's average. People in Group 2 had used B_{12}-fortified soymilk and ended up with higher lab values, averaging 389 pg/ml.

Table 7.1 Vitamin B_{12} Status after 1 to 28 Years on a Vegan Diet (Crane, U.S., 1994)

Subjects Studied	Dietary characteristics	Average lab results of Group Serum B12, pg/ml
Group 1a. 25 males, 22 females	Used no B_{12} supplements or fortified foods for 1 year prior to study	123
Group 1b. 16 males, 15 females	Used no B_{12} supplements or fortified foods for 1 year prior to study	288
Group 2 6 males, 6 females	Used B_{12}-fortified soymilk	389
"Normal" range		200–900

This study shows some important features of B_{12} in vegan diets. People have a range of responses to having no dietary intake of B_{12}. Some take longer to become depleted, due to efficient reabsorption of the vitamin. However, slowly but surely over time, serum levels drop without regular intakes. It also shows that some vegans have not recognized the need for dietary intake of this essential nutrient.

A 1999 California study by Haddad and coworkers compared B_{12} status in 25 vegans and 20 nonvegetarians; these were students and workers in the health field aged 20 to 60. The vegans had plenty of access to B_{12}-fortified foods (though they were not necessarily using them) and had avoided animal products for at least 1 and as long as 25 years. Haddad found that *on average*, serum B_{12} did not differ between the two groups. She did, however, find that in 10 of the 25 vegans, there was some evidence of vitamin B_{12} deficit shown by either macrocytosis (large cells), low serum B_{12}, or high MMA. She found that people with higher intakes of B_{12} through supplements had higher serum B_{12}.

A study that was done in Australia (1999) of 11 vegans that used no B_{12} supplements or B_{12}-fortified products showed B_{12} levels averaging 160 pmol/L. Normal reference range for the lab was 171-850 pmol/L (picomoles per liter.)

In earlier decades, few B_{12}-fortified products were available in Australia, New Zealand, Canada, much of Europe, and many parts of the U.S. This created a challenge for pioneers of vegan eating! However, with consumer interest and demand, the situation is changing fast. The range of products fortified with B_{12} and other nutrients is increasing, making it much easier for vegans to create a diet rich in B_{12} using a variety of fortified foods, supplements, or a combination.

> ### *Liquid Gold Dressing*
>
> *Two tablespoons of this dressing provides 3.8 g of omega-3 fatty acids (your day's supply, and then some) along with 40% of your B_{12} for the day (80% if you use the higher amount of yeast powder). This creamy dressing is packed with riboflavin and other B vitamins—plus it's very tasty.*
>
> ½ c flaxseed oil (120 ml)
> ½ c water (120 ml)
> ⅓ c lemon juice (80 ml)
> 2 Tbsp balsamic or raspberry vinegar (30 ml)
> ¼ c Bragg Liquid Aminos or tamari (60 ml)
> ¼ to ½ c Red Star Vegetarian Support Formula Nutritional Yeast powder or flakes (60-120 ml/25-50g)
> 2 tsp Dijon mustard (10 ml)
> 1 tsp ground cumin (5 ml)
>
> Blend until smooth. Dressing can be kept in a jar with a lid, refrigerated for 2 weeks. Makes 2 cups.
>
> *Per 2 tablespoons: calories 78, protein: 1 g, carbohydrate: 2 g, fat 7 g, dietary fiber: 0.4 g, sodium: 180 mg*

Food Sources and Fortification

To be sure of getting B_{12}, become a label reader if you're not one already! Get products that say "fortified" or "enriched" and then read nutrition panels to see specifically that they are fortified with B_{12}. In the U.S., the nutrient panel will show a percentage of the DV, also known as the U.S. RDA. (See page 117.) Current recommendations for B_{12} are about half the levels set when the U.S. RDA were developed. The DV for vitamin B_{12} is 6 mcg, so a food containing 50% of the DV contains 3 micrograms and will meet your B_{12} requirement for the day. Manufacturers change fortification levels from time to time, so once in a while check packaging on your food sources. Though all brands of nutritional yeast are high in other B vitamins, not all are fortified with B_{12}. The Red Star Vegetarian Support Formula brand, specified in Table 7.2, comes in large flakes, miniflakes, and powder (which is the same yeast, but more compact), and is fortified with B_{12}. This somewhat cheesy-tasting yeast is used in the Liquid Gold Dressing recipe above. In Table 7.2, you can see typical vitamin B_{12} levels in a variety of foods. **The B_{12} present in supplements and fortified foods can be relied on and is well absorbed.**

Unreliable Dietary Sources of B_{12}

Foods that have been reported to be B_{12} sources in health food pamphlets or popular literature include algae, spirulina, alfalfa, comfrey, amaranth, various

Table 7.2 Food Sources of Vitamin B_{12}

	Vitamin B_{12}, mcg per serving
Fortified Meat Substitutes★	
Yves Veggie Cuisine Slices, 1 serving (4 slices)	1.2-1.5
Yves Veggie Ground Round, 1 serving (⅓ cup/55 g) or Burger Burger, 1	1.4 g
Yves Veggie Wieners, Chili Dogs, or Jumbo Dog, 1	0.7-1.5
Red Star Vegetarian Support Formula Nutritional Yeast (T6635+)	
Nutritional yeast powder, 2 Tbsp (16 g) 8 mcg	8
Nutritional yeast, large flake, 2 Tbsp (8 g) 4 mcg	8
Fortified Soy and Grain Milks★	
Edensoy Extra, Silk, and Soy Dream, 1 c/240 ml	3
Rice Dream, 1 c/240 ml	1.5
So Nice and Vitasoy Enriched, 1 c/240 ml	0.9
Fortified Breakfast Cereals★	
Fortified Raisin Bran or Kelloggs Cornflakes, ¾ c/180 ml	1.5
Product 19, ¾ c/180 ml	6
Fortified Grapenuts, ¼ c/60 ml	1.5
Nutrigrain, ⅔ c, 160 ml	1.5
Total, 1 c/240 ml	6.2
For Comparison	
1 large egg	0.5
1 cup cow's milk	0.9

★Some products may be fortified in one country but not in another, or levels may differ.

greens (spinach, turnip greens), mushrooms, seaweeds (arame, wasake, kombu, nori), nuts and legumes, and fermented soyfoods (tamari, miso, tempeh). **Don't rely on these as B_{12} sources.** Here are some of the reasons we say this:

• One company that produces an excellent quality tempeh said that different lab tests for B_{12} done on their product showed a range from 0 to 4 mcg at different times, thus the tempeh could not be relied on as a B_{12} source. It is likely, however, that the fermentation does add some B_{12} at times.

• Some "B_{12}" reported in the foods listed above (e.g. algae and spirulina) has been shown to be analog forms. These are somewhat similar to cobalamin but are not useable to meet human requirements, unlike the real vitamin. These analog forms will not prevent B_{12} deficiency in humans. In fact, analog forms may even interfere with the action of real B_{12}.

• Plant foods can have bacteria and B_{12} *on* but not *in* them, for example as bits of dirt on the surface.

• The B_{12} content of sea vegetables, if any is present at all, seems to vary quite a bit, probably depending on growing conditions. Some raw seaweeds have been shown to have active B_{12}, along with analogs; dried seaweeds have been shown to have mostly analog forms.

For these reasons, it's better not to rely on these foods as a B_{12} source for you and your family.

THE ENERGETIC BS

In addition to B_{12}, there are six more B vitamins. These work as a team to convert carbohydrate, fat, and protein to useable energy, a process known as energy metabolism. These B vitamins (other than B_{12}) also tend to be present in the same foods: whole grains, legumes, green vegetables, nuts and seeds, and nutritional yeast. Whole grains are rich in these B vitamins and in minerals and fiber. When grains are refined, most of the B vitamins, minerals, and fiber are removed along with the bran and germ. When a grain or flour is "enriched," some of the B vitamins (thiamin, niacin, and in some cases folate and riboflavin) are added back along with iron. The other nutrients are not replaced. When the water used to cook vegetables and other foods is discarded, some of the water-soluble vitamins and minerals that were present in the food are poured away as well.

Following is a brief summary of functions, recommended intakes, food sources, and other characteristics of the B vitamins. Generally, excess B vitamins do not cause problems. If you are interested in more data on food sources of different nutrients, use the database at:

www.nal.usda.gov/fnic/cgi-bin/nut_search.pl

Thiamin (Vitamin B₁)   *Usually plentiful*

Function: Helps with conversion of carbohydrates to energy, amino acid metabolism, and nervous system function.

RDA:* 1.1 mg for women and 1.2 mg for men

Sources: Whole and enriched grains and whole grain products, legumes, nuts, nutritional yeast.

Special Issues: Vegans get plenty of thiamin; studies show higher than recommended intakes and good thiamin status.

Riboflavin (Vitamin B₂)   *Planning may be needed*

Function: Supports energy metabolism, health of skin, and normal vision.

**For definitions of the RDA, UL, and AI, see page 117.*

RDA: 1.1 mg for women and 1.3 mg for men

Sources: 1½ tsp. of nutritional yeast provides the RDA for riboflavin for the day. Many soymilks and cereals are fortified with riboflavin, so a bowl of cereal with soymilk can provide 33%-150% of the RDA. Other sources are leafy green vegetables, sea vegetables, asparagus, mushrooms, sweet potatoes, legumes, peas, almonds, peanuts, bananas, whole grains, breads, cereals, and other grain products. Enriched flour and cereals contain riboflavin, although enriched white rice does not. (Riboflavin was omitted to avoid the slight yellow tint it would give.)

Special Issues: Vegan intakes are generally adequate and equal to or slightly below intakes of nonvegans. Riboflavin can be destroyed by the ultraviolet rays of the sun or by fluorescent light, so it's a good idea to store riboflavin-rich foods, such as nutritional yeast, in a dark glass or opaque container or in a cupboard. In transparent glass, riboflavin will be destroyed. After taking a vitamin supplement, if your urine is yellow, you're seeing excess riboflavin.

Niacin   *Usually plentiful*

Function: Supports energy metabolism, health of skin, nervous system, and digestive system.

RDA: 14 mg for women and 16 mg for men; *UL (Upper Limit)* for niacin from fortified foods and/or supplements is 35 mg.

Sources: Whole and enriched grains and whole grain products, legumes, nuts, nutritional yeast. The synthetic niacin used in enriched grain products is well absorbed. Protein-containing foods provide niacin, since the vitamin can be made from the amino acid tryptophan which is present in all plant protein. Though corn is low in tryptophan and low in available niacin, the traditional Latin American practice of soaking corn in lime-treated water for making corn tortillas releases niacin, making it available for absorption. (This lime treatment also adds calcium to the tortillas.)

Special Issues: Studies of vegans show niacin intakes to be adequate.

Pantothenic acid (Vitamin B₅)   *Usually plentiful*

Function: Helps release of energy from carbohydrates and fat.

AI (Adequate Intake): 5 mg

Sources: All plant foods. Intestinal bacteria may synthesize this vitamin and further contribute to our intake.

Special Issues: Vegan intakes seem to be adequate, not surprisingly, considering wide distribution in plant foods.

Pyridoxine (Vitamin B$_6$)   *Usually plentiful*

Function: Helps with amino acid metabolism, fatty acid metabolism, and the building of hemoglobin protein for red blood cells.

AI (Adequate Intake): For women and men up to 50 years of age; 1.3 mg; women over 50, 1.5 mg; men over 50, 1.7 mg; *UL (Upper Limit)* 100 mg

Sources: Nutritional yeast, brewer's yeast, whole grains and whole grain products, legumes, soyfoods, soymilk, seeds, peas, potatoes, squash, green leafy vegetables, asparagus, avocado, okra, nori (seaweed), plantains, banana, figs, raisins, watermelon, elderberries, and tomato, orange, and prune juices

Special Issues: Need for this vitamin is linked with protein intake, thus requirement of vegans for this vitamin may be a little lower than for a general population with excessive protein intakes. In the limited studies that have been done, vegan intakes appear to be adequate.

Folate   *Usually plentiful—Planning may be needed early in pregnancy*

Function: Helps build new cells and the genetic material DNA (together with vitamin B$_{12}$). Helps in the metabolism of amino acids. Adequate intakes early in pregnancy help prevent neural tube defects.

RDA: 400 mcg (women and men); *UL (Upper Limit)* for folate from fortified foods and/or supplements is 1,000 mcg.

Sources: Leafy green vegetables, asparagus, avocado, broccoli, Brussels sprouts, cauliflower, corn, beets, parsnips, squash, sweet potatoes, tomato and orange juices, oranges, grapefruit, bananas, cantaloupe, strawberries, legumes, peanuts, sunflower seeds, sesame tahini, nutritional yeast, whole and folate-enriched grains and grain products.

Special Issues: Adult vegans and lacto-ovo vegetarians consume about 20% to 50% more folate than nonvegetarians. Being adequately nourished with iron and vitamin C helps in the proper absorption of folate.

Biotin   *Usually plentiful*

Function: Has coenzyme action (works with an enzyme to promote that enzyme's activity).

AI (Adequate Intake): 30 mcg

Sources: Grains, vegetables, soybeans and other legumes, nuts, seeds, brewer's yeast. Intestinal bacteria can synthesize this vitamin and further contribute to our intake.

Special Issues: Does not appear to be a concern for vegans. One study showed higher intakes in vegans than in lacto-ovo vegetarians and nonvegetarians.

VITAMIN D FOR DULL DAYS

Is vitamin D really a vitamin—or is it a hormone? In truth it can be either, depending on the circumstances. A hormone is a substance that we are capable of manufacturing in our own bodies and that subsequently makes its way to another part of the body to exert its effect. Since we make vitamin D in the skin (with the help of a little sunlight) and it travels to our kidneys, intestines, and bones to take effect, clearly it is a hormone. However, if you live in northern regions with little sunlight, are confined indoors as an invalid, or work in a submarine, the situation is different. For you, vitamin D is "a carbon-containing substance that is essential to life, is not burned for energy, and must be supplied in the diet." In these conditions, clearly it is a vitamin.

Vitamin D...Solution to the Mystery of Rickets

Vitamin D, or closely related compounds that can be converted to vitamin D, are present in significant amounts in few plant or animal foods. Over history, most humans have relied on sunlight as a major source of this vitamin. However, in northern climates people have tended to stay indoors during cold months, and there was less ultraviolet light during winter. One consequence of this was a childhood disease known as rickets in which bones did not become properly mineralized and legs bowed under the weight of the growing body. As early as the 1700s, it was recognized that rickets could be helped by cod liver oil, and people in Scandinavian and Baltic countries were aware of the therapeutic value of this oil. A hundred years later, a Polish physician realized that sunlight was helpful in preventing this condition; over the centuries, folk wisdom reflected an awareness that sunlight contributed to health in some way.

Nonetheless, the disease became so widespread that it was present in as many as 80% of children in northern urban areas such as London. With the advent of industrialization, closely packed buildings and coal smoke from factories blocked sunlight. Many children worked indoors from a very young age. German physicians noted that infants born in the fall were particularly vulnerable to the disease. (Animals tend to avoid rickets naturally, as they bear their young in the spring.) In the early 1900s, though the effectiveness of sunlight in preventing and curing rickets was recognized by some people, little practical help was available to get many of the urban children into sunlight. The effectiveness of cod liver oil in preventing and curing rickets was eventually demonstrated in a controlled study by Hess in 1917 with African American children in New York, among whom

> "In actual fact, rickets was the first air-pollution disease."
> W.F Loomis, writing of pollution and sunless alleys after the introduction of soft coal in Europe in 1650.

rickets was severe and almost universal. It was only after 1920 that the actual compound that could cure rickets, vitamin D, was identified and its dual origins understood.

Vitamin D: Its Names and Plant and Animal Origins

Two forms of dietary vitamin D are effective: D_2 (plant origin) and D_3 (animal origin). Both forms are made in nature from "previtamin" compounds, and both are available in fortified foods and supplements. A few plants contain previtamin D_2 that can be converted to vitamin D_2 by exposure to sunlight or other forms of

Table 7.3 Names of Plant and Animal Forms of Vitamin D

Plant-origin forms	
Previtamin D_2	ergosterol
Vitamin D_2	ergocalciferol

Animal (including human) forms	
Substance in skin that is transformed	7-dehydrocholesterol
Previtamin D_3	precalciferol
Vitamin D_3	cholecalciferol

ultraviolet light in a process known as irradiation. Previtamin D_2 is present in a few mushrooms, certain seaweeds, and yeast. Ergocalciferol, commonly referred to as vitamin D_2, is commercially produced from yeasts by irradiation. The various names for the forms of vitamin D will be of interest to vegans who wish to check whether the form used in a particular vitamin supplement or to fortify a product comes from a plant or animal source (Table 7.3).

When a fortified food or supplement label says "vitamin D_3" or "cholecalciferol," that means the origin was animal (generally fish, but sometimes from sheep wool, hides, or other animal parts such as cattle brains). Often milk or margarine, which may be thought of as vegetarian products, will contain vitamin D_3 of animal origin. We have even found supplements that are labeled "vegetarian," yet contain vitamin D_3; upon further inquiry, the suppliers were surprised to realize that the vitamin D used was of animal origin. Occasionally a soymilk can be found that uses D_3 instead of D_2, though most have chosen the D_2 (plant) form and clearly list D_2 on the nutrition panel.

How We Make Vitamin D

When our skin is exposed to sunlight (ultraviolet radiation), a compound derived from cholesterol that is present in oil glands throughout the skin is transformed to previtamin D_3. In further processes, this is converted to the active form of vitamin D that can perform many functions in the body.

Functions / What it Does

Vitamin D is a major player in a team of nutrients and hormones that keep blood calcium at optimal levels and support bone health during growth and

throughout life. It stimulates the absorption of the bone-building minerals calcium and phosphorus from the intestine and helps regulate the amount of
calcium in bone. It is important for proper functioning of cells throughout the
body (in muscle, nerves, and glands) that depend on calcium. If more blood calcium is needed, vitamin D is able to act in three places:

1) to reduce urinary calcium losses via the kidneys;

2) to absorb calcium from food more efficiently in the digestive tract;

3) to draw calcium from our bones, which serve as a storehouse of calcium.

In addition, vitamin D has roles in the immune system, skin, pancreas, and
perhaps in helping to prevent colorectal cancer.

As far as the body's eventual utilization is concerned, there is no practical
difference whether vitamin D is acquired from the action of ultraviolet light
on exposed skin or through the diet. Both D_2 and D_3 are effective as vitamins,
though it may take more dietary vitamin D_2 than D_3 to raise serum vitamin D
concentrations.

Deficiency/Effects of Too Little

Without vitamin D, absorption of dietary calcium is severely limited and bone
mineralization fails to take place adequately. As young children become heav-
ier and begin to stand and walk, the weights of their bodies bend bones, such
as those in the legs; these and other parts of the skeleton become misshapen in
a childhood condition known as rickets. Recall from the section on calcium
(page 90) that bone is composed of a somewhat flexible protein matrix which
becomes harder and more rigid with mineralization. Though rickets has been
eradicated as a widespread problem, the occasional case still turns up in
Toronto, Winnipeg, Vancouver, and Seattle. Cases have also been reported in
England, the Netherlands, and Norway. Generally these occur where there is a
problem of fat malabsorption (since this is a fat-soluble vitamin); however,
some cases are due to inadequate vitamin D from sun, diet, or supplement.

The adult form of rickets is known as osteomalacia, meaning "soft bones."
As one example, despite the sunny climate, women in the Middle East who are
entirely covered by clothing may become deficient in vitamin D. Their situation is made worse with calcium losses due to repeated pregnancies and
lactation; as a consequence, bones fail to be properly mineralized. Inadequate
vitamin D is a contributing factor to another, more common condition of the
bones: osteoporosis. In the latter, bones are brittle and porous (rather than soft)
and have lost a great deal of the calcium and other mineral content they once
had. (For more on osteoporosis, see pages 34–37 and page 98.)

Excess

Toxic effects of excess vitamin D have been observed with long-term intakes five times recommended doses and are a particular concern with growing children. (Parents and caregivers: don't leave vitamin/mineral supplements around!) The effects are overabsorption of calcium, leading to calcium deposits in the kidneys and other parts of the body and a variety of unpleasant symptoms. For this reason, limits have been set on the extent to which vitamin D fortification is permitted. You won't get vitamin D toxicity from too much sun, though excess sun exposure can lead to sunburn and skin cancer.

Getting Your Vitamin D from Sunlight

Going for a walk during your lunch break is a great way to get your vitamin D for the day! A number of factors affect our production of this essential substance. Here are the D-tails.

SKIN COLOR

For people with light skin, it takes about 10-15 minutes of sunlight a day on the face and forearms (or an equivalent surface area of skin) to build up previtamin D that can then be converted to vitamin D. Sun exposure (ultraviolet/UV radiation) beyond about 20 minutes does not seem to provide further benefit. People with dark skin require more exposure to sunlight (3–6 times longer) to get the same degree of vitamin D production, the darkest skin requiring the longest exposure in the sunlight.

The melanin pigment in dark skin absorbs some of the UV radiation and is a protective feature in the typically darker skin of people in sunny climates. It seems that over our evolution, as people moved from sunnier climates to northern latitudes, skin pigmentation decreased, allowing for adequate production of vitamin D in areas with less UV light.

AGE AND BODY FAT

Aging lowers the capacity for vitamin D production to about half that of young people. This may be particularly true for seniors who are very thin. Here's a situation where those with a little fat on their bones (or at least under their skin) have the advantage. These people seem to have more reserves of fat-soluble vitamin D to get them through gray winters.

USE OF SUNSCREEN

Sunscreen protection factors (SPF) of 8 and above can prevent vitamin D synthesis. People don't usually put on sunscreen nearly as lavishly as labels recommend; in fact surveys have shown that quantities applied are only about one-quarter of those used to measure the sun protection effectiveness. If this is the case, some vitamin D synthesis may occur using sunscreens above SPF 8.

> Our need for vitamin D must be balanced with the obvious need for protection from overexposure to the sun, especially during the hot hours of the day.

TIME OF DAY

For vitamin D synthesis, the amount of UV light in midmorning sun and through the afternoon is fine.

SUNLAMPS

The ultraviolet light from sunlamps can be used for vitamin D production. Limit to 20 minutes or use as recommended.

TYPE OF CLOTHING WORN

Vitamin D production varies with the amount of clothing one is wearing, which affects the surface area of skin exposed. Recommended times are based on exposure of face and forearms. If you bare a lot more, time can be reduced considerably.

TIME OF YEAR AND GEOGRAPHICAL LOCATION

Production of vitamin D varies with season and latitude, as these factors affect the amount of UV radiation. A summer day may bring us 16 times the UV rays of a winter day, and even cloudy summer days will stimulate some vitamin D production.

VITAMIN D WINTER IN NORTHERN LATITUDES

During summer, we store vitamin D for the months ahead; during winter, vitamin D production and serum vitamin D levels drop in adults. The time period during which this occurs is known as "vitamin D winter." Infants and children haven't built up reserves of this vitamin, and in northern regions their limited vitamin D reserves run out, so they need a fortified food or supplement. In Los Angeles (latitude 34° N), there is no vitamin D winter; however, in Boston (42° N), production drops off during December and January. In Edmonton (52° N), the period of little UV light extends from November to February. In Bergen, Norway (61°N), vitamin D winter extends for a full 5 months of the year, from October to March. Northern regions have historically relied on fish for much of their sources of vitamin D. People have also come up with creative solutions, such as wind-protected shelters in the Netherlands, that make it more comfortable to get sun exposure in colder months. In Russia, school children are exposed to ultraviolet light at day care centers and schools.

Recommended Intakes for Vitamin D from Food or Supplements

Recommendations are stated in micrograms, written as mcg or as µg, and are in the range of 5 to 15 mcg. You may also see intakes stated in International Units (IU), with recommendations in the range of 200 to 400 IU or more (1µg = 40 IU). The latest set of recommendations from the Institute of Medicine advises that intakes by the elderly be triple those of young people.

Toronto researchers Vieth and Trang suggest that vitamin D_2 may be about 60% as effective as vitamin D_3 in raising serum vitamin D levels. If this is the case, then it may make sense for vegans relying on vitamin D_2 from food or supplements to increase their intakes accordingly. (Multiply Adequate Intakes by 1.7.)

Adequate Intakes and Tolerable Upper Intake for Vitamin D		
Age	Adequate Intake, mcg	Tolerable Upper Intake Levels, mcg
0 to 1 year	5	25
1 to 50 years	5	50
Over 50 years	10	50
Over 75 years	15	50

Evidence has accumulated documenting vitamin D deficiency in elderly populations in the U.S. and Europe. According to researcher Michael Holick,

"Vitamin D is absolutely essential for the maintenance of a healthy skeleton throughout our lives. There is mounting evidence that vitamin D insufficiency and vitamin D deficiency in elderly people is a silent epidemic that results in bone loss and fractures. It is casual exposure to sunlight that provides most humans with their vitamin D requirement. Seasonal changes, time of day, latitude, aging, sunscreen use, and melanin pigmentation can substantially influence the cutaneous production of vitamin D. Although the recommended dietary allowance for vitamin D in adults is 5 micrograms (200 IU), there is mounting evidence that in the absence of exposure to sunlight the vitamin D requirement is at least 15 micrograms (600 IU) per day."

Lab Data

Vitamin D status is assessed by measuring serum vitamin D. Concentrations between 25 and 40 nmol/l (nano-moles per liter) reflect marginal vitamin D deficiency. At latitudes north of the continental U.S., 40 nmol/l is a typical winter *average* in adults.

Vitamin D Status in Various Populations

Surveys in recent decades have shown that in the general U.S. population, between 0.1 and 0.2% of the children showed signs of rickets. Often, these cases have resulted from combinations of contributing factors: for example, dark-skinned children whose exposure to sunlight was inadequate, were also lactose intolerant, and did not use fortified foods or supplements. In some macrobiotic families there has been a reluctance to use fortified foods or supplements, leading to cases of childhood rickets in Europe, the U.S., and Canada. Fortunately, some of the macrobiotic literature that led to these unfortunate situations has been recalled and revised.

Unlike "the naked ape," modern humans generally cover all but about 5% of their skin surface and seldom spend time in unshielded sunlight. Children tend to play in the house, go to school, or watch TV. Adults have indoor occupations, and rather than sunbathing, many take care to avoid sunlight, particularly after hearing skin cancer warnings. Even when they do go out, a protective layer of sunscreen may be worn. For these reasons, foods that are fortified with vitamin D are more important now than they were for predominantly agricultural populations, who were often outdoors.

Results from three studies (in Great Britain, Finland, and New Zealand) are summarized in Table 7.4. Note that vitamin D *intake* is not the whole story; this shows the vitamin D from food but is not a measure of skin production and so cannot be taken as an overall measure of adequacy.

Table 7.4 Average Vitamin D Intakes of Vegans and Nonvegans, mcg per Day,

Country, year	Vegan Intake, mcg (number and gender)	Vegetarian Intake, mcg (number and gender)	Nonvegetarian Intake, mcg (number and gender)
Great Britain, 1993	1.6 (20 females)	2.2 (36 females)	3.3 (377 females)
	1.9 (18 males)	3.0 (16 males)	4.2 (386 males)
Finland, 1993	0.3 (10 females + males)	2.2 (14 females + males)	4.5 (12 females + males)
New Zealand, 1994	1.9 (5 females)	2.2 (50 females + males)	3.4 (50 females + males)

Fortification

Vitamin D fortification of cow's milk was initiated in the 1930s in the U.S., a practice also adopted later in Canada. Milk was chosen because it was a calcium-rich food that could be used as a vehicle to get vitamin D into children. Fortunately the same levels of fortification are now available in soymilk in the U.S., Canada (since 1997), and many other parts of the world. With time, governments in some countries have recognized that it doesn't make sense to permit fortification of cow's milk but to refuse fortification of alternatives such as soy and grain milks. This would present an unfair hardship for vegans, children and adults with milk allergy or lactose intolerance, and for those who do not use dairy products for cultural and other reasons. In the U.S., U.K., and Canada, some soymilks, grain milks, and margarine are fortified with vitamin D; in the U.S. and U.K., cereals are fortified as well.

Vitamin D_2 from Food

It makes sense for vegans in northern latitudes to buy products that are fortified with vitamin D, or to use supplements, or a little of both. On U.S. food labels, the nutrient panel will show a percentage of the DV. The DV for vitamin D is 10 mcg (equivalent to 400 IU). So a cup of soymilk, containing 25% of the DV, provides 2.5 micrograms. Manufacturers change fortification levels from time to time, so check packaging.

A challenge that lies ahead for vegans is to contact companies (as potential consumers) and encourage them to use vitamin D_2 rather than D_3 in supplements and food products such as as margarine, which would otherwise be vegetarian. Vegan supplements with D_2 are available from Freeda Vitamins (N.Y.) at 1-800-777-3737. Other U.S. brands to check are Rainbow Light Just Once (Iron-Free), Country Life Support (N.Y.), and Nutribiotic 100% Vegetarian (Cal.). In the U.K., vegan-friendly supplements are listed at www.vegansociety.com/info/info41.html

Table 7.5 Food Sources of Vitamin D

Food	Vitamin D, per serving
Soy and grain milks	
Edensoy Extra, 1 c/240 ml	1
Enriched Rice Dream, 1 c/240 ml	2.5
Fortified Silk, 1 c/240 ml	2.5
Fortified So Nice ★, 1 c/240 ml	2.5
Enriched Soy Dream, 1 c/240 ml	2.5
Westsoy Plus, 1 c/240 ml	2.5
Vitasoy Enriched, 1 c/240 ml	2
Breakfast cereals	
Fortified branflakes, 1 c/240 ml	1.8
Fortified cornflakes, 1 c/240 ml	1.8
Fortified Grapenuts, ¼ c/60 ml	1.8
Margarine	
Fortified margarine★★	0.5
For comparison	
Fortified cow's milk★★	2.5

★*Canada and U.K.*

★★*Vitamin D_3, of animal origin, is often used in margarine and sometimes used in soymilks, cow's milk, and cereals.*

THE ANTIOXIDANT ARMY AND OTHER VITAMINS: A, C, E, K

Free Radicals and the Antioxidant Army

Oxygen supports our most basic life processes, yet this same substance can take the form of highly reactive, unstable oxygen molecules (free radicals). These molecules create yet more free radicals and chain reactions of damaged and damaging molecules, with some of our most serious health problems as the end results. Free radicals react with cell membranes, DNA, proteins, and cholesterol. As an example of their effects, oxidized LDL cholesterol leads to the formation of arterial plaque, a step towards heart disease, whereas unoxidized cholesterol does not cause this harm. Smoking and pollution increase free radical formation.

Diet can make tremendous contributions in defending cells and molecules from "oxidative stress." Whole grains and many other plant foods contribute zinc, selenium, niacin, and riboflavin which are essential for the protective action of enzymes. Proteins play important roles. Particularly effective are the antioxidants, including vitamins C, E, and selenium; beta-carotene (that we make into vitamin A) has antioxidant activity as well. In fact, plant foods contain hundreds of known antioxidants—and current knowledge is expanding fast. (See Chapter 8.) The antioxidants are a formidable team and are team players. For example, vitamin C promotes the activity of vitamin E, and vitamin E protects beta-carotene from oxidation. There is a lively field of research investigating the roles of antioxidants in reducing risk of cancer, cardiovascular disease, cataracts, macular degeneration, diseases of the nervous system (such as Alzheimer's and Parkinson's), and premature aging of skin due to ultraviolet light. Getting your antioxidants from foods, where a multitude of helpful substances are present, appears to be even more effective than using supplements.

Food Sources of Antioxidants

One important reason that vegetarians have less risk of some chronic diseases appears to be the considerably higher intakes of antioxidants in plant-based diets. Fruits and vegetables are the richest sources of vitamin C and beta-carotene and many other protective substances. Intakes from these food groups at the high end of the ranges in the Vegan Food Guide (pages 154-55) can be very effective in reducing oxidative damage. Virgin or extra-virgin olive oil contributes antioxidants to the Mediterranean diet and to many health-conscious eating patterns. The advantage of olive oil is that it is mechanically pressed rather than refined, thus the vast majority of vitamin E present in the olives is retained in the oil. Other unrefined plant oils are rich in natural vitamin E too, whereas the refined oils that line our supermarket shelves have much lower levels of vitamin E. Not surprisingly, intakes of fat-soluble vitamins may be less than optimal in low-fat diets.

The following section gives information on the vitamins not covered in the previous section. Though vitamins are essential to life, we can also get too much of a good thing in the concentrated doses available through supplements, so the RDAs and ULs (Tolerable Upper Intake Levels) are included. (See page 117 for more information.) Also included is vitamin K, which is not an antioxidant but is the last of the fat-soluble vitamins after A, D, and E.

Vitamin A (and Beta-Carotene)   *Usually plentiful*

Function: Important for eye health, growth of bones and teeth, and immune system support.

RDA: For women, 800 mcg; men, 1,000 mcg (These may also be expressed in RE/Retinol Equivalents.)

UL: Vitamin A (of animal origin), taken in supplements at many times recommended intake, can be toxic. High intakes of beta-carotene (from plant foods) will temporarily tint the skin an orange color without further effects.

Sources: Deep orange vegetables (carrots, peppers, pumpkin, squash, sweet potatoes, turnips, tomatoes and tomato products, yams), broccoli, green leafy vegetables, nori (seaweed), deep orange fruits (apricots, cantaloupe, mango, nectarine, papaya), persimmon, plantain, prunes.

Special issues: Beta-carotene and other carotenoids provide much of the beautiful orange, red, and yellow color in vegetables and fruits. These are present in green vegetables too, though the color is overlaid by the green of magnesium-rich chlorophyll.

Vitamin C (Ascorbic Acid)   *Usually plentiful*

Function: Helps absorb iron, resist infection, builds blood vessels and bone.

RDA: For women, 75 mg; men, 90 mg; Smokers add 35 mg.

UL: From both food and supplements is 2,000 mg.

Sources: Citrus fruit, potatoes, peppers, strawberries, cantaloupe, broccoli, vegetables in the cabbage family, leafy greens, tomatoes, papaya, mangos. (See also page 148.)

Special issues: Intakes of vegetarians tend to be about 150 mg per day (about 50% higher than intakes of nonvegetarians), and vegan intakes are higher still, with studies showing average intakes from 138 up to 584 mg/day.

Vitamin E (d-Alpha Tocopherol)   *Planning may be needed*

Function: Prevents oxidation of vitamin A and fatty acids, and stabilizes cell membranes.

RDA: For adults: 15 mg equivalent to 22 IU (International Units) of d-alpha-tocopherol, natural-source vitamin E (best choice) *or* 33 IU of the synthetic form "dl-alpha-tocopherol."

UL: 1,000 mg of alpha-tocopherol from supplements. People who consume more than the UL place themselves at greater risk of hemorrhagic damage because the excess vitamin E can increase risk of bleeding. On supplement labels, intakes may be listed in either IU or mg, the UL of 1,000 mg is equivalent to 1,500 IU of "d-alpha-tocopherol," or 1,100 IU of "dl-alpha-tocopherol."

Sources: Nuts, seeds, whole grains, wheat germ, leafy green vegetables, hijiki seaweed, and unrefined vegetable oils, especially olive and sunflower oils. Vitamin E protects the oils in plants from oxidation and is present in all plant foods in proportion to plant oils present.

Special issues: On average, the general public consumes only about 50% of the RDA for vitamin E, vegetarians about 50-100%. If you are using a vitamin

E supplement, take it with a meal that includes some fat (for example, salad dressing), because the oil supports the vitamin's absorption and transport to the cells where it is needed. Better still, use an unrefined, vitamin E-rich oil to make the salad dressing! (See Liquid Gold Dressing, page 127.)

Vitamin K   *Usually plentiful*

Function: Helps with blood clotting and regulation of calcium in blood.

RDA: For women 19-24, 60 mcg; age 25 and over, 65 mcg; For men 19-24, 70 mcg; age 25 and over, 80 mcg

Sources: Leafy green vegetables, broccoli, cabbage, asparagus, pumpkin, lentils, peas, soybean oil, nori, hijiki, and other seaweeds. A half-cup kale provides 179 mcg vitamin K;. 1 Tbsp. soybean oil provides 77 mcg. Vitamin K is also synthesized by bacteria in the colon.

Special issues: Average intake of the U.S. population has been estimated at 300-500 mcg; vegetarian intakes could be expected to be higher still. Vegan intakes appear to be abundant.

SELECTED REFERENCES

For a complete list see www.nutrispeak.com/veganrefs.htm. See also general references for the whole book on page 276.

Antioxidant DRIs (Daily Recommended Intakes) at www.nationalacademies.org. *(Do a search.)*

Crane, M. et al. "Vitamin B$_{12}$ studies in total vegetarians (vegans)." *J. Nutr. Med.* 4 (1994): 419-430.

Heaney, R. "Lessons for nutritional science from vitamin D." *Am. J. Clin. Nutr.* 69 (1999): 825-826.

Herbert, V. "Staging vitamin B-12 (cobalamin) status in vegetarians." *Am. J. Clin. Nutr.* 59:1213S-1222S.

McKenna, M.J. "Differences in vitamin D status between countries in young adults and the elderly." *Am. J. Med.* 93 (1992): 69-77.

Tucker, K. et al. "Plasma vitamin B-12 concentrations relate to intake source in the Framingham Offspring Study." *Am. J. Clin. Nutr.* 71 (2000): 514-522.

Vieth, R. "Vitamin D supplementation, 25-hydroxyvitamin D concentrations, and safety." *Am. J. Clin. Nutr.* 69 (1999): 842–56.

CHAPTER
8

Phytochemicals...
Powerful protection
from plants

I t is beginning to sound like a plot, an animal conspiracy to insure the untimely demise of carnivores and longer lives of vegetarians. They seek their revenge brilliantly. Just think about it. The more animal foods people eat, the greater their risk of dying of chronic diseases such as heart disease, cancer, and diabetes. When people switch to a diet of plants, their risk for such diseases miraculously diminishes. Animal foods are high in saturated fat and cholesterol, both important contributors to disease. Plant foods are low in saturated fats and completely free of cholesterol. Plant foods are rich in fiber which lowers blood cholesterol levels, improves blood sugar control, and reduces risk of gastro-intestinal disorders; animal foods are completely fiber-free. The protein in plant foods protects against heart disease and kidney disease; animal protein increases risk for these diseases. Plant foods are rich in antioxidant nutrients like vitamin C, vitamin E, and beta-carotene, which protect us from free-radical damage; animal foods contain few of these protective nutrients. Just when you'd imagine they'd be doing their victory dance, a whole new arsenal of secret weapons is summoned—phytochemicals. Needless to say, these little powerhouses are completely absent in animal foods.

While phytochemicals are not currently considered essential nutrients, volumes of research studies are accumulating to support their strong and consistent beneficial effects on health. In this chapter we will give you a glimpse of the real phytochemical champions and the feats they are capable of.

PHYTOCHEMICAL BASICS

Phytochemicals (phyto is Greek for "plant") are naturally occurring chemicals that give flavor, color, texture, and odor to plants. They also help to regulate plant growth and defend against attacks by insects or fungi.

Vegetables and fruits are considered our primary sources of phytochemicals. However, many legumes, whole grains, nuts, seeds, herbs, and spices provide impressive contributions to our intakes. There are literally thousands of different phytochemicals found scattered throughout the plant kingdom. Many plants contain over a hundred types of phytochemicals. The largest category of phytochemicals is *phenolic compounds*, a group of over 4,000 different chemicals. Within this category are several subgroups, the three most important being: *flavonoids* (flavonols, flavones, flavanols, and isoflavones) concentrated mainly in vegetables, fruits, green tea, and soybeans; *phenolic acids* (ferulic acid, caffeic acid, coumaric acid, ellagic acid, and gallic acid) found mainly in whole grains, berries, cherries, grapes, citrus, and other fruits; and *tannins* (catechin) found in lentils and other legumes, tea (black and green), grapes, and wine. Phenolic compounds have been found to have powerful antioxidant, anticancer, and anticardiovascular disease (CVD) effects.

Another large powerful group of phytochemicals is *terpenes*. They include *carotenoids* (lycopene, beta-carotene, and lutein) found in carrots, tomatoes, leafy greens, and other vegetables and fruits, and *limonoids* (limonin, nomilin, d-limonine) found in citrus fruits. These phytochemicals have been shown to have antioxidant, anticancer, and anti-CVD activity and to reduce the effects of aging and macular degeneration of the eyes.

A third major category of phytochemicals is the *sulfur-containing chemicals* such as *organosulfur compounds* in garlic and the *isothiocyanates*, such as sulforaphane in cruciferous vegetables. These substances have been shown to have powerful anticancer activity and immune-enhancing ability.

Lucky for us, when we eat plants, their powerful little protectors go to work on our behalf. Their potential for human health is quite remarkable, their mode of action varied and complex. Primary actions of phytochemicals are:

Anticancer activity
- blocking tumor formation
- reducing cell proliferation (multiplication of cells)
- inducing enzyme systems that detoxify carcinogens and promote their excretion
- reducing oxidative damage to tissues and to DNA
- antibiotic properties—acting against bacteria known to be associated with certain cancers (e.g., the bacteria Helicobacter pylori, which may increase risk for stomach cancer)
- antiestrogenic activity, possibly reducing hormone-related cancers

Anti-CVD activity (potentially reducing hypertension, heart disease, and stroke)
- lowering blood cholesterol levels
- lowering blood pressure
- reducing the conversion of arachidonic acid (AA) to prostaglandin E2 (PGE2), a potent eicosanoid that increases blood pressure, platelet stickiness, and vasospasm

- vasodilation: increasing openness of blood vessels
- antithromotic: reducing blood clot formation
- antioxidant activity: reducing oxidative damage to blood vessel walls and reducing the oxidation of LDL cholesterol

Antiestrogenic activity (potentially reducing estrogen-related cancers, osteoporosis, heart disease, and discomforts of menopause)

- reducing the production of the more potent form of estrogen (16-hydroxy derivative of estradiol) and increasing production of the less potent form (2-hydroxy derivative of estradiol)
- competing with potent estrogen for receptor sites, reducing its effects in the body

Anti-inflammatory

- reducing the conversion of arachidonic acid (AA) to prostaglandin E2 (PGE2), a potent inflammatory agent

Immune-enhancing activity

- increasing activity of cells that protect the body from microorganisms causing disease

Antioxidant activity (resulting in antiaging and reduced macular degeneration)

- neutralizing free-radicals that damage tissues and DNA

Antiviral, antibacterial, antifungal, antiyeast activity

- reducing the growth of potentionally harmful invaders

Antimotion sickness

To make matters even more complicated, phytochemicals often work synergistically with one another, producing certain benefits only when two or more compounds are present together.

Interest in phytochemicals has grown tremendously since their discovery in the early 1970s. The predictable result is a whole new market for phytochemical-rich foods and supplements. Some foods are being specifically engineered to have higher levels of phytochemicals or different mixes of phytochemicals. Companies are now extracting phytochemicals to sell as supplements. Some are concentrating whole plant foods to sell as phytochemical-rich supplements. There are a number of terms that have evolved as a result of these efforts. The definitions on page 146 will help you sort this out.

There is tremendous controversy about the value of designer foods and nutraceuticals. Will all of this messing with nature backfire? At present, we really don't know. What we do know is that in cancer studies, the antioxidants shown to reduce risk of cancer did so *only* when eaten in whole food form. On the other hand, in CVD studies, antioxidant nutrients (especially vitamin E) have demonstrated beneficial effects. At this time, we don't know enough about the complicated interactions of these dietary components to be confident that extracting them, concentrating them, or adding them to other foods will provide the same kind of protection offered by intact plant foods. The best thing any person can do to increase the phytochemical content of their diet in a safe and effective manner is to increase both the quantity and variety of whole plant foods eaten each day.

The New Wave of Foods

Phytochemical: Plant chemicals that contain protective, disease-preventing properties but are not presently considered essential to life.

Nutraceutical: A product isolated or purified from foods, not usually associated with food and demonstrated to have a physiological benefit or provide protection against disease. Nutraceuticals are generally, but not always, sold in pills, powders, potions, or other medicinal forms.

Functional Food: Any food or food ingredient that is similar in appearance to conventional foods and is consumed as part of a regular diet, but has been demonstrated to have health benefits. There are two main categories of functional foods:

Phytochemical-rich whole foods—this includes a huge number of plant foods such as garlic, soy, flax, broccoli, tomatoes, etc.

Designer Foods—processed foods supplemented with food ingredients naturally rich in disease preventing substances. Examples of designer foods include foods fortified with vitamin C or calcium, margarine with added plant sterols and stanols, and cereals with added herbs or psyllium. Another category of designer foods is genetically engineered foods (sometimes called "farmaceuticals"). They include crops grown to contain higher levels of certain nutrients or phytochemicals.

PHYTOCHEMICAL POWERHOUSES

Phytochemicals are present in all whole plant foods in varying amounts; however, some foods stand out as real powerhouses. While variety is your real key to a phytochemical-rich diet, making these foods a regular feature will turn your diet into a phytochemical feast. We'll take a look at each class of food—vegetables, fruits, whole grains, legumes, nuts and seeds, and even spices, and tell you which foods are particularly noteworthy in each. Remember that we are at a very early stage in our understanding of phytochemicals, so while right now there are some foods that stand out as being particularly protective, new discoveries will continue to pour in. Get set, you're in for a few surprises!

Vegetables

There is no question about it; vegetables stand out as being the most protective foods you can eat. They are also the most nutrient dense and, not surprisingly, the richest sources of numerous phytochemicals. Those that are particularly noteworthy include:

CRUCIFEROUS VEGETABLES

Cruciferous vegetables include, broccoli, cauliflower, cabbage, turnips, kohlrabi, Brussels sprouts, kale, collards, mustard greens, and turnip greens. The phytochemicals that make cruciferous vegetables stand out are:

Indoles: antiestrogenic activity potentially reducing risk of related cancers; *Isothiocyanates (including sulforaphane):* anticancer activity

UMBELLIFEROUS VEGETABLES

Umbelliferous vegetables include celery, carrots, parsnips, fennel, dill, anise, parsley, and cilantro. Principal phytochemicals in these foods are:

Coumarins: anti-CVD activity (inhibit blood coagulation); *Flavones:* antioxidant, anticancer, anti-CVD activity (Celery is one of the richest sources of two important flavones.); *Carotenoids (over 600 different carotenoids found in nature):* antioxidant activity (in lab tests although not proven in humans),. anticancer and immune-enhancing activity; *Phthalides and Polyacetylenes:* antitumor activity

---

Veggie Champions

✭ Kale ✭

Rated against 19 other vegetables, kale had the greatest antioxidant activity. It is also:

* ★ rich in lutein, a phytochemical that protects the eyes from macular degeneration
* ★ one of our best sources of flavonols
* ★ a great source of calcium

Note: Other deep green leafy veggies like collards offer similar benefits.

✭ *Broccoli Sprouts* ✭

Sprouting changes the phytochemical content of a plant significantly, and thus far, those changes look pretty impressive!

* • Broccoli is prized for its sulforaphane content.
* • Certain variety of broccoli sprouts contain anywhere from 10 to 100 times the amount of sulforaphane as mature broccoli.
* • Other sprouts appear to have elevated levels of phytochemicals as well.

ALLIUM VEGETABLES

Allium vegetables are the sulfur-containing vegetables of the garlic and onion family (including leeks, shallots, chives, and scallions). The most active components are:

Allicin: Anti-CVD activity; antiviral, antibacterial, antifungal, and antiyeast activity; anticancer activity. (Allicin gives garlic its smell)

Breakdown products of allicin: *Ajoenes:* antithrombotic activity (reduces PGE2 formation); *Vinyldithiins:* antiasthmatic and antithrombotic activity; *Allyl sulfides:* anticancer, anti-CVD activity.

☆ *Veggie Champion—Garlic* ☆

Hippocrates used garlic to treat pneumonia and infections. Wise man.

Garlic has much potential for health.

• CVD protection—may lower cholesterol, lowers blood pressure, reduces stickiness of blood cells, dilates blood vessels, and has high antioxidant activity.

• Cancer protection—destroys cancer cells and reduces cell division. Battles microbes that increase stomach cancer risk.

• Stimulates the immune system.

Better Raw or Cooked?

Cooking can alter the structure of phytochemicals, resulting in very different health effects. In some cases cooking increases the availability of phytochemicals, while in others it is reduced. For example, lycopene is better absorbed from cooked tomatoes than from raw tomatoes. Cooking can also change phytochemicals, giving them entirely different properties. For example, when garlic is cooked in water, vinyldithiins are produced; when cooked in oil, ajoenes are formed. It looks as though we are best to include a variety of both raw and cooked foods in the diet.

Fruits

While fruits have not been quite as impressive as vegetables in epidemiological studies on disease risk reduction, they are not far behind. Among the most phytochemical-packed fruits are:

CITRUS FRUITS

Citrus fruits include oranges, grapefruits, lemons, and limes. Not only do these fruits contain vitamin C and folic acid, they provide a wonderful array of phytochemicals. A single orange contains over 170 different phytochemicals, including:

Flavonoids (over 60 flavonoids): strong antioxidants; anticancer activity, anti-CVD activity; *Terpenes (over 40 different limonoids—major terpenes in bitter parts of citrus fruits):* d-limonene has anti-CVD activity (reduces cholesterol synthesis) and anticancer activity (stimulates detoxifying enzymes); **Carotenoids:** oranges contain about 20 different carotenoids with antioxidant activity

Grapes and grape juice

Rich in a variety of phenolic compounds:

Flavonols *(especially quercetin):* anticancer and anti-CVD activity; **Anthocyanins:** strong antioxidants; inhibit LDL cholesterol oxidation, promote growth and repair of connective tissue, anticlotting activity, anti–inflammatory activity;

Resveratrol: antioxidant, anticlotting activity, anticancer, and anti–inflammatory activity. (Grapes are the richest source, mainly in skins and seeds.)

> ★ *Fruit Champion—Blueberries* ★
>
> The primary active component in blueberries is a phenolic compound called anthocyanin. These substances give blueberries their rich blue color. (Deep shades of blue, purple, and red come from anthocyanin—great sources also include plums, deep purple grapes, and other berries.)
>
> Blueberries are not only one of the world's best-tasting foods, but they may also be one of the most protective:
> • neutralize free radicals that damage DNA
> • protect against urinary tract infections
> • may help reduce effects of aging
> • improve problems with tired eyes
>
> *U.S. Department of Agriculture's Center for Aging at Tufts University studied more than 40 vegetables and fruits measuring their Oxygen Radical Absorbance Capacity (ORAC). Of all the foods, blueberries came out on top—even above all of the vegetables! Indeed it had 5 times the ORAC of most other fruits and vegetables. (Prior, 1996)*

BERRIES

Rich in phenolic compounds:

Anthocyanins: strong antioxidants; inhibit LDL cholesterol oxidation, promote growth and repair of connective tissue, anticlotting activity, anti–inflammatory; **Flavonols:** anticancer and anti-CVD activity (high in cranberries); **Phenolic acids** *(Ellagic acid and gallic acid derivatives):* antioxidant, anticancer activity (high in raspberries and strawberries).

OLIVES

Flavonoids *(flavonols and flavones):* anticancer and anti-CVD (activity among the richest sources of flavonols).

Whole Grains

For most people, grains are not important contributors to their phytochemical intake. This is not because grains lack phytochemicals, but rather because they are generally removed before people eat the grains. Grain phytochemicals are mostly stored in the same places as vitamins, minerals, and fiber—the germ and bran. However, while we lose about 75% of the vitamins and minerals and 90% of the fiber during the refining of grains, we lose at least 95% of the phytochemicals. By selecting mostly intact grains, we can increase our phytochemical intake significantly. The phytochemicals most plentiful in grains are:

Phenolic acids *(ferulic, p-couramic, and caffeic acids)*: antioxidant, anticancer activity; **Lignans** *(compounds with structure similar to estrogen, also known as phytoestrogens)*: reduce antiestrogenic activity, possibly reducing risk of estrogen-related cancers; **Phytates:** function as antioxidants by binding with minerals such as iron, reducing their capacity to cause damaging free radical reactions; **Tocotrienols:** antioxidants (these are forms of vitamin E).

Legumes

Legumes are the protein powerhouses of the plant kingdom. They are the richest plant sources of iron, zinc and other trace minerals, and fiber. Not surprisingly, they come packaged with a number of phytochemicals:

Isoflavones *(phytoestrogens):* antiestrogenic activity, antioxidants; **Phenolic acids:** antioxidants, anticancer activity; **Tannins** *(catechin)*: anticancer activity. (Lentils are among the richest sources.) **Phytates:** function as antioxidants by binding with minerals such as iron, reducing their capacity to cause damaging free radical reactions.

★ Legume Champion—Soybeans ★

The legumes that reign supreme are soybeans. The principal phytochemicals in soy are isoflavones, mainly genestein and daidzein. They are also known as phytoestrogens, estrogen-like compounds with weak estrogenic or antiestrogen activity. They may reduce the risk of estrogen-related cancer, the discomforts of menopause, the risk of osteoporosis, and the risk of CVD. Isoflavones are powerful antioxidants and very effective inhibitors of the tyrosine kinase enzyme, a potent tumor promoter.

- Soy is a great source of phytosterols (plant sterols) that compete with cholesterol, reducing blood cholesterol levels.
- Soy is rich in saponins, antioxidants which may reduce cancer risk and CVD.

Which soyfoods are the best sources of isoflavones?

Soyfoods are sometimes categorized as "first generation" or "second generation." First generation soyfoods include whole soybeans and all products made from whole soybeans (i.e., tofu, tempeh, soy flour, roasted soybeans, some soymilks) and are generally rich sources of isoflavones. Second generation soyfoods include all products made from extracted soy protein (soy protein isolate, soy protein concentrate) and may or may not be rich in isoflavones. When the protein from second generation soyfoods is extracted using a water wash, the isoflavone content remains high; however, when they are extracted using an alcohol wash, most of the isoflavones are lost. The only way of knowing if the soy protein source is water- or alcohol-extracted is to check with the producer. For example, Yves products made with soy isolate are high in

Table 8.1 The Approximate* Isoflavone Content of Soyfoods

Food (per 100 gm/3.5 oz edible portion)	Genestein	Daidzein	Total Isoflavones**
Soy flour, full fat	97	71	178
Soybeans, green	72	68	151
Soybeans, roasted	66	52	128
Instant Protein Beverage (made from water washed soy protein)	62	40	109
Soy protein concentrate	56	43	102
Soy protein isolate	60	33	97
Soybeans, boiled	28	27	55
Tempeh	25	18	44
Miso	24	16	42
Soybean sprouts	22	19	41
Tofu, firm	13-16	10-13	25-32
Soymilk, selected	6-12	4-9	10-24
Soy protein concentrate, alcohol washed	5	6	12

* There are great variations depending on strain of soybeans, growing conditions, etc.

** Total isoflavones may include small amounts of other isoflavones such as glycitein.

Source: USDA—Iowa State University Database on the Isoflavone Content of Food—Release 1.1 1999. Available online: www.nal.usda.gov/fnic/foodcomp/Data/isoflav/isfl_tbl.pdf

isoflavones. Soy oil and soy sauce do not contain isoflavones. The isoflavone content of some common soyfoods are listed in table 8.1

Nuts and Seeds

There is good evidence that nuts and seeds reduce risk for CVD, and that at least part of the beneficial effects are due to the phytochemicals in these foods. While at present there is little evidence for cancer prevention, there is very good reason to believe that nuts and seeds will reduce risk due to their high content of anticancer phytochemicals. The primary phytochemicals in nuts and seeds are:

Flavonoids (quercetin, rutin, kaemperol): antioxidant properties, anticancer activity and anti-CVD activity; Phenolic acids (ellagic and caffeic acid): antioxidant and anticancer activity.

☆ Nut and Seed Champion — Flaxseed ☆

Flaxseeds are packed with health-promoting substances. Their uniqueness makes them true superstars:
• richest known source of lignans, containing over 100 times the lignans of most other plant foods (including nuts and seeds)
• highest alpha-linolenic acid content of any food (57% of the fat is omega-3 fatty acids, with anticancer, anti-CVD activities)
• among the richest sources of boron
• also rich in potassium and magnesium
• rich in soluble fiber (lignin)

(Walnuts are particularly high in ellagic acid, 98% of which is in the skin.) *Lignans:* antiestrogenic activity; *Phytic acids:* Anticancer activity; *Tocotrienols: (also known as vitamin E!):* antioxidants, antitumor activity, and hypolipidemic lipid-lowering effect.

Spices

GINGER ROOT

In 1982, a USDA study found ginger to be more effective for treating motion sickness than Dramamine, the most commonly used medication. It has also been used to relieve stomach aches, coughing, migraines, and fever. The active ingredients in ginger are:

Phenolic compounds (gingerols and diarylheptanoids): pungent principles that protect the stomach lining and combat motion sickness, potent antioxidants; *Terpenoids (oils that rapidly evaporate and give ginger its aroma):* anticancer activity; *Curcurmin:* antitumor activity.

TURMERIC

A popular spice in Indian and Middle Eastern cuisine, turmeric has tremendous potential as an anticancer agent. The active constituents of turmeric are:

Phenolic compounds (mainly curcumin): significant anticancer activity; strong antioxidant, anti-inflammatory properties.

SELECTED REFERENCES

For a complete list see www.nutrispeak.com/veganrefs.htm. See also general references for the whole book on page 276.

★Craig, W. *Nutrition and Wellness…A vegetarian way to better health.* Berrien Springs, Michigan: Golden Harvest Books, 1999.

——— *The Use and Safety of Common Herbs and Herbal Teas, 2nd edition.* Berrien Springs, Michigan: Golden Harvest Books, 1996.

——— "Phytochemicals: Guardians of our Health." *Issues in Vegetarian Dietetics.* 3 (1996).

Hasler, C. "Functional Foods: Their role in disease prevention and healthpromotion." *Food Technology.* 52, 11 (1998): 63-70.

King, A., and G. Young. "Characteristics and occurrence of phenolicphytochemicals." *J. Am. Diet. Assoc.* 99, 2 (1999): 213-218.

Kitts, D.D. "Bioactive substances in food." *Can. J. Physiol. Pharmacol.* 72 (1993): 423-434.

★These references can be ordered from: Andrews University Bookstore, Berrien Springs, MI 49104-0500 or from Dr. Craig at 616-471-3351.

CHAPTER
9

The Vegan Food Guide

I n earlier chapters, we covered the protein, fats, carbohydrates, fiber, minerals, vitamins, and phytochemicals that are central to good health. The Vegan Food Guide takes all of that information and translates it into practical eating advice for everyone four years of age and older. It is designed to help you build a balanced vegan diet with all the nutrients that your body needs.

The Vegan Food Guide is modeled after the U.S. Food Guide Pyramid,★ with three key differences:

- *All foods of animal origin have been replaced by plant foods that contain similar amounts of key nutrients.* In the vegan guide, the group that is particularly high in protein, iron, and zinc is called *Beans & Bean Alternates.* The high calcium foods are the *Fortified Soymilk & Alternates.*

- *The top triangle of the pyramid is "Other Essentials."* This group includes sources of vital nutrients that may not be supplied in adequate amounts from the other five food groups. These nutrients are omega-3 fatty acids, vitamin B_{12}, and vitamin D.

- *The recommended intake from Fortified Soymilk & Alternates is 6-8 servings.* This is more than double the number of servings from the Milk and Alternates group in the U.S. Food Guide Pyramid for two reasons. First, this allows a variety of calcium-rich plant foods to be included in reasonable serving sizes. In the U.S. Food Guide Pyramid, 1 serving = 1 cup of milk, while in the Vegan Food Guide, 1 serving = ½ cup of fortified soymilk, 1 cup of kale, and so on. Second, the number of servings of calcium-rich foods reflects the new higher Dietary Reference Intakes for calcium, which have increased from 800-1,200 mg/day, to 1,000-1,300 mg/day for those above the age of 8 years.

★*www.health.gov/dietaryguidelines/dga2000/DIETGD.PDF*

VEGAN FOOD GUIDE

DAILY PLAN FOR HEALTHY EATING

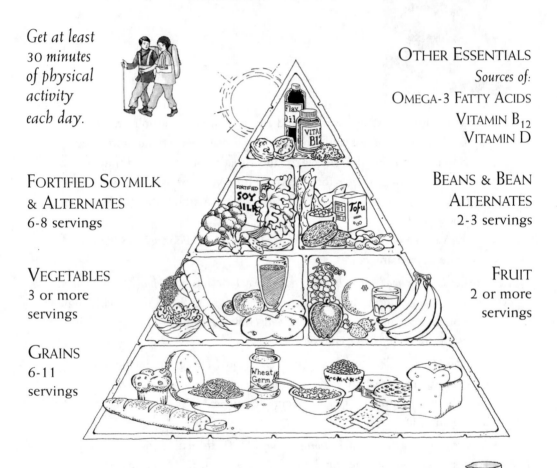

Get at least 30 minutes of physical activity each day.

OTHER ESSENTIALS
Sources of:
OMEGA-3 FATTY ACIDS
VITAMIN B_{12}
VITAMIN D

FORTIFIED SOYMILK
& ALTERNATES
6-8 servings

BEANS & BEAN
ALTERNATES
2-3 servings

VEGETABLES
3 or more
servings

FRUIT
2 or more
servings

GRAINS
6-11
servings

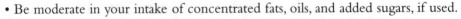
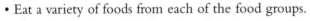
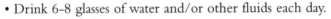

- Eat a variety of foods from each of the food groups.
- Drink 6-8 glasses of water and/or other fluids each day.
- Be moderate in your intake of concentrated fats, oils, and added sugars, if used.

Vegan Food Guide

Daily Plan for Healthy Eating

The ranges in servings allow for differences in body size, activity levels, and age.
For example, smaller and less active people need fewer servings, larger, more active people need more.

Food Group servings per day	What Counts As A Serving?	Important Comments
Grains (bread, cereal, whole grains and pasta) 6-11 servings	1 slice of bread 1 oz (28 g) ready-to-eat cereal ½ cup cooked grains, cereal, or pasta 2 Tbsp wheat germ 1 oz (28 g) other grain products	*Choose mainly whole grains.* Good examples are brown rice, barley, quinoa, millet, oats, wheat and kamut berries, as well as whole grain breads and cereals.
Vegetables 3 or more servings	½ cup (120 ml) vegetables 1 cup (240 ml) salad ¾ cup (180 ml) vegetable juice	*Eat a wide variety of colorful vegetables.* Include raw vegetables each day. Green vegetables are great sources of folate; many provide calcium too!
Fruit 2 or more servings	1 medium apple, banana, orange, pear ½ cup (120 ml) fruit ¾ cup (180 ml) fruit juice ¼ c dried fruit	*Select an assortment of fruits, including those rich in vitamin C.* Vitamin C-rich sources are citrus fruits, strawberries, kiwi, guava, papaya, cantaloupe, and mangos.
Beans and Bean Alternates (beans, tofu, nuts, and seeds) 2-3 servings	1 cup (240 ml) cooked legumes (beans, lentils, dried peas) ½ cup (120 ml) firm tofu or tempeh 1 serving veggie "meats" (1 burger or wiener, 2-3 lunch slices) 3 Tbsp (45 ml) nut or seed butter ¼ c (60 ml) nuts & seeds 2 cups (480 ml) soymilk	*For maximum benefit, eat a wide range of these protein-rich foods.* Eating vegetables or fruits that are high in vitamin C along with these foods increases iron absorption. Nuts and seeds provide vitamin E and minerals.
Fortified Soymilk and Alternates 6-8 servings	½ cup (120 ml) fortified soymilk ¼ cup (60 ml) calcium-set tofu ½ cup (120 ml) calcium-fortified orange juice ¼ cup (60 ml) almonds 3 Tbsp (45 ml) almond butter 1 cup (240 ml) cooked, or 2 cups (480 ml) raw, of high calcium greens, (kale, collards, Chinese greens, broccoli, okra) 1 cup (240 ml) high-calcium beans, (i.e. soy, white, navy, Great Northern, black turtle beans) ¼ cup (60 ml) dry hijiki seaweed 1 Tbsp (15 ml) blackstrap molasses 5 figs	*Get to know your calcium sources!* Many of these foods double as servings from the Bean and Bean Alternate group and the Vegetable group. Include calcium-rich foods with every meal. Foods should provide at least 15% of the DV per serving to be included as a serving in this group. (If a serving provides 10% of the DV, use 1½ servings.)
Other Essentials: Omega-3 fatty acids 1-2 servings Vitamin B_{12} to meet recommended intakes Vitamin D to meet recommended intakes *For more details on sources, see page 66 (omega-3 fatty acids), page 127 (vitamin B_{12}), and page 139 (vitamin D).*	*Omega-3 fatty acids★* Serving =1 tsp flax oil, 4 tsp canola oil, 3 Tbsp walnuts *Vitamin B_{12}★* Fortified foods or supplements supplying 2.4 mcg (adults); 2.6-2.8 mcg/day (pregnancy and lactation); 0.9-1.8 mcg/day (children) *Vitamin D★* Sunshine or fortified food or supplements supplying 5 mcg /day vitamin D_2 (10 mcg /day 51-70 yrs; 15 mcg 70+ years)	*Pay attention to these important nutrients.* The best source of omega-3s for vegans is flax oil. Use in salad dressings and on baked potatoes, vegetables, and grains! Look for foods fortified with vitamin B_{12}. (Red Star Vegetarian Support Formula nutritional yeast is a good example.) If you don't get enough sunshine, be sure to get vitamin D_2 from foods or supplements.

PRACTICAL POINTERS

These practical pointers will help you plan an excellent vegan diet using the Vegan Food Guide:

• Eat a wide variety of foods from each food group in the Vegan Food Guide. Variety helps to ensure sufficient nutrients, phytochemicals, and fiber. It also makes your meals a whole lot more interesting!

• Be moderate in your intake of concentrated fats, oils, and added sugars, if used. These foods are generally rich in calories but poor sources of nutrients. Excessive intakes of fat and sugar will crowd out foods that offer valuable nutrients.

• Get at least 30 minutes of physical activity each day. Physical activity, while not a component of "diet," is central to energy balance and overall health.

• Drink 6 to 8 glasses of water and other fluids each day. Fluids such as water, vegetable or fruit juices, and herbal teas help to maintain good health. Many of these beverages provide additional phytochemicals, vitamins, and minerals.

MEAL AND MENU PLANNING USING THE VEGAN FOOD GUIDE

Sample 1,600-4,000 Calorie Menus

Now that you are familiar with the food guide, let's put it to practical use. What follows are four menu plans with caloric levels designed to meet the needs of people with varying energy requirements.

Important Notes:

• These menus can be easily adapted to suit your personal preferences and adjusted to include slightly greater or lesser amounts of calories.

• You'll notice that in a well-designed, nutritionally complete menu, there's not a lot of room for extras that provide calories but little else. This is true whether you're following a vegan diet or not. If you have a higher activity level, you can add oils (approximately 45 calories per teaspoon) and sugars (15 calories per teaspoon).

• Using ready-to-eat and convenience foods tends to result in increased sodium intakes. To decrease sodium, balance your overall diet with more of the basic foods. In the nutritional analyses of these menus that is provided on page 161, the analysis is done using the first option in cases where optional menu items are listed.

1,600 CALORIE MENU

Perfect for those individuals who are small in stature and relatively inactive,
for those who are trying to lose weight, or for less mobile seniors.

• *Some foods items count as items in more than one food group.*
The food is italicized where it is mentioned in the second food group.

• *Remember to include 6 to 8 cups of water daily. This includes herbal teas and juice.*

Food group	Breakfast	Lunch	Supper	Snack	
	cereal with soymilk and fruit	lentil soup, crackers, veggies with dip/ dressing, and fruit	stir-fried greens and tofu on rice	banana shake and popcorn	*Total Servings from Food Group*
Grains	1 c/240 mL cooked cereal or 2 oz/60 g other grain product	3 rice cakes or crackers	1 c/240 mL cooked brown rice or other grain	3 c/720 mL popcorn with tamari and nutritional yeast	Grains 6
	(2 grain servings)	*(1 grain serving)*	*(2 grain servings)*	*(1 grain serving)*	
Vegetables		2 c/480 mL raw vegetables: carrots, celery, peppers, cherry tomatoes, cucumber	1 c/240 mL broccoli, 1 c/240 mL Chinese greens or Napa cab- bage in stir fry		Vegetables 4
		(2 vegetable servings)	*(2 vegetable servings)*		
Fruit	½ c/120 mL berries or other fruit	1 slice watermelon or 1 other fruit		1 banana	Fruit 3
	(1 fruit serving)	*(1 fruit serving)*		*(1 fruit serving)*	
Bean and Bean Alternates	1 c/240 mL fortified soymilk	1 c/240 mL cooked lentils in lentil soup	¼ c/60 mL firm tofu	1 c/240 mL fortified soymilk	Bean and Bean Alternates 2½
	(½ bean serving)	*(1 bean serving)*	*(½ bean serving)*	*(½ bean serving)*	
Fortified Soymilk and Alternates	*1 c/240 mL fortified soymilk*		*¼ c/60 mL calcium-set tofu, 1 c/240 mL broccoli, 1 c/240 mL Chinese greens or Napa cabbage*	*1 c/240 mL fortified soymilk*	Fortified Soymilk and Alternates 7
	(2 fortified soymilk servings)		*(3 fortified soymilk servings)*	*(2 fortified soymilk servings)*	
Other Essentials★		1½ Tbsp/22 mL Liquid Gold Dressing (page 127)			Other Essentials★ 1 (omega-3s)
		(1 omega-3 serving)			

★*Vitamin B$_{12}$ is supplied by Liquid Gold Dressing and vitamin D by fortified soymilk.*

2,200 CALORIE MENU

Designed for the majority of active women, children, and teenage girls,
and for many men who are less active.

• *Some food items count as items in more than one food group.*

The food is italicized where it is mentioned in the second food group.

• *Remember to include 6 to 8 cups of water daily. This includes herbal teas and juice.*

Food Group	Breakfast	Lunch	Supper	Snack	
	cereal and soymilk with juice or fruit	carrot or vegetable soup, pita with hummus	tofu and grain or rolls, green salad, dressing	soymilk, figs, or almonds	Total Servings from Food Group
Grains	1 c/240 mL cooked cereal or 2 oz/60 g other grain product	2 pita bread	1 c/240 mL cooked grain or 2 small rolls		Grains 6
	(2 grain servings)	(2 grain servings)	(2 grain servings)		
Vegetables		1 c/240 mL carrot or vegetable soup	4 c/960 mL salad containing 2 c/ 480 mL calcium- rich greens		Vegetables 6
		(2 vegetable servings)	(4 vegetable servings)		
Fruit	¾ c/180 mL juice or 1 fruit				Fruit 1
	(1 fruit serving)				
Bean and Bean Alternates	1 c/240 mL fortified soymilk	1 c/240 mL hummus, made without oil	4 oz/120 g firm tofu		Bean and Bean Alternates 2½
	(½ bean serving)	(1 bean serving)	(1 bean serving)		
Fortified Soymilk and Alternates	1 c/240 mL fortified soymilk	1 c/240 mL hummus	4 oz/120 g calcium- set firm tofu, 2 c/480 mL calcium- rich greens in salad	½ c/120 mL fortified soymilk, 5 figs, or ¼ c/ 60 mL almonds	Fortified Soymilk and Alternates 7
	(2 fortified soymilk servings)	(1 fortified soymilk serving)	(3 fortified soymilk servings)	(1 fortified soymilk serving)	
Other Essentials*			1½ Tbsp/22 mL Liquid Gold Dressing (page 127)		Omega-3s 1

Vitamin B_{12} is supplied by Liquid Gold Dressing and vitamin D by fortified soymilk.

2,500 TO 2,800 CALORIE MENU

Suited to teenage boys, many active men and some very active women.

The menu below totals 2,500 calories. To bring intake to 2,800 calories,

add 1 piece of fruit or small roll, plus 2 cookies.

• *Some foods items count as items in more than one food group.*

The food is italicized where it is mentioned in the second food group.

• *Remember to include 6 to 8 cups of water daily. This includes herbal teas and juice.*

Food group	Breakfast	Lunch	Supper	Snack	
	cereal and soymilk, fruit, toast with almond butter and blackstrap molasses	veggie club sandwich, orange juice	2 veggie burgers or baked beans or veggie chili, baked potato, squash, salad	trail mix (figs and walnuts)	*Total Servings from Food Groups*
Grains	2 slices toast 1 c/240 mL whole grain cereal *or* 2 oz/ 60 g dry cereal *(4 grain servings)*	3 slices whole grain bread *(3 grain servings)*			*Grains* 7
Vegetables		tomato slices, lettuce *(½ vegetable serving)*	1 baked potato 1 c/240 mL squash 2 c/480 mL salad *(5 vegetable servings)*		*Vegetables* 5½
Fruit	1 fruit *(1 fruit serving)*	1 c/240 mL calcium-fortified orange juice *(1 fruit serving)*		5 figs (½ c/120 mL) *(2 fruit servings)*	*Fruit* 4
Bean and Bean Alternates	2 Tbsp/30 mL almond butter 1 c/240 mL fortified soymilk *(1 bean serving)*	6 slices veggie bacon and veggie turkey *(2 bean servings)*	2 veggie burgers, or large serving of baked beans or vegetarian chili *(2 bean servings)*	walnuts, 3 Tbsp/45 mL *(1 bean serving)*	*Bean and Bean Alternates* 6
Fortified Soymilk and Alternates	2 tsp blackstrap molasses *2 Tbsp/30 mL almond butter 1 c/240 mL fortified soymilk* *(3 fortified soymilk servings)*	*1 c/240 mL calcium-fortified orange juice* *(2 fortified soymilk servings)*	*kale (in salad)* *(½ fortified soymilk serving)*	*5 figs* *(1 fortified soymilk serving)*	*Fortified Soymilk and Alternates* 7
Other Essentials*			3 Tbsp/45 mL dressing on salad and potato ★★	*walnuts, 3 Tbsp/45 mL* *(1 serving)*	*Omega-3 Fatty Acids*

*Vitamin B$_{12}$ is supplied by fortified products such as deli slices and soymilk, vitamin D by fortified soymilk.

★★If Liquid Gold Dressing (page 127) is used, this bring total servings for the day from Omega-3 fatty acids to 3.

4,000 CALORIE MENU

Constructed for athletes, men whose work or recreation involves a great deal of physical activity,
and some people who are trying to gain weight.

• *Some foods items count as items in more than one food group.*
The food is italicized where it is mentioned in the second food group.

• *Remember to include 6 to 8 cups of water daily. This includes herbal teas and juice.*

Food group	Breakfast	Lunch	Supper	Snack #1	Snack #2	Snack #3	
	cereal with soymilk, bagels with tahini and jam, orange juice	2 vegan burgers, fruit	tofu-cashew-vegetable stir fry over rice or noodles	basic Quick Shake (page 240) with banana and berries	power bar	granola with raisins and walnuts, soymilk or soy yogurt	Total Servings from Food Groups
Grains	2 bagels or 3 slices toast 1 c/240 mL cereal *(5 grain servings)*	2 rolls *(2 grain servings)*	2 c/480 mL noodles or rice *(4 grain servings)*			1 c/240 mL granola *(2 grain servings)*	Grains 13
Vegetables		tomato slices, lettuce *(½ vegetable serving)*	Vegetables in stir fry, including greens *(4 vegetable servings)*				Vegetables 4½
Fruit	1½ c/360 mL orange juice *(2 fruit servings)*	2 fruit *(2 fruit servings)*		1 banana, ½ c/ 120 mL berries *(2 fruit servings)*	1 power bar★★ *(1 fruit serving)*	2 Tbsp/30 mL raisins *(½ fruit serving)*	Fruit 7½
Bean and Bean Alternates	3 Tbsp/45 mL sesame tahini 1 c/240 mL fortified soymilk *(1½ bean servings)*	2 vegan burgers *(2 bean servings)*	¼ c/60 mL cashews ¼ c/ 60 mL calcium-set tofu *(2 bean servings)*	1 c/240 mL fortified soymilk *(½ bean serving)*	1 power bar★★ *(1 bean serving)*	1 c/240 mL fortified soymilk (or soy yogurt★) *(½ bean serving)*	Bean and Bean Alternates 7
Fortified Soymilk and Alternates	3 Tbsp/45 mL sesame tahini 1 c/240 mL fortified soymilk *(3 fortified soymilk servings)*		¼ c/60 mL calcium-set tofu *(1 fortified soymilk serving)*	1 c/240 mL fortified soymilk *(2 fortified soymilk servings)*		1 c/240 mL fortified soymilk *(2 fortified soymilk servings)*	Fortified Soymilk and Alternates 8
Other Essentials★★						3 Tbsp/45 mL walnuts *(1 omega-3 serving)*	Omega-3s 1

★ *Since soy yogurt is not calcium-fortified, it does not count as alternate for fortified soymilk.*

★★*Vitamins B$_{12}$ and D come from fortified soymilk; power bar and fortified veggie burgers may add B$_{12}$ (check labels).*

Table 9.1 Nutrients Provided in Various Menus

Nutrients	Minimum Recommended Adult Intake	1,600 Calorie Menu	2,200 Calorie Menu	2,800 Calorie Menu	4,000 Calorie Menu
Protein, grams	45–70 or more	71	85	115	143
Fat, grams	20–50	33	64	91	128
Omega-3 fatty acids, grams	2	3.6	4.1	8.6	2.09
Carbohydrate, grams	180–315 or more	280	362	420	618
Fiber, grams	Approx. 25–54 or 15–22 g per 1,000 cal	45	58	59	55
Percent calories from:					
Protein	10–15%	16%	14%	15%	14%
Fat	15–30%	18%	24%	28%	27%
Carbohydrate	55–75%	66%	62%	57%	59%
Minerals					
Calcium, mg	1,000–1,200	1,302	1,567	1,374	1,955
Iron, mg	14–32	25	33	32	43
Magnesium, mg	320–420	615	712	648	1,122
Potassium, mg	2,000	3,909	4,733	5,838	6,306
Sodium, mg	Aim for up to 2,400 on average	2,002	2,447	3,061	4,254
Zinc, mg	8–11	16	15	15.8	24
Vitamins					
A mcg (beta-carotene)*	800–1,000	11,746	11,115	10,476	15,399
Thiamin/B_1, mg	1.1–1.2	2.3	4.6	5.7	4.9
Riboflavin/B_2, mg	1.1–1.3	2.4	3.4	4.7	5.3
Niacin Equivalents, mg	14–16	16.7	43	43	58
Folate/Folic Acid, mcg	400	603	755	509	1,376
Pyridoxine/B_6, mg	1.3–1.7	3.4	3.9	5.2	4.6
B_{12}/Cobalamin, mcg	2.4	6.3	4.5	7.5	15
C/Ascorbic acid, mg	75–90	287	290	259	586
D, mcg (or sunlight)**	5–15	6	3	3	9
E/d-alpha tocopherol, mg***	15	5	9	15	16

*Intakes are high because source is beta-carotene; these intakes are fine.

** To meet recommended intakes, sunlight or vitamin D_2 from fortified cereal or other food is needed in some menus.

*** To meet recommended intakes, supplemental vitamin E is required in some menus.

CHAPTER
10

Building Vegan Dynamos
...pregnancy and lactation

You're pregnant, and being vegan (or near-vegan) just might create some concern among well-meaning friends, family, and health care providers. It may even make you begin to have doubts yourself. The last thing you want to do is to risk the health of your unborn baby. Before packing for a guilt-trip, read this chapter carefully, then move forward with confidence. Getting all the nutrients you need to grow the healthiest baby possible is not so difficult on a vegan diet—in fact, it is getting easier all the time.

The Proof is in the Pudding!

The largest study to date on the health of pregnant vegans and their pregnancy outcomes was completed in 1987 (Carter et al). In this study, the maternity care records of 775 vegan women from The Farm in Summertown, Tennessee, were examined. Two important findings came out of this research:

1. The vegan diet did not affect infant birth weight.

2. Vegan women were almost completely free of preeclampsia (only 1 out of 775 mothers, a rate of 0.1% compared to 5-10% for the general population).

The authors of this study concluded that it is possible to sustain a normal pregnancy on a vegan diet and that a vegan diet may possibly alleviate most, if not all, of the signs and symptoms of preeclampsia.

In a much smaller study by Thomas and Ellis (1977), birth weights of vegan infants did not differ from those of nonvegetarian mothers and there was little difference in the incidence of preeclampsia.

While there have been a few less favorable reports regarding pregnancy outcomes of mothers consuming vegan or near-vegan diets, the diets consumed were consistently low in calories, protein, and other nutrients (i.e., very restrictive). We must remember that most of the studies on pregnant vegans were carried out long before nutritious, convenient vegan food options became available (i.e., fortified soymilk, fortified veggie "meats," flavored tofu). The message we can take away from all of this is that vegan diets can support very healthy pregnancies, however, vegan mothers do need to take care to ensure adequate intake of energy and nutrients.

NUTRITION CONSIDERATIONS FOR PREGNANCY

Pregnancy is a time when proper nutrition is critical. After all, the nutrients your baby needs for growth come entirely from you. It is extremely important that you enter pregnancy with excellent nutrient reserves, as they will be drawn upon frequently during this time. This means that if you are planning to get pregnant any time in the next year or two, start making the necessary changes in your diet now. By the time you are pregnant, not only will your nutrient reserves be in good shape, you will have established eating patterns that will go a long way towards a lifetime of great health for your entire family.

While your energy needs during pregnancy increase only moderately (about 10-15%), your needs for several vitamins and minerals are increased by 20 to over 100%. That means that you need to pay special attention to your food choices during this time. Let's take a closer look at the challenges you face and most effective ways of handling them.

Weight Gain and Energy Needs

Your weight gain can have a tremendous impact on your baby's birth weight. If you fail to gain enough weight, your baby could end up being very small. Babies with low birth weight (under 5½ lbs/2.5 kg) are at higher risk for illness and death than are babies of normal weight. Weight gains associated with the healthiest pregnancy outcomes are listed in Table 10.1.

If you have a large body frame, aim for the upper end of each range, and if you have a smaller frame, aim for the lower end. If you are underweight or happen to be carrying more than one baby, it is very important that you gain a little extra weight. Adolescents also need to strive for higher weight gains, especially if they are still growing and/or are underweight. Women who are overweight do not need to gain "fat stores" for lactation, thus a slightly lower weight gain is

Table 10.1 Weight Gain in Healthy Pregnancy

Factors Determining Weight Gain Goals	Recommended Weight Gain
Normal Weight (BMI* 19-24.9)	25-35 lbs (11.5-16 kg)
Underweight (BMI less than 19)	28-40 lbs (12.5-18 kg)
Overweight (BMI more than 25)	15-25 lbs (7-11.5 kg)
Adolescent	30-45 lbs (14-20 kg)
Normal weight with twins	35-45 lbs (16-20 kg)

* Body mass index prior to pregnancy.

generally considered safe. It is important to note that many people assume that they are overweight when in fact they are within their healthy weight range. Check with your doctor or health care provider before you decide to limit your weight gain. You may unnecessarily compromise your nutrient intake and, consequently, the health of your baby.

In order to gain the appropriate weight, you'll need to increase your caloric intake. During the first trimester, strive for an extra 100 calories per day and during the next two trimesters, an extra 300 calories per day.

Tips for Great Gains

If you are having trouble gaining weight, don't give up. With a little extra effort, you can get those calories high enough to produce a healthy weight gain.

- Eat regular meals and snacks.

- If you have trouble eating more, try drinking more. Shakes are a perfect choice. (See Quick Shake, page 240.) Do include the optional flax oil to improve your omega-3 intake. Even fresh squeezed orange juice can provide a good supply of extra calories and nutrients.

- Increase your intake of low-bulk, high-fat plant foods. Eat more tofu, nuts, seeds and their butters, avocados, and soups or puddings made with soymilk.

- Use some concentrated oils. While oils have little nutritional value, they do help increase nutrient absorption and energy content of the diet.

- Use oil-based salad dressings and small amounts of oil in cooking.

- Enjoy nutritious baked items. Make nutrient-packed granolas, cookies, squares, muffins, and fruit crisps. Spike these foods with wheat germ, flaxseed, and soymilk powder for a real nutrition boost.

- Try our Sneaky Dad's Pudding (page 194)—we consider this a secret weapon which could almost come with a written guarantee!

Protein

You will undoubtedly be besieged with questions about how you can possibly get enough protein to support a baby's growth on a vegan diet. Fear not; you probably already eat close to the recommended intakes of protein for pregnancy. You need about 60-66 grams a day, an increase of about 10-20 grams above nonpregnant needs. (Recommended intakes for nutrients are provided in Table 10.2.) At least 60 grams of protein/day is recommended for the general population or for vegans who rely mainly on easy-to-digest plant foods, such as tofu and veggie "meats" as primary protein sources. Sixty-six grams/day (a 10% increase) is suggested for vegans who get much of their protein from harder-to-digest plant foods such as beans. This amount of protein comes very close to the average intakes of vegan women. However, if your diet is low in protein, you will need to make a concerted effort to include more protein-rich foods in your diet.

Those at greatest risk for insufficient protein intakes are people who don't eat enough calories and/or those who include few high-protein plant foods in their diet (i.e. tofu, legumes, nuts, seeds, or meat substitutes). This can be a problem particularly for people who switch from a nonvegetarian diet to a vegan diet by eliminating the meat and dairy products and not replacing them with foods of comparable nutritional value. Pasta and bread products are often staples in such diets.

To meet your needs for protein, add an extra serving from the beans and bean alternate group to your daily diet, bringing your total intake to 3 servings a day. A good rule of thumb is to include a serving of beans and bean alternates with each meal. A serving of beans and bean alternates equals a cup of beans, ½ cup of tofu or tempeh, 1 veggie patty, 3 veggie deli slices, 2 cups of soymilk, ¼ cup nuts or seeds, or 3 Tbsp. nut butter.*

Iron

Iron needs are greater during pregnancy because of the increased formation of red blood cells for both the mother and her infant. These needs are at least partially compensated for by increased iron absorption (from 10-20% to as much as 50%) and decreased iron losses (menstruation ceases). Iron deficiency anemia is associated with both low birth weight and preterm delivery. The incidence of iron deficiency anemia increases during the third trimester of pregnancy; however, it is suggested that this is due to hemodilution (expansion of blood volume without a parallel increase in red blood cells) and does not negatively impact the baby's birth weight or length of gestation.

Recommended iron intakes go up from 32 mg/day to 49 mg/day during this time, an amount that can be a challenge to obtain from either vegan or nonvegetarian diets. (Recall that the RDAs for iron are 1.8 times higher for vegetarians than for nonvegetarians.) There is currently little evidence to suggest that the risk for iron deficiency in pregnancy is any greater in vegans than it is in nonvegetarians. However, vegan iron stores are lower, so theoretically, risk may be increased. To help ensure sufficient iron intake, supplemental iron at a rate of 30 mg/day (60-120 mg/day if anemic) starting at the second trimester of pregnancy is generally recommended. Little evidence exists to

* *Nuts, seeds, and their butters are lower in protein than the other items listed; however, when a variety of items are selected, they average out to about 15 grams of protein per serving.*

show that iron supplements actually improve pregnancy outcome, although there is some evidence that iron status after delivery is better in women who have been supplemented during pregnancy.

Even if you are using iron supplements, it's still a good idea to include plenty of dietary sources too! Legumes, tofu, nuts, seeds, dried fruits, whole and enriched grains, and dark greens are great choices. (See chapter 6 for further information on iron sources.) Eating these foods with a source of vitamin C will improve absorption considerably, and cooking in cast-iron will help increase iron content of the food. To help ensure good iron status during pregnancy, avoid tea and coffee with meals, as they are high in tannins which interfere with iron absorption.

Zinc

Severe zinc deficiency in pregnancy has been associated with spontaneous abortion and congenital malformations, while milder forms of zinc deficiency have been associated with low birth weight, growth retardation, and preterm delivery.

The recommended intake for zinc during pregnancy is 11 mg a day, an increase of 3 mg above nonpregnant needs. These recommendations assume an absorption rate of at least 20%. In a vegan diet, zinc absorption generally ranges from 15-20%, and there is little indication that zinc absorption improves during pregnancy. In addition, total zinc intakes of pregnant women, whether vegans or nonvegetarians, rarely meet the recommended intakes.

While some studies suggest that zinc supplementation may improve infant birth weight and lengthen the duration of pregnancy, results have been highly inconsistent. Several recent studies have failed to find any improvements in infant birth weight or pregnancy duration, however, some suggest that other indicators of infant development may be improved. Although zinc supplementation is not routinely recommended (unless over 60 mg of iron/day are taken), it may be prudent for pregnant vegans to select a prenatal supplement that includes 10-15 mg of zinc. This supplement should also contain about 2 mg copper, as zinc can reduce copper absorption.

To maximize the zinc content of your diet, include plenty of whole foods such as legumes, nuts, seeds, and whole grains. Some fortified breakfast cereals and veggie meats are fortified with zinc (read labels). Also see chapter 6 for more information on zinc.

Calcium

Calcium helps ensure proper formation of your baby's bones and teeth, as well as their nerve, muscle, and blood functioning. Your body has huge calcium reserves (your bones!), so your baby will certainly get enough. To avoid using up your precious reserves, it is important that you eat sufficient calcium-rich foods.

While women used to be advised to substantially increase their calcium intakes during pregnancy, this is no longer considered necessary. The reasons are twofold: first, recommendations for calcium intake during adolescence and adulthood have been increased to 1,300 mg for those 14-18 years of age and 1,000 mg for those 19-50 years of age. Thus, if women are meeting recommended intakes, they enter pregnancy with great calcium stores. Second, during pregnancy, calcium absorption appears to be significantly increased. While there is some controversy as to whether vegans need as much calcium as nonvegetarians (due to lower protein intakes and lower sodium intakes), it is prudent for all pregnant women to meet the RDA until there is enough evidence to prove otherwise.

Getting enough calcium on a vegan diet need not be any more difficult than it is on a lacto-ovo vegetarian or nonvegetarian diet. You need 6-8 servings per day from the calcium-rich group. (See food guide on page 174.) The following food combinations each supply the equivalent of at least 6 servings from the calcium-rich group:

- 2 Tbsp. tahini, 1 Tbsp. blackstrap molasses, 1 cup calcium-fortified orange juice, and 1 cup fortified soymilk
- 2 cups fortified soymilk, ⅓ cup almonds, and 1 cup cooked broccoli
- 1 cup baked beans, 5 large figs, 1 tofu/fortified soymilk shake, and 1 cup cooked bok choy
- ⅓ cup hijiki seaweed, 2 cups black bean soup, 4 cups raw kale salad, 1 cup fortified soymilk

For those who have not previously consumed a calcium-rich diet or those who consume less than the recommended number of servings from the calcium-rich group, a calcium supplement may be warranted.

Calcium in most prenatal supplements ranges from about 100 to 250 mg, which is *insufficient* to meet the needs of those who are consuming few calcium-rich foods. If you need a calcium supplement, select one that provides about 500-600 mg/day. In addition to the calcium from your food, this should be sufficient.

Vitamin D

Vitamin D is calcium's partner, necessary to its absorption. Without sufficient vitamin D, infants can be born with rickets and tetany and mothers can develop osteomalacia (softening of the bones).

Recommended intakes of vitamin D are the same in pregnant and non-pregnant women—5 mcg per day (200 IU). For those living in colder climates (with no warm sunshine in the winter) or those who have little exposure to sunlight, an intake of 10 mcg per day (400 IU) is suggested.

There are two ways to get vitamin D: from sunshine or from food. Light-skinned women need about 10-15 minutes of warm sunshine on their face and forearms each day. Those with darker skin may need an hour a day or more. If you don't get enough sunshine, vitamin D–fortified foods or a vitamin D supplement should be used. Vitamin D fortification of foods varies considerably from country to country; however, in many areas soymilk is now being fortified with vitamin D_2 (the nonanimal form of vitamin D).

Vitamin B_{12}

The importance of getting sufficient vitamin B_{12} in pregnancy cannot be overstated. A lack of this nutrient during pregnancy means that your baby will be born with stores that are only about 10-25% that of mothers with sufficient vitamin B_{12} intakes. The stores of infants from adequately nourished mothers last about 6 months to a year, while the stores of infants from mothers with poor B_{12} intake will be depleted in very short order. If you breast-feed your infant and still do not have a reliable source of vitamin B_{12}, your infant may end up with severe vitamin B_{12} deficiency (weakness, loss of reflexes, failure to thrive, delayed development, muscle wasting, and irreversible brain damage). To add to the concern, recent research has demonstrated that high homocysteine levels during pregnancy may increase the risk for neural tube defects in infants. Homocysteine levels are elevated by a lack of both folate and vitamin B_{12}. Several prominent researchers have suggested that along with folate, B_{12} should also be added to foods. This may help to decrease the risk of masking B_{12} deficiencies with folate.

There is some uncertainty as to the impact of your vitamin B_{12} stores on the vitamin B_{12} status of your baby. Some studies suggest your stores are not available to the infant and that the key determinant of your baby's vitamin B_{12} status is your current intake, while others have shown that your stores may also effect your baby's B_{12} status. One thing that is very clear is that no one should rely on their B_{12} stores to provide the necessary B_{12} for their infant.

Aim for at least 3 mcg/day of vitamin B_{12} from fortified foods or supplements. (The RDA is 2.6 mcg/day.) The best dietary sources of vitamin B_{12} for vegans are Red Star Vegetarian Support Formula nutritional yeast (T-6635+), fortified nondairy beverages, cereals, and meat substitutes. (See chapter 7 for more information on B_{12} sources.) Seaweed and fermented soyfoods are not reliable vitamin B_{12} sources.

Folic Acid

Folic acid is a B vitamin that has been strongly linked to neural tube defects, including spina bifida and anencephaly. It is estimated that occurrence of these devastating diseases could be reduced by at least 50% by increasing folic acid intake prior to conception and during early pregnancy. It is recommended that all women of childbearing age consume at least 400 mcg of folic acid per day and that pregnant women consume 600 mcg of folic acid per day.

The use of folate supplements is a routine recommendation for all pregnant women. However, vegan diets are significantly higher in folate than nonvegetarian diets. In a recent study by Haddad et al (1999), female vegan folate intakes from food averaged 435 mcg per day, compared with 240 mcg per day for nonvegetarians. These findings are consistent with several earlier studies. Thus, there is a question of whether or not vegans need to take folate supplements during pregnancy. The concerns are this: with high folate intakes from plant foods and food fortification with folate and folate supplements, it is possible intakes of some vegans could become excessive. Very high intakes of folate can mask a vitamin B_{12} deficiency. Supplements of both folate and iron can also reduce zinc absorption. On the other hand, while average folate intakes of vegan women are high, there will undoubtedly be those who do not consume enough, especially those who eat few legumes and leafy greens. Thus, the most prudent advice would be to either increase dietary folate intake during pregnancy to 600 mcg of folic acid per day, or to take folate as part of a prenatal multi-vitamin preparation that also supplies vitamin B_{12} and zinc.

Essential Fatty Acids

Essential fatty acids include two nutrients—linoleic (omega-6) and alpha-linolenic acid (omega-3). Vegans generally get excess omega-6 fatty acids, but only about half the necessary omega-3 fatty acids. The lower omega-3 fatty acid intake is reflected directly by levels in the blood. The big concern about low omega-3 fatty acids in pregnancy is that there will be insufficient conversion of alpha-linolenic acid to a longer-chain omega-3 fatty acid called DHA, which is an integral part of all cell membranes and is important to brain development and visual acuity. Vegans have approximately one-half the DHA of nonvegetarians in their blood and breast milk. DHA not only influences the development and function of many different organ systems, but it is the predominant structural fatty acid of the brain and retina. (DHA accounts for 40% of the polyunsaturated fat in the brain and 60% in the retina.) The research on DHA and its impact on infant health has exploded over the past decade. There are now dozens of studies that confirm the beneficial effects of DHA on visual acuity and brain development in infants.

Why are vegan DHA levels so low? There are two main reasons. First, vegans and vegetarians consume little, if any, direct DHA. The primary dietary source for most people is fish. Second, vegans must rely on the conversation of alpha-linolenic acid to DHA, which is highly inefficient (about 2-5% for most people). The high levels of linoleic acid (omega-6) generally found in vegan diets can reduce the conversion of alpha-linolenic acid (omega-3) by 50%. DHA is maximized by keeping the omega-6 fatty acids in check and consuming generous portions of omega-3 fatty acid-rich plant foods. (See chapter 4.) Whether this will be sufficient to provide optimal DHA levels in pregnancy is still a question.

For this reason, many experts suggest that pregnant vegans take a direct source of DHA. Fortunately, the original source of DHA is microalgae (tiny sea plants). Today DHA-rich microalgae is being cultured and sold as a supplement. This source of DHA, unlike most fish, is free of contaminants. However, at the present time it is sold only in gel caps; companies are working on alternative ways of marketing DHA. (See sources, page 272.) You can purchase the caps and squeeze the oil out—it is quite tasteless. The suggested intake of DHA in pregnancy ranges from 200-300 mg/day. Regardless of whether or not you opt to supplement with DHA, it is important that you follow the guidelines for optimizing omega-3 intake (page 68). Your minimal requirements for alpha-linolenic acid are double during this time, thus you need to aim for about 4 to 5 grams per day (2 servings from the essential fatty acid group). Two teaspoons of flaxseed oil or two tablespoons of canola oil will provide sufficient omega-3 fatty acids for most pregnant woman.

Supplements for Pregnancy

Although vitamin and mineral supplements are not absolutely necessary if the diet is very well planned and the mother enters pregnancy well nourished, they are generally recommended.* There are some situations when supplements are necessary. Among the more common include:

• being undernourished, underweight, or otherwise nutritionally compromised at conception

• not consuming the necessary amounts of vitamin B_{12}-fortified foods to meet your recommended intakes

---

*Single nutrient supplements can be toxic to the developing baby and are generally best avoided unless medically indicated. There are three notable exceptions: calcium, vitamin B_{12}, and essential fatty acids (specifically DHA).

- not using adequate amounts of vitamin D fortified foods, and/or having limited exposure to sunlight

- having a history of poor iron status or iron levels that are presently below normal

- having a documented nutritional deficiency of any sort

- inability to consume the amounts of foods recommended in the food guide because of nausea, lack of appetite, or any other reason

- smoking. No amount of nutrients can counter the tremendous risk to your baby; however, if you choose to take that risk, supplements are advised.

Table 10.2 Nutrient Increases Recommended for Pregnancy and Lactation

Nutrient	Nonpregnant (19-50 years)	RDA or AI* (AI - in italics)		Percent Increase Over Nonpregnant Needs	
		Pregnant (19-50 years)	Lactating (19-50 years)	Pregnant (19-50 years)	Lactating (19-50 years)
Protein	46-50 g	60 g	62-65 g	20%	24-30%
	55 (+10% ★★)	66 g	68-72 g	20%	24-30%
Minerals					
Iron★★★	32.4 mg	48.6 mg	16.2 mg	50%	0
Zinc	8 mg	11 mg	12 mg	38%	50%
Calcium	*1,000 mg*	*1,000 mg*	*1,000 mg*	*0*	*0*
Magnesium	310-320 mg	350-360 mg	310-320 mg	13%	0
Selenium	55 mcg	60 mcg	70 mcg	9%	27%
Vitamins					
Vitamin A	700 mcg	770 mcg	1,300 mcg	10%	86%
Thiamin	1.1 mg	1.4 mg	1.4 mg	27%	27%
Riboflavin	1.1 mg	1.4 mg	1.6 mg	27%	45%
Niacin	14 mg	18 mg	17 mg	29%	21%
Vitamin B$_6$	1.3 mg	1.9 mg	2.0 mg	46%	54%
Vitamin B$_{12}$	2.4 mcg	2.6 mcg	2.8 mcg	8%	17%
Folic Acid	400 mcg	600 mcg	500 mcg	50%	25%
Vitamin C	75 mg	85 mg	120 mg	13%	60%
Vitamin D	*5 mcg*	*5 mcg*	*5 mcg*	*0*	*0*
Vitamin E	15 mg	15 mg	19 mg	0	27%

* RDA (Recommended Dietary Allowance, U.S.) – *Average daily intake levels sufficient to meet requirements of 97-98% of healthy people.*
AI (Adequate Intakes) – *A recommended daily intake used when RDA cannot be determined with confidence. Based on observations and research on a group (or groups) of healthy people. Nutrients for which AIs are indicated are in italics.*

** *10% is added on to allow for the reduced digestibility of whole plant foods in those individuals who get most of their protein from these sources as opposed to tofu, soymilk, meat substitutes, etc.*
***RDAs for iron are 1.8 times higher for vegetarians than for nonvegetarians.*

NUTRITION CONSIDERATIONS FOR BREAST-FEEDING

There is no better food for the mind and body of the human infant than the warm milk of his/her mother. It is exquisitely designed to provide the perfect balance of nutrients and protective substances for optimal growth and development. The rate of breast-feeding is significantly higher among vegan populations, and it continues for longer periods of time. In general, we recommend that you breast-feed your baby for a minimum of one year and preferably for two years or more.

Common Concerns of Nursing Mothers

How much does my diet affect the nutritional composition of my breast milk?

The nutrient composition of your diet definitely affects the composition of your milk, but not to the extent that many people would imagine. In general, minerals are not greatly affected by your diet (with the exception of iodine, manganese, and possibly selenium) and insufficient intakes result in depletion of your body stores. Vitamin levels in breast milk are affected by your diet (with the possible exceptions of folate and vitamin K) and a low dietary intake can mean insufficient amounts in your breast milk. It is interesting to note that what you eat doesn't have much of an impact on the total protein, carbohydrate, or fat content of your milk, but it has a huge impact on the type of fat in your milk. Vegans generally have only about one-half of the long-chain omega-3 fatty acids in their breast milk as nonvegetarians. The degree to which this affects the infant is not known. Formulas in the U.S. and Canada do not contain any of these long-chain fatty acids (although many other countries fortify formulas with these nutrients), so breast-fed vegan babies get considerably more than formula-fed infants. However, we are still uncertain about what is optimal, and from research studies to date, it appears that the higher levels of DHA are better for both visual acuity and brain development. Thus, getting sufficient omega-3 fatty acids in the diet is of utmost importance during this time.

What are the most serious potential pitfalls of a vegan diet for breast-feeding?

Without any doubt the two most common pitfalls are not insuring sufficient vitamin B_{12} or vitamin D. Recall that vitamin B_{12} stores in an infant of a mother with insufficient B_{12} intake will last only a short period. If sufficient B_{12} is not consumed during lactation, the infant will very likely end up with a deficiency (see section on vitamin B_{12} in pregnancy). The recommended intake of vitamin B_{12} in lactation is 2.8 mcg/day. Vitamin D deficiency is not uncommon in populations that have limited warm sun exposure and do not consume vitamin D-fortified foods or supplements. If you do not get sufficient vitamin D, your infant may end up with rickets unless he/she gets sufficient sunlight. Many authorities recommend that all breast-fed infants receive a vitamin D supplement of 5 mcg (200 IU) per day.

Do I need to take supplements while breast-feeding?

When you breast-feed your baby, your nutrient needs are similar to what they were during your pregnancy. (See Table 10.2). It is often recommended that lactating mothers continue on a prenatal vitamin supplement for a couple of months after the baby is born, then switch to a regular adult multivitamin/ mineral preparation with vitamin D and vitamin B_{12}. Some experts also recommend a DHA supplement of 200-300 mg/day to help ensure optimal levels of DHA in breast milk. (Milk levels of this nutrient respond very well to supplementation.)

Can my baby be allergic or sensitive to my milk or to foods that I am eating?

Allergy to breast milk is virtually nonexistent; however, your baby can certainly react to foods you eat. Indeed, your infant may become sensitized to a protein prior to birth.

If your baby has colic, eczema, chronic congestion, or GI distress, it could be something you are eating that is causing the reaction, particularly if there is a history of allergy in your family. The foods most commonly associated with these kinds of reactions are cow's milk (causing an estimated 75-80% of the cases), eggs, wheat, soy, citrus fruits, nuts, and chocolate. Try eliminating the offending food from your diet for seven days and observe the baby's reaction. It may take a little perseverance to track the down the offending food.

While most foods can be consumed during breast-feeding, some foods can cause distress, especially if eaten in large amounts. The foods commonly cited as causing problems are those with strong flavors, such as garlic, onion, hot spices, soda pop, MSG, licorice, and artificial sweeteners.

Are there any toxic substances that I need to take special care to avoid?

In general, the guidelines concerning toxic substances are much the same as they are for pregnancy. Caffeine and alcohol should be kept to a minimum. Infants should never be exposed to nicotine—it can cause gas, irritability, and difficulty sleeping in babies, in addition to reducing your milk supply. Stick to organic and local foods if at all possible. You will be delighted to know that vegans tend to have lower levels of pesticides such as DDT and PCBs in their blood and in their breast milk. In The Farm study mentioned earlier in this chapter, the highest level of 17 chemicals in the breast milk was lower than the lowest level in the general population. In fact, the vegans had only 1–2% of the amounts found in the nonvegetarians. These findings have been supported by at least three other studies, with no studies suggesting otherwise.

PLANNING AN ADEQUATE PRENATAL DIET

In planning an adequate diet for pregnancy and lactation, you need to increase your nutrient intake significantly, while only increasing calories moderately. The 2,500 kcal diet provided on page 159 is appropriate for most pregnant and lactating women. (This will need to be adapted for those requiring slightly lower or greater energy intakes.) By following this pattern, you can be confident that all nutrient needs are met. In general, you can follow the vegan food guide, but modify your number of servings as suggested in Table 10.3 below.

Note: If you are a very small person who is relatively inactive, you may need the lower ranges of servings for each group, while if you are a large-framed person who is very active, you may need more food than what is suggested here. Adjust your intakes to ensure sufficient weight gain.

Table 10.3   Food Guide Modifications for Pregnancy and Lactation

Pregnancy		Lactation	
Bean and bean alternates	3–4 servings	Bean and bean alternates	3–4 servings
Grain products	7–11 servings	Grain products	8–11 servings
Vegetables	4 or more servings	Vegetables	5 or more servings
Fruits	4 or more servings	Fruits	4 or more servings
Calcium-rich foods	6–8 servings	Calcium-rich foods	6–8 servings
Essential fatty acid sources	2 servings	Essential fatty acid sources	2 servings
B_{12} source	fortified foods or supplements	B_{12} source	fortified foods or supplements
Vitamin D source	fortified foods or supplements	Vitamin D source	fortified foods or supplements

SELECTED REFERENCES

See also general references for the whole book on page 276.

Sanders, T.A.B. and S. Reddy. "The influence of a vegetarian diet on the fatty acid composition of human milk and the essential fatty acid status of the infant." *J. Pediatr.* 120 No. 4 P.2 (1992):S71–S76.

Specker, B.L. "Nutritional concerns of lactating women consuming vegetarian diets." *Am. J. Clin. Nutr.* 59(suppl) (1994):1182S-6(S).

Suitor, C.W., C. Olson, and J. Wilson. "Nutrition care during pregnancy and lactation: New guidelines from the Institute of Medicine." *J. Am. Diet. Assoc.* 93 No. 4 (1993): 478–479.

CHAPTER
11

Growing Vegans...birth through adolescence

One of the greatest tests of the adequacy of a vegan diet arises when it is given to the most vulnerable among us—infants and toddlers. As parents, we are committed to nourishing our children well. As we set out to accomplish this task, we must remember that infants and children have very different nutritional needs than adults. They are growing rapidly and require more protein, fat, vitamins, and minerals per pound of body weight than adults. Vegan diets, which are naturally less energy-dense (higher in bulk and often lower in fat), need to be adapted to support the unique nutritional needs of our children. We must move away from the adult model, focused on the prevention of degenerative diseases, towards a model that places priority on optimal growth and development. In so doing, we can be confident that vegan diets can pass the test with ease.

VEGAN INFANTS AND TODDLERS... FORMULA FOR SUCCESS (0-3 YEARS OF AGE)

Babies will grow at an unprecedented rate during these first few years of life. Mother Nature gives us tremendous support in nourishing our children during this time of complete dependency. We must take it upon ourselves to gain a thorough understanding of the nutritional needs of human infants, the potential pitfalls of vegan diets, and how to build a vegan diet that really works.

The formula for success is not so much different that it is for nonvegetarian babies (although all babies are vegetarians for the first 6 to 8 months of life!). There are four parts to the formula:

Formula for Success

Breast Milk + Vitamins B_{12} and D + Appropriate Solids + Sufficient Calories
= One Healthy Vegan Baby

1. Breast-feed your baby.

Breast milk is the only food your baby needs for the first 4 to 6 months of life. Continue to breast-feed your baby for a minimum of one year and preferably for a full two years or more. Breast milk is specifically designed to meet the needs of the human infant, just as the milk of other mammals is specifically designed to meet the needs of their young. The advantages of breast-feeding extend far beyond an ideal balance of nutrients for your infant. It provides immune protection, reduces risk of allergies, decreases the incidence of respiratory, gastrointestinal, and other illnesses, helps to create a wonderful bond between you and your infant, and is extraordinarily convenient and economical—always ready and at the right temperature! The benefits of breast-feeding continue to provide these advantages for as long as you breast-feed. (Natural human weaning occurs between 2-4 years of age.)

If you stop breast-feeding or decrease the number of times that you breast-feed to less than three times a day, an iron-fortified commercial infant formula should be used as the replacement until your baby is at least one year of age. Many experts, including the Canadian Paediatric Society and Dietitians of Canada, recommend that vegans continue on breast milk or formula until they are at least two years of age. The rationale for using formula in the 12-24 month period is that commercial formulas are modeled after breast milk and thus include most of the nutrients provided by breast milk (with the exception of long-chain omega-3 fatty acids) in amounts that are especially suited to the growth and development needs of infants. Breast milk and formula contain the amino acids carnitine and taurine, which are not present in plant foods and may be beneficial for infants. These amino acids are produced from other amino acids in the body but the production appears to be reduced in infancy. If you do decide not to breast-feed or use formula during the 12-24 month period, fortified soymilk is your best alternative. It should contain calcium, vitamin B_{12}, and vitamin D.

Unfortified nondairy beverages should not be used as a primary milk source for infants. These milks will not provide the nutrients necessary for optimal growth and development and could lead to malnutrition, especially during the weaning period. Fortified nonsoy beverages contain minimal protein and are not generally recommended as primary milks during the second year of life.

2. Provide your baby with a reliable source of vitamin B_{12} and vitamin D.

Vitamin B_{12} and vitamin D deficiencies are two potentially serious pitfalls for vegan infants. It is extremely important that reliable sources of both of these nutrients be provided.

VITAMIN B$_{12}$

Breast-fed vegan infants should receive a vitamin B$_{12}$ supplement of at least 0.3 mcg per day from the second week of life until at least 2 years of age, or until such time that enough vitamin B$_{12}$ is provided by fortified foods.

There are no reliable plant sources of vitamin B$_{12}$. Unlike adults, infants do not have significant B$_{12}$ stores and can rapidly become deficient if a reliable source of vitamin B$_{12}$ is not provided in the diet. Severe B$_{12}$ deficiency results in weakness, nerve damage, muscular wasting, and potentially irreversible brain damage. Infant B$_{12}$ deficiency is a tragedy that is completely preventable. **Don't take chances—make sure your baby gets a reliable source of vitamin B$_{12}$.**

While it is possible for an infant to receive sufficient vitamin B$_{12}$ from a vegan mother's breast milk, the available B$_{12}$ appears to be dependent on the mother's intake. If the mother's intake is low, the baby could become deficient. Considering the devastating consequences of B$_{12}$ deficiency, experts advise supplemental B$_{12}$ for all vegan babies. If your baby is formula-fed, vitamin B$_{12}$ supplements are not necessary, as formula is fortified with this nutrient.

Vegan Alert!

The only acceptable alternative to breast milk in infancy is commercial infant formula. Unfortunately, there are no formulas (that we can find) on the market today that are completely vegan. Several soy-based formulas are available; however, they all contain vitamin D$_3$ (animal-source vitamin D) and some varieties also contain animal fat. It is also of interest that soybeans used in infant formulas are not organic and almost always come from genetically modified crops.

DO NOT MAKE YOUR OWN INFANT FORMULA.

If there is a "formula for disaster," homemade infant formula is it. Cases of malnutrition in vegan infants are frequently linked to homemade formulas. These milks have numerous inadequacies, the first and foremost being a lack of calories (Breast milk and formula provide about 63-71 cal/100 ml, while homemade formula contains as little as 14 cal/ 100 ml). In addition, homemade formula generally lacks protein, fat (including essential fatty acids), taurine and carnitine (important amino acids needed in infancy), vitamin B$_{12}$, vitamin D, iron, zinc, calcium, and numerous other vitamins and minerals.

VITAMIN D

Most breast-fed vegan infants should be given a vitamin D supplement of 5 mcg per day (10 mcg per day in northern climates), beginning during the first week of life.

There are three factors that affect an infant's vitamin D status: levels at birth, vitamin D intake, and exposure to sunlight. Status at birth is entirely dependent on the mother's vitamin D status. Vitamin D intake varies with the source of "milk" provided and with the amount of fortified foods used after solids are introduced. (Some fortified soymilks include the vegan form called vitamin D_2.) Breast milk is not a reliable source of this nutrient, and formula is fortified with vitamin D_3 (animal source). While warm sunlight can provide sufficient vitamin D, it is recommended that clothing or sunscreen be used to protect baby's sensitive skin from damaging ultraviolet light. However, infants exposed to warm sunshine will make some vitamin D, as sunscreens and clothing rarely provide complete coverage. The bottom line is that the most reliable source of vitamin D for vegan infants is a supplement containing vitamin D_2. (To find plant-source vitamin D, you may have to phone a few pharmacies; see Chapter 7 for more information.)

3. Introduce appropriate solid foods when your baby is four to six months.

Most infants have no need for solid foods before six months of age; however, some are ready by four or five months, particularly if they are growing very quickly. Many parents are tempted to delay solids well beyond six months. This is not generally advised, as solid foods provide extra energy and nutrients that are needed at this time (protein, iron, and zinc), and the experience of new foods is important to infant development in other respects. When your baby is ready for solids, you'll know it! Here are a few of the signs:

- constantly hungry, even after nursing 8 or 10 times in a day
- ability to sit up and give signs of satiety like turning his/her head away
- ability to move solids to the back of the mouth and swallow without spitting most of it out

There are no hard and fast rules regarding the order of introduction for solid foods after six months of age, although the sequence usually recommended is infant cereals, vegetables, fruits, then protein-rich foods. This sequence takes into consideration both the nutritional value of these first foods and the maturity of the infant's gastrointestinal system. The rationale for beginning with iron-fortified infant cereal is that it is highly digestible, has a relatively low allergenic potential, and is a good source of iron, which may be lacking at this stage. In breast-fed babies, iron stores start to decline after about six months of age and even earlier for premature babies. With the small amounts of highly absorbable iron from breast milk and the iron stores that are present in the newborn at birth, it is possible for infants to maintain normal iron levels until they are nine months old or more; however, iron deficiency is the most common nutritional deficiency in infants and even marginal deficiency can slow development and cause irritability.

Zinc is also a nutrient of concern in vegan diets as plant foods tend to be moderate sources of zinc and absorption is a little lower than from animal foods. A lack of zinc in the diet can result in growth failure. (See Chapter 6 for more information on zinc). The best zinc sources during the first year are human milk, soy formula, legumes, and whole grains. Nuts, seeds, and their butters are generally not advised during the first year due to potential for allergy and choking but are good zinc sources after that. Butters are fine in creams or foods for infants where allergy does not run in the family and who don't show allergic reactions to new foods. So how can parents ensure sufficient zinc for vegan infants? Keep breast-feeding; breast milk provides just under 1 mg of zinc per cup and the absorption is over 40%—higher than for cow's milk, for-

Table 11.1 Introducing Solid Foods

Age	Foods to Introduce	Specifics	How Much?
4-6 months	Iron-fortified infant cereal	Offer hypoallergenic single-grain cereals such as rice and barley first, followed by other single-grain cereals, then mixed cereals	Begin with 1 tsp. (5 ml) of cereal. Gradually increase to ¼ to ½ cup (60-120 ml).
6-7 months	Vegetables Fruits	Vegetables: cook and puree vegetables (straining is not necessary). Fruits: peel and mash soft, fresh fruits; cook and puree harder ripe fruits.	Begin with 1 tsp. (5 ml) vegetables, gradually increase to 2-4 Tbsp. (30-60 ml).
7-8 months	Protein-rich foods Fruit juices	Protein-rich foods: well-mashed tofu and well-cooked and pureed legumes Fruit juice: unsweetened fruit juice	Begin with 1 tsp. (5 ml) and gradually increase to 2-3 (30-45 ml) Tbsp. at a meal. Begin with an ounce, gradually increase to not more than 8 oz. (240 ml)/day.
8-9 months	Finger foods Teething foods Whole grains	Finger foods: cooked fruit and vegetable pieces; ripe fruits and vegetable chunks; bread crusts, dry toast, rusks, frozen bagel pieces. Whole grains: rice, quinoa, millet, pasta, or other well-cooked grains (mashed)	Offer 2-4 Tbsp. (30-60 ml) of fruit of vegetable chunks, ½ slice of dry toast, or ¼ bagel. Begin with 1 Tbsp. grains, gradually increasing to 2-3 Tbsp. (30-45 ml)/meal.
10-12 months	Family food Veggie "meats," Gluten Nut/seed butters/creams	Family food: stews, casseroles, etc. Veggie "meats": patties, lunch slices, etc. Gluten: commercial or homemade Nut and seed creams: blend nut butter with soymilk, water, or juice	Start with 1 tsp. (5 ml) of a new food. Gradually increase to provide a total of about ¾ to 1 cup (180-240 ml) of solid food per meal.

mula, and most other foods. Use whole grains, serve legumes every day and make Dad's Sneaky Pudding regularly (page 194).

ADDITIONAL CONSIDERATIONS WHEN INTRODUCING SOLID FOODS

Observe for allergies

Offer one new food at a time, leaving at least three to four days in between to observe for allergic reactions and to see how well the new food is digested. If there is a family history of food allergy, wait six to seven days before introducing a new food. If there is a strong family history of allergy to a particular food, it should be avoided for the first one to three years of life.

Ensure sufficient iron

If you do not wish to use commercial iron-fortified infant cereal, you can provide your infant with an iron supplement (1 mg/kg [2.2 lbs.] body weight per day) to a maximum of 10 mg/day until 12 months of age.

Avoid potentially harmful foods or beverages

- Serve foods without added sugar or salt.
- Avoid presweetened or fried foods or foods with added hydrogenated fats.
- Avoid foods commonly associated with choking. These include: whole grapes, hard candies, cough drops, whole tofu dogs (slice in half or quarters, lengthwise), popcorn, nuts and seeds, nut and seed butters, except as an ingredient in foods, until 12 months.
- Limit juice to about 8 oz. (240 ml) per day, as excessive juice can reduce intake of more nutrient-dense solid foods and cause diarrhea.
- Minimize pesticides and herbicides in the diet. Use organic foods when possible. Be sure to wash all produce very thoroughly, as it may be contaminated if manure is used as fertilizer.

Introduce textured foods before 9 months

Add finger foods and some textured (mashed) foods before nine months of age, as this is the critical age at which the baby develops preferences for different textures.

4. *Make sure your little one gets sufficient calories.*

A lack of calories is the main reason diets fail to adequately nourish vegan toddlers. Babies are most vulnerable right around the time of weaning (usually between one and three years). Poorly planned vegan diets can be too high in bulk and too low in fat and calories to support the rapid growth and development of infants and toddlers. Recall that breast milk, the ideal food for infants, derives approximately 54% of its calories from fat and contains about 175 calories per cup. This is nature's way of telling us that babies need a more energy-dense diet. As your baby begins to eat more solid foods and drink less breast milk, it is important to ensure that the foods selected provide an appropriate balance of fat, energy, and nutrients. To be sure that your baby gets enough calories and all the necessary nutrients, follow the Vegan Food Guide for Toddlers on the next page and see Table 11.2 for the recommended intakes of specific nutrients for the one- to three-year-old child.

ENERGY-PACKED TIPS FOR TODDLERS

- Continue to breast-feed or provide an alternate such as fortified soymilk. Breast milk (or alternate) is an excellent source of energy and nutrients, and is low in fiber.
- Include plenty of higher-fat foods in the diet. Tofu, smooth nut butters and creams, mashed avocado, soy yogurt, puddings, and soups made with fortified soymilk or formula, and moderate amounts of olive, canola, and flax oil are important sources of fat for the vegan infant.
- Avoid excessive fiber in the diet. Concentrated fiber products such as raw wheat bran, bran cereals, and bran muffins should not be used for vegan infants. Do use mainly whole grains, as they contribute important minerals to the diet. Lesser amounts of refined breads and cereals, such as enriched pasta, can help limit total fiber.
- Serve regular meals with snacks in between. Infants have very small stomachs and should be fed 5-6 times a day. A few energy-packed favorites include mashed bananas with soy yogurt, bread or crackers with tofu spread, and homemade muffins.
- Pull out all the stops and serve Sneaky Dad's Pudding (page 194).

The Vegan Food Guide for Toddlers
(1–3 years)

Include a wide variety of foods in the diet of your vegan toddler. By selecting foods according to this guide, you can be sure your little vegan dynamo is well nourished! (Quantities given in each food group are equal to 1 toddler-size serving.)

Calcium-Rich Foods
20–24 oz. (600–720 ml) of breast milk, commercial soy formula,
or full-fat fortified soymilk (or a combination)
This will allow for three 6–8 oz. (180–240 ml) servings of milk.

Breads and Cereals
4–6 oz. iron-fortified infant cereal
(can be mixed with porridge, cold cereals, pancakes, muffins, etc.)
PLUS
2–4 toddler-size servings of other breads and cereals per day:
½ slice of bread
¼ cup (60 ml) rice, quinoa, enriched pasta, or other cooked grain
½ cup (120 ml) cold cereal

Vegetables
2–3 toddler-size servings per day:
½ cup (120 ml) salad or other raw vegetable pieces
¼ cup (60 ml) cooked vegetables
⅓ cup (80 ml) vegetable juice

Fruits
2–3 toddler-size servings per day:
½–1 fresh fruit
¼ cup (60 ml) cooked fruit
¼ cup (60 ml) fruit juice

Beans and Bean Alternates
2 toddler-size servings per day:
¼ cup (60 ml) cooked legumes
2 oz. (55 g) tofu
½–1 oz. (14–28 g) veggie "meat"
(i.e., 1 deli slice; 2 Tbsp. veggie ground round)
1½ Tbsp. nut or seed butter

Vitamin B_{12}
Aim for 1 mcg B_{12} in fortified foods. (See page 128 for sources.)

Vitamin D
Get sufficient sunlight, or at least 5 mcg vitamin D from fortified foods or supplements

Essential Fatty Acids
Aim for 1.1 g of omega-3 fatty acids/day. (See page 66 for sources.)

VEGAN CHILDREN... THE CHALLENGES (4-10 YEARS OF AGE)

The primary dietary goal for vegan children is to ensure that the diet is nutritionally adequate. However, as parents we strive to provide the very best opportunity for optimal health—a diet that will enable our children to grow and develop to their fullest physical, mental, and emotional potential. We hope food will be a joy for them, something to appreciate and celebrate. Be assured that a vegan diet can accomplish all of these things—thousands of wonderfully healthy vegan children can testify to that!

Making sure a child is well nourished can be quite a challenge for parents who are faced with picky eaters, poor growth, food allergies, diarrhea, and a society that caters to nonvegetarians. In this section we will present various common challenges and how we can best overcome them.

Challenge #1: The Poorly Planned Vegan Diet

Ashley is 10 years old and has been a near-vegan for about eight months. She decided to eliminate animal products from her diet after doing a class project on the reasons people become vegetarian. She has always loved animals and didn't need much convincing to stop eating them. Ashley's current diet consists primarily of refined carbohydrates, fruits, and vegetables. She eats toast with margarine and jam in the morning; soda crackers, a granola bar, and some fresh fruit for lunch, and whatever nonmeat items her Mom makes for dinner (i.e., potatoes, pasta, rice and vegetables, bread). She drinks water, juice, soft drinks, and Kool-Aid. Ashley is normal weight (32 kg/70 lbs) and has a healthy appetite. However, her parents are very concerned about her refusal to eat foods that they have always considered to be essential in a healthy diet for children—milk, eggs, and meat. They wonder how Ashley will ever get the calcium, iron, and protein she needs to grow and build strong bones.

The Solution? Add substitutes for milk and meat to Ashley's diet.

Ashley is the perfect candidate for nutrition counseling from a registered dietitian who specializes in vegan and vegetarian nutrition. She/he will be able to teach Ashley how to get the important nutrients from plant foods that she used to get from meat and milk.

The pitfalls of Ashley's diet are among the most common that vegan and many nonvegan children face. Her food choices will jeopardize her health in the long term. Upon analysis of Ashley's diet, we find that she is consuming sufficient calories but getting too little protein, calcium, zinc, vitamin B_{12}, and vitamin D. While total iron intake is borderline, there is still reason to be concerned about her iron status. Among the most effective tools Ashley will find to improve the nutrient content of her diet are the Vegan Food Guide (pages 154-55) and the Dietary Reference Intakes for Children on page 193. Let's consider the primary nutrients of concern in her current diet.

PROTEIN, IRON, AND ZINC

Total protein needs are generally easily met by any diet that provides enough calories. However, with poor dietary choices (ie., eating foods that are mainly fat and sugar, and/or avoiding beans and bean alternates), insufficient protein intake may result. When total protein intake is questionable, specific essential amino acids may be lacking (especially lysine, methionine, and cysteine). Not surprisingly, this is exactly what was found with Ashley's diet.

Children need about 1-1.2 grams of protein per kg body weight. For vegan children, a little extra (10-20% for older children and 20-30% for children from 4-6 years) is added to the usual recommendations to help compensate for the reduced digestibility of plant protein. This increases recommended intakes to 1.1-1.6 grams protein per kg body weight. Considering Ashley's age and weight, she needs about 38 grams of protein a day (32 kg x 1.2 g/day), a protein intake easily achieved by most vegan children. Her diet provides about 28-30 grams of protein—about 10 grams less than what she needs. The specific amino acids methionine and cysteine are sufficient from all of the grains she is eating, but lysine is only about two-thirds of recommended levels. Lysine is high in legumes, but low in grains and most other plant foods and particularly important during growth.

Both the quantity and quality of protein in Ashley's diet can be improved by adding 1-2 servings of beans and bean alternates to her daily diet. One serving provides about 12-15 grams of protein, depending on her choices. Here are a few ways Ashley can get those beans and alternates added:

Breakfast

- Eat peanut butter or almond butter on toast in the morning.
- Have cereal with soymilk instead of toast for a change.

Lunch

- Instead of crackers, bring a sandwich with 2-3 veggie deli slices (4-5 g soy protein per slice).
- Use a spread on the crackers such as sunflower spread. (See the excellent spreads and other tasty recipes in *Cooking Vegetarian,* Melina and Forest, Wiley 1998.)
- Bring some soy yogurt and pistachios, pumpkin seeds, or almonds.

Dinner

- In place of meat, have a commercial veggie patty.
- Use veggie ground round in favorite dishes that call for hamburger.
- Add cubed tofu to stir fries, marinate it in any favorite sauce for the BBQ, or bake it in the oven.
- Use refried beans in tacos, tortillas, and as a dip for taco chips.
- Eat canned baked beans; experiment with less familiar beans in soups and stews.

By including these more concentrated protein foods, Ashley will automatically improve her intake of iron and zinc. While iron intake was marginally sufficient, the additional amount provided would help to compensate for poor absorption. The zinc in Ashley's diet is only about one-third of her recommended intake (about 3.4 mg). Adding legumes, tofu, nuts, and beans will significantly improve her zinc intake. In addition to the beans and bean alternates, Ashley could also add dried fruits, whole grains (instead of refined grains), and fortified breakfast cereals to her diet.

CALCIUM AND VITAMIN D

Ashley's total calcium intake is 381 mg or about 30% of what she needs (AI = 1,300 mg). Her vitamin D intake is 0.25 mcg, only 5% of her needs, although this may not be a concern if she is getting 10-15 minutes of warm summer sun on her face and forearms each day. With Ashley being very close to puberty, these low calcium and vitamin D intakes could seriously jeopardize her ability to build and maintain strong bones.

To improve calcium intake, Ashley can rely on food or a combination of food and supplements. It is highly recommended that food sources be her first option. Ashley needs to eat 8 servings from the Fortified Soymilk and Alternates group each day (1 serving = ½ cup/120 ml fortified soymilk). Great choices are calcium-fortified beverages (soymilk, rice milk, orange juice, etc.), calcium-rich greens, figs, almonds, and blackstrap molasses.

VITAMIN B_{12}

Plant foods are not reliable sources of vitamin B_{12}. The only ways that Ashley will get this vital nutrient is by eating fortified foods or taking a supplement. Vitamin B_{12} food fortification varies dramatically among countries. Significant dietary sources in North America include Red Star Brand Vegetarian Support Formula (formerly T-6635+) nutritional yeast, some cereals, meat substitutes, and nondairy milks. Ashley needs 1.2 mcg of vitamin B_{12} a day. (For Red Star yeast flakes, that amounts to about 1 rounded teaspoon.)

OMEGA-3 FATTY ACIDS

Omega-3 fatty acids tend to be low in the vegan diet. Ashley's food choices provide only about 25% of the minimal recommended intakes. Most children need about 2 grams per day. This amount of omega-3 can be obtained from 1 tsp. of flaxseed oil, 3 Tbsp. walnuts, or 4 tsp. canola oil.

Challenge #2: The Slow-Growing Child

Four-year-old Kevin was doing very well on his vegan diet (very near the 50th percentile for height and weight) until he stopped nursing about a year-and-a-half ago. Since then he has only gained 3 pounds and is now at the 10th percentile for height and weight. Kevin's parents are very health conscious vegans and provide him with an abundance of fresh organic fruits, vegetables, and their juices. They don't use any refined grains, but do use numerous whole grains including brown rice, oat groats, kamut and spelt berries, barley, millet, and quinoa. They enjoy a great variety of legumes and sprouts. Concentrated oils are not often used, but some sprouted nuts and seeds are added to patties and breakfast cereals. Kevin drinks 1½ cups of fortified soymilk each day and has a good appetite. He eats three meals plus two snacks and takes a multivitamin/mineral supplement including iron, zinc, vitamin D, and vitamin B_{12} every day. What more can Kevin's parents do to ensure he grows and develops as he should?

The solution? Add fat and calories and reduce bulk.

Kevin's parents have done so many things right; they are feeding him a wonderful mix of grains, legumes, vegetables, and fruits. They make sure he gets fortified soymilk twice a day, and they provide him with a supplement for extra iron, zinc, vitamin B_{12}, and vitamin D. While Kevin's diet provides a reasonable intake of protein, vitamins, and minerals, it is too high in bulk and too low in fat to support his caloric needs. On a quick analysis, Kevin's diet is only 17% fat and contains only 1,150 calories. At Kevin's age, he needs about twice as much fat and about 1,500-1,600 calories a day. To accomplish this:

- Increase fortified soymilk to 2-3 cups a day (a serving with each meal).
- Add higher-fat, lower-fiber plant foods. Tofu, avocados, and nuts, seeds, and their butters are all great options. You get them all rolled into one delicious package in Sneaky Dad's Pudding (page 194).
- Include some oil in the diet. Use oil in salad dressings and in baking and cooking.
- Use cooked vegetables and fruits in addition to raw. Make sure legumes are thoroughly cooked.

- Use some processed grain products such as bread, pasta, cereal, etc., instead of strictly whole grains. Children like these foods and will usually eat more spaghetti than kamut berries or quinoa, thus will end up eating more calories. These foods will also help to reduce the bulk in their diet.
- Offer appealing and wholesome snacks two or three times a day. Nutritious puddings, squares, muffins, loaves, cookies, crackers and soy cheese, mashed avocado,

> *What are percentiles for height and weight and how meaningful are they?*
>
> Height and weight charts tell you how your child's height and weight compare with the general population. If they are at the 50th percentile for height, it means that 50% of children are taller and the other 50% are shorter. The charts are based on the growth of nonvegetarian children and are on the web at www.cdc.gov/growthcharts. Some vegan children tend to grow a little more slowly after weaning, but catch up at around 10 years of age. Unless a child is under the 5th percentile, there is not generally a cause for concern. However, changes in your child's growth pattern can signal a problem. This is the case for Kevin—he was at the 50th percentile and is now down to the 10th percentile. His growth is faltering and it is important to determine why.

flavored tofu or nut butter, little sandwiches, soy yogurt with granola, soy shakes, and dried fruit and nut mixes all make great options. (Note: Eating dried fruits can lead to tooth decay; be sure to brush teeth after eating.)

Challenge #3: The Picky Eater

Five-year-old James has been a near-vegan for two years, prior to which he was a lacto-ovo vegetarian. James has always been a picky eater and tends to have a poor appetite. He refuses to eat dinner a good part of the time and demands his favorite foods. At the present time, it is peanut butter and banana sandwiches and orange juice. That's it for breakfast, lunch, and dinner! While he will usually eat a greater variety of fruits, he refuses most vegetables. James also usually drinks about two to three cups of fortified soymilk each day (although not since his latest food jag). His parents are terribly concerned about his nutrient intake, but they don't want to turn dinner into a battleground. They generally end up giving in and letting him eat whatever he likes. They figure at least this way he is eating something. How can James' parents improve his eating habits?

The solution? Provide a wide range of appealing, nutritious foods, and avoid short-order cooking.

Don't concern yourself with James' food jags. They are generally short-lived and the nutrient intake during these jags is rarely as bad as we as imagine. To provide some perspective on this, we analyzed James' diet of four peanut butter and banana sandwiches on whole wheat bread and three glasses of orange juice. He managed to get 1,400 calories, almost double the necessary protein, 43% of the iron, 114% of the zinc, 65% of the riboflavin, 168% of the niacin, and plenty of selenium, magnesium, potassium, and thiamin. He is definitely low in calcium, vitamin D, and B_{12}, but these are normally provided in his soymilk. So while eating such a limited diet is not ideal by any stretch, it is not worth losing any sleep over. Of greater concern is James' behavior around meal times. It is important to note that poor appetite can be the result of a zinc deficiency, so this should be ruled out. If poor zinc status is part of the problem, zinc supplementation will be required. Zinc supplements can interfere with other nutrients, so unless medically indicated, don't provide him with a single nutrient zinc supplement. If you want to give extra zinc just to see if it helps, use a multivitamin/mineral supplement that includes 5-10 mg zinc; also see the list of zinc-rich foods on page 115. If zinc intake is fine, begin to work on the food behaviors. The following ideas will help to make meal times less of a struggle for all of you.

• Do not short-order cook. James is no dummy. He has learned that if he refuses dinner items, he will get his favorites. Breaking the cycle may take a little perseverance. Serve what you have prepared for dinner. If James completely refuses to eat, calmly remove the dishes after everyone is finished eating. You may wish to cover his plate, store it in the refrigerator, and offer it later should he want something to eat. Don't fall into the trap of letting him have whatever he wants an hour after dinner. Don't worry, James won't starve himself.

• Let James decide how much he is going to eat. You control what foods are being served—let him have control over how much he is going to eat. This will do a great deal to avert mealtime battles.

• Consider food preferences when meal planning. Do include at least one item that your child enjoys at each meal. Everyone has likes and dislikes, and these should be respected. However, they are usually limited to a few foods and should not extend to a whole group from the Vegan Food Guide (pages 154-55). If food dislikes seem excessive, they are probably more about power struggles than about food.

• Make food appealing. Include a variety of colors, textures, and flavors with meals. For example, very moist mashed potatoes, crispy barbecued tofu, and raw or steamed carrots and broccoli.

• Reinforce desirable behavior. Pay attention to James when he is not complaining about dinner. Include him in your conversations.

To improve vegetable and fruit intake:

- Encourage an interest in vegetables and fruits by growing some in your own garden or on your balcony. Get James involved in preparing vegetable salads.
- Provide a plate of raw veggies, with or without a dip. Don't make a big deal of it, just put it out. Little veggie plates are a great complement to a meal or may be set out prior to dinner, when youngsters wander by the kitchen to see what's cooking. Children who aren't so keen on cooked vegetables are often glad to munch on finger foods like carrot sticks, raw broccoli, and red peppers.
- Add grated carrots and/or zucchini to baked goods such as muffins and to loaves and patties.
- Puree vegetables to make "cream soups" and to add to spaghetti sauces.
- Throw out the rule book about how meals should look. If James wants frozen peas and raw carrots instead of cooked, great! He'll save on the nutrients that would have been lost in the cooking water.

Challenge #4: Soy Allergy

Five-year-old Adrian has an allergy to soy. His response to soy exposure has included abdominal cramps, diarrhea, vomiting, irritability, and hives. Adrian's mom breast-fed him for almost four years and avoided soy in her diet during this time. Adrian eats a wide variety of foods but rarely eats very large portions of anything. How can Adrian's parents be sure he gets enough high-quality, digestible protein without using soy?

The Solution? Determine if the allergy still exists, and if it does, find substitutes for soy.

It is important to recognize that most allergies in infancy are due to an immaturity of the digestive lining which allows proteins into the bloodstream. The lining matures at about four years of age, and the allergy generally disappears. When an allergy develops after the age of three years, it is less likely to be outgrown, especially with potentially life-threatening anaphylactic reactions (although anaphylactic reactions to soy are extremely rare). So, as difficult as it might seem, it is important Adrian be challenged to see if the allergy has disappeared. A challenge involves giving a small amount of soy (e.g., soymilk in a muffin) and if no reaction occurs, gradually increasing the dose. His parents may be very pleasantly surprised to learn that Adrian's allergy is gone. *Note: Challenges should never be done for any food suspected of causing an anaphylactic reaction, unless medically supervised.*

If the allergy persists, it is worth challenging small amounts of soy in foods such as soy lecithin, soy oil, or miso to see if these might be safe. If you are certain soy has got to be removed completely, do not despair. There are over 20 varieties of legumes commonly used, and several fortified nondairy, grain, and potato-based beverages available.

REPLACEMENTS FOR SOY

- *Instead of soymilk*: Use fortified rice milk or other fortified nondairy milks. As grain and potato-based milks are lower in protein and trace minerals, Adrian needs to get these nutrients from other foods such as legumes, nuts, and seeds.
- *Instead of tofu and soy-based "meats"*: Use legumes; you have huge options here, many of which can be sprouted; also include nuts, seeds, gluten and commercial grain/ vegetable patties.
- Legumes come in many different flavors and textures, so try a wide variety to see which ones are especially appealing to Adrian. Legumes may be sprouted or cooked. (For improved digestibility, cook well.) They make a great base for loaves, patties, dips, and sandwich spreads and wonderful additions to soups and stews.
- Nuts and seeds are great on their own, as butters or creams, patties and loaves (ground nuts provide excellent binding power), and in baked goods.
- Gluten, made from wheat protein, is quite low in fiber and also makes wonderful vegan roasts, cutlets, and veggie burgers. You can add chick-pea flour to homemade gluten to improve its nutrient content.

The Question of Supplements

Vegan children have no need for nutritional supplements if the Vegan Food Guide (pages 154-55) is followed and appropriate amounts of fortified foods are used. If fortified foods are not used in sufficient quantity, the following supplements are required:

- *Vitamin B_{12}:* 2 mcg/day
- *Vitamin D:* 5 mcg/day or 10–15 minutes of warm sun on forearms and face (more for dark skin).
- *Calcium:* Enough to supply needed amounts after dietary intake has been accounted for. (See Table 11.2.)

For vitamins B_{12} and D, a multivitamin/mineral supplement is suitable (read labels). If using this type of supplement, check to make sure it also contains zinc.

HEY TEENS!

So, you've decided to become a vegan—that's great! Your strong stand just may rub off on friends and family. The impact you have will depend somewhat on how you take care of yourself. It's hard to convince someone of the benefits of a vegan diet if you are sick all the time. Getting the right food is not such a big deal. These simple suggestions will get you past the biggest hurdles.

1. Eat something! It would be great to see you sit down to a big breakfast of scrambled tofu, veggie bacon, whole grain toast, and freshly squeezed orange juice. But we totally understand that breakfast may not be one of your top priorities. It is far better that you eat a granola bar and a juice box on your way to school than nothing at all.

2. Replace meat with protein-rich plant foods. These foods give you the important nutrients you used to get from meat, without all the fat, cholesterol, and other stuff that you don't want anyway. Here's how:

Try veggie "meats."	*Give tofu a chance!*
Make a burger with a veggie patty.	Try dessert tofu.
Add a pack of veggie ground round to a can of spaghetti sauce for pasta or Sloppy Joes.	Buy flavored tofu for snacks or sandwiches.
Veggie ham, turkey, bologna, and pepperoni make sandwiches a snap.	Add tofu to stir fries and shish-kabob.
Cook veggie bacon or sausages for breakfast.	Scramble tofu for breakfast.
Buy some veggie dogs.	Throw soft tofu into a shake.
	Dip firm tofu into your favorite sauce (sweet and sour, BBQ, etc.), and bake or fry it.

Eat beans in all sorts of foods.	*Go nuts!*
Eat bean salad and bean soup.	Spread peanut butter or other "nut" butter on toast, crackers, apples, or celery.
Go for bean burritos or tacos.	Snack on nuts and seeds.
Try flavored soynuts as a snack.	Add nuts and seeds to stir fries or salads.
Make or buy chili with kidney beans.	Put nuts and seeds in your granola.
Buy some hummus from the deli.	Pack nuts along for an instant snack.
Open a jar of baked beans.	Use nuts in baking.
Throw some chick-peas into a green salad.	

3. Replace cow's milk with fortified soymilk. You get the same key nutrients as you do from cow's milk, but without the fat and cholesterol. Aim for at least 2-3 cups a day.

• Use soymilk on your cereal.

• Drink soymilk. There are lots of different flavors to try. Make a soy shake.

• Use soymilk in your puddings, soups, muffins, or any other cooking you do that calls for milk.

- Make sure you buy fortified soymilk—there are huge differences in the calcium content of fortified and unfortified soymilks. If you don't like soymilk, try other fortified nondairy beverages such as rice milk or use fortified orange juice more often.

4. Eat your veggies. Now where have you heard this before? On this count, your mom is definitely right.

- Include some raw veggies with your lunch. (It can be as simple as a carrot.)
- Eat greens—add them to salads, stir fries, soups, etc.
- Add lots of veggies to vegan pizza.
- Make some vegetable soup, even if it means just opening a can.
- Use spaghetti sauce instead of eating your pasta plain.
- Think about what vegetables are your favorites—even the old standbys like frozen or canned corn or peas are better than nothing!

5. Buy some Red Star Vegetarian Support Formula Nutritional Yeast. It not only tastes great; it is loaded with vitamin B_{12}, the one nutrient that we don't get from plants.

- Sprinkle nutritional yeast on popcorn.
- Add it to your stir fries or scrambled tofu.
- Use as a coating for baked or fried tofu. First dip tofu slices in soy sauce, tamari or Bragg Aminos, then dip in nutritional yeast and Spike (a great seasoning).
- Use nutritional yeast like Parmesan cheese on spaghetti, salad, or anything else.

6. Use flax oil. There are some very nutritious fats that vegans and many other people don't seem to get enough of. Flax oil is loaded with good stuff, so give it a try. It will make a big difference in the long haul. Aim for about a teaspoon a day.

- Sprinkle flax oil on pasta or vegetables. Try a flavored flax oil!
- Add it to bottled salad dressing or make some of our easy Liquid Gold Salad Dressing (page 127).
- Pour a little into mashed potatoes.

Note: Don't cook with flax oil—it is very easily damaged by heat.

7. Take a multivitamin/mineral supplement. Technically, if you eat really well and use foods fortified with vitamin B_{12} and vitamin D, you don't need a supplement. However, take a supplement if you:

- regularly skip breakfast
- eat lots of foods from packages
- are not real keen on vegetables

- use less fortified soymilk than you should

- eat mostly pasta, bagels, pretzels, popcorn, fruit snacks, or

- miss out on beans, tofu, veggie-meats, nuts, and seeds

If none of these apply to you, we wholeheartedly applaud you. For all others, take an adult multivitamin/mineral supplement.

8. Use the Vegan Food Guide on pages 154–55.

This guide was designed to help you plan a diet that will ensure that all of your nutrient needs are met. Check it out.

Table 11.2 Dietary Reference Intakes for Selected Nutrients in Children

Nutrient Needs/Day	1-3 Years	4-8 Years	9-13 Years	14-18 years
Energy	1,300	1,800	2,000	2,200 (F) 2,500–3,000 (M)
Protein (RDA)	16 g (1.2 g/kg)	24 g (1.2 g/kg)	28 g (1 g/kg)	45-59 (.8-1 g/kg)
RDA + 10%	18 g (1.5 g/kg)	27 g (1.3 g/kg)	31 g (1.1 g/kg)	50-65 (.9-1.1 g/kg)
Iron* (RDA)	12.6 mg	18 mg	14.4 mg	27 mg (F) 19.8 mg (M)
Zinc (RDA)	3 mg	5 mg	8 mg	9 mg (F) 11 mg (M)
Calcium (AI)	500 mg	800 mg	1,300 mg	1,300 mg
Iodine (RDA)	90 mcg	90 mcg	120 mcg	150 mcg
Vitamin A (RDA)	300 mcg	400 mcg	600 mcg	700 mcg (F) 900 mcg (M)
Vitamin C (RDA)	15 mg	25 mg	45 mg	65 mg (F) 75 mg (M)
Vitamin D (AI)	5 mcg	5 mcg	5 mcg	5 mcg
Folate (RDA)	150 mcg	200 mcg	300 mcg	400 mcg
Vitamin B_{12} (RDA)	0.9 mcg	1.2 mcg	1.8 mcg	2.4 mcg

*RDAs for iron are 1.8 times higher for vegetarians than for nonvegetarians.

Sneaky Dad's Pudding

This recipe was created by Louisville lawyer John Borders, who said, "The point is to get fruits, veggies, essential fatty acids, fats, and protein all in a tasty pudding. I haven't felt guilty about feeding this to my daughter Mattie almost every night, and she loves making it with me. It's great bonding time for us. And if that weren't enough, she LOVES the taste. She is THE quintessential picky eater. If she eats it, most kids will."

1½ cups frozen strawberries (360 ml/330 g)

1 banana, cut into 4 pieces

1-2 tsp carob or cocoa powder (5-10 ml)

2 tsp flaxseed oil—try butterscotch flavor! (10 ml)

3-5 Tbsp nut butter (preferably cashew or almond) (45-75 ml)

2-3 Tbsp orange juice or other healthy juice, like carrot juice (30-45 ml)

2 Tbsp fortified soymilk, any flavor (30 ml)

⅛-¼ avocado, peeled, cut into a wedge

Optional ingredients: ¼ tsp. spirulina, ⅛ tsp. multidophilus,
or 2 Tbsp cooked carrots.

Set your little companion up on a stool beside you, ready to toss in the ingredients and push the button. Place all the ingredients in a food processor or blender. This works best in a food processor; you might add a bit more juice or soymilk if you use a blender. Blend until smooth.

Makes 2 servings.

Per half basic recipe: calories: 336, protein: 7 g, carbohydrate: 40 g, fat: 19 g, dietary fiber: 6 g, calcium: 60 mg, % calories from: protein 7%, fat 48%, carbohydrate 45%

For a toddler aged 1-3 years, using 3 Tbsp. cashew butter for the whole recipe, a serving of this pudding provides approximately:

- *the entire day's requirement for magnesium, folate, vitamin C, and essential fatty acids*
- *two-thirds of the requirement for copper and potassium*
- *half the requirement for pyridoxine and fiber, and 42% of the protein*
- *a quarter of the requirement for calories, iron, and selenium*
- *17% of the zinc (more minerals with more nut butter)*

CHAPTER
12

The Prime of Life...
reaping the rewards

Good nutrition during the later years is a major factor in maintaining health and quality of life, allowing you to truly experience your prime at this stage. As we now recognize, being well nourished does not simply mean getting enough. Too much of a good thing can be a health hazard, and excess calories, fats, protein, minerals, and vitamins are not an advantage. In fact, a diet that is nutritionally adequate yet rather low in calories compared to typical eating patterns in affluent countries may help you to live longer and decrease your risk of chronic disease.

Though our focus in this book is nutrition, other lifestyle factors are also key to achieving good health: the habit of regular exercise, the maintenance of loving relationships—whether of long-term family or of new-found friends—plus a positive attitude and a great sense of humor!

> "Of all the self-fulfilling prophesies in our culture, the assumption that aging means decline and poor health is probably the deadliest."
> Marilyn Ferguson,
> The Aquarian Conspiracy

In this chapter, we look at some of the nutrition-related changes that occur with aging, not just for vegans but for anyone. Indeed, there are too few life-long vegans for much research to have accumulated.

HOW NUTRITIONAL NEEDS CHANGE AS YOU AGE

As you get older, your requirements for various nutrients change. Fewer calories are necessary to maintain body weight, and perhaps less of certain B vitamins like riboflavin and thiamin that are linked to caloric requirements. At the same time, your diet should include as much or more of other nutrients— calcium, vitamin D, vitamin B_{12}, and perhaps protein—as it did when you were younger. What does this mean in terms of your food choices? Simply, it means that you need to get "more bang for your buck." Despite reduced caloric intake, aim for intakes of protein, minerals, and most vitamins that are the same as or a little higher than when you were younger.

Decreased requirements

Our need for calories decreases for two primary reasons:

1. Reduction in muscle mass. The amount of muscle tissue, or lean body mass, tends to shrink as you get older. This has the effect of reducing your metabolic rate and overall caloric requirement. At age 65, men may have 26 pounds (11.8 kg) less muscle tissue and women may have 11 pounds (5 kg) less muscle tissue than they had 40 years earlier. You may continue to lose 2 or 3 pounds of muscle tissue each decade.

2. Decreased physical activity. Though you may look forward to hiking and outdoor activities during retirement, for most people, unfortunately, the amount of physical exercise actually decreases.

Dr. Wendy Kort of the Division of Geriatric Medicine of the University of Colorado Health Sciences Center noted that:

"The technological advances of the past century have resulted in a remarkable reduction in the level of physical activity. In fact, in wealthy nations it has become customary to think of sedentary behavior as normal and of exercise as an intervention (in other words, as an artificial or therapeutic measure)."

Dr. Kort makes the point that some changes, such as adult onset diabetes, are actually linked to inactivity and increased fat in the abdominal region, rather than to age.

Physical activity also helps retain muscle mass, resulting in a wide range of benefits. According to Rosenburg,

"No single feature of aging can more dramatically affect basal metabolism, insulin sensitivity, calorie intake, appetite, breathing, ambulation, mobility, and independence than muscle mass."

If you do not gradually cut calories as the years go by, especially if physical activity decreases, the result will be unwanted weight gain.

Above the age of 70, getting *enough* calories may be more of a problem for reasons discussed on page 199 under "Changes that may affect food intake."

Increased requirements

Due to decreased absorption or less efficient usage, dietary requirements for calcium and vitamins D and B_{12} increase, and protein needs may stay as high as those for younger people or increase.

PROTEIN

Recall from Chapter 3 (page 40) that protein needs are stated in terms of grams protein per kilogram body weight. In actual fact, your protein requirements are closely related to the amount of muscle tissue in your body, which drops as you age. However, the absorption and utilization of protein that is in your diet becomes less efficient. Overall, protein needs in grams per kilogram body weight may be the same as when you were younger or they may be higher than those of younger people. Though there is not an age-specific protein RDA for seniors, some experts suggest that requirements may be in the range of 1 or 1.25 grams of protein per kilogram of body weight instead of 0.8-0.9 g protein/kg. Soyfoods and legumes are good protein sources. Quick Shakes (see recipe, page 240) can be a pleasant way for elderly people to get protein and can be made with soymilk or with tofu. Cooked cereal should not be discounted as a protein source: 1 cup of oatmeal with ¾ cup soymilk provides 11 grams of protein, which may be 25% of the day's requirement. You'll get the same amount from an English muffin with 2 Tbsp. almond butter.

CALCIUM

The efficiency with which we absorb calcium may decrease considerably as we age; for example, from age 40 to 60 it may drop as much as 25%. *Adequate Intakes of calcium recommended for those over 50 years of age increase to 1,200 mg per day* from 1,000 mg for adults below age 50. This amount of calcium is provided in 4 cups of fortified soymilk or 3 cups of fortified beverages plus about ½ cup calcium-set tofu (check labels). Of course, you can count on additional calcium from greens, almond butter, figs, and other foods. (See pages 100-01 and 154-55.) For most people, these intakes are most easily achieved by adding supplements to the amount derived from food.

VITAMIN D

This vitamin, which can be derived from the effects of sunlight or from fortified foods, stimulates the absorption of calcium. *Adequate Intakes of vitamin D double to 10 mcg per day for those between 50 and 70 years of age and triple (15 mcg) for those over 70.* Above the age of 70, it is difficult to achieve these intakes from fortified foods alone, so supplementation is advised. A variety of causes contribute to the low serum vitamin D levels of many elderly people. The following checklist will help you to determine if you need a vitamin D supplement. If you check any of the following items, you need to take a supplement of 10 mcg/day (ages 50-70 yrs) and 15 mcg/day (70 years +).

• Insufficient consumption of vitamin D-fortified foods—less than 3 cups (720 ml) of fortified beverages per day. Four servings of fortified foods is better and may include vitamin D-fortified breakfast cereals (in the U.S. and U.K.) and margarine (though it is not easy to find vegan margarines fortified with vitamin D_2).

- Insufficient exposure of face and forearms to warm sun. Minimum is about 20 minutes per day, 4 or more times a week. Better still is 20-minute exposure on more than 4 days per week; people with darker skin may require more. Of course, avoid excess sun exposure.

- Use of laxatives.

- Use of prescription medications such as steroids (usually for arthritis), anticonvulsants, or others. Ask your doctor or pharmacist about any possible nutrient/drug interactions.

VITAMIN B_{12}

Several physical changes associated with aging affect absorption of this vitamin and the subsequent risk of vitamin B_{12} deficiency. (For more on absorption and laboratory tests, see pages 123–25.)

- *Reduced production of Intrinsic Factor by the lining of the stomach.* Intrinsic Factor is necessary to the absorption of B_{12}, thus a decrease in Intrinsic Factor production can lead to severe deficiency and megaloblastic anemia.

- *Reduced production of gastric acid and enzymes by the lining of the stomach.* Hydrochloric acid and the enzyme pepsin are needed for digestion and absorption of many nutrients, including B_{12}. As you get older, the stomach lining produces less acid and pepsin, reducing your ability to release the vitamin B_{12} present in animal foods (for those who eat animal foods). This decrease in acid production does not affect absorption of crystalline vitamin B_{12} (cobalamin, the form of B_{12} used by vegans) found in supplements and fortified foods.★

- *Bacterial overgrowth.* Because of decreased acid production by the stomach, there can be an overgrowth of bacteria in the stomach and small intestine. These bacteria may bind vitamin B_{12} for their own use, making it unavailable.

A decrease in stomach acid production creates a more gradual depletion of B_{12} than occurs with the drop in production of Intrinsic Factor. For someone whose vitamin B_{12} status is marginal, conditions that can further deplete B_{12} are intestinal surgery, use of nitrous oxide during surgery, use of laxatives, antacids, and alcohol, diminished thyroid function, and deficiencies of iron, calcium, and vitamin B_6.

Mild vitamin B_{12} deficiency may affect as many as 25–30% of the general population. Since B_{12} is needed for a healthy nervous system, symptoms such as confusion, disorientation, and memory loss may be due to shortage of this vitamin. Other symptoms can be fatigue, depression, irritability, mood swings, restlessness, apathy, insomnia, and perhaps poor hearing. Laboratory diagnosis

---

★*For examples of B_{12}-fortified foods, see Table 7.2 on page 128.*

may show low serum vitamin B_{12} levels or elevated serum methylmalonic acid and homocysteine levels.

The 1998 RDA (recommended dietary allowance) for vitamin B_{12} is 2.4 mcg. To ensure adequate absorption for elderly people, the best form of vitamin B_{12} is that in supplements or fortified foods. Where there is decreased production of Intrinsic Factor, people should receive B_{12} by injection. (See your physician.)

Other Important Aspects of Diet for Seniors

ANTIOXIDANTS

Vitamins A and C (from fruits and vegetables), vitamin E, and the mineral selenium (found in nuts, seeds, and whole grains) are powerful protectors against free radical damage. Antioxidants are linked to a reduced risk of cataracts, macular degeneration, heart disease, various forms of cancer, and even wrinkles. Vegans tend to have excellent intakes of these antioxidant-rich foods and the amounts of vitamins A, C, and selenium provided by following the Vegan Food Guide on pages 154-55 will be ample. A vitamin E supplement in the range of 200-400 mg/day may provide additional protection. If dental problems develop, fruit and vegetable intakes may be reduced; however, soft fruits, cooked vegetables, and fresh squeezed vegetable or fruit juices can take the place of foods that are more difficult to chew.

FLUIDS/WATER

Though we don't need more fluid as we get older, we do need the usual 6-8 cups (1.5 to 2 liters) each day. With age, one's sensitivity to thirst decreases, so it's important to drink water even when one is not particularly thirsty. Fear of incontinence may also lead to decreased fluid intake. Dehydration can result in constipation and other health problems, so it's important to drink water, juice, soy or grain beverages, and herbal teas. All of these count towards the 6-8 cups.

Changes that may affect food intake

Many factors in the lives of elderly people can have an impact on food intake. This is not an exhaustive list, but it touches some common problems that are encountered.

DENTAL PROBLEMS

If teeth are in poor repair or dentures fit improperly, it may be difficult to eat nuts, seeds, whole grains, and raw vegetables and fruits. Yet there is need for these nutritious foods. In place of nuts and seeds, nut and seed butters may be well accepted. Spread them on whole grain or enriched toast or bread with or without jam or a thin layer of blackstrap molasses; use them in baked goods and add them to puddings, soups, and sauces.

It's entirely possible to get excellent nutrition on a soft foods or "cut up" diet. If eating more crunchy fruit and vegetables is difficult for you, try softer options. Use ripe fruits such as papaya, peaches, nectarines, mango, pears, bananas, melons, kiwi, and berries. Occasionally bake fruit, and grate harder fruits such as apples for salads. You may find well-cooked vegetables easier to eat: try soft-cooked squash, yams, sweet potatoes, zucchini, eggplant, mashed potatoes, and other veggies, and nicely marinated or seasoned tofu. Invest in a good juicer. Get quite creative with Quick Shakes; the recipe on page 240 is just a beginning. Use your imagination to come up with delicious combinations of fruit and soymilk or tofu.

If health is failing or someone is depressed, there can be less inclination to keep teeth clean and floss. Good home care will make a big difference in future dental health, food intake, nutritional status, and even the ability to speak and socialize.

DECLINING TASTE SENSITIVITY

At the age of 70, people have just 30% of the taste buds that they did as young adults. Zinc deficiency can contribute further to loss of ability to taste. Zinc is found in nut and seed butters, legumes, soyfoods, and whole grains.

Loss of taste and smell can mean that people pile on the salt just to get some flavor into the food. It's a better idea to flavor foods with herbs, spices, lemon juice, and other low-sodium seasonings.

OTHER FACTORS

In addition, there are many aspects of declining health or other challenges that can have an impact on how well nourished an elderly person is; high blood pressure, diabetes, digestive difficulties, and swallowing problems require dietary modifications beyond the scope of this book. Other problems are lack of transportation, the effects of medications, shortage of money, and isolation.

> *If the Fountain of Youth is discovered, we can certainly expect that its location will be close to vegetable patches, fields of grain and seeds, and groves of fruit and nut trees, and that the fountain itself will be bubbling with soymilk.*

COMMUNITY SUPPORT FOR SENIORS

Vegetarian Associations

Growing numbers of communities have lively vegetarian associations. Membership spans the whole spectrum from newborns to those arriving by wheelchairs, those in their nineties, and beyond.

> ### Seniors Online
> • For helpful information on everything from heartburn to quick, inexpensive meals, look at the Vegetarian Resource Group's website at http://vrg.org/
> • Do a search for "seniors"or any other topic of interest.

Practical Assistance for Housebound Seniors

If you are housebound or have difficulty getting around or preparing meals, food delivery programs such as Meals-on-Wheels may be just the answer. These programs may cater to vegetarian and vegan clients, depending on the local demand—do inquire. Many supermarkets, including some natural foods stores, offer grocery delivery services.

Vegetarian Food in Care Facilities

If you or a loved one are in search of a suitable care home with expertise in vegan or other vegetarian food preparation, check those run by the Seventh-day Adventists. (See tele-

> ### Resources on quantity cooking
> see *Vegan in Volume,* "The Vegetarian Journal's Food Service Update and Quantity Cooking Information"
> Information at http://vrg.org/fsupdate/

phone listings; a local Seventh-day Adventist church can help you out.) In other facilities, you may be pleasantly surprised to find that kitchen staff is willing and able to accommodate a vegan or vegetarian senior, especially if you help them to figure out some good practical solutions to the challenges of preparing vegan entrées, such as marinated tofu, soy burgers, and frozen individual portions.

Vegan and Vegetarian Diet Specialists

Dietetic associations in the U.S., U.K., and Canada list consultant dietitians who specialize in vegetarian and vegan nutrition. Generally, names of specialists in your area are available through dietetic association websites and national offices.

VEGETARIAN EATING: A GROWING INTEREST IN A GROWING POPULATION GROUP

Twenty percent of the U.S. population is above the age of 65. The age group whose numbers are growing most quickly is the segment 85 years of age and older. Thus, health interests of seniors are drawing more attention, and it is becoming apparent to many people that vegan and vegetarian diets offer many potential health benefits. This is true for those following low-fat dietary guidelines for the reversal of heart disease, those exploring the benefits of vegetarian eating in relation to various forms of cancer, and for those who simply want to maintain the good health they are currently enjoying. A 1992 poll showed that 40% of vegetarians are over the age of 40.

Research to Date on the Health of Elderly Vegetarians

Information on studies of vegan health overall are reported in Chapter 2, though there is little information available yet on the health status of elderly vegans.

One study compared two groups of women: 23 vegetarians with an average age of 72 years and 16 nonvegetarians with an average age of 71 years. All had similar lifestyles other than diet—for example, they were in good health, took part in regular exercise, and did not smoke. The results showed that *"Vegetarian elderly women were found to have nutrient intakes that conformed more closely to recommended nutrition guidelines than nonvegetarian elderly women."* In both groups, intakes of zinc and vitamin D were low. Otherwise, the vegetarians consumed less cholesterol, saturated fat, and caffeine and the vegetarian diets were higher in carbohydrate, fiber, magnesium, manganese, copper, vitamins E and A, thiamin, and pantothenic acid. The distribution of calories between protein, fat, and carbohydrate was found to be closer to recommended patterns in the vegetarian diets. In other respects, nutrient intake was similar for the two groups.

Potential Advantages of Vegan/Vegetarian Diets in the Senior Years

The combination of a diet based on the Vegan Food Guide, regular exercise, and stress management offer great potential for slowing down or preventing changes that have been associated with aging. We can decrease blood pressure and cholesterol levels, avoid obesity, digestive problems, and constipation, reduce bone loss, and improve breathing capacity and heart function. Signs of aging such as skin damage and wrinkling can be slowed in their onset and joint flexibility retained. With improved health and fitness, sexual functioning can be maintained Getting all the nutrients you need even helps avoid mental confusion.

> *"Populations of vegetarians living in affluent countries appear to enjoy unusually good health, characterized by low rates of cancer, cardiovascular disease, and total mortality. These important observations have fueled much research and have raised 3 general questions about vegetarians in relation to nonvegetarians:*
>
> • *Are these observations the result of better nondietary lifestyle factors, such as lower prevalences of smoking and higher levels of physical activity?*
>
> • *Are they the result of lower intakes of harmful dietary components, in particular meat? and*
>
> • *Are they the result of higher intakes of beneficial dietary components that tend to replace meat in the diet?*
>
> *Current evidence suggests that the answer to all three questions is 'Yes.' "*
>
> Walter C. Willett, Department of Nutrition,
> Harvard School of Public Health, Boston

EASY-TO-PREPARE VEGAN MEALS

It is not uncommon to hear a senior proclaim that she or he is tired of cooking. After all, making the same kinds of dishes year after year can get boring. Some people lack the motivation to cook for themselves, and others are just so busy doing other things, they don't want to spend time in the kitchen. The trick to renewing your spirit in the kitchen may be as simple as taking a walk on the wild side. Explore fast and easy options that you would usually shy away from.

Great Flavors from Around the World!

• Italian: pizza crust with prepared sauce, your favorite vegetable toppings, and optional veggie pepperoni or deli slices.

• Mexican: refried beans, chopped tomatoes, onions, and shredded lettuce with salsa on soft or hard tacos.

• Chinese: stir fry of Chinese greens, red peppers, and firm tofu cubes or gluten served with brown rice.

• East Indian: cooked lentils, greens, and onions with curry paste.

• Polynesian: "haystacks" made by piling peanuts, sliced peppers, chopped pineapple, green onion, and toasted or dried coconut on low-fat taco chips or rice.

Almost Instant

- Soups: canned, instant, or tetrapack soups, or take-out soups from delis (regular or low-sodium).
- Vegetarian burgers, with or without the bun.
- Sneaky Dad's Pudding (recipe, page 194).
- Marinated three-bean salad (three types of canned beans, Liquid Gold Dressing, page 127, or other favorite dressing).
- Peanut butter, almond butter, or other nut/seed butter sandwich (on bread, roll, or bagel). Keep loaves of bread in the freezer for freshness, to toast whenever you want a slice or two.
- Pasta with tomato sauce and vegetarian "ground round."
- Vegetarian baked beans with sliced veggie wieners.
- Baked potatoes with Liquid Gold Dressing (recipe, page 127) and cooked or raw veggies.

Super Soyfoods

- Tofu marinated in barbecue sauce and baked in the oven.
- Stir-fried, cubed, or grated tofu, seasoned with tamari and herbs, over salad.
- Veggie "bacon" slices, tomato, and lettuce sandwich.
- Pureed tofu with vegetables to make a nutritious, high-protein cream soup.
- Crumbled tofu mixed with vegan mayo and seasonings to make sandwich filling.
- Cooked or ready-to-eat cereal and soymilk (any time of day).
- Rice or grain pudding with soymilk and raisins.
- Quick Shake (recipe, page 240).

NUTRITION GUIDELINES FOR VEGAN SENIORS... INVESTING IN VITALITY!

Despite decreased caloric needs and reduced food intakes, needs for certain nutrients increase. This can make it a challenge to meet needs for protein, vitamins, and minerals whether one is vegan, vegetarian, or nonvegetarian. The following guidelines will help you to ensure that you achieve and maintain excellent health.

• *Follow the Vegan Food Guide* (pages 154-55).

    Grains: Go for cooked whole grains that are soft and easy to digest (i.e. barley, millet, rice, quinoa, and oats). Use whole grain flour, ground flax, and wheat germ in muffins⋆ and other baked goods.

    Vegetables: Aim for variety and color; be sure to include greens regularly.

    Fruits: Bananas and oranges are great, but also include less familiar fruits such as mango and melons.

    Beans and Bean Alternates: Opt for super-convenient ready-made patties, flavored tofu, and delicious, mineral-rich nut butters.

    Fortified Soymilk and Alternates: Make calcium-fortified nondairy beverages and fortified orange juice a regular feature in your diet. Include plenty of calcium-rich plant foods such as greens, almonds, figs, and blackstrap molasses too.

    Other Essentials: Pay particular attention to vitamins B_{12} and D, and include either fortified foods or supplements. Use flaxseed oil on vegetables, rice, and baked potatoes and in salad dressings.

• *Drink plenty of fluids, especially water* (6-8 cups/1.5-2 liters per day).

• *Limit sweets, salty foods, alcohol, coffee, and tea; avoid concentrated fats* (vegetable oils and margarine) as much as possible.

• *Consider using some nutritional supplements.* Calcium, vitamin D, and vitamin B_{12} are often needed.

• *Keep physically active.* Aim for a minimum of 30 minutes of activity each day.

• *Contact a vegan/vegetarian specialist* through your national dietetic association, if individual diet consultation is required.

SELECTED REFERENCES

For a complete list, see www.nutrispeak.com/veganrefs.htm. See also general references for the whole book on page 276.

Carmel, R. "Cobalamin, the stomach, and aging." *Amer. J. Clin. Nutr.* 66 (1997): 750-759.

Potter, S. et al. "Soy protein and isoflavones: their effects on blood lipids and bone density in postmenopausal women." *Amer. J. Clin. Nutr.* 68 (1998): 1375S-1379S.

Seventh-day Adventist Dietetic Association. "Nutrition for Vegetarian/Vegan Seniors." pages 7-1 to 7-7 in *The Vegetarian/Vegan Resource* (an annex to *Diet Manuals 1997-1998)* Roseville, Cal.: Adventist Health.

⋆*For excellent muffin recipes see* Cooking Vegetarian *by Melina V, Forest J, Wiley, 1998, and* Becoming Vegetarian *by Melina V, Davis B, Harrison V, The Book Publishing Company, 1995.*

CHAPTER 13

Overweight

Humans are remarkably efficient animals. In our hunter-gatherer days, that efficiency meant survival. Today, amidst abundance, our fat-storing efficiency often leads to obesity* (severe overweight), disease, and death. Indeed, obesity is now considered the second leading cause of death in North America. From 1950 to the mid-1990s, overweight increased from 25% to almost 55%. The most dramatic increase was in the prevalence of obesity during the last decade. Dr. George Blackburn, widely recognized authority on obesity, suggested that by 2025, at this rate, 75% of the North American population would be overweight. "The State of the World 2000 Report" (World Watch Institute) indicated that for the first time in history as many people are overweight as underfed—1.2 billion each.

DETERMINATION OF HEALTHFUL WEIGHTS

The most accurate way of assessing whether or not you are overweight or obese is to calculate how much of your body weight is fat. A body fat level greater than 17% in men and 27% in women indicates overweight, while a body fat level of greater than 25% in men and 31% in women indicates obesity. Unfortunately, getting accurate body fat measurements can be difficult and costly. Thus, a simple tool called body mass index (BMI) is commonly used for estimating total body "fatness." It is recommended for people between the ages of 20 and 65 years, and is not considered valid for children, pregnant or nursing women, or for those with very large muscle mass, such as weight lifters or body builders. To find your BMI, plot your height and weight on the BMI table on the next page.

BMI does not factor in muscle mass; thus, people with large muscle mass will have a high BMI but low body fat. In addition, very short people (less than

Overweight=10% above healthy body weight; Obesity=20% above healthy body weight.

Table 13.1 Body Mass Index Relative to Height and Weight																
Height in Inches																
Wt/ lbs	60	61	62	63	64	65	66	67	68	69	70	71	72	73	74	75	76
100	20	19	18	18	17	17	16	16	15	15	14	14	14	13	13	12	12
105	21	20	19	19	18	17	17	16	16	16	15	15	14	14	13	13	13
110	21	21	20	19	19	18	18	17	17	16	16	15	15	15	14	14	13
115	22	22	21	20	20	19	19	18	17	17	17	16	16	15	15	14	14
120	23	23	22	21	21	20	19	19	18	18	17	17	16	16	15	15	15
125	24	24	23	22	21	21	20	20	19	18	18	17	17	16	16	16	15
130	25	25	24	23	22	22	21	20	20	19	19	18	18	17	17	16	16
135	26	26	25	24	23	22	22	21	21	20	19	19	18	18	17	17	16
140	27	26	26	25	24	23	23	22	21	21	20	20	19	18	18	17	17
145	28	27	27	26	25	24	23	23	22	21	21	20	20	19	19	18	18
150	29	28	27	27	26	25	24	23	23	22	22	21	20	20	19	19	18
155	30	29	28	27	27	26	25	24	24	23	22	22	21	20	20	19	19
160	31	30	29	28	27	27	26	25	24	24	23	22	22	21	21	20	19
165	32	31	30	29	28	27	27	26	25	24	24	23	22	22	21	21	20
170	33	32	31	30	29	28	27	27	26	25	24	24	23	22	22	21	21
175	34	33	32	31	30	29	28	27	27	26	25	24	24	23	22	22	21
180	35	34	33	32	31	30	29	28	27	27	26	25	24	24	23	22	22
185	36	35	34	33	32	31	30	29	28	27	27	26	25	24	24	23	23
190	37	36	35	34	33	32	31	30	29	28	27	26	26	25	24	24	23
195	38	37	36	35	34	33	32	31	30	29	28	28	27	26	25	24	24
200	39	38	37	35	34	33	32	31	30	30	29	28	27	26	26	25	24
205	40	39	37	36	35	34	33	32	31	30	29	29	28	27	26	26	25
210	41	40	38	37	36	35	34	33	32	31	30	29	28	28	27	26	26
215	42	41	39	38	37	36	35	34	33	32	31	30	29	28	28	27	26
220	43	42	40	39	38	37	36	35	34	33	32	31	30	29	28	27	27
225	44	43	41	40	39	37	36	35	34	33	32	31	31	30	29	28	27
230	45	43	42	41	39	38	37	36	35	34	33	32	31	30	30	29	28
235	46	44	43	42	40	39	38	37	36	35	34	33	32	31	31	29	29
240	47	45	44	43	41	40	39	38	36	35	34	33	33	31	31	30	29
245	48	46	45	43	42	41	40	39	37	36	35	34	33	32	32	30	30
250	49	47	46	44	43	42	40	39	38	37	36	35	34	33	32	31	30

Understanding your BMI:

BMI less than 19: May indicate underweight

BMI 19–24.9: Healthful weight for most people

BMI 25–29.9: Indicates overweight

BMI more than 30: Indicates obesity

Fast Facts (North America)

Prevalence of Excess Weight

Percentage of adults that are overweight: 55%

Percentage of adults that are obese: 33%

Percentage of children ages 6–17 that are overweight: 33%.

Percentage of children ages 6–17 that are obese: 20%.

Weight of Vegetarians

Difference in body weight of lacto-ovo vegetarians and nonvegetarians:

lacto-ovo vegetarians are 5% lighter

Difference in body weight of vegans vs. lacto-ovo vegetarians: vegans are 5% lighter

Difference in body weight of vegans vs. nonvegetarian: vegans are 10% lighter

Cost of Excess Weight

Health care costs directly attributable to obesity: over $100 billion/year

Money spent on weight-reduction programs and special foods: over $35 billion/year

Popularity, Success, and Failure of Weight Loss Diets

Proportion of adult women trying to lose weight: 50%

Proportion of adult men trying to lose weight: 30%

Proportion of weight regained after 1 year by 97% of the population: $\frac{1}{3}$–$\frac{2}{3}$

Proportion of the weight regained after 3 years in 97% of the population: most or all

Health Consequences of Overweight and Obesity

Increased all-cause mortality

Increased risk of:

CVD • lipid disorders •hypertension • stroke

gallbladder disease • Type 2 diabetes • osteoarthritis

sleep apnea • respiratory problems • certain cancers

5 feet) may have higher BMIs than would be expected relative to their size. There is also far greater variability in healthful body weights than what we once thought. A person may be significantly larger than current "ideals" and still be at a very "healthful weight" for their build.

Body Fat Distribution: "Pears" vs. "Apples"

It is not only the amount of fat you carry that affects health, but also the distribution of that fat. Women typically collect fat in their hips and buttocks, resulting in what we call a "pear" shape. Men more often accumulate fat around their bellies, resulting in an "apple" shape. People with more abdominal fat are at greater risk for health problems associated with obesity.

The best way to determine your body shape is to measure the circumference of your waist, which is more useful than the waist-to-hip ratio (WHR) as a marker of abdominal obesity. A waist circumference of greater than 35 inches (88 cm) in women and 40 inches (102 cm) in men is associated with an increased risk of diabetes, heart disease, and hypertension.

The Root of the Problem

Technically, overweight and obesity are caused by taking in more energy than you expend. Popular opinion suggests that they are the products of poor willpower—overweight people eat too much and exercise too little. In fact, overweight people do not necessarily eat more than thin people; some eat less. Our current popular opinion serves only to pour salt on the wound.

If you are an overweight vegetarian (especially a vegan), you may feel cheated by your body. After all, vegetarians are usually lean and sometimes downright skinny. While a vegetarian or vegan diet is an effective means of achieving and maintaining a healthy body weight for many people, there are no guarantees. The reason is that food is rarely 100% of the problem—physiological, environmental, and psychological factors are all important contributors.

Inherent differences in your metabolism and fat-processing systems can affect energy needs and body weight. If you eat moderately and are active but still overweight, you may have an exceptionally efficient body and require less energy than the average person. That gives you a great survival advantage in times of famine, but unfortunately, in times of abundance you need to be diligent with exercise and energy intake to avoid excessive weight gain.

In this society of convenience and super-sizing, it is easy to overeat and underexercise. Vegan and vegetarian options are more widely available than ever, both in supermarkets and restaurants. It is easy to overindulge when good food is so abundant and tasty.

Physical activity also has a huge impact on your body weight. If you get to and from work in a car, sit at a desk most of the day, and relax in front of the television at night, chances are that your inactive lifestyle is an important contributor to your overweight.

Your weight struggles may have as much to do with self-preservation as with genetics or environment. Food never judges and always comforts. It has the power to build a wall protecting you from intimacy and pain. The intense pressure from society to be thin usually serves only to make matters worse. The result is often discontentment with your body and years of yo-yo dieting. For some people, this triggers a self destructive, obsessive/compulsive relationship with food. In extreme cases, severe eating disorders result, such as binge-eating disorder. No amount of "dieting" is effective in such a situation, and professional assistance is generally advised. (See Chapter 15.)

BATTLE OF THE BULGE

While some overweight individuals are content with their weight and shape, the far greater majority eagerly engage in the infamous "battle of the bulge." The list of potential allies is mind boggling: diets and diet aids by the thousands, drugs, teas, herbal formulas, fat-burning paraphernalia, and surgery. Unfortunately, over 95% of weight loss battles fail in the long-term, and the fallout is staggering. Just think of the countless hours spent in search of a miracle that might have been better spent running barefoot in the sand with someone you love. The losses extend far beyond your pocketbook directly to your heart and soul. Spare yourself the misery—let your most trusted ally be your own common sense!

Weight Loss Diets

It would seem as though you could go on a different diet every week for the rest of your life, though the vast majority of diets are just a new variation on an old theme. Those that remain among the most popular are listed below.

PERSONALIZED PROGRAM BY A REGISTERED DIETITIAN

Description: Programs vary; emphasis is on comprehensive lifestyle changes and nutritionally balanced eating.

Pluses and Pitfalls: Personal attention. Nutritional and health status monitored. Nutritionally sound. Attention to mind and body, includes exercise, but costly.

The verdict: Works as long as you follow the program.

★★★*This is the best option for personal attention.*

WEIGHT WATCHERS

Description: Comprehensive lifestyle changes. Points system based on energy, fat, and fiber. Group support.

Pluses and Pitfalls: Meets nutritional requirements. Great vegetarian and vegan programs. Reasonable cost. Excellent support. Challenges addressed, includes exercise. Can be tedious (involves calculating points for each food consumed). You pay a weekly fee, whether or not you attend the weekly meeting.

The verdict: Works as long as you follow the program.

★★★*This is the best of the best for those wanting group support.*

WEIGHT LOSS CLINICS

Description: Low-calorie diets. Often include prepackaged meals.

Pluses and Pitfalls: Good personal support. Emphasis on lifestyle changes. Regular follow-ups. Costly. Emphasis on prepared foods rather than learning how to make healthy meals yourself. Some lacto-ovo vegetarian options; few vegan options.

The verdict: Works if you follow the program! When special foods are no longer used, weight may be regained.

★★*A reasonable choice for those who prefer very close personal monitoring.*

VERY-LOW-FAT, HIGH-FIBER VEGETARIAN

Description: 5–10% fat, vegetarian or vegan diets. Emphasis on whole plant foods. Examples: Eat More Weigh Less (Dr. Ornish), Maximum Weight Loss, (Dr. McDougall).

Pluses and Pitfalls: Vegan and near-vegan programs. Nutrient dense. Larger serving sizes. Encourages permanent, positive change. Considers food behaviors, exercise, and lifestyle changes. Unnecessarily removes higher-fat vegan options (e.g., nuts and seeds) which, when eaten moderately, are an excellent addition to a vegan diet. May reduce absorption of important nutrients Potentially deficient in EFAs. Can be difficult to follow over the long term.

The verdict: Works if you follow the programs!

★★*Good options but lower in fat than is necessary or optimal for most people.*

FASTING OR MODIFIED FASTING

Description: Consumption of only water (fasting) or fluids such as juice, herbal tea, and broth (modified fasting).

Pluses and Pitfalls: Takes willpower, empowers dieter. Can reduce symptoms of several chronic diseases. Loss of lean body tissue. (Up to a third of weight loss is muscle.) May lead to deficiencies. May cause dizziness and fatigue. Can lead to liver and kidney problems. Slows metabolism. Doesn't improve eating habits in the long term.

The verdict: Works—if you don't eat, you lose weight, in the short term. However, weight is generally quickly regained when eating is resumed.

★*Has useful applications for disease; not generally recommended as a weight loss diet.*

HIGH-PROTEIN, HIGH-FAT, LOW-CARBOHYDRATE DIETS

Description: Based on the theory that carbohydrates cause excess insulin production, triggering hunger and overeating. 800–1,500 cal/day. 30% protein, 10–40% carbohydrates, 30–60% fat.

Pluses and Pitfalls: Plans that allow 40% of calories from carbohydrates improve blood sugar and triglycerides in some people. Some programs encourage exercising, drinking lots of water, eating plenty of vegetables, and replacing refined grains with whole grains. Ketosis leading to dizziness, headaches, nausea, fatigue, and bad breath. Vitamin deficiencies. Insufficient fiber leading to constipation and bowel disorders. Excessive saturated fat and cholesterol increasing risk for chronic diseases. Excessive protein may contribute to osteoporosis, liver and kidney problems. Reduced athletic endurance.

The verdict: Most of these diets will produce weight loss but at a cost to health.

No Stars. These diets are a vegan's nightmare. They sell because they justify the type of diet that many people want to eat—one loaded with animal foods.

MIRACLE FOOD DIETS

Description: Centered on "miracle foods" touted as having unique properties (e.g., Grapefruit Diet).

Pluses & Pitfalls: There's no guessing involved; the rules are clear cut and many people like that. Boring! Nutritionally inadequate. Teach nothing about life-long healthy eating habits.

The verdict: Works only in the short term.

No stars. These diets are definitely not worth the effort!

The Bottom Line: If you cut back on calories enough, no matter what you eat, you'll lose weight. The objective of the diet guru is to offer the most appealing method of reducing energy intake. There is one sure way of determining if a diet has any hope of success on a long-term basis. Ask yourself this question:

Could I eat this way for the rest of my life?

If the answer is no, don't waste your time or money. The only thing the average diet is almost guaranteed to do is to feed our sense of failure.

Pills, Potions, and Poppycock

Want to melt pounds overnight without dieting? Want to eat whatever you like without absorbing the fat? No problem! The promise of popping a pill each day or drinking a special herbal tea and watching fat melt away is universally appealing to dieters. It comes as no surprise that those who seek a solution with wallet in hand will have a few thousand options to choose from. But think about it for a moment. If a safe and simple "cure" for obesity really existed, would 50% of the population be overweight?

PRESCRIPTION DRUGS

The most common prescription medications used in treating obesity are appetite suppressants. They work by reducing appetite or increasing feelings of fullness. Few long-term studies have evaluated their safety or effectiveness. Only a few years ago, the most popular of these drugs were withdrawn from the market due to their reported association with valvular heart disease.

Common side effects of these medications include dry mouth, headaches, constipation, insomnia, and slight increases in blood pressure.

One of the newest prescription drugs on the market is a fat blocker sold under the name Xenical (Orlistat). It works by inhibiting enzymes responsible for fat breakdown, reducing fat absorption by about 30%. The side effects of Xenical are much the same as fake fats such as Olestra, namely diarrhea, malabsorption of fat-soluble vitamins and phytochemicals, anal leakage, and urgency.

The Verdict: Prescription medications come with a risk of serious side effects, are rarely effective in the long-term, and are best avoided.

NONPRESCRIPTION DRUGS, HERBS, TEAS, ETC.

Medicinal herbs are largely unregulated; thus, effectiveness and safety of these products can be highly variable. While some may help kick-start weight loss efforts, they are not necessary, nor are they ever the answer to long-term healthful weights. While we don't have space to do an exhaustive list of products, this will give you some idea of what is available and what to avoid.

Metabolic Stimulants: Herbal fen/phen is an over-the-counter replacement for the popular prescription medications recently removed from the market. It is made from a combination of extracts often including ephedra (ma huang) and St. John's wort. The FDA has proposed a ban on marketing supplements containing over 8 mg of ephedra per dose because of reports of adverse effects (over 900 reports including almost 50 deaths). Using preparations that also include caffeine, kola nut, or guarana seed can result in anything from nervousness, headaches, tremors, insomnia, high blood pressure, and chest pain to heart attack, stroke, seizure, and death. There is little clinical evidence supporting St. John's wort as an effective weight loss aid.

Several spices, including red pepper, ginger, mustard seed, cinnamon, and cardamom, are also thought to boost metabolic rate. Kelp and other sea vegetables are said to increase metabolism by virtue of their iodine content and thyroid stimulation. While evidence demonstrating their effectiveness is lacking, these herbs and seaweeds are considered relatively safe.

Appetite Suppressants: Chickweed is probably the least harmful of the appetite suppressants. Garcinia cambogia is rapidly gaining respect in the weight loss world as both an appetite suppressant and fat burner. The active ingredient is hydroxycitric acid (HCA), and while research is limited, it also appears quite harmless.

Fat blockers: Sold under names such as "Fat Absorb," "Fat Magnet," "Fat Blocker," and "Fat Trapper," chitosan is derived from chitin, a polysaccharide found in the exoskeleton of shellfish such as shrimp, lobster, and crabs—a definite turn-off to vegans and vegetarians. Chitosan can reduce the absorption of fat-soluble vitamins and phytochemicals, doing more harm than good (to both people and shellfish!).

Laxatives: While it may seem a little odd to be discussing laxatives under a weight loss supplement section, they are used as such with considerable regularity. Laxatives fall into two main categories: stimulants and bulking agents. Stimulants work by irritating the system, often causing cramps (e.g., senna, cascara sagrada, and buckthorn). Stimulants can be useful in cases of severe constipation, but long-term use leads to sluggish bowel function and dependence. Bulking agents, when consumed with sufficient water, increase feelings of fullness and help improve bowel function. They are gentler than stimulants but completely unnecessary for active people eating a high-fiber, plant-based diet.

The verdict: Don't rely on any supplement to provide an answer to your weight concerns. If you want to play around with supplements, stick to herbal appetite suppressants, spices, and psyllium or flax (bulking agents) with lots of water. But remember, your best allies will always be whole foods, water, and exercise.

The Vegetarian Advantage

The vegan diet is a natural for promoting healthful weights. It is less calorie-dense and more nutrient-dense than typical North American diets. The advantages of vegetarian, and especially vegan, diets where weight control is concerned are well recognized.

HIGHER FIBER INTAKE

The average North American nonvegetarian consumes 10-15 grams of fiber a day. Current recommendations are 27-40 grams a day. Vegans meet and exceed recommended intakes, averaging about 40-50 grams of fiber a day. Fiber increases food volume without adding calories. It also helps speed food through the digestive system, resulting in moderately reduced energy absorption. In addition, fiber reduces hunger and improves satiety.

HIGHER CARBOHYDRATE INTAKE

Diet gurus often claim that carbohydrates are the source of all evil, but science tells us another story. Carbohydrates are not the enemy unless we first refine them. Some evidence indicates that complex carbohydrates may speed resting metabolic rate. One intriguing study found that young male vegetarians had an 11% higher metabolic rate than nonvegetarians with similar energy intake. Carbohydrates also enhance the synthesis and release of serotonin, which in turn suppresses further cravings, leading to better portion control. Vegans eat about 55-65% of their calories as carbohydrates, most of which is unrefined, while nonvegetarians generally eat less than 50%, much of which is refined.

IMPROVED FAT INTAKE

Vegetarians eat less fat, which may prove advantageous for weight control. Evidence suggests that people eat a larger quantity of food when provided with high-fat meals than they do with low-fat meals. Fat is more than two times more concentrated in energy than carbohydrates or protein (100 calories per tablespoon vs. 40 calories for carbohydrate or protein). Thus, very modest portions of high-fat foods can be very energy dense.

HEALTHY MIND, HEALTHY BODY

The best way to achieve a life-long healthy body weight is to lead a healthy lifestyle. It requires a balance of body, mind, and spirit, and a deep appreciation for their connection. Recognize that every small step taken in the right direction goes a long way towards well-being. Your shift towards a vegan diet is a brilliant beginning. These guidelines will help to keep your focus where it really needs to be:

10 Simple Steps to a Slimmer You

1. Make great health your goal.

Dump the dieter's mentality of "thinness at all costs." Thinness is a shallow goal based on fickle ideals of the fashion industry. Instead, make great health your goal. With health as your focus, you'll not only end up with a better body weight, but more energy and reduced risk of chronic disease.

2. Center your diet on whole plant foods.

Make vegetables, fruits, legumes, whole grains, and small amounts of nuts and seeds the foundation of your diet. Select a wide variety of fresh, whole foods, processed without added fat, sugar, or salt. Minimize your use of refined and processed foods. It is that simple.

3. Listen to your body.

It is so tempting to eat because there is food around or you're bored, tired, or stressed out. Learn to recognize real hunger and respect it. Don't eat if you aren't hungry but don't deprive yourself if you are. Learn to deal with boredom, fatigue, and stress in healthier ways—join a new club, have naps, go for long walks with a friend. Pay attention to how foods affect your digestive system. Be mindful of your body when you make your food selections.

4. Build healthful habits.

Examine your habits and replace those that undermine your goals with better choices. Write down your challenges and your goals. Take them on one by one. If you end up "backsliding," don't consume yourself with guilt or shame. You simply made a choice; don't let it become more than that. Work on ways to make the new, more healthful habits even more enjoyable.

5. Eat regular, modest meals—slowly!

Skipping meals can compromise your performance and leave you so hungry that you overeat at the next meal. People who eat breakfast burn more calories during the day and perform better than those who don't. Watch your portion sizes—the more food on your plate, the more you end up eating. Eat slowly—it not only enables you to better appreciate your food, it can help reduce the amount you eat and improve digestion.

6. Make physical activity a priority in your life.

Physical activity increases stamina, energy output, and metabolism. Avoid laborsaving devices when you can (e.g., take the stairs instead of an elevator). Try to exercise at least 5 or 6 days a week. Your best choice for weight loss and overall health is moderate aerobic activity such as brisk walking, combined with moderate resistance training such as light weight training. Aim for 30 to 60 minutes a day. Be adventurous. Don't avoid an activity because of your size—others will benefit from the fine example you set.

7. Enjoy your wonderful body.

Are you so caught up in self-loathing of your body that you forget all of the great things that it enables you to do? Take a moment each day to appreciate unfailing efforts of your feet, hands, or eyes. Celebrate your strength, stamina, or agility and any little improvements you might observe. No matter what your size or shape, pamper yourself. Have a nice long bubble bath, get a facial, go for a new haircut, or splurge on that outfit you deserve!

8. Leave the scales where they belong—on fish.

Weight scales tell only one part of the story. Weight naturally fluctuates from day to day and from morning to night. With increased physical activity, muscle mass increases, and muscle weighs more than fat. Thus, while your weight may be unchanged, you are actually leaner. You can count on the way your clothes fit far more than what a scale reads! Whenever you step on the scales, you tend to judge yourself according to the number you see. This is contrary to your ultimate healthy mind/healthy body goal. Your value is far beyond any number on a scale.

9. Be realistic.

Think about your goals, both long- and short-term. Write them down. Be sure to include lots of minigoals you are confident that you can achieve. Don't expect to lose 30 pounds overnight. For permanent weight loss, aim for no more than 1 to 2 pounds a week. Appreciate every little bit of progress you make. Walking an extra 5 minutes a day, being content with a slightly smaller serving size, or watching a half-hour less television—every positive change you make is worth celebrating.

10. Take care of your inner being.

Health can only be realized when you take care of your inner being. It may involve making difficult, but necessary, changes in your life. It may mean facing struggles, both past and present, that are yet unresolved. It may also involve seeking out a support group or therapist who can help you deal with depression, abuse, or anger. Until these underlying issues are addressed, it will be much more difficult for you to realize your ultimate health goals and fully appreciate the person you are.

POUND-WISE PYRAMID POINTERS

The Vegan Food Guide is an excellent tool for helping to ensure that your diet provides you with the right balance of all essential nutrients. The following pointers will help you make the best choices within each food group.

Go for whole grains; avoid refined grain products!   (5 to 7 servings/day)

Whole grains are more slowly digested, leaving you feeling fuller for longer.

- Best choices: intact whole grains (millet, quinoa, barley, brown rice).
- Good choices: whole grain bread, cereal, or pasta. Look for bread with whole grain flour as the first ingredient and at least 3 grams of fiber per slice.
- Poor choices: refined grains (white bread products, white pasta, and white rice). These foods contribute to overeating and poor nutrition. Use sparingly or not at all.

Pile on the vegetables!   (3 or more servings/day)

Vegetables offer the most nutrition for the least calories. You can pile them on without blowing your diet. Including large servings of vegetables at mealtime makes you feel like you've eaten a big meal, even when your caloric intake is quite moderate.

- Eat as many low-carbohydrate vegetables as you like. Limit higher-carbohydrate vegetables (potatoes, corn, and peas) to 3 or fewer servings a day.

- Stick with fresh vegetables when you can. Raw vegetables are especially filling and loaded with phytochemicals and other protective dietary components—eat them every day.
- Grill or roast vegetables with little or no oil for intense flavor. You can also stir fry using only a few drops of oil with fresh garlic, Bragg Liquid Aminos (lower in sodium than soy sauce), and white wine.

Treat yourself to nature's candy…pick fruit!   (3 to 5 servings/day)

Fruit is a perfect treat. While it is wonderfully sweet, it contains almost no fat and is loaded with vitamins, phytochemicals, and fiber.

- Include a wide variety of fruits in the diet because their calorie and nutrient content varies considerably.
- Go for whole fruit instead of juice! It is more filling and takes longer to eat. (If you do drink fruit juice, squeeze the fruit yourself).
- Select fruit as a snack often—it is portable, convenient, and tasty.

Think green for calcium.   (6 servings/day)

Your lowest-calorie sources for calcium are green vegetables from the land and the sea (bok choy, collards, kale, broccoli, and certain seaweeds). Other excellent choices are calcium-fortified nondairy beverages and calcium-fortified orange juice.

- Add calcium-rich greens or seaweeds to salads, patties, potatoes, soups, casseroles, and pasta dishes.
- Always use calcium-fortified soymilk on cereal and in cooking.
- If you drink orange juice, always buy varieties fortified with calcium.
- Use smaller portions of higher-fat calcium choices such as tofu, almonds, and tahini.

Get powered by legumes!   (2 to 3 servings/day)

Whole legumes are more nutrient-dense (more nutrients per calorie) than the higher-fat bean alternates such as nuts and their butters. They are also loaded with fiber, helping you to feel fuller for longer.

- Experiment with all kinds of legumes. Sprout them, stew them, add them to salads and loaves, or just eat them as a side dish.
- Try some of the great-tasting deli slices, burgers, and veggie dogs on the market. Most are very low in fat—read the labels.
- Include smaller portions of higher-fat choices (tofu, nuts, and seeds).

Don't forget omega-3s and vitamins B₁₂ and D!

These important nutrients are too often forgotten. Be sure you get yours!

- Omega-3 fatty acids: Your best choices are whole foods such as walnuts, flaxseeds, and greens. If using oil in salad, use flaxseed oil. Most people can meet their omega-3 needs with only a teaspoon.

- Vitamin B_{12}: Use fortified foods such as Red Star Vegetarian Support Formula nutritional yeast or supplements.

- Vitamin D: You need 10 to 15 minutes of warm sun per day or sufficient vitamin D from fortified foods or supplements.

Use concentrated oils, sweets, and salty foods with discretion.

Most of these products offer little but calories.

Fruits are your best bet for natural sweets. If you want something sweet after dinner, how about trying frozen berries or grapes, dried fruits, such as cherries, strawberries, or cranberries, or some fruity or herbal tea.

Fat provides more than two times the energy of carbohydrates or protein, so use vegetable oils and other fats sparingly. Avoid deep-fried foods or foods rich in high-fat ingredients.

Salty snack foods keep us coming back for more. If you want a salty snack, stick to air-popped popcorn, seasoned rice cakes, vegan sushi, Oriental seaweed crackers, or pretzels.

Use beverages to your advantage!

Beverages can wreak havoc with your weight loss goals. A single cup of juice can have up to 150 calories, as can a cup of soymilk. Soda pop is loaded with sugar—10 teaspoons per 12-ounce can—and contains between 120 to 200 calories. By consuming 6 calorie-rich beverages a day, you could take in almost 1,000 calories. Instead, make water your principal beverage—go for 6 to 8 glasses of water per day. For variety, use herbal teas or vegetable juices.

Take a multivitamin/mineral supplement.

- Diets that are low in energy can have marginal levels of a number of nutrients. Taking a daily multivitamin/mineral supplement can help ensure that these nutrients are present in sufficient quantities for optimal health.

- Select a supplement with vitamin B_{12}, vitamin D, zinc, and other trace minerals.

  For an excellent sample menu for weight loss, check out the 1,600 calorie menu on page 157. You can adjust the menu slightly to increase or decrease energy intake.

  May your efforts be well rewarded!

CHAPTER
14

Eating Disorders

D
o you constantly think about food and eating, weight and shape? Do these thoughts affect your physical or emotional state and ability to effectively function on a day-to-day basis? If so, you may have an eating disorder.

When people hear the words "eating disorder" they generally think of young women with anorexia nervosa or bulimia nervosa. However, eating disorders are not determined by body weight or gender but rather by state of mind. There are many eating disorders distinct from anorexia nervosa or bulimia nervosa that are even more common. One example is binge-eating disorder, which fits into a third class of eating disorders referred to as "eating disorders not otherwise specified" (EDNOS). All of these disorders are powerful and consuming but completely curable. If you think you or someone you care about may be at risk, please read on.

TYPES OF EATING DISORDERS

Anorexia Nervosa

Anorexia nervosa is an eating disorder characterized by the relentless pursuit of thinness resulting in extreme thinness. Those suffering from anorexia nervosa lose between 15% to 60% of their usual body weight. About half of anorexic individuals achieve weight loss by restricting food intake (anorexic restrictors), while the other half achieve weight loss through a combination of dieting and purging (anorexic bulimics). Affected individuals go to great lengths to achieve weight loss, often building strange rituals around food, eating, and exercise. They have an intense fear of gaining weight and see themselves as fat, even when they are dangerously thin. Anorexics generally categorize food into good/safe foods (very-low-fat, low-calorie foods) and bad/dangerous foods (high-fat or high-calorie foods). As many as 50% of anorexics become vegetarian/vegan as a means of justifying the elimination of "bad foods." Anorexia nervosa is most commonly seen in young female women.

Bulimia Nervosa

Bulimia nervosa is an eating disorder in which recurrent cycles of binge eating are followed by purging in an effort to prevent weight gain. Binge eating involves the uncontrollable consumption of large amounts of food, often in secret. Purging is accomplished through self-induced vomiting, use of laxatives, enemas, diet pills, diuretics, or exercise. A diagnosis of bulimia is made when there are at least two bulimic episodes per week for three months. However, bulimics often average 14 binge-purge episodes a week, and the frequency of binge-purge episodes is often much higher. The primary distinguishing feature between anorexia nervosa and bulimia nervosa is body weight. Bulimics have normal to high-normal weights and thus do not suffer from the effects of starvation. Some individuals develop variations on what would be considered "classic" bulimia nervosa. One example is the the male athlete (e.g., wrestler, horse jockey) who becomes bulimic during the competitive season to meet weight requirements, but resumes normal eating patterns off-season. In such cases many of the characteristics common to persons who develop these disorders are absent.

Fast Facts (North America)

Prevalence of Eating Disorders

Prevalence of anorexia nervosa in young women: 1%
Prevalence of bulimia nervosa in young women: 2-3%
Anorexics or bulimics who are male: 5-15%
Prevalence of binge eating disorder in the general population: 3-4%
People with binge eating disorders that are male: 40%
Increase in anorexia nervosa between the mid-1950s and mid-1970s: 300%

Behaviors and Attitudes

Women who dislike their overall appearance: 56%
Men who dislike their overall appearance: 43%
Those with anorexia nervosa who develop bulimic patterns: 50%
Anorexics who eat a vegetarian or vegan diet: 50%

Mortality and Recovery Rates

People who die as a result of a serious eating disorder when
no treatment is received: up to 20%
People who die as a result of a serious eating disorder when
treatment is received: 2-3%
People who fully recover from an eating disorder: 60%
People with eating disorders who make only partial recoveries: 20%
People with eating disorders who do not recover: 20%
Young women who die of anorexia nervosa in the U.S. every year: 1,000

Eating Disorders Not Otherwise Specified (EDNOS)

There are numerous eating disorders that meet some, but not all, of the diagnostic criteria for anorexia nervosa or bulimia nervosa. Still others are quite unique and clearly distinct from either of these disorders. The body weights of people suffering from EDNOS can range from seriously underweight to morbidly obese. The most common EDNOS are binge eating disorder (uncontrollable binge eating without purging) and chronic overeating disorder (chronic excessive food consumption). In both cases, sufferers are overweight and sometimes morbidly obese. These individuals are at high risk for chronic diseases such as heart disease, diet-related cancers, hypertension, gallbladder diseases, and others. While these disorders are even more common than anorexia nervosa or bulimia nervosa, they are less widely recognized and less often treated. Fortunately, eating disorders organizations have embraced those with EDNOS and have come a long way in their education efforts.

THE CAUSES

Eating disorders are complex and no single reason explains their presence in anyone. In most individuals, eating disorders are the product of an interplay of biological, psychological, family, and cultural factors and a manifestation of unresolved emotional struggles.

Certain biological factors appear to increase risk for eating disorders. If your mother had an eating disorder, your risk is increased up to eight times. Abnormal levels of certain brain chemicals can contribute to perfectionism and obsessive/compulsive behaviors, both increasing your risk for eating disorders.

Numerous psychological factors may also affect your risk. Among the most common are perfectionism and an obsessive/compulsive personality. Those at highest risk for eating disorders tend to be very concerned about how others perceive them. In spite of their intelligence, work ethic, and notable achievements, they see themselves as inadequate, even worthless. They may lack a sense of personal identity and independence. Their eating disorder may provide a sense of being in control of their own lives.

Families can contribute to eating disorders by being overprotective, rigid, and enmeshed. This strongly reinforces the problems with self-esteem and personal identity. There are often difficulties resolving conflict, and family members fail to share doubts, anxieties, and fears. Parental expectations are generally very high and physical appearance is extremely important. In some cases, sexual or physical abuse is present.

Our culture contributes to eating disorders in major ways and many experts believe this is the most important factor of all. Television, movies, mag-

Red Flags for Eating Disorders in Vegetarians

If you think you or someone you care about might have an eating disorder, go through this list of red flags. The more red flags, the greater the risk. While many of the behaviors described below are not unusual in our thin-obsessed society, they cannot be considered normal or healthy. If after going through this list of red flags you believe that you or someone you care about may have an eating disorder, seek professional assistance. The chances of recovery are vastly improved if you do. As a first step, talk to your family physician or counselor. That takes some courage on your part but it is vital to your recovery. Please be assured there is help out there!

Food

❑ refusal to eat energy-dense vegetarian foods (e.g., nuts)
❑ refusal to eat foods with visible or added fat (e.g., oil-based salad dressings)
❑ eating mainly very-low-calorie, nonfat foods (e.g., vegetables, fruits, air-popped popcorn, rice cakes)
❑ refusal to eat foods that were former favorites
❑ refusal to eat out
❑ drinking diet sodas, tea, coffee, or other noncaloric beverages constantly
❑ severely restricting calories and knowing caloric content of everything
❑ skipping meals, eating like a bird
❑ having unlimited excuses not to eat (sore stomach, already ate, will eat later, etc.)
❑ exhibiting strange eating behaviors (chewing food and spitting it out, cutting food in tiny pieces, arranging food on plate)

Bingeing (with or without purging)

❑ uncontrollably consuming large amounts of food
❑ preferring to eat alone or in secret
❑ nervous/jumpy response if "caught" eating
❑ frequently purchasing special binge foods
❑ making trips to the bathroom right after a meal
❑ running water in bathroom to cover sounds of vomiting
❑ smell of vomit or obvious remains of vomit around toilet
❑ using excessive amounts of mints, mouth washes
❑ frequently purchasing laxatives, diuretics, or diet pills
❑ numerous, unsuccessful dieting attempts
❑ getting up at night to eat

Appearance and body image

❑ tremendous fear of weight gain
❑ wearing many layers of clothes to hide fat, hide thinness, or stay warm
❑ excessive concern about clothing size
❑ having a distorted body image (imagining the body larger than it really is)
❑ spending much time in front of the mirror
❑ hating specific body parts
❑ equating personal worth with body weight
❑ having unusual weighing routines

Exercise

❑ compulsive exercising beyond what is necessary or healthy
❑ exercising constantly, even while watching TV, doing chores, etc.
❑ taking time from work or school to exercise
❑ never satisfied with exercise accomplishments, always pushing to do better

Social behavior

❑ becoming socially isolated (often not present prior to the disorder)
❑ avoiding friends and activities, especially those involving food
❑ denying feelings
❑ becoming moody and irritable
❑ trying to take care of everyone else, but ignoring personal problems
❑ avoiding sexual activity or situations that could lead to it (anorexics)
❑ becoming more sexual or even sexually promiscuous (bulimics)
❑ becoming rigid and controlling (anorexics)
❑ lacking impulse control, leading to poor decisions about money, sex, careers, shoplifting, etc. (bulimics)

azines, books, and billboards all send a message to women that thin is society's standard for beauty. In contrast, men are encouraged to be strong and athletic. Thinness is so highly valued in women that it profoundly affects success, employment, power, popularity, and romance. The pressure towards achieving and maintaining very low body fat is especially prevalent in athletes such as dancers, gymnasts, skaters, and distance runners. The term "female athlete triad" is commonly used to describe female athletes who exhibit eating disorders, amenorrhea, and eventual osteoporosis.

For those who are predisposed, a full-blown eating disorder can be initiated by a seemingly insignificant trigger, such as a thoughtless comment from a family member or friend about weight or shape. For some, the trigger is a major event, such as a relationship breakup, a death, a rape, or a change in one's life—new school, job, or graduation. The disorder is usually precipitated by a period of increased challenges or responsibilities that the individual feels ill-equipped to handle.

Do vegetarian diets increase risk for eating disorders?

Research indicates that as many as 50% of those suffering from anorexia nervosa or bulimia nervosa are vegetarian. On the basis of such figures, it has been argued that vegetarians are a high-risk group for eating disorders. Indeed, a recent Minnesota study matching 107 vegetarian teens with 214 comparable nonvegetarians found that the vegetarian teens were twice as likely to eat fruits and vegetables, one-third as likely to eat sweets, and one-fourth as likely to eat salty snack foods more than once a day. However, the vegetarians were also twice as likely to diet, four times as likely to practice self-induced vomiting, and eight times as likely to use laxatives.

The obvious question that arises is: "Do vegetarian and vegan diets contribute to or cause eating disorders?" While this may seem a logical conclusion, it is important to consider which came first, the vegetarian diet or the eating disorder. Research indicates that the large majority of vegetarian or vegan anorexics and bulimics chose this eating pattern after the onset of their disease. The "restricted" vegetarian or vegan eating pattern legitimizes the removal of numerous high-fat, energy-dense foods such as meat, eggs, cheese, ice cream, sour cream, whipping cream, and butter. It is an appealing diet for anyone wanting to reduce these types of foods for whatever reason. However, the eating pattern chosen by those with anorexia or bulimia nervosa is far more restrictive than a healthful vegan diet, eliminating nuts, seeds, nut butters, avocados, and limiting overall caloric intake.

The Consequences of Eating Disorders

The potential physiological and psychological consequences of eating disorders arise from starvation, purging, and bingeing leading to obesity.

Starvation

Weight loss leading to emaciation

Amennorhea (absence of menstruation),
   Infertility

Heart Failure

Electrolyte imbalances

Hypertension

High cholesterol

Liver and kidney damage

Constipation, bowel spasms

Increased surgical morbidity

Low blood sugar

Digestive problems, deficiency of digestive
   enzymes, malabsorption

Edema of the abdomen

Increased susceptibility to infection,
   reduced immunity

Depression, mood swings

Muscle atrophy

Decreased sex drive

Malnutrition, anemia

Growth of lanugo (fine, downy hair)

Bone loss, osteoporosis

Dry blotchy skin, brittle hair and nails,
   loss of hair

Coldness (hands and feet)

Seizures

Purging

Weight fluctuations (loss or gain)

Irregular periods

Bradycardia (reduced heart rate)

Hypotension

Heart disease

Liver and kidney damage

Chronic watery diarrhea (with laxative
   abuse)

Dehydration

Low blood sugar

Swelling of face and neck

Reduced immunity

Depression, mood swings

Muscoloskeletal disorders

Severe stomach or esophageal problems

Sleep disturbances, bad dreams

Malnutrition

Callused or bruised fingers (from self-
   induced vomiting)

Erosion of teeth

Redness in hands, feet, face

Binge Eating (without purging)

Weight gain leading to obesity

Hormonal imbalances leading to menstrual
   problems

Heart failure

Liver and kidney damage

Constipation or diarrhea

Dehydration

Type 2 diabetes mellitus

Gallbladder disease

Edema of legs and feet

Breast, bowel and reproductive cancers

Depression, mood swings

This is quite a different situation from that of an individual who commits to a vegetarian or vegan diet out of concern for personal health, animal rights, or environmental advocacy. People who make strong ethical choices that are contrary to popular cultural opinion tend to be self-assured, independent thinkers. Research suggests that vegetarian/vegan diets do not increase risk for eating disorders, but rather those with eating disorders tend to follow severely restricted diets that they describe as vegetarian.

If you have an eating disorder, ask yourself this question: Was your decision to become vegetarian influenced by your desire to achieve a lower body weight? Be honest with yourself. Recovery does not require that you begin eating animal foods again. While returning to an nonvegetarian diet is a part of recovery for some individuals, it is not necessary for everyone. Many who select a vegetarian/vegan diet as a means of eliminating fattening food end up becoming convinced of the ethical, ecological, or health arguments in favor of this pattern of eating. If this is the case for you, be assured that you can achieve complete recovery without forsaking your beliefs and values.

CLAIMING BACK YOUR LIFE

The first step to claiming back your life is recognizing that you have a serious disorder. You may resist taking this first step because you are terrified that getting help means getting fat. You may be afraid to risk losing what seems like the only part of your life you really control. If you take nothing more from this chapter, please take this.

You are not in control of your life when you have an eating disorder.
The eating disorder is completely in control of you.

It's ironic, isn't it? Just when you think you finally have control over something in your life, it traps you like bird in a cage. It masquerades as your friend, filling your head with voices that remind you of all your failings, "You are so fat, ugly, and worthless." It convinces you that it is your only hope for being a slim, beautiful, and valuable human being.

Don't fall for this message! It is a pack of lies.

Your eating disorder is not your friend; it never has been and never will be. It is a powerful, destructive enemy. It is a trap that robs you of your time, your friends, your spirit, and your life. It does not keep its promises. Trust me. I have heard those voices and I remember that cage. I mourn the years that it robbed from my life and the lives of the people I love. If I could, I would take a giant cage cutter and set you free. I would rejoice with all my heart to see you fly, laugh, and love again. There is just one problem—the cage can only be opened from the inside. You have the power to set yourself free. You are, you were, and you always will be stronger than your disorder.

If you choose to dedicate your life to being the thinnest of the thin, you will have sacrificed all the gifts you could offer the world as a trade for that thinness. Is that what your life is really all about? Who will it benefit? Who will be hurt? Think about it. There are no rewards for reaching 60 pounds. Your family and friends will not celebrate the moment. No one will stand in awe of your will power or envy your emaciated body; they will only pity your weakness and pray for your return.

Deep down inside you is a spirit who wants to make a real difference in this world. What are your passions? Do you want to put an end to child slave labor? Do you want to protect the chimpanzees sacrificed in the name of science? It feels infinitely more satisfying to be cherished for the light you bring to those around you rather than being resented for your darkness and despair. Eating disorders make it very difficult to commit yourself to anything other than your personal quest for thinness. You are far too precious to be wasted on such a useless cause. You are one of a kind—intelligent, compassionate, and creative. When you free yourself from your eating disorder, your true inner spirit will shine and you will make this world a better place. Do not deprive those around you of that privilege.

If you suffer from binge eating disorder or chronic overeating disorder—some of the previous material applies but there is more. Your pain is among the worst of those with eating disorders. Health professionals may tell you that all you need to do is lose a little weight, just cut back on fattening foods, and do some exercise. They may not recognize your problem as they would anorexia or bulimia. Thinness is esteemed in our society, while overweight is maligned. Thus, disorders leading to obesity are looked upon with less sympathy and compassion that those which lead to thinness. This is not just and with education and perseverance that will change. The reality is there is little difference between the torment of an anorexic or a binge eater. They are separated by a very fine line.

The road to recovery

Eating disorders begin as psychological disorders that can produce serious physiological consequences, thereby becoming diseases of both mind and body. To treat only the mind can be a grave error, as malnutrition can in itself create alterations in the mind. Treating only the body is an even more serious error, as it neglects the root of the problem and in so doing we may mask the symptoms but aggravate the condition. You can make a complete recovery; however, the healing process may take many months or even years. An effective treatment program requires a holistic approach that addresses causes and consequences at many levels. This is best accomplished with a multidisciplinary team offering consistent, ongoing support.

Begin by seeing your family doctor. He or she will refer you to the appropriate treatment center. There you will get a medical assessment to determine the physiological and psychological consequences of your disorder. Initiation of appropriate treatment and monitoring by an experienced eating disorders team is necessary for many affected individuals. If you have anorexia nervosa, hospitalization is often required for initial treatment, while bulimics rarely need this type of crisis intervention. If you have binge eating disorder or another eating disorder (EDNOS) that is less well recognized by health professionals, collect information before seeing your doctor.

Soon after medical assessment is completed, individual counseling with an experienced therapist should begin. This is the part of your treatment that addresses the underlying issues of control, ineffectiveness, and autonomy. It will assist you in building self-confidence and independence, getting control over your life. Some people also benefit from group therapy, which can help build relationships and break down feelings of isolation and alienation.

Family therapy, while not essential for everyone, is extremely important for younger patients for whom the family is still a strong influence. It helps all family members understand what the patient is going through and how they can best support her recovery. The many destructive patterns of interaction that feed the disease are addressed, creating new and healthier family dynamics.

Drug therapy is also often used for patients with eating disorders. While some success has been achieved with the use of antidepressant medications, they have generally not been effective in treating anorexia nervosa. It is important to remember that medication will not cure your disorder but can help to get you through a crisis or improve your physiological or psychological functioning.

Nutrition counseling is an integral part of your recovery. This is the part of your treatment that directly addresses food and eating behaviors. The primary goal is the "normalization of eating." This means the consumption of a wide variety of foods in amounts that are supportive of appropriate body weight. Normal eating helps to restore your nutritional status, emotional state, and overall well-being. For vegetarians/vegans, this part of the treatment regime can be especially difficult. The next section will explore this part of therapy in more detail. It is meant not as a substitute for an experienced registered dietitian but as a guide to get you started.

NORMAL EATING FOR VEGETARIANS

The goal of normalization of eating is to re-establish healthful eating patterns. It is important for the treatment team to carefully examine the reasons a vegetarian diet was chosen before determining the appropriate nutrition therapy. It is equally important that the individual with an eating disorder be completely honest about their motivation if recovery is to take place.

If you chose a vegetarian diet solely to reduce calories or fat, a return to a mixed nonvegetarian diet will be an important part of your recovery. Please don't feel guilty about that. There may come a time after you are healed when you want to explore the vegetarian lifestyle for other reasons.

If you were vegetarian before the onset of your disease or have become an ethically committed vegetarian since the onset of your disease, there is no reason for you to begin eating meat or go back to eating meat. Some experts are convinced that recovery for those who ate meat prior to the onset of the disorder depends on eating a mixed nonvegetarian diet. This can be counterproductive and disrespectful to those who have since become ethical vegetarians. Millions of vegetarians and vegans enjoy normal eating, with a wonderful balance and variety of wholesome foods. Those individuals recovering from eating disorders can too!

Follow the steps to normal eating listed below, and refer to the Vegan Food Guide on pages 154-55 for further guidelines. Love and joy to you in your journey towards better health.

Guidelines for Normalizing Eating

OVERCOME RESTRICTIVE EATING

Eat small, regular meals each day

- Eat at least 3 meals a day plus 1 to 3 snacks.
- Aim for 5 to 6 small meals per day.

Practice "mechanical eating" until your body heals itself.

Your hunger and satiety signals may not be working too well. Until they kick in, eat set amounts of food at predetermined times. A registered dietitian can help you set up a program that meets your nutritional needs and is acceptable to you. Your program will look something like this:

- Breakfast (7:00 am): 1 cup cold whole grain cereal, ¼ cup granola, 1 cup fortified soymilk, and ½ cup berries
- Morning Snack (10:00 am): one fresh orange, one small carrot muffin

- Lunch (12:30 pm): tofu salad sandwich, vegetable sticks, fruit juice
- Afternoon Snack (3:00 pm): soy yogurt and a banana
- Dinner (5:30 pm): veggie patty, potato, and a mixed vegetable stir fry
- Evening Snack (9:00 pm): one apple and 1 oz. walnuts

Reintroduce "unsafe foods" slowly.

"Unsafe food" usually means any food that is high in fat or energy. For most vegetarians with an eating-disorder that includes nuts, seeds, avocados, olives, oils, legumes, and many grain products. For lacto-ovo vegetarians it also means dairy products and eggs. It is easiest to reintroduce these foods slowly and in small portions. Slice avocado in a salad, toss some toasted almonds into your stir fry, or add black beans to the soup.

Focus on what you can eat rather than what you eliminate.

It is important to focus on the wonderful variety of foods you can eat, rather than on what you can't. This means exploring the world of vegetarian options that is growing every day. There are numerous patties, loaves, sandwich slices, nondairy yogurts, and frozen desserts. Also look to other cultures for ideas. You will be amazed at the bounty that awaits you.

Stop buying diet foods.

Buy foods because you enjoy them and they help nourish your body, not because of their fat or calorie content. Instead of buying diet salad dressing, make a dressing with flaxseed oil or extra-virgin olive oil and fresh lemons. (See recipe, page 127.) Instead of diet soda, drink freshly squeezed juice.

Forget counting calories.

Don't count calories. Instead, learn to listen to your body. As it heals, your body will begin to function as it should. It will let you know when you need to eat and how much to eat. Give yourself the opportunity to enjoy these pleasures once more.

Let food be your medicine.

Food is your ally, not your enemy. Let it be your medicine. Food is the fuel that fills you with boundless energy. It nourishes you and restores your health.

ELIMINATE BINGE EATING

Do not skip meals or otherwise allow yourself to become famished.

Hunger is the most powerful binge trigger of all. The more severely you restrict calories, the higher your risk of a binge. Skipping breakfast or lunch can be disastrous. If you do this, you are setting yourself up for a binge. Eating more frequently will help ensure that you do not get too hungry. Eat 4 to 6 small meals each day.

Normalize serving sizes.

When you are a binge eater, it is easy to forget what normal portions look like. It can help to eat with other people and notice usual portion sizes. Better yet, have a registered dietitian develop an eating plan that gives you specific foods and quantities for each meal and for snacks.

Lead yourself not into temptation.

During your recovery, if you have a trigger food such as potato chips, don't keep it in the house. If you really want a certain food, share some with a friend or go to a restaurant where you can order a single portion. That way, you won't feel deprived and you'll see that you can enjoy even "forbidden food" in reasonable portions.

Develop a plan of action to get through binge urges.

The most effective plan may require that you leave the house—take the dog for a walk, go shopping, visit a friend, make a trip to the library. If you can't get out, call a friend, meditate, or read a book. You may start a woodworking project, needlepoint, or some other craft or art work that will keep your hands busy. When you feel that urge, pick up your project. Keep some mints or chewing gum handy—they can help to get you through that difficult moment.

If your plan of action fails, go to plan B, a reasonable, nonbinge snack.

Be prepared for those times when you are really hungry and are at risk for a binge. Write a list of 5 or 6 reasonable snacks and stick to them. Select foods that take a little effort to consume. Some great choices would be:

• a bowl of shredded wheat cereal with some grape nuts sprinkled on top

• a slice of toasted pumpernickel bread with almond butter and an apple

• a bowl of popcorn and a pomegranate

• 8 crackers with veggie pepperoni, veggie cheese, and pickles

Don't eat standing up.

Whenever you eat, make a point of setting a place at the table or setting a nice tray with utensils, a napkin—the whole nine yards, especially when you are alone. Make the food look attractive. Don't begin eating until you are sitting down. Eat slowly and savor every bite. Drink a big glass of water or herb tea with your food.

Break the cycle of eating in secret.

Eating in secret is an invitation to binge. As far as is possible, eat with other people. Eat in public places more often. Bring your lunch to a park; plan regular potlucks with friends. If you have avoided restaurants, make a point of going to one with a friend. It will be a real breakthrough for you.

Learn to appreciate and enjoy great food.

Spend time preparing wonderful meals. Take pride in the effort you put into making things from scratch. Set a pretty table. Light some candles. Share your food with family and friends. Avoid eating alone when you can, but if you are alone, do make it extra special—you are worth it!

REPLACE DESTRUCTIVE BEHAVIORS WITH HEALTHY ONES

Get rid of your scales.

Scales do not measure human value. They only serve to feed your disorder.

Get involved in nonfood-related activities.

- Think about all the things that you love to do or have dreamed of doing.
- Rekindle those loves. Take a pottery class. Join a canoe club. Get certified for scuba. Learn to parachute. Become a volunteer. Enjoy your every accomplishment.

Be conscious of your exercise activities.

If you exercise excessively, change your routines a little. Cut back on aerobic activity to about 30-40 minutes 3 or 4 times a week and add in some strength-building activities. You'll begin to look healthy and fit instead of weak and wasted.

If you are a nonexerciser and are overweight, consider all the exciting options available to you. You don't have to join a gym to get exercise. Join a hiking club, take up tennis, find a walking partner. Your options are endless. Aim to exercise at least 3 or 4 times a week.

Don't beat yourself up if you make a mistake.

Everyone makes mistakes. If you blow it, don't be too hard on yourself. Think about how things went wrong and learn from your mistake. Being a perfectionist is simply setting yourself up for failure. No human has ever been or will ever be perfect. Instead, aim to be a balanced, compassionate, and loving person. Not only is that possible for you, it will be easier than you imagine.

Celebrate each and every step in the right direction.

Make a big deal about every positive step you take. If you eat a good meal and don't vomit, reward yourself. If you eat a food that you have avoided for many months or years, have a party. Celebrate the food that can once again bring you pleasure; celebrate your newfound strength; celebrate life.

Supporting the vegetarian with an eating disorder

As a family member or a friend of a person with one of these disorders, there are a number of things you can do to help support recovery and to avoid making things worse.

• Encourage the person to seek professional assistance.

• Accept the person's right to make decisions concerning his/her disorder.

• Remember that they are seeking control over their own life.

• Make the person responsible for any behavior they might do that affects others.

• Encourage involvement with nonfood related activities.

• Reinforce positive characteristics that do not involve food and/or weight.

• Avoid making comments about weight or appearance.

• Let the person decide what he/she will or will not eat.

• Avoid buying special foods to accommodate the person with an eating disorder.

• Do not use bribes of money or privileges to control the person's eating behavior.

• Try to maintain as much normalcy in your family life as possible.

• Participate in family therapy if it is recommended.

• Take care of yourself and seek support if you need it.

Information on eating disorders, organizations, websites, support groups and recovery centers abound. To get the necessary information, just do an Internet search of "eating disorders" or go to your local library.

When I developed anorexia nervosa in 1976, information and support was so scarce that I had never even heard of the disease, nor had any of my family or friends. Today the support systems are amazing. Please use them. May you be healed inside and out.

Brenda Davis

CHAPTER
15

Underweight

A re you desperately trying to gain weight? Do people constantly remark on your excessive thinness, while others envy your ability to eat anything and not gain weight? It can be every bit as challenging for someone who is underweight to gain a pound as it is for someone who is overweight to lose a pound. Underweight can be particularly frustrating, as it is not always recognized as a problem. The general consensus in this society is that "you can never be too rich or too thin." This is especially true for women, in whom thinness is prized. By contrast, men strive for a lean but muscular, athletic build. Many men who are not technically underweight consider themselves too skinny and go to great lengths to build a "better body."

If you believe you are underweight, this chapter is for you.

Determination of Underweight

Underweight is generally determined using a tool called Body Mass Index (BMI, page 206). The two sets of cut off figures most commonly used are:
- less than 20.7 for men and less than 19.1 for women
- less than 18.5 for both men and women

While these figures provide useful guidelines for the determination of underweight, other factors such as your state of health and body frame can help to determine if your low body weight poses a health risk. If you are in poor health (you lack energy, are often sick, are slow to recover from illness, etc.) chances are your body weight is too low. On the other hand, if you are in excellent health, chances are that your body weight is healthy for you, even if your BMI suggests otherwise. Using the BMI, small-framed people often appear underweight when they are at a healthy weight, while large-framed people may appear at a healthy weight when, in fact, they are underweight.

Causes of Underweight

Underweight is relatively rare in this culture of abundance. It is most commonly seen in conjunction with serious diseases such as cancer, Chron's disease, or eating disorders. It is more common in children than in adults, and in men than in women (except in case of eating disorders—see Chapter 14). Technically, underweight is the result of insufficient energy intake relative to energy output, just as overweight is the result of excessive energy intake relative to energy output. However, the causes of weight imbalances are far more complex than textbook calculations might suggest. Individuals experience underweight for many reasons.

Physiological Factors	*Environmental Factors*	*Psychological Factors*
• genetic predisposition	• inadequate access to food	• stress
• high metabolism	• overactive lifestyle	• depression
• hormonal abnormalities	• lack of time to eat	• pressure from society to be thin
• disease states affecting nutrient absorption, metabolism, or appetite	• loneliness, isolation	• personal perception of your body (Men tend to be more highly motivated to correct underweight than women.)
• nutritional deficiencies affecting appetite (e.g., zinc deficiency)	• habitual meal skipping	
	• poorly planned diet	
	• use of medications drugs, alcohol, or cigarettes	

WEIGHT GAIN MARKETPLACE

The market for weight gain aids is surprisingly large. The vast majority of these products are geared towards those who have embarked on a body building program and are seeking rapid increases in muscle mass, many of whom are not technically underweight using BMI cutoffs. These weight-gain aids are, however, appealing to almost anyone who is interested in putting on weight. While some of these products may be of benefit, many are not only a waste of money, they are potentially harmful. Here's a quick run-down on the most popular offerings.

Diets

The vast majority of weight gain diets recommend an increase in energy intake of at least 500-1,000 calories per day. In the past most of these diets were very high in fat (40-50% of calories) with an emphasis on high-fat meat and dairy (cheese, cream, etc.). Today, with the push for increases in lean body mass, weight gain diets tend to be low in fat (15-30% of calories) and high in protein.

Supplements

Many consumers assume that if something is in the store, it must be safe. Not so! There is no guarantee that a supplement being marketed is safe, contains what it claims to contain, or is effective. It is completely up to the consumer to educate him/herself. The information provided below is intended to make that task a little easier.

AMINO ACID SUPPLEMENTS

Single amino acids and combinations of two or more amino acids are said to increase lean body mass. To date, numerous studies have failed to demonstrate any influence on body composition or strength.

Amino acid tablets containing a variety of amino acids are often based on egg-white, thus are of no use to vegans. Dry roasted soynuts are cheaper and far tastier anyway!

PROTEIN POWDERS

Protein powders are probably the most popular of all weight gain aids Yes, vegan options are readily available! They are loaded with both protein and calories—just one shake can provide about 25-50 grams of protein and 300-700 calories (depending on your choice of powder and what you like to throw in) without adding a lot of bulk to the diet. But before you jump on the protein powder bandwagon, calculate your requirements and your current intake. (See "How much protein do you really need to gain muscle mass?" on page 238.) It's easy to go overboard. When you consume more protein than you require, it is converted to sugar to be used as energy or stored as fat. The conversion process generates nitrogen, which puts stress on the kidneys. In addition, excess protein can contribute to urinary calcium loss and osteoporosis.

CREATINE MONOHYDRATE

Creatine is among the most popular ergogenic aids used to enhance power, size, and endurance. The only dietary sources of creatine are meat and fish. (A pound of meat contains 1.5-2 g.) However, it is synthesized in the body from two amino acids, and experts agree that most people make enough to meet their needs.

Vegetarians have lower creatine muscle stores than nonvegetarians and some studies suggest that we have the greatest uptake of creatine and the greatest increases in weight from these supplements. Thus, it is often assumed that vegetarian athletes or vegetarians attempting to gain weight would benefit from creatine supplements.

Scientific research assessing the effectiveness of creatine has had inconsistent results, with some studies demonstrating increases in muscle mass and improved performance, while others have shown no benefit at all. Observed improvements in muscle mass are thought to be due to fluid retention in the muscle, which is quickly lost when the supplement is discontinued.

Questions remain about the long-term safety of creatine, particularly for the heart, kidneys, and liver. Reports of increased muscle cramping, joint soreness, muscle tears, elevated heart rate, increased blood pressure, and GI problems are fairly common with regular use. Given the high price, questionable benefits, and potential side effects, it is probably not worth using.

Trace Minerals: Chromium, Vanadium, Boron, and Magnesium

• Trace Minerals: A variety of trace minerals including chromium, vanadium, boron, and magnesium are necessary for muscle building, thus are often marketed in supplement form as anabolic aids. Scientific studies have failed to demonstrate significant benefits from supplemental chromium or vanadium, while research on boron is too limited to draw any conclusions at this time. There is some evidence that magnesium may be useful, especially in those with poor status.

• Beta-Hydroxy-Beta-Methyl Butyrate (HMB): HMB is thought to increase muscle mass, however, only one study to date has confirmed such benefits and they were very modest. While HMB does not appear to be a health hazard, it is expensive and not overly effective.

• Testosterone boosters: Various "pro-hormone" substances (naturally occurring hormone building blocks) have become popular alternatives for anabolic steroids. These substances, collectively known as "andros," may have the potential to cause health problems similar to those caused by anabolic steroids, though less severe. Avoid them.

GREAT GAINS FOR VEGANS

The most effective approach to weight gain is not so different than it is for weight loss: make permanent changes in your diet and lifestyle.

Body Stuff…Simple Steps to a Bigger Body

SET REALISTIC GOALS

If your natural body type is tall and skinny, don't expect to turn into The Hulk. You can gain muscle but it may take more work than it would for a person with a naturally muscular build. Consistency is the key to producing the results you're after.

DO RESISTANCE TRAINING.

Even if you have no desire to build big muscles, moderate resistance training will help ensure that the weight you gain includes a healthy balance of muscle and fat. You may prefer to do pull-ups, pushups, dips or other resistance exercises. However, for many people, using weights will be the training of choice. A professional trainer will help to tailor a program to meet your personal goals.

BE MODERATE WITH AEROBIC EXERCISE.

It is really tough to gain weight when you are training for a marathon. Keep aerobic exercise to 2-3 times a week for about 30-60 minutes each time. Aerobic exercise will help keep body fat low and contribute to better overall health, so don't forsake it!

MAKE REST AND RELAXATION A PRIORITY.

Simplify your life! Do at least a half-hour of stress management each day. Take up yoga, meditation, or tai-chi. Get a good night's sleep. For most people 7-9 hours is a reasonable goal.

AVOID ADDICTIVE SUBSTANCES.

Addictions to alcohol, cigarettes, or other drugs are not only damaging to health, they can alter metabolism and interfere with appetite. If you are addicted to some harmful substance, chances are very good that the addiction is a contributing factor to your weight problem. Take your first positive step in the right direction—seek professional help.

How much protein do you really need to gain muscle mass?

Sedentary to moderately active individuals: 1 g/kg body weight★

Athletes: 1.5 g/kg body weight★ (1 kg = 2.2 pounds)

★ *These are average figures chosen for ease of calculation. Reduced digestibility of plant protein has been accounted for. Needs may be greater for highly competitive athletes.*

Example:

Assuming a weight of 154 pounds, protein requirements would be:

154 lbs. ÷ 2.2 = 70 kg

70 x 1 = 70 grams of protein (moderately active)

70 x 1.5 = 105 grams of protein (athlete)

For anyone consuming a very-high-calorie diet, protein intakes in this range are easy to achieve. However, if you have difficulty taking in enough protein and calories, protein powders may be a reasonable option for you.

LISTEN TO YOUR BODY.

Recognize that our bodies are all unique and function optimally at different sizes and shapes. If you are constantly tired, your body is giving you a message. If you are always sore, you are probably overworking your muscles. Overtraining does not allow your muscles sufficient time to recuperate and grow, but sets you up for injury.

Food Stuff...Sensible Steps to a Better Diet

MAKE HEALTH YOUR #1 GOAL.

The foods that best support a healthy body weight are those that provide not only calories, but an abundance of nutrients and phytochemicals. With a focus on health, you reduce your risk of falling prey to seductive sales pitches that are often not only worthless, but potentially harmful. Even if weight gain doesn't happen as quickly as you might have hoped for, you'll appreciate the benefits of a healthier lifestyle—increased energy, better strength, improved concentration, and fewer illnesses.

If your nutrient intake is questionable, consider using a multivitamin/mineral supplement.

EAT MORE!

Servings for weight gain:	
Grains	10-12+ servings
Beans and Bean Alternates	4-8+ servings
Calcium-Rich Foods	6-8+ servings
Vegetables	4+ servings
Fruits	4+ servings
Essential Fatty Acids	4+ servings

You need to add at least 500–1,000 calories per day to your diet to gain 1–2 pounds per week. Follow the Vegan Food Guide on pages 154–55, but aim for the highest numbers of servings in each food group and then some! This will help to bring your total caloric intake in the range of 2,500–3,000 calories a day (more will be needed for competitive athletes) and ensure that all your nutrient needs are being met.

Extra high-quality oil will help to further increase caloric intake. Two to three tablespoons a day is reasonable).

BE GENEROUS WITH CARBOHYDRATES.

Try these high-carbohydrate winners:
- hummus and whole wheat pita bread
- whole grain cereal with soymilk
- baked potatoes with bean sauce
- whole grain pilafs
- whole grain pasta dishes
- vegan muffins or other nutritious baked goods

The single most important dietary strategy affecting weight gain (including lean body mass) is increasing total energy intake. A high carbohydrate diet allows for the best recovery of muscle glycogen stores, enabling muscles to work harder for longer periods of time. In addition, the best way to accumulate protein is to increase your energy consumption, as this serves to improve nitrogen retention. If the energy supply is insufficient, protein will be used to meet energy needs and not to increase muscle mass.

PUSH PLANT PROTEIN.

For weight gain, it is recommended that 15% of total calories come from protein, or 1.0-1.7 g of protein per kg body weight. For most people, that amounts to between 70-130 g/day depending on current weight and weight gain goals. It is not uncommon for poorly planned vegan diets to be low in protein. Popular foods like bagels, cereal with rice milk, French fries, and pasta with tomato sauce provide little protein. The best way to ensure an

Food	Serving Size	Protein (grams)
Pumpkin seeds	½ cup	37
Soy nuts	½ cup	34
Soybeans	1 cup	29
Field Roast	3 oz.	23
Tofu (firm)	½ cup	20
Just Like Ground, Yves	4 oz.	20
Peanuts	½ cup	19
Veggie lunch slices, Yves	4 slices	16-20
Seeds (not pumpkin)	½ cup	15-20
Beans, most	1 cup	15-20
Veggie dogs, Yves	2 dogs	18
Tempeh	½ cup	16
Nuts (most)	½ cup	8-15
Veggie burgers, Yves	1 burger	12
Soymilk	1 cup	6-10

adequate protein intake is to include a reasonable source with each meal. If you have difficulty consuming enough food, vegan protein powders are an option. Look for a supplement that is a nonalcohol-extracted, soy-based product.

EAT HIGHER-FAT WHOLE VEGAN FOODS.

Vegan diets tend to be bulky and low in fat—not an advantage when you are aiming to put on weight. Use vegan foods that are less bulky and more energy dense to your advantage. Among the most useful foods are nuts and seeds, soy nuts, tofu, soymilk, avocados and nutritious baked goods. Their energy content might surprise you:

Quick Shake

Basic shake:
1 banana, fresh or frozen (unpeel before freezing)
1 cup soymilk (240 ml)

Optional ingredients:
1 cup berries, peaches, or other fresh or frozen fruit (240 ml)
¼-1 cup soy yogurt (60-240 ml)
1 Tbsp. flax oil (15 ml)
¼ cup soy protein powder (60 ml)
Process all the ingredients in a blender until smooth. If
desired, add 2 to 3 ice cubes before blending. Makes 2 cups.
(Provides over 40 grams of protein and 500 calories if all optional ingredients listed above are used.)

Nuts, seeds and their butters
Add ½ to 1 cup nuts and seeds to your
daily diet:

Food	Serving Size	Energy (calories)
Nuts (not peanuts)	½ cup	360–480
Peanuts	½ cup	415
Soy nuts	½ cup	390
Tofu (firm)	½ cup	183
Soymilk	1 cup	120–160
Avocado	1 medium	340
Carrot cake	1 slice	400
Pumpkin muffin	1 large muffin	400
Hearty cookie	2 cookies	300

- Keep a bag of nuts and/or seeds where-ever you spend most of your time.
- Add nuts and seeds to veggie roasts, pat-ties, and stir fries.
- Sprinkle roasted nuts or seeds on salads.
- Add nuts and seeds to baked goods.
- Eat nut/seed-based power bars.
- Use nut butters on toast, bread, and in sauces.
- Try soy nuts for a change. They are loaded with high-quality protein.

Tofu

Tofu is a wonderfully versatile, low-bulk vegan food. To increase it in your diet:

- Add soft tofu to shakes.
- Scramble tofu for breakfast.
- Use flavored tofu in sandwiches and salads.
- Put tofu in soups and stews.
- Use tofu as a base for veggie roasts and patties.
- Include tofu in desserts such as puddings, tofu cheesecake, cakes, muffins, and cookies.

Soymilk and soy yogurt

Soymilk has more calories and protein than most other nondairy beverages. Include regular, fortified soymilk in your diet more often.

- Drink soymilk and use it on your cereal.
- Cook cereals in soymilk instead of water.
- Use soymilk in pancakes, waffles, breads, muffins, puddings, soups, etc.
- Make shakes using soymilk and/or soy yogurt.
- Use soy yogurt as a snack with fruit and granola.

Avocados

Avocados pack an awful lot of calories into a small fruit. Eat them more often.

- Dress up a salad with a few slices
- Mash with lemon juice for dips, sandwich spreads, and toppings
- Add avocado chunks to salsa.

- Use avocado pieces in vegetable pita sandwiches.
- Add diced avocado to pasta or quinoa salads.

Baked goods

Baked goods can be so much more than white flour and hydrogenated fat. If you start with the right stuff, they can make valuable contributions to the diet.

- Use whole grain flour and enrich with extra wheat germ.
- Add nuts, seeds, and nut butters.
- Use soymilk or soymilk powder in baked goods instead of water.
- Use dried fruits in place of sugar. (Cooked, mashed dates work well).
- Use high-quality oils instead of hydrogenated fats in baking.

EAT MORE OFTEN.

Eat at least 5-6 times a day, including at least 2-3 hearty snacks. When you eat infrequently, it is hard to meet energy needs. Don't skip meals or go to bed on an empty stomach. Just including one additional snack of 500 calories each day could result in a weight gain of a pound a week. Here are a few snack options with about 500 calories each:

- ¾ cup trail mix (nuts, seeds and dried fruits)
- ⅔ cup nuts
- A fruit smoothie
- 1 almond butter and banana sandwich plus 1 cup soymilk
- 1 cup shredded wheat, ¼ cup granola, 1½ cups soymilk
- 20 crackers, 2 oz. vegan cheese, 4 veggie slices, and 10 olives
- 1 large vegan muffin, a cup of soy yogurt, and an apple
- 2 oz. taco chips, salsa, and ½ mashed avocado

DRINK BETWEEN MEALS

Fluids are very important but if you drink with your meals, it can reduce the amount of food you are able to eat. When the chosen fluids provide little if any calories (i.e., clear soups, coffee, and tea), they can sabotage weight gain efforts. The beverages you choose can make a significant difference to your overall energy intake. Just one cup of fruit juice provides 120-150 calories (fresh squeezed is best), one cup of soymilk about 120-160 calories, and a soy/fruit shake about 300-500 calories. Including these calorie-rich fluids will help increase total energy intake with little effort.

ADD CALORIES TO LOW-CAL, BULKY FOODS.

Fruits and vegetables are important components of any nutritious diet. However, these foods are bulky and low in calories. When they predominate in the diet, it can be tough to gain weight. By eating higher-energy foods along with them, you will not only improve their energy content, but make them even more delicious:

• To salads, add nuts, seeds, soy bits, tofu, avocado, and dressing.

• Sauté vegetables in olive oil, and top with toasted nuts or seeds.

• Add tofu, nuts, or seeds to stir-fries, casseroles, and pasta dishes.

• Add a cashew cheese sauce to steamed vegetables.

• Cut up fruits and top with soy yogurt and granola.

HONOR YOUR HUNGER!

Try to eat a little more than you need to be satisfied. Be sure good food is accessible at work, in the car, or wherever else you spend a lot of time. Keep a few energy bars or other nonperishables on hand in case you forget your snacks. Pay attention to what foods cause you digestive difficulties, and limit your intake of those foods. Eating foods that cause distress will only reduce your appetite. If they are key items for weight gain (i.e., nuts, tofu, etc.), you may need to keep serving sizes moderate. Experiment with eating these foods at various times of the day. You may find that your system is more able to handle these foods when it is functioning at its best. For some people that is in the morning, for others it is at night.

FOCUS ON FOOD.

If you never seem to have food around and only eat what comes out of a box or bag, perhaps it's time to consider making food more of a priority in your life.

• Make a weekly menu, prepare a list, and select a weekly shopping day.

• If you can order in bulk, go for it. Look into co-ops, buying clubs and organic delivery services. Take advantage of them!

• If you can't cook, take lessons. Go with a friend and make it fun.

• Buy a crock-pot. In the morning, throw in your grains, veggies, beans and/or tofu, and let it cook all day.

• Share meals with a friend.

• Plan for the time to prepare nutritious meals and snacks. For nutritionally complete weight-gain menus, check out chapter 9. For most women, the 2,800 calorie menu will be sufficient (although some people need more). For most men, the 4,000 calorie menu will be required to ensure desired weight gain.

CHAPTER
16

The Vegan Athlete

C an you become vegan and expect to maintain or improve athletic performance? You bet! Not only is it possible, it happens all the time. Just ask world class athletes such as six-time ironman champion Ruth Heidrich, professional and Olympic skating sensation Charlene Wong Williams, U.S. national team synchronized swimmer Kim Wurzel, power-lifting champion Pat Reeves, or any one of the thousands of other successful vegan and near-vegan athletes. The key to fueling peak performance is getting the right balance of energy and nutrients. If you are an athlete, whether a weekend warrior or serious competitor, you'll want to maximize your potential with the best nutrition possible.

ENERGY TO BURN

There are two main sources of energy that fuel muscles—glucose and fatty acids. Moderate levels of these fuels are present in the bloodstream from the foods you consume. Small amounts of glucose are stored in the liver and muscle tissues as glycogen, although glycogen stores in athletes can be twice as high as in sedentary people. These glycogen stores are generally sufficient to support daily activity but must be constantly replenished by carbohydrate intake. Stores of fatty acids provide greater energy reserves. (Fat stores vary dramatically among people, but they are generally sufficient to last for many hours of exercise.)

The fuel of choice for your muscles depends on the type, intensity, and duration of the activity performed and the fitness levels of the person performing the activity. The body has two distinct systems that unlock energy: the aerobic system and the anaerobic system.

VO₂ max

VO_2 max

A measure of the maximum volume of oxygen the muscles can use per minute of activity. The more oxygen a person consumes and uses per minute, the more fit they are.

When the heart and lungs are able to provide sufficient oxygen to your muscles, *aerobic metabolism* (aerobic meaning "with oxygen") is used to meet energy needs. The primary fuels used in aerobic activities are fatty acids and, to a lesser extent, glucose. The aerobic system predominates in endurance sports using large muscle groups, such as distance running, swimming, or biking. Aerobic activities improve cardiovascular fitness and help to reduce body fat. They train the lungs and cardiovascular system to deliver oxygen more quickly and efficiently to every part of the body. As a result, a fit individual can work longer, more vigorously, and achieve a quicker recovery at the end of the aerobic session.

When the your heart and lungs can't provide muscles with sufficient oxygen, the muscles have to rely on *anaerobic metabolism* (anaerobic meaning "without oxygen") to meet energy needs. When insufficient oxygen is delivered to cells, glucose is the only fuel that can be used for energy. Anaerobic metabolism does not completely metabolize glucose, and fragments of lactic acid build up, causing a burning pain and muscle fatigue. When sufficient oxygen becomes available, lactic acid can be completely broken down or converted back to glucose. The anaerobic system predominates in the first few minutes of any exercise and when exercise is so intense that energy demands outstrip the oxygen supply. It is also the primary system used in speed sports such as sprinting, basketball, and hockey. Power sports involving sudden intense movements, such as weightlifting and wrestling, also rely largely on anaerobic metabolism.

FUELING THE VEGAN ATHLETE

Energy Needs

The energy needs of vegan athletes vary with body size, weight, composition, metabolism, gender, age, and the amount and type of physical activity preformed. Physical activity increases energy needs and can also increase basal metabolic rate (BMR) by up to 30%. (BMR accounts for about 60-75% of total energy needs). Exercise can lead to increased energy output for up to 24 hours after the exercise is stopped. This is a very minor increase, but it can make a difference in the long term. In addition, eating a whole foods vegan diet may increase energy requirements by up to 10-15% due to reduced overall digestibility of high-fiber whole foods.

For individuals exercising casually a few times a week, energy needs increase only slightly, if at all. For those training more intensely several times a week, energy needs can be as high as 3,000-6,000 calories a day or more.

If you are constantly lacking energy, the problem may be that you are eating too little. Many athletes restrict energy intake in an effort to maintain a low body weight. Interestingly, this can seriously impair performance by lowering meta-bolic rate and reducing energy available for activity. When you increase food intake, your metabolism generally returns to normal and your energy levels sky-rocket. In fact, athletes have been known to increase energy intakes by 1,000 calories or more per day, vastly improve performance, and not gain an ounce.

Is it possible to get 3,000-6,000 calories a day on a vegan diet?

It is entirely possible to take in "big" calories eating vegan foods. However, plant foods tend to be bulky, so it is important that vegan athletes with high energy needs include plenty of energy-dense vegan options such as tofu, soy shakes, nuts, seeds and their butters, and power bars. (See pages 239-43 for many helpful ideas on how to increase energy intake, and pages 159-60 for 2,800-4,000 calorie menus.)

ENERGY-GIVING NUTRIENTS...THE RIGHT BALANCE

After all of the hoopla in the popular press about being in "The Zone," one might assume the optimal balance of energy-giving nutrients for athletes is 30: 30: 40 (protein: fat: carbohydrate). It may come as a bit of a surprise but there is very little debate about this issue in the scientific community. Sports nutri-tion and medical experts agree that carbohydrates are the preferred fuel for athletes and an inadequate supply leads to poor performance. The American and Canadian Dietetic Association and Dietitians of Canada, in their Position on nutrition for physical fitness and athletic performance for adults, state:

> *"In general (i.e., for most athletes), it is recommended that 60-65% of total energy should come from carbohydrate. Athletes who train exhaustively on successive days or who compete in prolonged endurance events should consume a diet that provides 65-70% of energy from carbohydrate."*

They also recommend that fat not exceed 30% of total calories. For endurance athletes, fat is gener-ally in the 15–20% range.

> *Recommended intakes for carbohydrates, protein, and fat as a percent of your total calories:*
> Carbohydrates: 60–70%
> Protein: 12–15%
> Fat: less than 30%

Carbohydrates

In 1968, classic research demonstrated that a high–carbohydrate diet could triple an athlete's endurance, and nothing to date has refuted these findings. High car-bohydrate intakes allow for maximum glycogen stores, helping to improve energy reserves for both aerobic and anaerobic activities. The result is that you can work harder for longer periods of time before becoming exhausted.

Glycogen stores become depleted after about 90-120 minutes of exercise at 60-80% of VO_2max. At higher intensities, depletion occurs even faster.

Endurance training increases muscle capacity to store glycogen; however, it is essential that sufficient carbohydrate be consumed in order to replenish glycogen reserves. Most athletes require approximately 6–8 grams of carbohydrate per kg (2.2 lbs.) of body weight. That works out to about 400–800 grams (1,600–3,200 calories) of carbohydrate per day.

How do I maximize my glycogen stores?

The best way to improve your glycogen stores is to follow a good aerobic training program and eat a high carbohydrate diet. To maximize glycogen stores in preparation for an endurance competition involving 90 minutes or more of continuous activity, the modified "carbohydrate loading" regime outlined in table 16.1 is recommended.

Table 16.1 Modified Carbohydrate Loading for Endurance Events of 90 Minutes or More

Time before event	Exercise	Diet
Days 8 or before	Usual training	Usual diet (60–75% carb.)
Day 7	90 min. intense (70–75% VO_2max) (glycogen depletion phase)	50% carb. diet (4 g/kg)
Days 5–6	40 minutes, moderate	70% carb. (8–10 g/kg)
Days 2–4	20 minutes, moderate	70% carb. (8–10 g/kg)
Pre-event day	Rest	70% carb. (8–10 g/kg)

TIPS FOR MODIFIED CARBOHYDRATE LOADING

- On your depletion phase (day 7), do the same activity you will be doing for the event.

- On day 4 to competition (especially on the pre-event day), reduce fiber intake and intake of any foods that tend to cause you GI distress; use refined carbohydrate foods.

- Exercise intensity can be reduced or maintained (personal preference) after the depletion phase on day 7 until the day prior to the event. However, exercise *time* must be reduced, especially in the last three days prior to the event.

What are the best sources of carbohydrates for an athlete?

Whole plant foods should serve as the primary source of carbohydrates for athletes. Whole grains, vegetables, fruits, legumes, nuts, and seeds come packaged with a vast array of important vitamins, minerals, and phytochemicals—all extremely important to peak performance. Refined carbohydrates and sugars can contribute to overall carbohydrate intake for athletes but they should account for not more than 10% of total carbohydrate calories, though higher intakes are of value immediately prior to events. For most athletes, that works out to about 7-15 tsp. of sugar per day. While this seems like a lot, one 12-oz. sugar-based beverage contains about 10 tsp. of sugar!

Protein

It is widely believed that the most important nutrient for athletes is protein, and the more, the better. While protein is a very important nutrient for athletes, it contributes only about 3-6% of the total fuel used and is needed in smaller amounts than the other energy-giving nutrients. Athletes who eat carbohydrate-rich diets use even less protein for fuel than those who consume higher-protein and fat diets. (Carbohydrate has a protein-sparing effect.) In addition, more highly trained athletes tend to use less protein for fuel during exercise, depending on type of activity, caloric intake, intensity of training, etc.

How much protein does a vegan athlete really need?

Protein requirements for athletes are greatest during early stages of training. For those wanting to increase muscle mass, the limiting factor for protein deposition is energy intake, not protein intake.

The general recommendation of 12-15% protein is appropriate for most vegan athletes, although for those with low caloric intakes (athletes attempting to keep body weight low), 15-20% may be necessary. For those with extraordinarily high caloric requirements (such as ironman athletes), 10-12% may be sufficient. For example, a 50 kg (110 lbs.) gymnast who requires about 1.4 g protein/kg body weight needs about 70 g protein per day. If she eats only 1,600 kcal/day, her protein needs would be 17.5% of total calories. On the other hand, a 70 kg endurance athlete who requires 1.4 g protein/kg body weight needs about 98 g protein/day. If he eats 4,000 calories/day, his protein needs would be about 10% of total calories.

When receiving protein solely from plant foods, as is the case for vegans, protein requirements may be higher than for nonvegetarians due to a reduced digestibility of certain plant proteins. For those consuming more highly processed and soy-based plant proteins (veggie "meats," tofu, and soy shakes), no increase in protein intakes above nonvegan athletes is generally required. For those relying more on whole foods (legumes, nuts, and seeds), an increase of 10-15% will compensate for the reduced digestibility of these foods. Using a variety of protein sources will help to ensure a reasonable protein intake.

Protein Needs for Vegan Athletes	
Standard	1.0-1.2 g/kg
Endurance	1.2-1.7 g/kg
Power/Speed	1.2-2.0 g/kg
Early Training	2-2.3 g/kg

Do I need to use protein powder shakes or bars to get sufficient protein?

It is not necessary to use protein powder shakes or bars to get sufficient protein. However, if you have difficulty meeting energy and protein needs, they can be helpful, for example, for noncooks or especially while traveling. They are also convenient prerace meals when you don't want a lot of bulk, or for those times when you want a quick and easy energy and protein supply.

Can I get too much protein?

Absolutely! While it is uncommon for vegans to get too much protein, even when eating a variety of foods, including beans, tofu, and veggie "meats," it is possible. The new low-fat, soy-based lunch slices, burgers, wieners, etc., are highly concentrated protein sources. If these are staples at almost every meal, in addition to tofu, beans, and soymilk, protein intake can be excessive. However, it is more common to see excessive protein intake when protein supplements are added to an already high-protein vegan diet. Eating excessive amounts of protein will not increase muscle mass or improve athletic performance but could be detrimental to performance and to overall health. Surplus protein gets converted to fat and stored or oxidized for energy. Amino acid oxidation increases the risk of dehydration, because by-products of protein metabolism must be excreted via the urine. Conversion of protein to fat for storage is also inefficient. (For more information on protein, see Chapter 3.)

Fat

Fat is the "enemy" in the eyes of many athletes who worry that dietary fat will lead to body fat. They are partly right. Dietary fat becomes body fat much more efficiently than carbohydrates or protein. However, this only happens when energy intakes are excessive. Fat is a major source of energy during distance events, contributing up to 75% or more of the total energy requirements. Fat is also the source of essential fatty acids and a carrier of valuable fat-soluble vitamins (A, D, E, and K), minerals, and protective phytochemicals. The body is able to store far more energy as fat than as glycogen. Fat is stored both around the body's cells (fat stores) and within muscle cells. The fat stored within muscles is immediately available to fuel aerobic activity.

With fat being such an important fuel source, you may wonder why we don't need more fat and less carbohydrate. The reason is that we have limited storage capacity for carbohydrates, thus we must constantly replenish our stores. By comparison, even thin, muscular people store substantial amounts of fat and need not worry about replenishing them in the same way. In addition, at higher intensities, you can't use fat as your major fuel and you *must* rely on carbohydrates.

How much fat do athletes really need?

The amount of dietary fat recommended for athletes depends on the carbohydrate and protein needs. Assuming a protein intake of 12-15% of calories, fat intake would vary according to carbohydrate intake as shown. Table 16.2 provides guidelines for appropriate levels of fat intake with different levels of carbohydrate intake.

Table 16.2   Fat Needs at Varying Levels of Carbohydrate Intake

% Carbohydrate in Diet	% Fat in Diet	Fat in 2,000 kcal diet	Fat in 3,000 kcal diet	Fat in 4,000 kcal diet	Fat in 5,000 kcal diet
70%	15-18 %	33-40 g	50-60 g	66-80 g	83-100 g
65%	20-23%	44-51 g	67-77 g	88-101 g	111-128 g
60%	25-28%	56-62 g	83-84 g	112-124 g	139-156 g

What are the best sources of fat for vegan athletes?

The best sources of fat for vegan athletes are the same as they are for anyone—whole plant foods. When fat comes from nut butters, tofu, and avocados, it provides many other beneficial dietary components. However, some oil can be helpful for those with higher energy needs. The best oils to use are flaxseed oil, extra-virgin olive oil, and canola oil. Using these oils will help to ensure an appropriate balance of essential fatty acids. (See Chapter 4.)

Is it true that low to moderate intensity exercise is best for fat burning?

Low to moderate intensity exercise is often promoted as being optimal for fat burning. While it certainly makes sense when you consider that in order to use fatty acids as a fuel you must be working aerobically (getting enough oxygen to muscles), total energy expenditure plays an important role in this equation. At 25% of VO_2max (walking), almost all of the fuel comes from fat, while at 65% of VO_2max (jogging), only about half the energy comes from fat. Because the rate of energy expenditure is about 2½ times higher with jogging than with walking, the total amount of fat used for fuel is actually greater. For example, a person weighing 150 lbs. would burn about 312 calories walking at 3.5 mph for 1 hour. The same person would burn about 790 calories jogging at 7 mph for 1 hour. Most of the 312 calories burned on the walk would be fat, as compared to about half of the 790 calories on the jog, or 395 calories!

VITAMINS AND MINERALS FOR VEGAN ATHLETES

Not surprisingly, an athlete's needs for vitamins and minerals is often higher than it is for a sedentary individual. This is because many of these nutrients play key roles in the use of body fuels. Vegan diets are naturally higher in certain vitamins and minerals and lower in others. The following section addresses the potential impact of these differences on athletic performance.

Vitamins

Most B vitamins (including thiamin, riboflavin, and niacin) are involved in the metabolism of energy-giving nutrients; thus, requirements for these nutrients are proportional to energy intakes. Vitamin B_6 is necessary for processing amino acids, so needs increase with protein intake. Vitamin B_{12} and folate are involved in new cell synthesis, including red blood cells. Insufficient intake of most B vitamins can impair aerobic power by reducing the breakdown of lactic acid. While getting enough of these nutrients is very important to peak performance, there is no evidence that taking large amounts of any B vitamins will enhance athletic performance. Indeed, niacin supplements may speed glycogen depletion. Some athletes take B_{12} shots to improve endurance prior to competition, although there is no good science to support this practice. Vitamin B_{12} is, however, of special concern to vegan athletes, as plant foods are not reliable sources of this nutrient. Fortified foods or supplements are essential for all vegans, whether athlete or nonathlete!

Vitamin C is necessary for the production of collagen (the chief protein in connective tissue), synthesis of carnitine, and the transport and metabolism of other nutrients. Studies suggest that athletes have increased vitamin C requirements, and even slight deficiencies can impair physical performance. Vegan athletes generally consume several times the recommended intake for vitamin C and about 50% more than nonvegetarians. Vitamin C is one of the most popular supplements for athletes; however, research is still inconclusive regarding its possible benefits to performance. Taking massive doses of vitamin C could backfire, contributing to kidney stones, GI upset, and iron overload, especially in susceptible individuals, as it increases iron absorption. If you take extra vitamin C, limit doses to not more than 500 mg/day.

Of the fat-soluble vitamins, vegan diets easily meet recommended intakes for vitamin A (primarily from colorful vegetables) and vitamin K (found mainly in green vegetables). Vitamin D can be in short supply if fortified foods are not used and/or sunshine exposure is inadequate. Vitamin E may be limited, especially if total fat intake is low (mainly from nuts, seeds, grains, and vegetable oils). There is some evidence that vitamin E supplementation may protect athletes against free radical damage and improve response to exercise-induced injury. While intakes of up to 400 IU per day are often suggested for athletes training at moderate to high intensity levels, further research is needed before more specific recommendations can be made. There is no evidence indicating that supplements of other fat-soluble vitamins are of benefit to athletes if needs are met through diet. (See Chapter 7 for more information on vitamins.)

Minerals

An athlete's mineral status can have profound affects on performance. While it is entirely possible to meet needs on a vegan diet, there are some minerals that warrant special attention by vegan athletes.

Iron deficiency is the most common mineral deficiency among athletes. Iron is needed for the transport and handling of oxygen; thus, athletes' requirements are increased due to their high oxygen demands. In addition, intense physical activity can induce iron losses through sweat and destruction of red blood cells during high-impact exercise. Studies have demonstrated that at similar levels of iron intakes, vegetarian female athletes have reduced iron status compared to nonvegetarian female athletes, so they are generally considered a high-risk group for iron deficiency. While research on the iron status of vegan athletes is virtually nonexistent, vegans tend to have better iron status than lacto-ovo vegetarians.

In general, athletes have lower hemoglobin levels and iron stores than nonathletes. Low hemoglobin levels in athletes is known as "sports anemia." This term is somewhat misleading, as the reduction in hemoglobin levels is a natural consequence of increase in blood volume and a dilution of red blood cells caused by exercise. Vegan athletes (especially menstruating females and endurance athletes) can help ensure sufficient iron intake and absorption by consuming plenty of iron-rich plant foods and iron-fortified foods, and consuming them with a rich source of vitamin C. Some individuals absorb iron very efficiently, resulting in high iron levels. Excessive iron can act a pro-oxidant, damaging tissues and negatively affecting physical ability. Thus, it is best to have your iron status checked before taking iron supplements.

Zinc is necessary for the metabolism of energy-giving nutrients and for healing of injuries. Zinc requirements are also increased by intense exercise, as zinc can be lost in perspiration. Achieving recommended intakes for zinc can be a challenge for anyone but may be even more difficult for vegans. However, studies have not shown zinc status to be related to aerobic capacity, and there is little evidence to suggest that supplementation improves performance. Plant foods provide moderate amounts of zinc but it is not as well absorbed as it is from animal foods. It is important that vegan athletes make an effort to include plenty of zinc-rich plant foods in their daily diet, including legumes, nuts, seeds, and whole grains.

While it is often assumed that young athletes will achieve high peak bone mass due to vast amounts of weight-bearing exercise, osteoporosis is a growing problem among this population, particularly in sports where weight and caloric intakes are restricted. When the level of body fat drops too low in female athletes, amenorrhea occurs and the risk for osteoporosis escalates. This situation is often associated with eating disorders. When eating disorders, amenorrhea, and osteoporosis occur together, they are referred to as the "female athlete triad." While a disproportionate number of individuals suffering from this syndrome call themselves vegans or vegetarians, it is not the plant-centered diet that causes the disorder. Rather, women suffering from this disorder become vegan or vegetarian as a means of eliminating fatty foods from their diet. (For more information on eating disorders, see Chapter 14.) Studies have suggested that vegetarians have increased menstrual disturbances when compared with nonvegetarians. However, a more recent study which controlled for many of the confounding variables (i.e., oral contraceptives, body weight, exercise frequency, age, childbirth, cycle length, and alcohol consumption), showed no such relationship in the population studied (long-term, weight-stable vegetarians with normal BMIs).

Calcium is critical to bone health, muscle contractions, nerve impulses, and numerous body reactions. It is important to ensure that vegans achieve the recommended intakes for calcium of 1,000-1,300 mg or 1,500 mg/day for those with amenorrhea or other risk factors. This generally means incorporating some fortified nondairy beverages such as calcium-fortified soymilk and orange juice into the diet, in addition to calcium-rich plant foods.

Other minerals of concern to vegan athletes are chromium, copper, magnesium, and the electrolyte minerals (sodium, potassium, and chloride). Exercise increases losses of all of these minerals from both urine and sweat; thus, endurance athletes have increased needs.

Chromium is necessary for the action of insulin and the metabolism of carbohydrates, so athletes have higher requirements than sedentary individuals. Some evidence also indicates that exercise may increase urinary chromium losses; however, it is not known whether additional dietary chromium is needed or whether retention increases as a response to the loss. Athletes ingest more food (thus more chromium), which may be sufficient to supply increased needs. There is concern that athletes who limit energy intake to maintain a low body weight could be compromising chromium status. In the general population, chromium intakes fall short of recommended levels and information about the chromium status of vegan athletes is lacking. Vegan athletes are well advised to consume nutritional yeast and chromium-rich foods such as nuts, seeds, and whole grains, as much of the chromium is missing in refined foods.

Copper is involved in oxygen transport, so a deficiency can lead to problems for athletes. However, vegans tend to have higher copper intakes than nonvegetarians, as legumes, nuts, and seeds are among our richest sources. If using a zinc supplement, it is best taken as part of a multivitamin with copper, as zinc can impair copper absorption.

Magnesium deficiency can cut muscle gains associated with training in half. While this nutrient is clearly a problem for some athletes, vegans may be at an advantage since their intakes can be 2-3 times the recommended levels, especially in those consuming 3,000 kcal or more. The richest sources of magnesium are plant foods such as nuts, legumes, greens, and whole grains.

Requirements for electrolyte minerals, including potassium, sodium, and chloride, are highly variable among athletes, depending on their fluid losses. While potassium is generally plentiful in vegan diets, sodium and chloride quickly become depleted during intense exercise, and insufficient repletion of these nutrients can seriously impair performance. (See Chapter 6 on minerals.)

VITAMIN AND MINERAL SUPPLEMENTS

It is commonly assumed that athletes need to take vitamin and mineral supplements in order to meet their needs for these nutrients. However, when the diet is well-planned and energy needs are met, the increase in nutrients that accompanies increased energy intakes is generally sufficient. This is true for all athletes, including vegans. The menus on pages 159-60 (2,800 kcal and 4,000 kcal) meet and exceed all recommended nutrient intakes. Indeed, at the 4,000 kcal level, most of the vitamins and minerals are close to or in excess of 200% of the recommended amounts. However, many athletes still opt to take supplements to ensure needs for all nutrients are consistently met. When you consider the increased free radical reactions and nutrient losses induced by exercise, taking some supplements may be an advantage, especially for athletes who eat a lot of processed foods or have low energy intakes. If you decide to take vitamin/mineral supplements, here are a few simple guidelines.

• Take a high-quality multivitamin/mineral supplement. Include iron if you are at risk for iron deficiency (often the case with females); exclude it if you are at risk for iron overload (more likely to be the case with males).

• Calcium supplements are warranted where calcium intakes are below recommended levels. Choose a supplement with magnesium and vitamin D, unless a multivitamin/mineral supplement with these nutrients is used. Aim for 500-1,000 mg elemental calcium, 200-400 mg magnesium, and 5-10 mcg vitamin D.

- If you decide to use an antioxidant supplement, select a combination antioxidant such as ACE selenium, which contains the three antioxidant vitamins plus selenium. If you prefer a single antioxidant vitamin, stick to vitamin E (up to 400 IU/day).

- Do not take single nutrient supplements of niacin or vitamin B_6.

- Avoid supplements containing more than 10 times the recommended intakes for vitamin A or any mineral, and 5 times the recommended intakes for vitamin D—these can be toxic in excess.

- Rather than using supplements in pill form, many athletes opt for fortified power bars or shakes. These are good choices, especially for athletes needing extra calories.

ERGOGENIC AIDS FOR VEGAN ATHLETES

The supplement story only begins with vitamins and minerals. There are literally hundreds of compounds packaged and sold as performance enhancers. Among the most popular are herbs (ma huang [ephedra], ginseng, guarana, and schizandra); amino acids and their metabolites (branched-chain amino acids, HMB, creatine and L-carnitine); "vitamin-like" substances (CoQ10, inositol, lipoic acid, pangamic acid, and laetrile); hormone-like substances (DHEA and "andros"); and others, including caffeine and pyruvate. The science behind the vast majority of these supplements is inconclusive and further research will be necessary before any solid recommendations can be made. For some, while benefits appear impressive, they come at a cost. Caffeine is a good case in point. Moderate doses of caffeine (about 2-3 mg/lb or 4-6 mg/kg body weight) appear to increase performance by stimulating the release of fatty acids into the blood early in exercise, thus sparing glycogen. However, caffeine has numerous potential side effects, including stomach upset, nervousness, sleeplessness, irritability, headaches, diarrhea, and dehydration. Caffeine is a diuretic and a special concern for those exercising in hot temperatures. Other supplements, such as ma huang, DHEA, and andros, are not recommended due to the numerous reports of serious adverse consequences. To add insult to injury, many ergogenic aids are derived from animal products (bee pollen, royal jelly, gelatin, carnitine, and others), and thus are not suitable for vegan athletes.

QUENCHING THE ATHLETE'S THIRST

Our needs for water are much greater than they are for any other nutrient. A sedentary person living in a cool climate loses about 1½ liters of fluid per day.

An athlete can lose 2-4 liters in a single hour of heavy exercise, especially in warm climates. Even a fluid loss of as little as 1% of body weight results in impaired physical performance. A 4-5% loss of body weight can reduce muscular work by 20-30%. An 8% loss of body weight can cause dizziness, mental confusion, and heatstroke.

The increased fluid requirements of athletes depend on the intensity and duration of their exercise, and the temperature at which they are exercising. Dehydration impairs peak performance at any level. Thus, it is important to begin exercise adequately hydrated, to ensure sufficient hydration during the exercise, and to replenish fluids when the activity is finished. The following guidelines are adapted from the Position of The American College of Sports Medicine. These guidelines are especially important for athletes who live and/or train in warm climates.

Guidelines for Maintaining Hydration During an Event or Training Session

24 hours prior to an event or training session
Drink plenty of fluids.
Keep well hydrated.

2 hours prior to an event or training session
Drink about 2 cups (480 ml) of fluids.
Drink 2-4 oz. (60-120 ml) of fluids every 15 minutes up to event time.

During event or training session
Drink 4-8 oz. (120-240 ml) fluids every 10-15 minutes.
Events less than 1 hour: water or sports drink.★
Events greater than 1 hour: sports drink.

Immediately following exercise
Drink 2 cups (480 ml) fluid for each pound lost or 150% of lost fluids.

★*Sports drinks should contain 4-8% carbohydrates, sodium chloride, and potassium for long distance events. The form of carbohydrate should be a combination of several sugars such as glucose, glucose polymers, sucrose, and fructose. Beverages that use fructose as the main carbohydrate source are not recommended because fructose is slowly absorbed and must be converted to glucose by the liver before it can be metabolized by muscle. High intakes of fructose can also cause cramping and diarrhea.*

PRACTICAL POINTERS FOR PEAK PERFORMANCE

What does all this mean in terms of real food?

Eat sufficient quantities of a wide variety of nutrient-dense whole foods as described in the Vegan Food Guide (pages 154-55), and stay well hydrated.

Sound simple? It is. If you don't eat enough nourishing food, you'll lack energy and vital nutrients. If you don't drink enough, you could end up dehydrated—either way performance takes a nosedive!

The following chart gives you a good idea of how much food from each food group you will need to eat in order to achieve your desired energy intake and meet all nutritional requirements. The breakdown of carbohydrate, protein, and fat for all of the patterns listed below is 64-66% carbohydrate, 14-15% protein, and 19-21% fat. Also see the menus on pages 157-60.

Food Group	Serving Size	2,000 kcal	2,500 kcal	3,000 kcal	4,000 kcal	5,000 kcal
Grains, 80 kcal	1/2 c grains, 1 sl bread	10	13	15	20	25
Beans, 170 kcal	1 c beans, 1/2 c tofu, 1/4 c nuts	3	4	5	6	8
Vegetables, 30 kcal	1 c raw; 1/2 cup ckd	6	7	8	10	12
Fruits, 60 kcal	1 med; 1/2 cup	6	7	8	12	14
Calcium-rich foods	1/2 c fortified bev, 1 c kale	6	7	8	9	10
Oils, 45 kcal	1 tsp.	3	4	5	7	9
Total estimated calories		1,985	2,540	3,055	3,955	4,965

Making the most of each food group

GRAINS

The number of servings looks huge, but remember one serving is only ½ cup of grains or a slice of bread. It is easy for big eaters to get 6 servings of grains in one meal (for example 2 cups of rice and some hearty grain-based dessert or a roll). It helps to include grains at each meal and with at least one snack each day.

BEANS AND BEAN ALTERNATES

In our calculations we assumed an intake of several different foods from this group, including beans, tofu, veggie "meats," seitan, nuts and seeds, and soymilk. Protein-rich vegan choices have huge variations in carbohydrate and fat content, so it is a good idea to select a variety of these foods. The differences in composition of these products are listed here.

• Veggie "meats" are protein-rich but usually low in fat and carbohydrates.

• Tofu is protein-rich, moderately high in fat, and low in carbohydrates.

• Beans are carbohydrate-rich, moderate in protein, and low in fat.

• Nuts and seeds are fat-rich, fairly low in protein, and moderate in carbohydrates.

VEGETABLES

If you have difficulty achieving the recommended number of servings from this group, try to include vegetables at lunch as well as dinner, and use a mixture of raw and cooked vegetables. (Cooking condenses the vegetables and makes it easier to eat larger amounts.)

FRUITS

The easiest ways of increasing fruit consumption are to bring them with you as a snack, use several in a fruit shake, cook them for puddings and cereals, and juice them.

CALCIUM-RICH FOODS

All of the foods that fit into the calcium group also fit into other food groups. Therefore, when calculating calories, we do not include this group, since they are already accounted for elsewhere. For example, fortified soymilk, calcium-set tofu, and almonds fit into the bean group, kale and broccoli fit into the vegetable group, and calcium-fortified orange juice fits into the fruit group. One of the best ways of getting the recommended servings here is to always select calcium-fortified soymilk and fortified juice. Just ½ to ¾ cup of either of these is a serving. It adds up very quickly!

OILS

While not a food group, oils need to be considered in calculations for overall energy intake. Although it is not necessary to use oil (you can get enough from nuts, seeds, avocados, olives, etc.), it can help you to meet your energy needs and can make meals more enjoyable.

FACING THE CHALLENGES HEAD ON

Being a vegan athlete can present a few unique challenges. With your ingenuity and fortitude, it will be no sweat. Here are a few suggestions on how to deal with some of the most common questions that arise for vegan athletes.

I am a competitive athlete and I dread trying to get a decent meal when I'm on the road. What can I do to ensure I get enough good food when travelling?

First and foremost, always bring nonperishable food with you. If you are lucky enough to have a little refrigerator in your hotel, pack some soymilk, a pack of lunch slices, or some vegan "cheese." Bring fresh and dried fruit, bread (including Wasa bread, rye crackers, pappadoms [Indian crackers], or some other nutritious cracker), nuts, seeds, nut or seed butter, granola or other cereal of your choice, power or sports bars, and beverages. If you don't have a fridge, opt for some dehydrated tofu or soymilk powder. Pack some dehydrated vegan soups and min-imeals in cardboard containers—just add boiling water. Don't forget your plate, bowl, and some utensils.

Buy a few nonspill containers of various sizes from an outdoor equipment store. Take along Liquid Gold Salad Dressing (recipe, page 127) to add to baked potatoes, rice, vegetables, and salads that are widely available, and fortified soymilk for cereal (or use little soymilk tetrapacks). Also use these containers for takeout soups and stews from restaurants along the road. (See page 273 for tips and resources for vegan travelers.)

If there are no vegetarian restaurants, try ethnic. Most offer legume or tofu dishes. Don't hesitate to ask for a custom-ordered meal. If you are in an American-style restau-rant with nothing vegetarian on the menu, ask for a couple of baked potatoes or some rice and a very generous portion of vegetables (with beans or nuts, if available).

If you are travelling by air, be sure to order vegan in-flight meals. These meals often include tofu, vegetables, and rice, with fruit for dessert. Breakfast can be very disap-pointing, a white bagel and a banana. Be sure to bring a few extras such as nuts, seeds, and dried fruits to help supplement the meals.

What can I eat at sporting events? I can't find much at the concession stands.

Generally you can't depend on concession stands other than for peanuts, pretzels, and beverages. It's best to pack along whatever you need. Invest in a large, wide-mouth metal thermos and bring leftovers from dinner, such as soup, stew, chili, etc. Many din-ner items are also tasty cold. Snacks such as fresh fruit, muffins, soy yogurt, power bars, trail mix, and soy nuts will also be welcome treats.

I am a body builder and everyone at my gym, including my trainer, says there is no way I can achieve the kind of muscle gains I want on a vegan diet. I am sick and tired of trying to defend my choice. Is there anything I can do to put their minds at ease?

There are a couple of things you can do. First, lend them some reading material—including this book. Second, have a nutritional analysis done by a registered dietitian specializing in sports and vegetarian nutrition. Share it with your colleagues. When they see what you are actually taking in, they might relax a little. Finally, prove them wrong. There are plenty of vegans who are the envy of everyone at the gym.

RECOMMENDED RESOURCES

For a complete list, see www.nutrispeak.com/veganrefs.htm. See also general references for the whole book on page 276.

Dorfman, Lisa. *The Vegetarian Sports Nutrition Guide.* N.Y.: John Wiley and Sons, 1999

Gatorade Sports Science Institute: www.gssiweb.com/

The Veggie Sports Association: www.veggie.org/main/vegetarian.shtml

CHAPTER
17

Vegan Diplomacy

Becoming vegan can be a profound and rewarding physical, emotional, and spiritual journey. As any traveler knows, being prepared for difficult situations can make them a lot less daunting. In other chapters, the focus is nutrition and achieving an optimal vegan diet. Here, we consider intelligent solutions to the challenges of human interaction.

As a vegan, your dietary choice has immense impacts: the preservation of dwindling resources, powerful protection for health, and dramatic reduction in the pain and suffering of animals. There are few choices in life that offer such diverse, positive outcomes. It's enough to make you want to spread the word to the entire nonvegan world! In the past, when you got this excited about a discovery, your parents, siblings, and friends may have rejoiced and celebrated with you. This time, instead of being delighted, they may be distant and defensive. The very people with whom you most want to share your insights see these changes as an intrusion into their culture and an affront to your relationship. Becoming vegan challenges the foundation of our society, and that makes people uncomfortable. Given these realities, your interactions will depend a great deal on your attitude and approach. While there is a place for fire and brimstone, that style goes over better when preaching to the converted. For all others, a little vegan diplomacy goes a long way!

WHAT IS VEGAN DIPLOMACY?

Diplomacy is the fine art of honoring your own ethical principles and social consciousness without judging, condemning, or otherwise injuring another person. It is highly dependent on effective communication. Since people who follow a vegan lifestyle aspire to practice "harmlessness," being a vegan diplomat requires avoiding insult, contempt, and intimidation in one's interactions with others.

In a society that exploits animals for everything from toothpaste to entertainment, is it possible to be a diplomatic vegan?

Yes. It's not only possible; it's an invaluable set of skills for a vegan to acquire. While being vegetarian, which is often adopted for health reasons, is widely understood and accepted, becoming vegan is likely to bring a new level of challenge because considerations of ethics will almost inevitably arise. Some people will respect your decision and your personal integrity. Others will likely feel threatened, no matter what your intentions. Your clarity, warmth and kindly humor will also go a long way towards challenging people without making them feel judged or otherwise threatened. However, there are times when you might choose not to be diplomatic and that's OK. It may be that your colleague has dangled his 12 oz. porterhouse in front of you just one time too many. We have all been subjected to thoughtless comments or actions that isolate, ridicule, or otherwise hurt us. When this happens, it is tempting to be very nondiplomatic in your response. Sometimes that's just what is needed to get the other party to really hear what you are saying.

Be assured that there is no one right way or wrong way to deal with each and every sticky situation. Both gentleness and shock can be effective in communicating thoughts and feelings. However, consider why another person might react so negatively to your being vegan. Perhaps it is because it forces them to examine their own choices when they have a great deal else on their minds, and it makes them feel very defensive or uncomfortable. This situation and challenge are captured by the words of Dr. Albert Schweitzer, one of the greatest humanitarians of all times:

"The thinking man must oppose all cruel customs, no matter how deeply rooted in tradition and surrounded by a halo. When we have a choice, we must avoid bringing torment and injury into the life of another, even the lowliest creature; but to do so is to renounce our manhood and shoulder a guilt which nothing justifies."

MASTERING THE FINE ART OF DIPLOMACY

So how can one go about being a diplomatic vegan? Just keep reminding yourself of what being vegan is really all about—reverence for life. Recall the essence of Ahimsa referred to in Chapter 1—dynamic harmlessness. It is the active participation in nonharming and noninjuring of humans and animals. With these principles guiding your words and actions, diplomacy becomes automatic. However, for most of us, diplomacy does not come so naturally. If you are among the diplomatically challenged, here are some simple guidelines that you may find helpful.

Guidlines for the Diplomatically Challenged

Do unto others…

You know this. Let's face it, this is the golden rule and the heart of diplomacy. If you want your brother to respect your deeply held convictions about animal issues, you need to respect his deeply held convictions about religion, politics, or whatever he is passionate about. (This doesn't mean you have to agree with one another!)

Do not judge.

Judging implies approval or disapproval of someone else's convictions, statements, etc. It usually takes the form of criticism, name-calling, labeling, or analyzing. When you do this, it sabotages communication and generally results in the other person becoming defensive or resentful. Judgements usually involve "you" statements such as: "You are so narrow-minded." Instead use "I" statements such as "I feel unheard when you tune me out every time I mention anything about animal food." Positive "I" statements help to turn very negative expressions into honest reflections of your thoughts and feelings.

Avoid the "I'm good, you're bad" mentality.

When you categorize people into "good and bad" or "saint and sinner," you undermine any chances for effective communication. Moralizing rarely results in anything more than resistance. Most people sincerely want to do the right thing, but it is not always easy for them, given their current circumstances. Always give people the benefit of the doubt, and appreciate the good they do.

Listen with your heart

Most people can hear, few really listen. Listening involves more than the sensory physiological process that sends auditory messages to the brain. It takes us a step further—into the heart, where psychological involvement with the other person occurs. Effective listening can involve reflecting thoughts and feelings back to the person you are speaking with, but it also means being attentive, having appropriate eye contact, being aware of your body language, and not questioning everything that is said. Listening with your heart lays the foundation of trust and respect between two people.

Be assertive.

Assertiveness is about protecting your personal space and your ethical and social commitments in a way that is not destructive to yourself *or* to other people. It allows you to live your own life, to defend yourself, and to meet your needs while respecting those around you. Being assertive is quite different from being submissive, an action that communicates that you don't really matter and that your feelings are unimportant. Submissive people may express themselves but they do so apologetically and as a result are rarely taken seriously. By contrast, aggressive individuals express their feelings at the expense of others. They often come across as being controlling, rude, overpowering, abusive, or offensive. Aggression serves only to alienate people. It creates fear, hostility, and anger and does not encourage people to consider your viewpoint.

Be genuine.

Being genuine means being authentic; it is the polar opposite of being phony. Genuineness means awareness of your own feelings, accepting those feelings, and sharing them responsibly. When you are genuine, you allow people to connect with you on a level playing field. You remove threat and fear from your interactions.

Empathize.

Empathy is crucial to truly understanding another person. It allows you to walk in another person's shoes or see through her eyes without losing your sense of self. Empathy requires sensitivity. It makes people feel accepted and understood. It fosters constructive change. When someone acts or thinks differently from you, there can be a temptation to distance oneself; however, it is connection that encourages change. Empathy is different from sympathy; the latter puts the receiver in a "one down" position.

Celebrate every little step in the right direction.

We are all at very different places in our lives. For some, the thought of completely giving up ice cream seems insurmountable. For others, avoiding the most minute amounts of animal by-products in bread or a shampoo is second nature. If we are to encourage a massive mainstream shift towards plant-based diets, we need to encourage people for every little step in the right direction. Instead of focusing on their inability to say no to Aunt Edith's blueberry pancakes, we need to celebrate their success in switching from cow's milk to soymilk. When someone tells you that they hardly eat meat anymore (even if you know that they eat at McDonald's twice a week), recognize that they are trying to connect with you. Seize the opportunity to share some heart-warming story with them, or offer to lend them a book. Building bridges works far better than burning them when your goal is helping people across to your side of the river.

Make your example your most powerful ally.

Of all the tools at your disposal, none is as powerful as your example. It is hard for someone to argue about how dangerous a vegan diet is if you are the only one in the office that doesn't have a serious health problem, such as high blood pressure, high cholesterol, or diabetes. Myths about vegans having trouble getting enough protein will evaporate if you are the fittest person in your circle of friends or business associates. Instead of trying to convince someone that vegan foods taste wonderful, invite them for dinner or bring something special to the company get-together. It is amazing what you can accomplish without saying much at all.

Breaking it to them respectfully.

Telling people that you don't eat or use animal products can be a daunting task. Food is central to most celebrations and traditions. Sharing food is an important way of connecting. Family members may fear that you are pulling away or condemning the values with which you were raised. Your friends may be uncomfortable because they're not sure how to relate to you anymore. Your dietary choice may bring up a host of feelings, including guilt, sadness, and anger. Yet with time, your disclosure may lead to a new closeness, and a deeper sharing than you've ever had before. A key to a positive outcome is respect. Even if your world is almost entirely nonvegan, it is populated with many who are trying, in their own ways, to make the world a better place. If you wish to share your insights with others, it will help if you also allow time and space for *their* responses and expression of deeper values. These suggestions may help.

- Select a time when you're both in good spirits and relaxed, instead of when you have just had a disagreement or are stressed out.
- If verbal communication is difficult, write a thoughtful letter.
- Share what your commitment involves and how it affects your life.
- Make food sharing easy: bring your own food or prepare vegan meals together.
- Let others know what you do and don't eat. A verbal or written list might include:

    I *do* eat grains, vegetables, fruits, beans, tofu, vegan meat substitutes, nuts, and seeds.

    I *don't* eat meat, poultry, fish, dairy produts, eggs, gelatin, or honey.
- Changes of the heart and soul rarely happen overnight, but they do happen. Express appreciation for the consideration shown by the other person.

STICKY SITUATIONS

You will undoubtedly find yourself in situations that are more than a little uncomfortable. Your responses will depend, at least in part, on where you are along the path to becoming vegan. Over time, you'll become adept in a range of situations. At first you may just avoid everything that is obviously derived from animals—like cheese in a casserole or eggs in a salad. Later, you may pay closer attention to food labels and also eliminate animal by-products, such as casein in soy cheese. You may choose to eat only vegan foods at home but not be so careful when dining out. Eventually, you may decide you'd rather go hungry than eat anything with a trace of animal products in it. The following situations are familiar to most of us in one form or another. The choices suggested are not intended as right and wrong answers but options that can be adapted to your situation.

The Hidden or Not-So-Hidden Animal Ingredients

You're invited to your aunt's house for lunch. She assures you all the food will be vegan and serves a lovely vegetable soup and homemade bread. You thoroughly enjoy your lunch and are down to your last bite of soup when you spot a piece of chicken on the bottom of your bowl. When you ask her what it is she says, "Oh, I hope you don't mind, I thought I'd throw in a chicken bone. It isn't like adding real meat, it was just a bone after all." You...

a) *tell her not to worry about it, and avoid any food-related activities with her in future;*

b) *yell at her so she'll never make that mistake again;*

c) *tell her that vegans don't eat any traces of meat at all and give her some good reading material.*

PROBABLE OUTCOME:

a) *Tell her not to worry:* She'll continue to misunderstand what being vegan is all about and/or to believe that it is just another fad diet.

You have to make a judgement call depending on the personality you are dealing with. If you believe that it doesn't matter what you do or say, and nothing will change how she sees things, then this option is reasonable.

b) *Yell at her:* She'll think you're totally ungrateful and write you out of her will.

Name-calling will only serve to alienate your aunt, put her on the defensive, and cause bad feelings in your family.

c) *Explain vegan:* She'll understand vegan a little better and appreciate your commitment to this cause. She may even be inspired to move towards a more plant-based diet after reading suitable materials.

Being assertive but considerate is your best bet in this type of situation. To avoid completely losing it, do a quick empathy exercise in your mind. Why do you think your aunt used a chicken bone in what she called "vegan" soup? Do you think it was a malicious act or simply ignorance on her part? Assume that her intentions were the best. She really wanted to have a nice lunch with you. Why did she put the bone in her soup? Probably because she was afraid if she didn't use a bone, the soup wouldn't taste good enough to serve a guest. You simply need to let her know that all meat, even by-products of meat, are unacceptable to you and why. Do so with compassion. Offer to share a video or book with her so she can understand your choice a little better.

Happy Birthday to You!

When you started your new job a couple of weeks ago, you decided you would avoid making your animal rights agenda public right away (but wait a month or so until they like you). You never suspected that your boss would take notice of the birth date on your application form. On your special day, everyone at the office surprises you with a big, beautiful cake with your name on it. Your coworkers light the candles and start singing "Happy Birthday to You." You...

a) eat the cake and say nothing;

b) tell them you have a stomach ache, and ask if you could bring a piece home;

c) tell them that you are most grateful for their thoughtfulness, but you are vegan.

PROBABLE OUTCOME:

a) Eat cake: Next it will be ice cream, then fried chicken. You get the picture.

You may choose this option if you don't mind eating the occasional bit of eggs and dairy. However, if you want to avoid animal products, then eating the cake will backfire. By not telling your colleagues that you don't wish to eat these foods, you are saying that these choices are unimportant. You are being submissive rather than assertive, which undermines your personal integrity and their respect for you.

b) Stomach ache: You'll compromise the trust and respect your colleagues have for you.

Being dishonest about your ethical beliefs suggests that you are ashamed, embarrassed, or uncertain about those beliefs. Honesty is important in gaining the respect that is an essential part of connecting with other people.

c) You are vegan: Your colleagues may be surprised, but they will appreciate your being straight with them now.

If you are really committed to being vegan, this is your only option. How you break the news is important. First, acknowledge the gift and the thoughtfulness of your coworkers. Admit your oversight in not telling them sooner, perhaps in a light-hearted way. They'll not feel rejected when they sense your genuine warmth and when you shift your attention from the cake to the circle of people around you.

Thanksgiving Dinner

In your family, Thanksgiving dinner is a big deal. In the past, it always involved a 20-pound turkey, dressing, cranberry sauce, mashed potatoes, sweet potato casserole, gravy, Brussels sprouts, glazed carrots, Waldorf salad, your Mom's homemade pickles, pumpkin pie, and whipped cream. Only two items were ever vegan: the pickles and cranberry sauce! Even the Brussels sprouts are coated with butter. It has become uncomfortable for you to partake in the meal. Several vegan friends gather together to celebrate life with a stuffed squash or tofu unturkey; this year you would really rather share Thanksgiving dinner with them. You . . .

a) go to the family dinner because you know how upset your parents will be if you don't show up. You bring your own little patty and ask Mom to leave a few potatoes and Brussels sprouts aside before adding milk and butter;

b) attend the family dinner, but bring a centerpiece dish (stuffed squash or tofu unturkey), vegetarian gravy, and salad;

c) tell your family that you are not comfortable eating meat-centered meals but will be happy to do nonfood activities;

d) say you are having Thanksgiving dinner with friends but would love to come for a visit.

PROBABLE OUTCOME:

a) Go anyway and bring a patty: You end up resentful, your family senses your uneasiness, and everyone is uncomfortable.

Meals with family are among the most difficult situations to deal with, whether it's Thanksgiving, Easter, Christmas, Hanukkah, someone's birthday, anniversary, or family reunions. It is understandable that you want to be part of these occasions, yet honor your rights and values. Think of things that will make you more comfortable. This will help your family to respect your ethical commitments.

b) Go anyway, but bring delicious vegan food: It gives you a feeling of celebration and your relatives are impressed with how tasty the food is.

This is a good compromise if you are willing to share a meal where meat is served. (Otherwise, it's clearly not an option.) By making a big contribution, you don't feel isolated and deprived. Your family is introduced to wonderful vegan food, may add it to future feasts, or even switch to the vegan dishes over time. This option keeps the doors open and may impact your family in ways you may never have dreamed possible.

c) No more eating with you: This could cause some difficulties with family relationships and be taken as personal rejection. For some vegans, it is the only option they can live with.

You know your family well enough to hazard a guess as to how they will respond. At first it may seem that to celebrate together, you'll have to be around meat. However, solutions will surface: vegan Jewish foods during Hanukkah, Chinese vegan food on Christmas Eve or New Year's Day, or an Easter brunch with vegan waffles, fresh fruit sauces, and an afternoon hike. There are many ways of showing your family how important they are to you.

d) Dining with friends this year: You feel less stressed, and your family may feel fine too.

As much depends on *how* you say things as on *what* you say. When telling your family about alternate plans, be positive and genuine. Share your excitement about this vegan celebration. Tell them about the menu and your contribution. Sometimes elderly parents can even be included, either for this meal or for a future outing to a vegetarian restaurant. They may be delighted to meet your friends.

Difficult Transition to a Vegan Diet

Two months ago you became near-vegan overnight after going to a compelling lecture on the ethics of eating. Prior to this, your nine-year-old daughter, Sarah, was raised much like any nonvegetarian child. Her favorite foods are Dairy Queen sundaes, McNuggets, fries, ham and pineapple pizza, and orange pop. Sarah understands why you want to be vegan, but she is not very happy with the food. Sarah doesn't like the soymilk you buy, so she eats her cereal plain. She doesn't like the mushy tofu you add to the spaghetti sauce, so she eats spaghetti noodles plain too. You are worried that, while health was part of your reason for becoming vegan, Sarah's diet is even worse than before. At least when you had milk and meat in the fridge, Sarah was getting calcium and protein. Sarah has been begging you to let her have milk for her cereal and some cheese. You . . .

a) agree to buy milk and rennet-free cheese for her;

b) say she can eat what she likes when out, but at home it's strictly vegan;

c) refuse to let her eat any animal foods at all.

PROBABLE OUTCOME

a) Buy milk and cheese: Sarah is happier; you are not so happy about purchasing and having nonvegan food around the house.

It's tough for anyone to make a sudden change and tougher still when it wasn't her choice. Allowing Sarah to adjust at her own pace will help her feel less resentful. Chances are good that Sarah will drop these foods in time. Though your feelings are mixed, it's important for Sarah to have control over her food choices.

b) Vegan at home: Sarah may start wanting to eat out a lot more; however, you can divert this by incorporating new, tasty vegan dishes into your daily diet.

This gives Sarah some control over her choices and she will appreciate that you respect her rights.

• *Make vegan versions of formally favorite foods.*

Instead of cereal, buy bagels, nut butters, and jam; some mornings make vegan pancakes, scrambled tofu, veggie bacon, blueberry muffins, fruit salad, or Quick Shakes (page 240). Use veggie turkey, bologna, or ham for sandwiches. Send nuts, dried fruits, soy puddings, or yogurts in lunch bags. Veganize her favorite dinner meals by using veggie ground round instead of tofu in spaghetti sauce and shepherd's pie. Experiment with burgers (we know of 30 different vegan burgers), veggie dogs, and fresh buns from the bakery. Make oven fries with fresh veggies and dip as side dishes. Buy marinated tofu and bake it in the oven until crispy.

• *Encourage Sarah to be your assistant cook.*

This will help to increase her interest and enjoyment in the food.

• *Don't go overboard with eliminating fun foods.*

It's tough enough to be near-vegan amidst friends who love cheeseburgers; help her figure out vegan options for the mall: fries, falafel, and bean burritos.

c) No choice vegan—Sarah will become very resentful of this new lifestyle and may well rebel against it.

You know how it goes. Whether big or little, people don't like being controlled. Prohibiting her favorite foods may make them more appealing. It is probably better to come to a compromise that you both can live with.

You'll likely encounter many variations of these challenges. With experience, your skill at responding will increase. Fortunately, the world is becoming more vegan-friendly, offering a multitude of resources outlined on page 270 to 273.

Closing Thoughts

When your daily choices are made out of reverence for life,
And respect for the connection among all things,
This world becomes a better place
*It **is** that simple.*

APPENDIX: *Vegan Resources*

There are inventive and thoroughly livable solutions to the various dilemmas that face people who have a desire to live more lightly on the planet and make vegan choices that affect their diet and other aspects of their lifestyle. Here are some websites, books, and other materials that will help tremendously, wherever you are, wherever you go, and whatever you are doing.

THREE KEY WEBSITES

These will open the door to a world of vegan-friendly resources:

www.ivu.org	International Vegetarian Union
www.vrg.org	Vegetarian Resource Group
www.vegansociety.com	Vegan Society, U.K.

Foods, Ingredients, and Shopping

If you can't tell what an ingredient is on a food label, check the Vegetarian Resource Group's *Guide to Food Ingredients*, available by calling 1-410-366-VEGE or from their website. Fact sheets and information on ingredients, production of "free-range" eggs, dairy, and honey can be found at:

www.vrg.org/nutshell/faqingredients.htm
www.ivu.org/faq
www.peta-online.org/mc/facts

MAIL ORDER SOURCES FOR INGREDIENTS:

The Mail Order Catalog
P.O. Box 180
Summertown, TN 38483
800-695-2241
931-964-2241
www.healthy-eating.com

Red Star nutritional yeast, textured soy protein, organic flaxseeds, egg replacer, powdered soymilks, soy isolates, seitan mixes, vegan baking mixes, soy pudding mixes, vegan cookbooks.

Choices Market
2627 West 16th Ave.
Vancouver, B.C., V6K 3C2
Canada
604-736-0009
604-736-0011 (fax)

Natural foods, soyfoods, vegan products, volume discounts, COD anywhere in Canada.

LONG-CHAIN OMEGA-3 FATTY ACIDS

(DHA, unfortunately only in gel caps to date):

OmegaTech   Martek Biosciences Corp.

301-381-8100   410-740-0081

www.omegadha.com   http://bio.com/home/martek

MEALS AND MENUS

Whether you're confident and experienced in the kitchen, a beginner, or a non-cook, here are are resources to support your vegan meal and menu creation.

The Vegan Handbook (D. Wasserman, R. Mangels, The Vegetarian Resource Group, 1996), provides a one-week menu and many recipes. It even has a 30-day menu for people who don't like to cook, developed by C. Stahler.

Cooking Vegetarian (V. Melina, J. Forest, Wiley 1998, Macmillan Canada 1996) combines the expertise of a dietitian and professional chef in a complete range of delicious recipes; every recipe is vegan as first option.

Simply Vegan (D. Wasserman, The Vegetarian Resource Group, 1996) includes a nutrition section by R. Mangels.

Conveniently Vegan (D. Wasserman, The Vegetarian Resource Group, 1997) shows creative use of convenience foods and is simpler still!

For other vegan recipes:

The Vegan Kitchen (F. Dinshah, The American Vegan Society, 1997)

Table for Two (J. Stepaniak,) and *Instead of Chicken, Instead of Turkey,* (K. Davis), both from Book Publishing Company.

If you're stuck for lunch ideas, here are helpful resources:

The Natural Lunchbox (J. Brown, Book Publishing Company, 1996)

Soups On! Vegetarian Soups, Muffins, and Accompaniments (B. Bloomfield, Book Publishing Company, 1997)

The Uncheese Cookbook (Book Publishing Co, 1994) (Joanne Stepaniak) People will often say "I'd like to be vegan, but I'm not sure that I could give up cheese." Fortunately, Joanne has made a real contribution here in capturing the flavor of favorite cheeses in recipes that you can make yourself.

What's For Dinner?

Does making vegan meals seem a challenge? In fact, revolutionizing your diet is easy, according to Dr. Neal Barnard. In the foreword to *Cooking With PETA* (Book Publishing Company, 1997), he makes the point that most people have eight or nine favorite recipes they return to again and again. Start with three favorites that are already vegan (cheeseless burritos, spaghetti with tomato sauce, meatless chili with beans), add three that are easy to make vegan (split pea or lentil soup, sub sandwich with vegan deli slices, or one from the list of Eay-To-Prepare Meals, pages 203–04). Add three new recipes from the cookbooks listed above or any of those available from The Mail Order Catalog (1–800–695–2241 or www.healthy-eating.com).

BOOKS, MAGAZINES, AND PERIODICALS

Buy books through www.ivu.org/books and 5% of your normal purchase price goes to the International Vegetarian Union.

For history:

• Joanne Stepaniak's *The Vegan Sourcebook* (Lowell House, 1998)

• Colin Spencer's *A Heretic's Feast* (University Press of New England, 1995)

• Also see www.ivu.org/history

For helpful, practical information for vegans and other vegetarians, an excellent scientific update column by registered dietitian Dr. Reed Mangels, a nutrition hotline by registered dietitian Suzanne Havala, recipes from around the world, and excellent practical tips, see *The Vegetarian Journal*, www.vrg.org

For delicious vegan recipes, food photography, and well-researched articles:

• *Veggie Life*, www.veggielife.com or 1–800–777–1164

For articles that are helpful for new vegetarians:

• *Vegetarian Times;* www.vegetariantimes.com

For nutrition research:

• Messina, M., and V. Messina *Dietitians' Guide to Vegetarian Diets* (Aspen Pub., Gaithersburg, Md., 1996). Look forward to the revised edition by coauthors Mark and Virginia Messina and Reed Mangels in the autumn of 2001.

• The Vegetarian Nutrition Dietary Practice Group of the American Dietetic Association publishes a quarterly newsletter, *Issues in Vegetarian Dietetics,* that is a tremendous help in keeping updated on the latest vegetarian-related research topics. (Subscriptions are also available for nonpractice group members.) For fact sheets and selected articles, see:
    www.vegetariannutritiondpg.org

• *The Vegetarian Health Letter* is another excellent source of reliable nutrition information, published by Loma Linda University, Loma Linda, Cal.; contact vegletter@sph.llu.edu

- *VegNews* at www.vegnews.com or call 408-358-6478.

RESTAURANTS, TRAVEL, HOLIDAYS, AND RELATED INTERESTS

- *The Vegetarian Journal's Guide to Natural Foods Restaurants in the U.S. and Canada* (Avery Publishing) Over 2,000 restaurants, juice bars, delicatessens, and vacation spots (revised every few years).

- www.vegdining.com: Just click on the country you're going to, print a list of vegetarian restaurants, pack your bag, and things couldn't be simpler!

Also see www.vegeats.com/restaurants

- www.ivu.org/global for the IVU's global directory.

In the U.S., also check out www.vegetarianusa.com/vegan2.html

- Airlines are becoming accustomed to meal requests using one or other of these phrases: "strict vegetarian," "pure vegetarian," "nondairy vegetarian," or "vegan."

- Invest in containers of various sizes with tight-fitting, spill-proof lids (available from outdoor equipment stores) so that you can bring with you fortified soymilk, protein-rich food (soup, hummus, or marinated tofu) or a little salad dressing. With these three items, the rest of your meal will come together fairly easily and be very tasty.

CELEBRATIONS, FESTIVALS, SUPPORT ORGANIZATIONS

- World Vegetarian Congress (www.ivu.org/congress) and international and national Vegan Festivals are held in different countries every few years. These stimulating, inspiring celebrations provide great ways to see the world!

- Summerfest, in a beautiful U.S. setting with well-organized workshops, excellent vegan meals, warm friendships, one-week getaway, and great speakers on a wide range of topics: www.navs-online.org

- EarthSave potlucks, cooking classes, speaker presentations, and turkey-free Thanksgiving dinners; larger groups located in Vancouver, Seattle, and Louisville sponsor an annual "Taste of Health" (a healthy food festival). Vegetarian Starter Kit also available: www.earthsave.org

- Visit VegSource's website to see announcements for events: www.vegsource.com/events

Table 18.1 Instead of Dairy, Egg, Meat, and Sugar: Substitution Basics

Nonvegan Food	Vegan Substitute
Instead of Dairy Products	
1 cup cow's milk	1 cup fortified soymilk or grain milk
1 cup buttermilk	1 cup soymilk plus 2 tsp lemon juice or white vinegar
1 cup yogurt	1 cup soy yogurt
1 oz cheese	1 oz of casein-free soy cheese
1 cup cottage cheese (in recipes)	1 cup mashed tofu (drained medium works well)
½ cup cream cheese (4 oz)	½ cup soy cream cheese (4 oz)
1 cup ricotta cheese (as in lasagne)	1 cup mashed tofu (firm works well)
1 cup ice cream	1 cup frozen soy or rice dessert, vegan fruit sherbet, or sorbet
1 cup whipping cream	12 oz firm silken tofu + ¼ c maple syrup + 1 Tbsp lemon juice + 1 tsp vanilla, blended (*Cooking Vegetarian*, V. Melina, J. Forest, Wiley/Macmillan Canada)
1 Tbsp butter	1 Tbsp olive oil, vegan margarine, soy spread
Instead of Egg	
(Note that sometimes just leaving out 1 egg in a recipe makes very little difference.)	
1 egg	2-4 Tbsp soft tofu 1 Tbsp ground flaxseed mixed with 3 Tbsp water ¼ cup mashed, very ripe banana or applesauce 1 tsp EnerG "Egg Replacer," for baking. ⅛ teaspoon baking powder mixed with dry ingredients, to replace leavening action of 1 egg or egg white in baking
Instead of Meat Products	
1 Tbsp gelatin	1 Tbsp agar flakes (thickens 1 cup liquid) ½ tsp agar powder (thickens 1 cup liquid)
1 cup meat or chicken stock	1 cup liquid vegetable stock or 1 c water + vegetable stock cubes or power (see package directions) Bragg Liquid Aminos or tamari (to taste) mixed with water Miso mixed with water (to taste)
1 serving meat, chicken, fish	Equal weight or volume of meat substitutes, beans, tofu, marinated tofu, tempeh, gluten (seitan), gluten-based meats from Oriental restaurants Equal volume of portobello mushrooms
1 cup ground beef	1 cup veggie ground round (Yves or other) ½ cup dry textured soy protein + (½ c less 1 Tbsp) boiling stock or water, stirred and soaked for 10 minutes
1 serving sausage or smoked meat	equal weight or volume of meat substitutes, equal weight or volume of crumbed, seasoned tofu (season with sage, savory, thyme, parsley, garlic, fennel seeds, and liquid smoke)
Instead of Sugar*	
1 cup white sugar 1 cup brown sugar, or ¾ c honey	⅔ to 1 cup dried cane juice granules ¼ cup blackstrap molasses plus ½ cup sweet molasses 1 to 1½ cups barley malt syrup or rice syrup (or to taste; these are less sweet)

**Cane sugar is sometimes whitened using animal bones*

Basic Shopping List

Grain Products

- ❑ Brown rice
- ❑ Quinoa
- ❑ Bulgur
- ❑ Dry cereal
- ❑ Mixed cereals
- ❑ Whole grain bread
- ❑ Pasta
- ❑ Barley
- ❑ Millet
- ❑ Other grains
- ❑ Oatmeal
- ❑ Popcorn
- ❑ Whole grain crackers
- ❑ Wheat germ
- ❑ Flours (whole wheat, unbleached, other)

Vegetables and Fruits

- ❑ Fresh greens (kale, collards, Chinese/Napa cabbage, broccoli,
- ❑ Garlic and onions
- ❑ Seasonal vegetables
- ❑ Seasonal fruits
- ❑ Tomato sauce, paste, and canned tomatoes
- ❑ Canned water-packed fruits
- ❑ Raisins, figs, apricots, dates, prunes, dried fruit
- ❑ Frozen vegetables
- ❑ Frozen fruit and juices

Beans & Lentils & Products

- ❑ Dried legumes (navy beans, garbanzos, pinto beans, kidney beans, lentils, split peas, etc.)
- ❑ Canned legumes (garbanzos, pinto beans, kidney beans, baked beans, etc.)
- ❑ Prepared bean dishes such as soups and chili.
- ❑ Tofu, tempeh
- ❑ Instant dried legume dishes (humus, soups, casseroles, refried beans, etc.)
- ❑ Meat substitutes, vegetarian patties, soy wieners, veggie slices, sausages, veggie ground

Nuts, seeds and butters

- ❑ Nuts (raw cashews, almonds, walnuts, pecans, filberts, peanuts)
- ❑ Nut butters
- ❑ Seeds (flax, pumpkin, sesame, sunflower)
- ❑ Seed butters (tahini)

Soy and grain beverages and related products

- ❑ Fortified soy or grain milks
- ❑ Vegan soy cheese
- ❑ Soy yogurt

Herbs and Spices

- ❑ Fresh parsley, cilantro, basil
- ❑ Fresh ginger
- ❑ Oregano, sage, savory, thyme
- ❑ Chili powder or other chili
- ❑ Cinnamon, allspice, nutmeg, cumin, curry
- ❑ Mustard (Dijon type), prepared or powder
- ❑ Salt and pepper

Sweeteners

- ❑ Blackstrap molasses,
- ❑ Barley malt, rice syrup, maple syrup
- ❑ Jams and conserves
- ❑ Dried cane sugar

Beverages

- ❑ Cereal grain beverages
- ❑ Fruit and vegetable juices
- ❑ Leaf and herbal teas
- ❑ Organic coffee

Fats and Oils

- ❑ Flaxseed oil
- ❑ Virgin olive oil
- ❑ Canola, high-oleic sunflower or safflower oils
- ❑ Nut oils (hazelnut, walnut)
- ❑ Toasted sesame oil
- ❑ Soy spread
- ❑ Vegetable or lecithin spray

Seasonings, Condiments, and Other

- ❑ Vegetarian Support Formula Nutritional Yeast (formerly Red Star brand T 6635+)
- ❑ Seaweed (hijiki, wakame, nori, agar)
- ❑ Miso
- ❑ Bragg Liquid Aminos
- ❑ Tamari or soy sauce
- ❑ Bottled sauces (teriyaki, barbeque, sweet and sour, other)
- ❑ Vegetable broth powder or cubes, or chicken-style seasoning
- ❑ Vinegar (rice, wine, balsamic, or apple cider vinegar)
- ❑ Frozen lemon juice
- ❑ Patak's or other curry paste

GENERAL REFERENCES

For a complete list see
www.nutrispeak.com/veganrefs.htm

Agren, J.J. "Fatty acid composition of erythrocyte, platelet, and serum lipids in strict vegans." *Lipids* 30 (4) (1995): 365-9.

American Dietetic Association and Dietitians of Canada, Vegetarian Nutrition chapter, *Manual of Clinical Dietetics*. 2000.

Brown et al. *State of the World 2000*. Worldwatch Inst. www.world watch.org

Draper, A. "The energy and nutrient intakes of different types of vegetarian: a case for supplements?" *Br. J. Nutr.* 69 (1) (1993): 3-19. erratum *Br. J. Nutr.* 70 (3) (1993): 812.

ESHA. *The Food Processor Nutrition Analysis Program*, www.esha.com 1-800-659-3742.

Fraser, G.E. "Diet and coronary heart disease; beyond dietary fats and low-density-lipoprotein cholesterol." *Am. J. Clin. Nutr.* 59 (5 Suppl) (1994): 1117S-1123S.

Groff, J. et al. *Advanced Nutrition and Human Metabolism*. St Paul, Minn.: West Publ. Co., 1995.

Haddad, E.H. et al. "Dietary intake and biochemical, hematologic, and immune status of vegans compared with nonvegetarians." *Am. J. Clin. Nutr.* 70 (3) (1999): 586S-593S.

Janelle, K., and S. Barr. "Nutrient intakes and eating behavior scores of vegetarian and nonvegetarian women." *J. Am. Diet. Assoc.* 95 (2) (1995): 180-6, quiz 187-8.

Kies, C.V. "Mineral utilization of vegetarians: impact of variation in fat intake." *Am. J. Clin. Nutr.* 48 (3 Suppl) (1988): 884-7.

Key, T.J. "Dietary habits and mortality in 11,000 vegetarian and health conscious people: results of a 17 year follow up [see comments]." *BMJ* 28;313 (7060) (1996): 775-9.

Key, T.J. et al. "Mortality in vegetarians and nonvegetarians: detailed findings from a collaborative analysis of 5 prospective studies." *Am. J. Clin. Nutr.* 70 (suppl) (1999): 516S-24S.

Krajcovicova-Kudlackova, M. "Plasma fatty acid profile and alternative nutrition." *Ann. Nutr. Metab.* 41 (6) (1997): 365-70.

McDowell et al. "Energy and macronutrient intake of vitamins, minerals and fiber of persons ages 2 months and over in the United States." *Third National Health and Nutrition Examination Study*. Phase 1, Number 255. National Center for Health Statistics. November 1994

Marcus, E., *Vegan, The New Ethics of Eating*. McBooks Press, 1998.

Messina. M., and V. Messina., *The Dietitians' Guide to Vegetarian Diets*. Gathersburg Md.: Aspen Publ., 1996.

"Meat or wheat for the next millenium?" (Conference) *Proceedings of the Nutrition Society* 58 (1999).

Mills, P.K. "Cancer incidence among California Seventh-Day Adventists, 1976-1982." *Am. J. Clin. Nutr.* 59 (5 Suppl) (1994): 1136S-1142S.

Nieman, D.C. "Vegetarian dietary practices and endurance performance." *Am. J. Clin. Nutr.* 48 (3 Suppl) (1988): 754-61.

Ornish, D. et al. "Can lifestyle changes reverse coronary heart disease?" *Lancet* 336 (1990): 129-33.

Report of the Scientific Review Committee. *Nutrition Recommendations*. Health and Welfare Canada, 1990.

Sanders, T. "The nutritional adequacy of plant-based diets." *Proc. Nutr. Soc.* 58 (2) (1999): 265-9.

Subcommittee on the 10th Edition of the RDAs, Food and Nutrition Board, National Research Council. *Recommended Dietary Allowances, 10th ed.* Washington, D.C.: National Academy Press, 1989.

Snowdon, D.A. "Animal product consumption and mortality because of all causes combined, coronary heart disease, stroke, diabetes, and cancer in Seventh-Day Adventists." *Am. J. Clin. Nutr.* 48 (1988): 739-48.

Spencer, Colin A. *Heretic's Feast*. Hanover, N.H.: University Press of New England, 1995.

Stepaniak, Joanne. *The Vegan Sourcebook*. Lowell House, 1998.

"Third International Congress on Vegetarian Nutrition." *Am. J. Clin. Nutr.* (1999) 70 (Supplement: entire issue).

USDA Nutrient Database for Standard Reference www.nal.usda.gov/fnic/cgi-bin/nut_search.pl

"Vegetarian Diets." *J. Amer. Diet. Assoc.* 97 (11) (1997): 1317-1321.

Vegetarian Nutrition Dietary Practice Group of the American Dietetic Association. *Issues in Vegetarian Dietetics*. www.vegetariannutritiondpg.org

Vegetarian Nutrition Health Letter, Loma Linda University, Loma Linda, Cal. vegletter@sph.llu.edu

Vieth, R. "Vitamin D supplementation, 25-hydroxyvitamin D concentrations, and safety." *Am. J. Clin. Nutr.* 69 (1999): 842–56.

World Cancer Research Fund in Association with American Institute of Cancer Research. *Food, Nutrition and the Prevention of Cancer: a Global Perspective*. Menasha, Wis.: Banta Book Group, 1997.

WHO Study Group on Diet, Nutrition and the Prevention of Non-communicable Diseases. "Diet, Nutrition and the Prevention of Chronic Diseases." *Tech. Report* 797. Geneva: World Health Organization, 1991.

Yates, A. et al. "Dietary Reference Intakes" *J. Amer. Diet. Assoc.* 98 (6) (1998): 699-705.

INDEX